P9-APQ-050

Reform and the Non-State Economy in China

Private and foreign economic sectors (termed non-state sectors in China) have been the main engine of China's phenomenal economic growth. Built on rich data analyses, this book offers a fresh and in-depth explanation of how China's pro-reform leaders successfully launched controversial policies to promote these dynamic sectors, managed leadership conflict, and ensured reform in the provinces and rapid growth in the nation.

Hongyi Lai is a research fellow at the East Asian Institute, National University of Singapore. His research covers China's political economy and external policies. In addition to three co-edited and translated books and three book chapters, he has published over ten articles in scholarly journals, including *Modern China, China Journal, The Third World Quarterly, Issues & Studies, Provincial China, American Asian Review, Asian Journal of Political Science, Copenhagen Journal of Asian Studies,* and *China Review.*

Praise for *Reform and the Non-State Economy in China*

"Hongyi Lai adds to the now standard insights that China's economic reform has succeeded by its decentralized and gradualist approach. He provides the crucial insight that Chinese leaders carefully chose, using criteria we can now identify, *where* to initiate reforms. Not all coastal provinces were first encouraged to experiment with reforms, nor were all sectors involved. By identifying and explaining how Deng and his associates chose their targets and sustained a reform-tolerating coalition at the top, Lai adds immeasurably to comparativists' understanding of just how the 'Chinese miracle' was crafted. To all students who pursue the pressing moral question of how countries can be lifted rapidly out of poverty, Lai offers compelling and important new answers. Lai's detailed, in-depth, and utterly convincing analysis of this crucial case supplies the complement to the great debates and theories of scholars like Easterly, Sachs, and Stiglitz."
—Ronald Rogowski, Interim Vice Provost, Director of the Center for International Relations, Professor of Political Science, University of California, Los Angeles

"How did China's political leaders manage to introduce and sustain market reforms and opening? This study helps answer this important question by exploring the interconnections between economics and politics. It is a valuable contribution to the literature on China's reforms."
—Susan L. Shirk, Graduate School of International Relations and Pacific Studies, University of California, San Diego

"Hongyi Lai has produced a wonderful study of China's reform process, stressing the way in which leadership strategies and divisions shaped the growth of the economy. It was leadership, Lai argues, that led China out of the Maoist wilderness and into a period of sustained growth. Divisions within the leadership generated ups and downs in the course of reform, but ultimately it was Deng Xiaoping, who, in the course of adopting strategies to moderate this conflict, found a way to move forward incrementally, minimizing conservative opposition. This book is an important contribution to our understanding of the political economy reform."
—Joseph Fewsmith, Professor of International Relations and Political Science, Boston University

Reform and the Non-State Economy in China

The Political Economy of Liberalization Strategies

Hongyi Lai

REFORM AND THE NON-STATE ECONOMY IN CHINA
© Hongyi Lai, 2006.

First published in 2006 by
PALGRAVE MACMILLAN™
175 Fifth Avenue, New York, N.Y. 10010 and
Houndmills, Basingstoke, Hampshire, England RG21 6XS
Companies and representatives throughout the world.

PALGRAVE MACMILLAN is the global academic imprint of the Palgrave Macmillan division of St. Martin's Press, LLC and of Palgrave Macmillan Ltd. Macmillan® is a registered trademark in the United States, United Kingdom and other countries. Palgrave is a registered trademark in the European Union and other countries.

ISBN-13: 978–1–4039–7418–1
ISBN-10: 1–4039–7418–7

Library of Congress Cataloging-in-Publication Data

Lai, Hongyi, 1965–
    Reform and the non-state economy in China : the political economy of liberalization strategies / Hongyi Lai.
        p. cm.
    Includes bibliographical references and index.
    Contents: Economic transition and the case of China—Policies toward the non-state sectors, 1978 to the present—Elite conflict, reformist strategy, and policy cycles—Extending the open policy : the nationwide approach—Provincial reform initiatives : causes for variation—Divergent reform paths in two provinces—How China's leaders made reforms happen.
    ISBN 1–4039–7418–7
    1. China—Economic policy—1976–2000. 2. China—Economic policy—2000– I. Title.
HC427.92L34 2006
338.951—dc22   2006047446

A catalogue record for this book is available from the British Library.

Design by Newgen Imaging Systems (P) Ltd., Chennai, India.

First edition: December 2006

10 9 8 7 6 5 4 3 2 1

Printed in the United States of America.

To my parents

Contents

List of Tables   xi

List of Tabulations   xiii

List of Figures   xiv

List of Acronyms and Abbreviations   xvi

Preface   xviii

**1 Economic Transition and
the Case of China**   **1**

Big Bang and Incremental Approaches to Transition   2
Big Bang and Incremental Views of China's Success   5
Political Studies on Reforms   9
Alternative Explanation of China's Reforms: Strategies
for Overcoming Constraints   12
A Synopsis of the Chapters   27

**2 Non-State Sectors Policies,
1978 to Present**   **31**

Policies toward Rural Enterprises   33
Policies toward Private Businesses   39
Policies toward Foreign and Joint Ventures   45

**3 Managing Elite Conflict
and Policy Cycles**   **61**

Top Leadership and Factionalism   62
Reformist Strategy of Overcoming Opposition   67
China's Political Business Cycles   69
Views on Sources of Cycles in Post-Mao China   74
From Elite Division to Policy Cycles   76

Factional Conflict and Dynamics of Cycles   77
Features of Cycles   86
Conclusion: Cycles and Reformist Approach
to Elite Conflict   87

4 **Installing Technocratic Young Leaders**   **91**

The Formation and Power of the Politburo   94
Changes in the Politburo and Implications   95
Conclusion   107

5 **Selective and Showcase Liberalization**   **109**

The Early Years of the Open Policy   111
Existing Explanations of the Open Policy   112
Environment, Initiatives, Patronage,
and Strategy   116
Politics of Selecting the First Open Areas   128
Consolidating the Open Policy   131
Conclusion   138

6 **Extending the Open Policy**   **141**

Existing Explanations   143
Other Explanations   150
Conclusion   163

7 **Provincial Reform Initiatives**   **167**

Significance of Provinces and Provincial
  Differences in Policies   167
Possible Explanations   172
Effects of National Policies on the
Provincial Policies   187
Conclusion   188

8 **Divergent Reform Paths in Two Provinces**   **191**

Methodology for Comparative Studies   191
Provinces for Comparison   192
Evolution of Policies toward Non-State
  Sectors in Shandong and Jilin   198
Causes of Divergence in Reform Policies   205
Conclusion   224

9   How China's Leaders Made Reforms Happen   **231**

China's Reform Strategies   232
Flaws in China's Reform Strategies   243
Major Problems in the Wake of High
Growth and Remedies   246

Notes   253

Data Sources   263

Bibliography   266

Index   281

List of Tables

1.1 Constraints and strategies of China's
   incremental reforms   15
1.2 Gross industrial output value and share
   by ownership (%)   23
2.1 China's FDI inflows and exports in the
   reform era, 1979–2004   50
2.2 Share of state and non-State sectors in
   gross industrial output (provincial total = 100) (%)   58
3.1 Coding of ideological control and fiscal
   policies in China: 1978–1999 (coding: 0:
   conservative; 1: liberal)   79
3.2 Growth rates and inflation of five periods (%)   86
4.1 Size, age, generation and membership of the
   Politburo, 1977–1992   96
4.2 Ideological orientation of Politburo members,
   1977–1992   98
4.3 Functional and educational backgrounds of
   the Politburo members   101
4.4 Central or local experience of the Politburo members   103
4.5 Regional backgrounds of Politburo members   103
4.6 Provincial backgrounds of Politburo members   104
5.1 Leaders in Guangdong: Regional backgrounds   124
5.2 Central leaders and officials with close ties
   with Guangdong   126
5.3 Exports, FDI, and GDP growth after the
   Open Policy   135
6.1 Coding of provincial leadership in reforms and
   provincial opening index   149
6.2 National patrons of provinces, 1980–1993   151

6.3   Trade potential of provinces with nearby
      economies in 1985   155
6.4   National economic ministries (bureaus at the
      provincial level), 1981–1983   159
6.5   Correlation coefficients of national opening of
      provinces with likely factors   164
7.1   Measure of the provincial policies toward
      non-state industry: change in share of non-state
      sectors in provincial industrial output (%)   172
7.2   Correlation coefficients of provincial reform
      with likely factors   184
8.1   Tax rates on major types of non-state enterprises
      in Shandong and Jilin   193
8.2   Possible factors in Shandong's and Jilin's
      reform policies   197
8.3   Shandong's and Jilin's fiscal arrangements with
      the center, 1980–1993 (milllion yuan)   207
8.4   Public employees and officials in Shandong and
      Jilin (1000)   211
8.5   Size of non-state sectors in Shandong and Jilin   219
8.6   Industrial output by ownership in Shandong and
      Jilin (billion yuan)   227
8.7   Reform policies and economic conditions in
      Shandong and Jilin (Data in parentheses stand
      for rank in the nation.)   228

List of Tabulations

3.1   Statistical analysis on the dynamic of sequences   81

3.2   Did low inflation trigger higher growth in the
following year?   85

6.1   Equation on relationship between the remittance
rate and provincial opening   146

List of Figures

1.1 Industrial output by ownership in China, 1978–1997   22
3.1 GDP per capita growth rate and inflation in China,
1976–1998   71
3.2 Dynamics of cycles   84
6.1 Revenue remittance and opening of provinces,
1980–1993   146
6.2 Distance from Beijing and opening
of provinces, 1980–1993   148
6.3 Provincial leadership and opening
of provinces, 1980–1993   150
6.4 National patrons and opening of
provinces, 1980–1993   152
6.5 Trade potential and opening of
provinces, 1980–1993   156
6.6 Distance from sea port and opening
of provinces, 1980–1993   157
6.7 Employment in light industry and
opening of provinces, 1980–1993   161
6.8 Employment in non-state sectors and
opening of provinces, 1980–1993   161
6.9 Size of provincial bureaucracy and
opening of provinces, 1980–1993   163
7.1 Distance from Beijing and provincial
reforms, 1978–1993   173
7.2 Distance from sea port and provincial
reform, 1980–1993   174
7.3 Trade potential and provincial
reforms, 1978–1993   176
7.4 Revenue remittance and provincial
reforms, 1978–1993   178

7.5   Provincial leadership and reform in provinces,
        1978–1993   179
7.6   National patrons and provincial reforms,
        1978–1993   181
7.7   Size of provincial bureaucracy and
        provincial reforms, 1978–1993   185
7.8   Employment in light industry and
        provincial reforms, 1978–1993   185
7.9   Employment in non-state sectors and
        provincial reforms, 1978–1993   185
7.10   Pre-reform size of non-state sectors and
        provincial reforms, 1978–1993   186
7.11   National opening of provinces and
        provincial reforms, 1978–1993   187
8.1   Bank loans to the collective sector in
        Shandong, Jilin, and the country   194
8.2   Total tax rates on rural industry and income
        tax rates on the collective sectors in Shandong,
        Jilin, and the country   194
8.3   Income tax rates on the private and
        foreign sectors in Shandong, Jilin, and the country   195
8.4   Economic conditions of Shandong and Jilin   195
8.5   Additional economic conditions in
        Shandong and Jilin   196

List of Acronyms and Abbreviations

BICA	Bureau of Industrial and Commercial Administration
BSLI	Bureau of the Second Light Industry
CBEs	Commune and Brigade Enterprises
CCCCP	Central Committee of the Chinese Communist Party
CCP	Chinese Communist Party
CMC	Central Military Commission
FAI	Fixed asset investment
FDI	Foreign direct investment
GDP	Gross domestic product
GDPPC	Gross domestic product per capita
GIOV	Gross industrial output value
GNP	Gross national product
IHB	Individual household business
IHEs	Individual household enterprises
IMF	International Monetary Fund
JPG	Jilin Provincial Government
MLI	Ministry of Light Industry
MOFTEC	Ministry of Foreign Trade and External Cooperation
NPC	National People's Congress (the legislature)
NSOI	Non–state-owned industry
NSOS	Non–state-owned sector
PES	Private enterprises
PLA	People's Liberation Army (the military in China)
PRC	People's Republic of China, official name of mainland China
R&D	Research and Development
RMB	Renminbi, Chinese currency
SETC	State Economic and Trade Commission
SEZ	Special Economic Zone
SMSE	Small- and medium-sized enterprises

SOEs	State-owned enterprises
SPC	State Planning Commission
SPG	Shandong Provincial Government
SSB	State Statistical Bureau
TVEs	Township and village enterprises
UCEs	Urban collective enterprises
UCS	Urban collective sector
UN	United Nations
WTO	World Trade Organization

Preface

One of the most profoundly important events at the turn of the millennium is the rise of China. China's phenomenal economic rise has been propelled by economic reform installed by Deng Xiaoping. While numerous studies and insights have emerged on China's economic reform, China's political strategy for managing reform has not been systemically examined. As Nobel Laureate for economics Joseph Stiglitz states, building a market economy is essentially a political process, for which textbook economics cannot be referred to as a manual. Ironically, that is why the Chinese, who are not known for their theorizing talent, but have an instinctive propensity for practical solutions, have engineered the most fruitful economic reforms. In contrast, Russians who are adept at theoretical arguments, as well as Indians who are blessed with great talents in economics have been much less impressive in their endeavors in the past decades. A close analysis of Chinese political strategies for reform is thus meaningful and much needed.

My analysis benefits from four valuable sources of knowledge—my personal insights from my childhood, teenage, and recent travels in Guangdong, the pioneering province in China's opening and reform; my experience with student movements and Chinese politics from 1983–1989 as a student at Beijing University; my doctoral training in political science and methodology at the University of California at Los Angeles (UCLA); and my field work, interviews, and empirical knowledge about local China in the recent decade.

My research and writing have benefited with help from scholars and colleagues. I would like to thank the following people for their helpful comments and suggestions on my research in its early stage— Ron Rogowski, Jean-Laurent Rosenthal, Barbara Geddes, Cindy Fan, Dan Treisman, Jeff Frieden, Richard Baum, Dali Yang, James Tong, and Ajit Kumar Jha. Others but not the only people I thank include

Shijun Liu, John Longdregan, Dan Posner, Mariam Golden, David Goodman, David Allison, Eric Zusman, Eric Stump, Hiroki Takeuchi, Carlo Tognato, Ward Thomas, Dong Wang, Sha Liu, Rebecca Emigh, Wei-I Wang, Wendy Belcher, and Michael Lin.

My research and writing also benefited from help from grants and institutions. Part of my data collection for the research was funded by grants by National Science Foundation (NSF) (grant number SBR-9709813) and a Social Science Research Council (SSRC). My data collection at the Universities Service Center (USC) at the Chinese University of Hong Kong was facilitated by Jean Hung, Kuan Hsinchi, the USC staff, and Mr. and Mrs. Wong in Hong Kong. Zhou XH, Liang SD, and acquaintances and officials in Jilin, Shandong, and Guangdong Provinces offered me generous help in my field research in China. Although I might not share all their views, I learned a lot from them about reform and economic development in these localities. Early writing was supported by the Graham Fellowship of the Department of Political Science at UCLA. Substantial revision and finalization of the book, as well as part of the data collection benefited from my research post and facilities at the East Asian Institute, National University of Singapore.

I thank the referee(s) for Palgrave Macmillan for their comments. I also thank Maran Elancheran for his copyediting. In particular, I am grateful to Senior Editor Anthony Wahl at Palgrave Macmillan for his valuable advice and support and Heather Van Dusen and Elizabeth Sabo for their services regarding editing or production. Jessica Loon kindly helped me to make a map. Finally, I thank my parents for their support. I dedicate the book to them as gratitude for decades of their love and sacrifices.

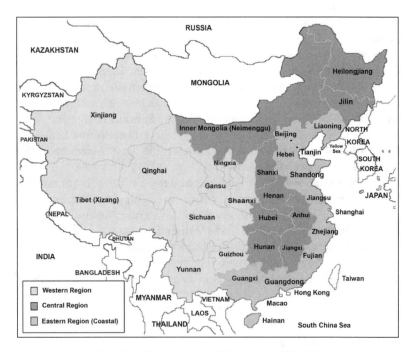

Map: China's Provinces and Neighbors, 1978–1996

Notes: Shaded areas stand for China's provinces and regions, and capitalized names China's neighboring countries. Hainan became a province in 1988.

Economic Transition and the Case of China

Economic reform has become an important and interdisciplinary research field in recent decades. Involved in the historical transition to the market economy are thirty-two former planning economies, which accounted for nearly 30 percent of the world population and over 17 percent of the world gross domestic product (GDP). In 2000, an International Monetary Fund (IMF) report pronounced: "The rise and subsequent failure of central planning ranks among the most significant events in the twentieth century, posing major challenges to both economic theory and policy from Prague to Beijing" (IMF 2000: 84, 89, 187). Studies on transition have become a new field crossing over political science and economics and have witnessed the production of a flurry of works.

China's success in economic transition in the past two and half decades has been phenomenal. Its economic reform started in 1978. Between 1978 and 2004 China's per capita GDP grew at 8 percent a year (SSB 2005b: 23). In the countryside alone, the share of the population in poverty decreased from 40 percent in 1980 to about 14 percent by the mid-1990s. The vice-president of the World Bank for the Asia-Pacific Region commented in 2004: "Since 1980, China has achieved poverty reduction on a scale that has no parallel in human history" (Lai 2005b: 6, 20). China's development in the wake of reform has transformed the country from an underdeveloped economy to a manufacturing and exports powerhouse. A scholar even coined the China model the "Beijing consensus" (Ramo 2004). Chinese leaders' management of economic reform is attracting attention from scholars, policy analysts, and policy makers of developing countries. This book attempts to shed light on the topic and draw lessons from China.

Big Bang and Incremental Approaches to Transition

How to make successful reforms happen has naturally become a top issue for policy makers in transitional economies as well as for interested scholars. The significance of reform strategy is further underscored by a stark contrast in the miraculous success of China's incremental reforms and the less promising results from the more radical transition in Eastern Europe and especially the former Soviet Union (the former Soviet bloc in short). Scholars holding a liberal perspective maintain that an optimal reform path should comprise a radical overhaul of the planned economy and its institutions, immediate liberalization, privatization, marketization, and deregulation, as well as a decisive closure of all inefficient state firms. This school tended to see the Chinese success as merely a result of favorable prior conditions. A number of scholars, on the contrary, hold that the incremental or gradualist approach is preferable. They point to the uncertainties over reform and emphasize political support for reform, the role of institutions, and the time it may take for new institutions to take shape. They attribute the Chinese success not only to prior conditions, but to a greater extent, to China's reform policies and right strategy. They insist that the key to the Chinese miracle is their patient efforts to gradually phase out old components of the command economy, actively promote market players, and incrementally build governmental, legal, and economic institutions that buttress the market economy.

Both incrementalists and shock therapists rightly suggest that prior conditions also matter a great deal. On the whole, the incrementalist perspective seems to fit better into the real experience of transitional economies in terms of the significance of institutions, the lengthy process of institutional evolution, and disruptive effects of a comprehensive economic shock therapy.

Both approaches, however, have concentrated primarily on the economic philosophy and measures in reforms. They have not paid sufficient attention to the subtle political strategy and state institutional arrangements that China's leaders have adopted in starting and sustaining reforms. They have not adequately explained how China's reformist leaders overcame stern opposition from influential conservative leaders and eased worries from a wary population. Neither did they reveal how Deng Xiaoping, China's paramount reformist, installed young power holders who backed his economic reforms. Nor did they demonstrate how China's reformists selected provinces for initial liberal experiments and demonstrated to other provinces the appeals of reform; they also failed to reveal how China's reformists carefully made fiscal arrangements to stimulate reforms in selected provinces (against the inaccurate impression of favoring all the coastal provinces). In other words, we still need to know what political, fiscal, and local arrangements enable reforms to take off in China. This book provides an in-depth account of how China's reformers accomplished their reform project in these aspects.

The shock therapy and incremental models diverge greatly in four economic attitudes, namely, uncertainty, complementarities and focus of reforms, as well as the reform of state-owned enterprises (SOEs).[1] As these differences have been covered in a large body of literature, they will be only briefly discussed here. First, big bang advocates possess misplaced confidence in their full knowledge of neoclassical economics and of market engineering. They believe that they know fully well about how to build a market economy from scratch.[2] Evolutionary scholars are more modest. Gradual change, they propose, is a safer choice in treading the unknown and complex territory of reform and policy makers can only learn many things about reforms by conducting reforms themselves (Murrell 1991; Stiglitz 1999).

Second, shock therapists view liberal measures as systemically complementary and interlocked. Any single reform cannot succeed without a set of corresponding measures (Ickes 1990), and therefore "the reform process must be comprehensive" (Lipton and Sachs 1990: 99). Incrementalists, on the other hand, argue that a few transitional measures and institutions can lead to more efficient allocation of resources than before. Reforms can make allocation of resources in a few targeted sectors efficient and accelerate their growth (Chen, Jefferson, and Singh 1992; Pomfret 1997), as evidenced in the case of China (McMillan and Naughton 1993; Stiglitz 1999; Qian 2003).

Third, in the vein of the second point, big bang advocates believe with undue optimism that with liberalization of prices and trade, financial stabilization, and privatization of SOEs in place all at once, markets will develop spontaneously (Lipton and Sachs 1990; Wolf 1991). Scholars of the evolutionary school suggest instead that three aspects of the transition should be the focus. They include an improved incentive structure for inducing efficient behavior of entrepreneurs and officials, liberalized entry and competition at the markets for fostering new private sectors and forcing SOEs to be competitive, and the development of institutions necessary for a market economy (Gelb, Jefferson, and Singh 1993; McMillan and Naughton 1993;

Qian 2003). These scholars stress that institutional arrangements such as legal framework and business network are crucial for the growth of markets, but they take a long time to build (Stiglitz 1999).

Fourth, big bang scholars maintain that inefficient SOEs need to be closed down immediately to avoid aggravation of debts and inefficiencies. Incrementalists, however, suggest that SOEs should be restructured to improve their performance and that meanwhile, private businesses should be promoted to reduce the absolute dominance of SOEs (McMillan and Naughton 1993; Naughton 1996; Stiglitz 1999).

These two schools also clash over four political aspects of reforms—irreversibility of reform, partial reform, democratization, and the role of the state.[3] First, big bang proponents propose that reformers could face possible delays in reforms due to popular opposition (Lipton and Sachs 1990: 100). Therefore, a comprehensive reform package can preempt this conservative coalition and create irreversibility in reforms (Fischer and Gelb 1991: 104). Incrementalists, on the other hand, argue that by sequencing reforms in a certain way, current and continuous support for reforms should be ensured, especially when economic compensation for full reforms is very costly (Dewatripont and Roland 1992). Rush privatization advocated by shock therapists may allow people with access to political and economic resources to steal assets from the state (Stiglitz 1999).

Second, both schools disagree markedly over partial reforms. Radical reform proponents charge that partial reforms will only encourage rent seeking (Shleifer and Vishny 1998; Aslund 2002), corruption, and crony capitalism (Murphy, Shleifer, and Vishny 1992). Over an extended period partial reforms will lead to a decay of state institutions (Aslund and Dmitriev 1990; Solnick 1998) and the capture of the state by people with political access and control of existing sectors (or rent seekers)(Winiecki 1990; Hellman and Schankerman 2000; Gustafson 1999), and eventually result in a decline of outputs (Murphy, Shleifer, and Wishny 1992) and of the economy (Winiecki 1990).

Incrementalists, on the other hand, argue that through permitting growth of market players, progressive rectification of inefficiencies, and right sequencing of reforms or right institutional arrangements partial reform can sustain popular support and its own momentum and can progress over time. The Chinese experience suggests that this is indeed possible (Putterman 1992; Griffin and Khan 1994; Lin and Cai 1996; Qian 2003).

Third, big bang scholars hold that economic and political reforms should go hand in hand. Rapid privatization transfers ownership into private hands; liberalization dissipates rents. Both could create a large number of supporters for full liberal packages. Democratization could empower this large segment of population who supports thorough reform for their general welfare and defeat oligarchic enterprises, party apparatchiks, and economic bureaucrats who prefer partial reforms (Winieck 1990; Hellman 1998).

The evolutionary school, however, suggests that the piecemeal changes can generate support for liberalization from beneficiaries of reforms. The latter include a middle class in the wake of a rising living standard, private entrepreneurs who take advantage of liberalized market entry (Roland 2000: 330–37), local governments whose revenue grows after decentralization, and even bureaucrats who benefit from their regulatory power over the markets.

Last but not least, both schools diverge on the role of the state in reforms. Shock therapists hold an excessively negative view of the state, seeing the bureaucracy that is used to the planned economy as largely interventionist and instinctively conservative (Lipton and Sachs 1990: 88). A strong state can only disrupt emerging markets. In addition, a powerful communist party, even at the central level, may become a base camp of conservatives who supported partial reforms. Big bang scholars thus believe that the size of the bureaucracy and the party as well as their power should be minimized.

Incrementalists believe that the state has an important role to play in guarding the markets through setting and enforcing law and norms and through securing property rights (Murrell 1991: 5; Stiglitz 1999; World Bank 1997a, 2002; Roland 2000: 330–45). Politicians do confront a dilemma in reforms. Fixing a broken economic system would inevitably inflict short-term welfare losses on the population, inviting the population to blame the reformers and demand their ouster (Przeworski 1991). The state should remain autonomous and free of pressure from the segments of population that suffer from reforms, until reforms bear fruits and create popular followings (Evans 1992; Williamson 1994; Haggard and Kaufman 1995). A weakened state can lead to asset stripping, unrestrained grabbing hands, and economic and political anarchy (Stiglitz 1999).

Big Bang and Incremental Views of China's Success

Few scholars dispute the fact that China outperforms in economic terms all other transitional economies. While all of these economies in Eastern Europe and the former Soviet Union suffer a steep decline in economic output for years after their reforms, China's economy continues to grow at an average 8 percent for over two decades. However, scholars disagree over the causes of China's successful economic reforms.

Advocates of the big bang approach largely attribute China's success to results of the following four favorable economic conditions before reforms and amicable political conditions during reforms. They insist that reform measures help only slightly and that incremental strategies do not help at all. First, China has a large rural sector and a huge rural population. It also started reforms at a low level of industrialization. Therefore, industrialization in the course of reforms is bound to generate substantial growth. In addition, China's heavy industry was much smaller compared with that in the former Soviet bloc. The disruption of reforms on heavy industry in China is thus milder (Sachs and Woo 1994; Woo 1994). However, these scholars forget that many developing countries with a large rural sector fail to engineer rapid growth. Thus sound government policies are a necessary condition for China to generate rapid growth in the reform era. Second, shock therapists argue that China also carried out its own mini big bang in conducting some critical reforms. For example, agricultural decollectivization was done drastically within a few years (Sachs and Woo 1994; Woo 1994). However, they fail to acknowledge clear limits for China's so-called big bang agrarian reform: Peasants were still required until the early 1990s to hand over quota grain to the state; land continues to be owned by villages, not by individual peasants. Third, Chinese state institutions remain intact and are capable of containing rent seeking, while those in the Soviet Union are weakened in the wake of democratization and permit officials and insiders try to embezzle state assets (Murphy, Shleifer, and Vishney 1992; Solnick 1996). This argument unambiguously admits that shock therapists err in failing to foresee that radical economic reforms or simultaneous political changes can undermine state institutions and eventually the reform course, as like what happened in Russia. Fourth, after rounds of mass denunciation and political cleansing during the Cultural Revolution, Chinese bureaucrats were not entrenched in the economic planning upon the start of reforms and were less resistant to reforms. In contrast, after decades of institutionalization and empowerment, bureaucracies in the former Soviet bloc had been deeply entrenched and were ready to choke off reforms (Woo 1994). Big bang advocates even claim that China's conditions were so favorable that even a mindless strategy could produce wonderful results (Woo 1994).

Incrementalists and mainstream China scholars, on the other hand, credit China's success much to China's gradualist strategy and a number of delicate institutional arrangements. First, the removal of inefficiencies in a few specific sectors at a time is preferable to comprehensive assaults of the command economy all at once. The former can produce efficiency gains in a few sectors at a time, allow the economy to maintain its vibrancy, and avoid a sudden fall in output (Lin and Cai 1996; Putterman 1996, 1992). Shock therapists, on the other hand, do not foresee such a drop in economic output in their programs (Lipton and Sachs 1990), which constitutes some of the most severe setbacks for the former Soviet bloc (Roland 2000: 336).

Second, decentralization helps to create a right incentive structure for local governments and enterprises for reform. The center, through fiscal arrangements, allowed local officials to claim a share of fiscal returns including the profits of rural enterprises.[4] This gave officials a strong incentive to foster growth of local economy and non-state firms (Montinola, Qian, and Weingast 1995; Walder 1995; Oi 1999).

A group of scholars even suggest that by allowing bureaucrats to supervise the economy and transition, the state has given officials both the power and incentives to engage in liberalization for the welfare of their communities and themselves. Scholars credit this developmental bureaucratism, bureaucratic entrepreneurship, or rent seeking by local officials with the breakdown of the economic planning and helping to make reforms irreversible (Gore 1998; Wedeman 2003).

In addition, a string of literature provides testimony to China's leaders' political skills in mobilizing local support and the constructive role the local government and the coast provinces have played in reforms. Shirk argues that in fighting against a conservative coalition of heavy industry, its governmental representatives, and inland provinces, national reformists devolved power to and played to a pro-reform coalition comprising light industry, its governmental agencies as well as coastal provinces (Shirk 1985; Shirk 1993). Localities engaged in "competitive liberalization" in order to reap economic and fiscal benefits from reforms (Montinola, Qian, and Weingast 1995; Yang 1997). The center also abandoned egalitarian yet unproductive interior developmental strategy and shifted to a coastal developmental strategy (Yang 1990).[5] Under liberal leadership and blessed with economic and political networks, coastal provinces responded enthusiastically to central calls for liberalization (Cheung et al. 1998; Chung 2000; Huang 1996; Zweig 2002). The center utilized its controls of appointment of local officials to maintain political unity and supervise their performance (Huang 1996).

Third and finally, two incremental economic strategies have helped China to sail through the perfect storms of transition. China adopted a dual track system in deregulating price control. It shifted away from price control step by step by allowing market prices gradually to replace state-fixed prices. In addition, the Chinese state also liberalized entry to markets while restructuring and overhauling instead of privatizing SOEs. Liberalized entry allowed productive non-state firms to emerge, improve, and expand. Balanced creation of new elements and controlled destruction of old elements allows the economy to continuously operate and renew itself (Gelb, Jefferson, and Singh 1993; Naughton 1996; Qian 2003) and permits robust economic growth.

In summary, both schools agree that initial political and economic conditions matter. China has benefited from an underutilized industrial society, swift agricultural decollectivization, and strong state institutions. However, while big bang scholars give little or no credit to China's incremental approach, the evolutionary school maintains that this approach is the key to China's stable and sustained growth.

The shock therapy argument has obviously been undermined by several pitfalls. It is unduly confident in its design of a new economic system and underestimates the output falls, as well as economic, social, and political disruption of radical reforms. It simplistically dismisses the plausibility of incremental yet persistent reforms. It also fails to foresee that market-enhancing institutions, norms, and even private firms take a long time to develop. Perhaps most importantly, it fails to appreciate the significant role appropriate reform strategies as well as state institutions can play in reforms. World Bank reports pointedly suggest that effective and reasonable state institutions (like those in East Asia) provide a backbone for growth by providing political stability, protecting and enforcing property rights, channeling information, fostering competition, and supporting markets (World Bank 1997a: 1–15, 2002: 3–30). As to be elaborated, the Chinese reformists followed prudent and pragmatic strategies in reforms. They placed market-sympathetic and technocratic officials in the key national and provincial positions, created successful examples of reforms in a few provinces as a powerful demonstration of liberalism, promoted efficient non-state ownership, and encouraged efforts to produce efficient and services-oriented government. These moves paved the way for the market economy in China. The Chinese experience also suggests that incrementalists have made right arguments over the sustainability of properly designed incremental reforms and the constructive role of institutions, the state, and market players for reforms and growth.

Political Studies on Reforms

It is also helpful to review studies on reforms carried out by political scientists. The existing political literature on economic reforms emphasizes two distinct sets of factions—interest groups and coalitions on the one hand, and political institutions on the other. Inefficient policies are believed to result from failure of collective action on the part of the general population and effective mobilization of small groups (Olson 1971). Special interests could plunder the state and lower public welfare through rent-seeking (Krueger 1974), corruption-dominating regulation (Peltzman 1976) or protectionist tariff policies (Nelson 1989). They are responsible for distortions in Africa's agricultural policies (Bates 1981, 1989a), Latin America's exchange rates (Frieden 1991), and trade policies around the world (Frieden and Rogowski 1996). Entrenched interests could lead to a decline of nation-states (Olson 1982). Following this line of argument, scholars model reforms in terms of interest groups' conflict over how costs of reform should be assigned (Alesina and Drazen 1991; Velasco 1994, 1998; Tornell 1995), or in terms of divergence of groups' preferences contingent on the likelihood of change in the government (Roubini 1991; Cukierman, Edwards, and Tabellini 1992), as well as on the strength of opposing social forces (Nelson 1990).

Echoing the incrementalist argument, a second body of literature argues that institutions play a key role in starting and consolidating reforms. Institutional factors conducive to earlier and persistent reforms include an autonomous or centralized executive, technocratic competence (Nelson 1989, 1990; Haggard and Kaufman 1992), legislative delegation, insulated agencies, party supports, links between leaders and supportive private sectors (Haggard and Kaufman 1992; Haggard 2000), and decision-making rules (Snyder 1999). While authoritarian regimes do not guarantee smoother reforms than democratic ones, new democracies do appear to have difficulties in consolidating reforms (Nelson 1990). Election cycles also shape the timing of reforms (Nelson 1990; Haggard and Kaufman 1992). Some cognitive (or soft) factors of institutions, such as leaders' perception of crises (Nelson 1989) and their beliefs, can also shape the course of reforms (Haggard and Kaufman 1992; Snyder 1999).

A few recent articles also reinforce the institutional argument. Specifically, accountability of state institutions can help resist corruption and state capture by powerful interests, increasing the chance for the success of economic reforms (Manzetti 2003). Manzetti's finding on the sixteen countries contravenes the earlier conclusion on the basis of three countries that economic liberalization progresses when powerful businesses collude with the state (Schamis 1999).

The existing literature on transition offers rich arguments on reforms and confirms the role of state institutions. However, it also suffers from a number of serious defects, especially regarding the reforms in China. Incrementalism, a potentially useful approach, lacks a careful analysis of political strategies for reform and thus could easily degenerate into a vague and unpractical conception. Our understanding of the political process of and the political ingredients for the most successful reforms has been handicapped in several ways. First, with a few exceptions (Waterbury 1989), thorough analyses are still needed on reformers' political strategies. The existing literature focuses on why reforms proceed differently and what structural and predetermined factors and economic strategies led to contrasting processes and outcomes. Inadequate attention is given to what political strategies reformers followed in launching and sustaining reforms.[6] For example, as in the context of the Chinese case, it has yet to be clearly shown how reformists outmaneuvered conservation leaders of opposition, dominated policy making, managed setbacks in liberalization, and won and sustained support for reforms from the population or local officials. Scholars, analysts, and policy makers will learn a great deal from an analysis of the political finesse of China's reformers in propelling the reforms into an economic miracle.

Second, the literature helpfully illustrates the role of preconditions in economic transition, such as crises (Nelson 1990, Haggard and Kaufman 1992, Bates and Krueger 1993). It also expounds the challenges of pursuing reforms when benefits are diffused and costs are concentrated (Nelson 1989, 1990), and suggests social and political conditions that help or hurt reforms (Przeworski 1991; Haggard and Kaufman 1992). However, it largely fails to demonstrate how policy makers' choice can turn these preconditions or current social and political conditions into advantages. For example, advantages such as a large rural population do not automatically translate into growth. This is evidenced in the widespread poverty in many countries with a large rural sector. Only through sensible and effective policies can China tap into and fully exploit these favorable conditions. Without them, advantages may simply be a baggage.

Third, the literature has yet to clearly show how sound reform strategies help the rise and consolidation of market-enhancing institutions including an efficient government, as well as market-enhancing norms and laws to emerge and consolidate. Prudent institutional arrangements could in turn produce an incentive structure that rewards creative and productive economic activities on behalf of officials, localities, and enterprises. The existing analyses on decentralization, for example, are too general to be either persuasive or empirically illuminating. For example, it has been argued that China's decentralization has stimulated provincial reform efforts, especially by giving all provinces fiscal discretion and claims to residual surplus. However, it is too simplistic to assume that the center gave the same amount of fiscal discretion to all provinces or even all the coastal provinces. In practice, the fiscal arrangement in decentralization has been varying and complex. In addition, there is a crucial difference between fiscal and political decentralization. The former can stimulate growth whereas the latter may have undermined national unity.[7]

Fourth, institutional and interest-groups approaches that are discussed above can be complementary, though the former may carry greater explanatory power. In my analysis, I lean toward the institutional approach by focusing on the leaders' reform strategies and institutional arrangements. I also give credit to certain concepts used by the interest-group approach when looking at coalitions for and against reforms as well as reformists' tactics to forge links with and empower liberal sectors and ownership.

All in all, these problems highlight the importance of politics and its interaction with economics in reform studies. A number of prominent scholars on economic transition have also recognized these problems. Gelb, Jefferson, and Singh (1993: 127), for example, remarked that "perhaps the most important lesson from China is that political economy, rather than simply economic theories, lies at the heart of the process of socialist transition." Their view is echoed by Fischer and Gelb (1991: 103), who specified what was lacking in the studies on transition: "Economic theory offers relatively little guidance on some important questions," such as "the extent to which the state should play an active role." "The most important strategic choices arise, however, out of the interplay between economics and politics . . . Technocratic solutions for optimal transitions cannot be designed without taking account of the political constraints." Stiglitz (1999) puts it in blunter terms: "Textbook economics may be fine for teaching students, but not for advising governments trying to establish from anew a market economy . . . W[w]hile due obeisance was paid to 'political process'. . . in fact, little understanding of these political processes was evidenced." Therefore, attention should be paid to the political process, constraints, and leaders' choice in circumventing these obstacles, stimulating reform efforts, and maintaining reform momentum.

Alternative Explanation of China's Reforms: Strategies for Overcoming Constraints

In this book, I aim to fill the inadequacy in the existing research by examining the reform strategies and reform-accelerating institutional arrangements in China. It addresses two sets of questions. The first set of questions is important and is implied by Roland in his excellent summary and critique of the literature on economic transition—What are the political constraints and conditions that shaped the process and dynamics of Chinese incremental reform? (Roland 2000: 337). In the case of China, what political strategies did the Chinese leaders adopt in order to sustain incremental reform, instead of allowing partial reform to be installed? Scholars on incremental and shock-therapy reforms have also asked similar questions in their debates on reforms, but gave no satisfactory answers (Dewatripont and Roland 1992; Rodrik 1995; Roland 2000). The second set of questions relates to the first set. It also has bearing on the political economy of reforms and on central-local relations in China's reform—What were the political economic factors that drove the Chinese national and provincial reform policies? Where in China did the reform progress earlier? How was competitive liberalization among Chinese provinces generated?

For politicians managing reforms these questions are critical and determine whether reform policies are executable and endurable. Centuries ago Machiavelli discussed extensively the politics of governing in his less-read masterpiece *Discourses*. His insightful view can shed some light on our study of reforms. He argued that the purpose of politics was to promote the common good. Leaders' successful efforts toward this end should take into account *necessita* (necessary tasks) and *fortuna* (contingencies or luck) and fully exploit their *virtu* (their own strength, charisma, and skills as statesmen) (Machiavelli 1970). In the case of reform, leaders try to promote the reform course, a *necessita*, which could more or less be conceived as a common good for the population in general and extend the economic freedom of the people. When implementing reform, leaders confront historical context and existing institutions specific in their own countries as well as changing situations and unexpected outcomes of reforms (*fortuna*).

They also need to make the right choice (*virtu*) to turn preconditions, institutions, and changing situation to their advantage and to sustain public support for the reform course.

In a similar vein, contemporary political studies also point to the importance of leadership and choice. Bunce (1980), in a careful study, concludes that leadership matters under democratic and communist regimes. She demonstrates that leaders may initiate new policies for the sake of consolidating their power in the course of succession. It has also been suggested that while institutions constitute constraints on rational actors, actors can still make appropriate choice to advance their interests (Lake and Powell 1999).

For the above reasons, in order to well comprehend reform strategies, sufficient attention should be paid to political and economic constraints, leaders' strategic choice, and coalition building. This is also true in the Chinese case.[8] For Chinese leaders, how to start and sustain incremental reforms has been arguably the most daunting task in the reform era. They needed to decide which reform measure should be adopted first, and where to implement it earlier. As seasoned politicians, they needed to make wise political choice regarding the sequencing of reform and the choice of localities for reform that were appropriate in the Chinese settings. With the right choice, leaders could turn China's political and economic constraints to their advantage, mobilize political support for each major reform measure, and lock reform into a set direction.

Briefly stated, my argument is that the Chinese economic reform was incremental and successful because of reformists' strategic and tactical choices to overcome political and economic constraints and to sustain reform. Confronted with constraints such as factional conflict among decision makers and a backward economy, Chinese reformists liberalized the economy incrementally, skilfully managed elite conflicts and to promoted technocrats, selected as early starters provinces that had a higher likelihood of success, and made delicate fiscal arrangements to induce a few provinces to launch pilot reforms.

Specifically, because of division between reformists and conservatives among decision makers, Chinese reformers chose an incremental approach that would be tolerated by conservatives. China's reformists also adopted clever strategies to win approval for reforms at the national and local level. They made tactical retreats when reforms produced unfavourable outcomes and met strong oppositions. They picked the provinces where marketization reforms would most likely succeed first to try out reforms. This strategy helped demonstrate the appeal of reforms and encouraged other provinces to follow suit.

China's leaders also adopted two economic strategies that could turn China's backwardness into advantages for reforms. First, seeing existing significant non-state sectors as movers of marketization and supporters for reforms, they relaxed restrictions on these sectors and encouraged their growth, allowing these sectors to eventually replace the state sector as dominant economic players. This strategy can be termed "growing out of the state sector." They also opened up initially provinces that had a larger pro-market non-state economy, rallying support from these sectors for marketization. Second, as China's pre-reform planned economy was decentralized, duplicated, and rudimentary compared to the Russian counterpart, China's central reformists could easily devolve economic power to localities. Through economic decentralization, they stimulated local reform initiatives and local competition and encouraged other provinces to emulate successful local initiatives. The following sections discuss these constraints and strategies in detail.

Political Constraints and Strategies

The Chinese reformist leaders confronted two sets of major constraints, one political and the other economic. Though they may not make up an exhaustive list of constraints, they are the major ones that influenced reform strategies. Reformist leaders adopted corresponding strategies that allowed them to make good use of these constraints and changing conditions to their advantage. The main components of these strategies, such as allowing the non-state economy to expand, granting targeted provinces preferential treatment to facilitate reform there, grooming young technocratic leaders, and pushing forth reforms boldly but retreating when facing setbacks, were adopted in the 1978–1980 period. The reformist leaders refined strategies and adjusted technical aspects of these strategies in the following years in the changing circumstances. My analytical framework, consisting of constraints and strategies, is summarized in table 1.1.

The first political constraint is strong opposition from the majority of the influential veteran leaders against thorough marketization. During 1980–1993 leaders more or less fell into two camps—reformists who supported market-oriented reforms vis-à-vis conservatives who backed cosmetic fine-tuning of the planned economy. Although they supported limited marketization, conservatives were ready to halt reforms when

Table 1.1   Constraints and strategies of China's incremental reforms

Political Constraints

1. Division among decision makers (into moderate and orthodox reformists and conservatives)
2. Popular opposition to slow income growth, high unemployment and inflation
3. The Party's dominance in major policies and personnel affairs
4. Varying provincial proclivity toward reforms

Economic Constraints/Conditions

1. Relatively significant non-state sectors
2. Decentralized, duplicate, and rudimentary planning system among provinces

Strategies for Building Support for Reform

1. Zigzag reforms ("Two Steps Forward, One Step Back" and emphasis on growth to overcome elite and popular opposition)(chapter 3).
2. Promoting liberal technocrats into the Politburo to oversee reforms (chapter 4).
3. Installing skillful and liberal leaders to start reforms in targeted provinces (chapter 5).
4. Picking the most advantaged provinces to be the early winner (allowed provinces that were liberal minded and externally linked and had a smaller state sector to reform first in order to demonstrate the attractiveness of marketization)(chapter 5).
5. Using carefully structured fiscal incentives, opening provinces, favoring local good governance, and promoting cadres to encourage reforms in coastal provinces (chapters 5–8).
6. (Economic strategies) Turning backwardness into advantages: Liberalizing market entry and promoting growth of non-state businesses (growing out of the state sector); decentralizing economic power and encouraging competitive liberalization. Permitting local policy exploration for a national solution (experimentalism, or "groping for stones to cross the river") (chapters 2 and 5–8).

liberal policies created serious economic, political, and social problems and seriously undermined central planning and when they saw the danger of losing political control (Baum 1996).

In addition, as is to be discussed, the central group of the first-tier leaders during 1978–1994 comprised eight veteran leaders. Only two of them (including Deng Xiaoping and Yang Shangkun) were clearly reformists and were committed to marketization. The rest were by and large conservative over economic reforms. Managing conflict with conservatives thus constituted a crucial yet delicate issue for reformists.

Severe conservative opposition and occasional setbacks in the reforms posed severe challenges for Chinese reformists in their endeavors at marketization.[9] Reformists, especially Deng Xiaoping, followed a zigzag reform path that helped to safeguard their liberal course. When conditions were favorable, Deng pushed for dramatic liberal policies. When conditions turned adverse, when results from reforms were disappointing, and when conservative forces were on the rise, Deng retreated moderately and waited for fresh opportunities for restarting liberal initiatives. When conservative policies did not work out, Deng would step out, criticize conservatism, and launch a new round of reform initiatives. This calculated strategy, coined by Lenin as "two steps forward, one step back," has allowed reformists to maintain the direction of incremental reforms despite adversities at times.

Deng also took pains to consolidate the support from conservative veteran leaders for his paramount leadership. He forged an important alliance with the latter through supporting the Party's monopoly of power and foiling any attempts to challenge the Party. These attempts included demands and protests by liberal intellectuals and vocal students. By doing so, Deng demonstrated to veteran conservatives that his embrace of marketization was a genuine effort at salvaging the political regime, instead of undermining it. Hence, even though conservative veterans might disagree with Deng's liberal economic policies, they did not challenge his leadership. In turn Deng used his undisputable leadership to push for a liberal economic program even though it caused conservatives to raise their eyebrows.

Deng also carefully consolidated his control of the military, the ultimate arbitrator in Chinese politics. In 1981, for example, he rejected a negative version of the Party's assessment of Mao Zedong and allowed only partial exposures of Mao's errors in order to appease a large number of military leaders who were loyal to Mao's ideology (Baum 1996: 134–37). In 1992, with military support Deng was able to launch his final assault on the conservative economic program and eventually reversed the post-Tiananmen retrenchment in reforms that was engineered by conservatives.

Reformists headed by Deng also made good use of their power to recruit young technocratic and liberal leaders who helped manage and sustain reforms. In the 1980s, reformists demoted Maoist provincial cadres and promoted reform-minded cadres. Liberal and competent cadres were installed in top national positions to supervise and support the reform course. With political skills and commitment to reforms, these national reformists served as openminded daily managers of economic and political affairs. Some of them, such as Qiao Shi and Li Ruihuan, were also quick to rally on Deng's calls for bold marketization in 1992. Young, liberal, and technocratic leaders also helped to sustain Deng's marketization agenda after him.

The aforesaid "two steps forward one step back" strategy also helped reformists to circumvent the second political constraint, that is, the population's discontent with sluggish growth in income, high unemployment, and inflation. Between 1978 and 1994, a period this study focuses on, slow income growth and high unemployment usually resulted from retrenchment engineered by conservatives. A reformist drive toward liberalization tended to result in surging inflation. The populace was averse to and was easily discontented with these economic problems. This popular economic preference often reinforced the above-discussed division among decision makers. Reformists and conservatives also pointed to these popular resentments over by-products of policies in order to undermine their opponents and to promote their own policy agenda. Reformists tried to adopt reform measures that would noticeably increase the people's living standard and used a rising living standard in the wake of reforms to educate the public about the virtues of reforms. As stated, when confronting run-away inflation due to economic liberalization, reformists tactically retreated from their liberal agenda in order to retain popular support. When a conservative program resulted in stagnation in the living standard of the nation, reformists would step out and argue in public about the need for reforms in order to achieve higher incomes. To elaborate further, reformists also purposefully allowed reform to start in a few provinces where the level of personal consumption would be lifted rapidly and where many jobs would be created. The success of these provinces compelled other provinces to follow suit, or risk losing their talents and economic clout.

The third political constraint is that of the political dominance of the Party, as well as that of the coordinating authority of the central government. This constraint arose out of the beliefs of conservatives and orthodox reformists among the national leadership. It is true that the Party's domination might have been a political liability and that it had led to sluggish political reform. Nevertheless, the Party could also use its power to advance the reform course. For example, the Party could become a valuable coordinator of reforms in the nation. It can help to maintain national unity and political stability. Similarly, the Party remained the dominant force in coordinating and sanctioning reforms in the provinces. After 1983 the Department of Organization of the Party controlled its appointment of local cadres mainly at the provincial level (Huang 1996). The central government used this power to promote provincial leaders whose liberal measures had rapidly expanded the local economy and significantly improved the local population's well-being. It made economic growth a primary criterion for judging performance of local officials and for determining their official promotion. This gave tremendous incentives for local officials to adopt marketization measures, liberalize the local economy, and generate growth in their localities. This incentive structure for promotion also encouraged local cadres to become political entrepreneurs.[10] In addition, the center also targeted specific regions with favorable conditions for earlier opening and reforms. This national selection of particular provinces and regions for earlier reform and development paved the way for successes of these early reforms and prevented possible chaos and waste of valuable resources in unmanaged reforms nationwide. This point will be elaborated later.

China's ability to coordinate local reforms is in stark contrast with the failure of the national government in the former Soviet Union. As Huang (1996: 323–25) pointed out, in the former Soviet Union Gorbachev pursued political opening and decentralization in order to push on marketization. His approach had weakened the national authority's power in coordinating economic reform across the republics and had led to their growing political and economic power. This is a key cause for the breakup of the Soviet Union and chaos and impasses in economic reforms. In contrast, the center in China, especially the Chinese Communist Party (CCP) has retained its final say in provincial cadre appointment. The state has maintained political unity, supervises reform implementation, and controls corruption in transition. The CCP tried to reduce localism through circulating cadres and monitoring their performance (Huang 1996: 92–93).

The last political constraint is that provinces varied in their inclination toward reforms. The underlying reason was that some provinces were better positioned to construct the market economy, whereas others might face considerable shocks and run into economic difficulties. The former would embrace reforms, while the others might prefer to wait and see before committing to liberal policies. The task for decision makers, especially reformists, was to design a strategy that could motivate provinces to embark on marketization and reward them for doing so.

National reformists employed a sophisticated tactic to promote reforms in the provinces. They picked the easy winner for provincial reform in order to create a domino effect. For example, in choosing provinces to open up to foreign business in the first phase, they deliberately selected provinces with the highest chance of success and gave them favorable fiscal arrangements. In addition, they encouraged these provinces to promote rapid growth of the non-state economy and light industry, thus creating sectoral support for opening and generating fiscal windfalls in these provinces. This helped to stimulate demands from other provinces to follow suit. For example, Guangdong, a province right next to Hong Kong whose capitalists were desperately looking for cheap labor and markets, was opened up first. Light industries and non-state businesses were also permitted to develop extensively. As a result, local fiscal revenue rapidly increased, and personal consumption and number of jobs grew. Other provinces were quickly impressed with the success of Guangdong and demanded similar policies from the national government. This strategy of picking the winner and creating showcase examples served to overcome varying inclination toward reforms among provinces. The following paragraphs will elaborate on this strategy after discussing economic constraints.

The center also carefully designed three sets of fiscal arrangements to ensure both central fiscal income and to stimulate local reforms. First, it had allowed provinces with certain fiscal capacities and making moderate remittance to the center to retain a higher share of their revenue. In doing so, it gave these provinces an enormous incentive to reform their economies, generate rapid growth for the non-state economy, and reap fiscal windfalls. Over the years, these provinces would have a much larger tax base and become large contributors for the center. Second, it required provinces with a relatively advanced economy such as Shanghai to make large contributions to the center by remitting heavily to the central coffer. This was a strong disincentive for local reforms. By so doing, however, central leaders ensured that its revenue would not be significantly disrupted. Third, the center continues to subsidize a number of provinces with limited fiscal capacities and underdeveloped economies. This helps maintain these provinces' allegiance to the center and maintains political stability. As to be elaborated in chapter 8, these prudent yet clever fiscal arrangements generated strong local initiatives for reforms in the first type of provinces. Much larger contribution from these provinces enabled the center to reduce the remittance from the second type of provinces (formerly heavy remitters) in later years, allow the second-type provinces to retain a large share of revenue, and generate robust reforms and growth in these former heavily remitting provinces. Thus the reform wave moved from first-type provinces to second-type over the years.

Economic Constraints/Conditions and Strategies

Even though this book focuses on political constraints and strategies for reform, it is worthwhile to discuss the economic conditions and strategies. The first constraint or condition, which this study examines, is that of China having a much larger non-state economy prior to reforms than did the Soviet one. On the eve of China's reforms toward marketization in 1978, the state sector accounted for only 24 percent of total employment and 78 percent of urban employment. In contrast, on the eve of the marketized reform in 1988 in the Soviet Union, the state sector was a highly dominant player in the economy, accounting for 88 percent of total employment and 96 percent of urban employment (SSB 1990b; IMF et al. 1991: 220).

These economic constraints hindered the functioning of China's pre-reform central planning. Non-state sectors of considerable size created substantial problems for officials and agencies in planning and coordinating economic activities at the national level. However, reformists realized that they turned this disadvantage in economic planning into advantages in reforms. China's leaders purposefully promoted the non-state economy and turned it into a key component and ingredient of China's economic reforms. As Samuelson and Nordhaus noted in their popular textbook *Economics* (1998: 550):

> To spur economic growth, the Chinese leadership has taken dramatic steps such as setting up "special economic zones" and allowing alternative forms of ownership . . . In addition, China has allowed collective, private, and foreign firms, free from central planning or control, to operate alongside state-owned firms. These more innovative forms of ownership have grown rapidly and by the mid-1990s were producing more than half of China's GDP.

The promotion of non-state businesses follows a path of liberalization without privatization and bears a birthmark of the incremental reform scheme. China's leaders have allowed non-state sectors to enter the market since 1978, yet have not sold off at a massive scale state enterprises to individuals, institutions, and foreign owners. Non-state sectors have profoundly changed China's economy. Non-state sectors are composed of collective firms (owned by local groups, townships, or villages and dominated by rural enterprises), foreign-owned or joint ventures, private business, and mixed sectors. They are subject to more effective oversight by their owners than state firms (McMillan and Naughton 1993: 132); they enjoy no state protection, have to survive competition at the market and are thus more cost-effective; they are more dynamic than state firms and make a larger contribution to growth than state firms in the reform era (Gelb et al. 1993: 111).

The national and local governments introduced a number of measures to help non-state businesses (private, rural, and urban collective, and foreign ownership) to expand. In 1978, the state lifted its ban on private business. Since then, its policies relaxed gradually despite cyclical changes. The state offered constitutional protection to small private business in 1982, eased restrictions on large private firms in 1987, and promoted private business after 1992. During 2001–2003, the Party and the state openly embraced private business. It offered constitutional protection to private business in 2003 (Lai 2004a, 2004b).

In 1979, the State Council formulated the first regulation regarding rural enterprises (called commune and brigade enterprises) and offered the state's protection and fiscal and financial support for them. As rural decollectivization in the 1980s led to a surge in rural surplus labor and capital and the growth of rural enterprises, the ministries and bureaucracy representing SOEs and economic planning pressed for restrictions on rural enterprises. In 1987 Deng praised rural enterprises. With central acquiescence and local governmental active promotion, rural enterprises boomed in a number of provinces. In these areas local officials saw the expansion of rural collective and private enterprises as a new engine of growth in the local economy and fiscal revenue (Oi and Walder 1999; Byrd and Lin 1990).

The most noticeable promotion of non-state businesses is the Open Policy. In 1979, the central government approved the setup of special economic zones (SEZs) in Guangdong and Fujian Provinces to attract overseas investors, especially those from Hong Kong and Macao. From 1984 to 1990, the largest cities and key economic areas in the coast were gradually opened up. During 1992–1993, dozens of inland provincial capital cities, border ports and prefectures were also opened up (Howell 1993; Chen Xuewei 1998: 284–301).

This policy of liberalized entry to markets has produced far-reaching economic changes. Non-state sectors accounted for only 22.4 percent of the gross industrial output in 1978. Thanks to the government's promotion, this share increased to 53 percent in 1993 (figure 1.1 and table 1.2). Among non-state sectors, collective-owned enterprises accounted for 34 percent, private business 8 percent, and enterprises of foreign and mixed ownership the remaining 11 percent (table 1.2). During 1978–1997, China's gross industrial output grew nearly sixfolds (figure 1.1). By 2003, over 70 percent of China's GDP came from the non-state economy.[11]

The bulk of the strong growth of the economy in China comes from the miraculous expansion of non-state businesses. How China promoted non-state sectors across its provinces over time thus constitutes a good case for examining the political economy of China's incremental approach. Thus this book focuses on the politics of carrying out this reform measure while discussing a variety of liberal policies.

The second economic constraint for China's reforms is a decentralized, duplicated, and rudimentary planned economy, which has been studied in detail in the existing literature. Here I will discuss this issue in the context of constraints and strategies for reforms. As Huang (1994) pointed out, China's planning system was more rudimentary than the Soviet Union's due to a lack of qualified administrative, managerial, and technical personnel, as well as less developed infrastructure and technology. The Chinese central planning was more susceptible to macroeconomic instability, and more costly to maintain.

China's planning system was also organized differently from that in Eastern Europe and Russia. In China, each province had its own industrial clusters. In contrast, the Soviet system was divided into

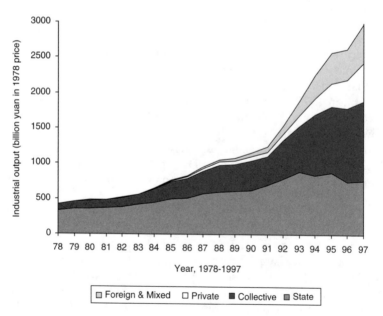

Figure 1.1.   Industrial output by ownership in China, 1978–1997.

Table 1.2   Gross industrial output value and share by ownership (%)

Year	Total (current price) (billion yuan)	State-owned or state-controlling share holding %	Collectively Collectively owned %	Individuals or private- owned %	Other types of ownership %
1952	35	42	3	21	35
1957	70	54	19	1	26
1962	92	88	12	0	0
1965	140	90	10	0	0
1970	212	88	12	0	0
1975	321	81	19	0	0
1978	424	78	22	0	0
1980	515	76	24	0	0
1985	972	65	32	2	1
1990	2392	55	36	5	4
1991	2663	56	33	5	6
1992	3460	52	35	6	8
1993	4840	47	34	8	11
1994	7018	37	38	10	15
1995	9189	34	37	13	17
1996	10741	34	37	14	15
1997	12067	30	36	17	17
1998	12699	26	36	16	21
1999	13607	26	33	17	24
2000	*8567*	*47*	*17*	*6*	*30*
2001	*9545*	*44*	*14*	*9*	*36*
2002	*11077*	*41*	*12*	*12*	*35*
2003	*14227*	*38*	*7*	*15*	*41*
2004	*18722*	*35*	*6*	*17*	*43*

Notes: Data in italics represent incomplete data. Data are based on computation from statistics in the sources below. The total outputs from 1996 to 1999 (A) are recalculated by summing up the output by each type of ownership (B) provided in SSB 2000, table 13–3. Shares of each type of ownership are also calculated by dividing A by B. The original official totals were smaller than the sum of each component and were thus not used. Data on 2000, 2001, and 2002, as suggested in the text, only include large enterprises and underestimate smaller enterprises, which tended to be non-state enterprises. The numbers are thus smaller than the output between 1995 and 1999. Collective enterprises comprise collectively owned industry and cooperative enterprises. The category "Other Types of Ownership" includes foreign and mixed ownership.

Sources: SSB 2000, table 13–3; 2002, table 13–3; 2003, table 13–1; *China Statistical Abstract 2005*, p. 127.

functional ministries such as machinery and mining and division of labor was carried out clearly and strictly between East European countries and especially among the Soviet republics. Qian and Xu (1993) called the Chinese economy the M-form and the Soviet economy the

U-form. The main disadvantage of the M-form is the duplication of industries across provinces, whereas the U-form is characterized by clear and more efficient central planning, which was an advantage prior to reforms.

In addition, the planned economy in China was also more decentralized than its Soviet and Eastern European counterparts due to a less sophisticated bureaucracy, less skillful labor, and Mao's policies and political campaigns. A highly centralized command economy, like the one in the USSR, required intensive coordination between different economic sectors and regions. A sophisticated bureaucracy would draw up economic plans; a developed infrastructure would help to exchange information and goods; skilled labor would help execute the plans. In the 1950s when China was building its command economy, its bureaucracy and infrastructure had been less developed and its labor was less skillful than those in the Soviet Union. The ministries were weakened by Mao Zedong during the Great Leap Forward in the late 1950s. The Cultural Revolution of 1965–1976 further devastated the bureaucracy, the educational system, and the central planning system (Naughton 1996: 39–40). In 1979 only 791 goods were under the national planning in China, whereas the production of 1.2 million goods was included in the Soviet economic planning in the late 1970s (Qian and Xu 1997: 51).

During the reform, reformist leaders turned the decentralized economy from a disadvantage into an advantage. They allowed ministries and localities to experiment with various measures to solve pressing economic problems. Several tactical considerations underlined this reform experimentalism and economic decentralization.

First, reformists tried to find out in the short run the best approach to reforms for the nation through local experiments. A serious challenge for countries in reform is "little prior knowledge before transition," a lack of readily available remedies to long-existing or new problems, and highly uncertain results of reform policies (Roland 2000: 1–2). Through experiment leaders could compare and assess different solutions and choose the optimal ones. If they failed, lessons were learned and similar mistakes could be saved. Deng called this strategy "groping for stones to cross the river."

Second, different reform solutions might suit various localities in the intermediate term, and contending local approaches to reforms might eventually result in the best approach for the nation in the long run. For example, two local approaches to promoting non-state firms had attracted the greatest attention from other provinces—collective-owned rural enterprises in southern Jiangsu and private firms in Wenzhou, Zhejiang. Prior to the early 1990s, the southern Jiangsu model had been regarded as the most dynamic and socially beneficial. Since the late 1990s, as collective rural enterprises in Jiangsu ran into problems and had to be privatized, the Wenzhou model had earned widespread respect.

Third, as stated, China's M-form economy permitted a successful policy to be transplanted easily from one province to another (Qian and Xu 1993). A rudimentary planning system also made it more worthwhile to reform rather than tickling with the pre-reform economy (Huang 1994). Fourth, under a decentralized economic system, China's reformists could delegate to the provinces greater power in managing the local economy in return for the provincial support for the reform agenda, without disrupting national economic development (Shirk 1993).[12]

As stated, this book focuses on China's reform strategy, especially strategies for managing elite conflict, leadership orientation, and central-local interaction. It uses national and provincial reform policies regarding non-state sectors (i.e., individual and private business, rural enterprises, and foreign enterprises) as the case for study. It analyzes political conflict among the leadership over reform, leaders' strategy in jump-starting reform and fostering competitive liberalization among provinces, and provincial considerations in pursuing local reforms. It explains how China's leaders made prudent strategic choices to advance favorable policies toward non-state sectors across provinces. It traces the province in which the national government first promoted reform and which provinces were the most active in helping non-state firms.

In order to gain a solid understanding of the process of China's reforms, I examine carefully the data and empirical aspects regarding China's promotion of foreign and domestic non-state sectors and uncover the underlying dynamics and pattern. In discussing China's policy cycles I record the ups and downs in the reform drive between 1978 and 1994. I explore the interacting political and economic forces that generated the cycles. I also discuss Deng's grooming of young leaders who could support and sustain his reform by examining in detail the profile and background of Politburo members from the late 1970s to the early 1990s. Moreover, I examine systemically the national pattern of central opening of the provinces to the world economy and reform initiatives in the provinces. In discussing the national pattern of the opening of China, I present time-series data on national policies toward reforms in twenty-seven or more provinces and reform policies in these provinces, which is rarely seen in the existing literature. I then conduct statistical analyses in order to uncover factors that shape the complex pattern of opening.

My statistical study in two chapters aims to address the following deficiencies in the literature on reforms in China's provinces. First, nationwide statistical analyses of national and provincial policies, as well as methodologically grounded comparative studies would generate methodologically sound conclusions and avoid over-generalizing conclusions that are based on only a couple of casually assembled cases. Existing studies on China's provinces are insightful and informative; but for careful methodologists, many of them suffer from serious methodological defects. A significant number of these studies only focus on one province. Some that focus on several provinces are often carried out without careful consideration of methodology for case selections and comparative studies. Given the great diversity in economic conditions among Chinese provinces, inference based on a couple of provinces, especially those studies without sound research design, may not be generalized as representative of the nation.[13] Our understanding of reform in China's provinces can thus be strengthened by a nationwide study that uses available data on all or most of the provinces. In this study, I carefully design my research, based on important political economic data on twenty-seven to thirty provinces, and apply statistical analyses so as to explain the nationwide pattern of reforms. In addition, I conduct a methodologically conceived comparative analysis of two provinces in order to demonstrate why reform policies differed widely in localities with comparable conditions.

Second, I apply and test the existing explanations of the center's differentiated policies toward reforms in provinces and provinces' differing reform initiatives. I hope that by evaluating contending arguments we can have a sense of their explanatory power in accounting for the nationwide pattern of the most important reform measure, that is, promotion of non-state businesses. I also hope to shed more light on the dynamics of reforms at the national and local levels. This solid empirical understanding can help me to develop a coherent account of China's reform strategies. Nevertheless, my analysis is presented in plain and easy-to-follow terms.

I focus on the period between 1978 and 1994 when the economy was largely decentralized and when provincial authorities exerted extensive influence over the local economy. In particular, central-local fiscal arrangements varied widely across provinces, giving the center considerable clout over designing so-called particularistic contracts with individual provinces. Provinces also possessed tremendous power in determining taxation and bank lending which affected the operation of non-state sectors. Since 1994 the tax-sharing system has replaced the central-local contracting system. Tax arrangements across provinces have become more uniform and less variant. The provincial discretion in tax rates has thus been reduced.

A Synopsis of the Chapters

The chapters in this book elaborate on the Chinese reform strategies that contributed to the success of the Chinese incremental reforms. Chapter 2 gives an overview of China's policies toward primary non-state sectors from 1978 to the present as well as their effects on the expansion of these sectors. Specifically, policies toward rural enterprises, private businesses, and foreign enterprises are mapped and explained, and growth of each of these sectors over the past twenty-seven years is briefly discussed.

Chapter 3 examines China's top leadership, its factions, and periodic changes in national reform policies especially toward non-state sectors over the decades. The cyclical changes in policies and the economy are also known as China's political-business cycles. This chapter builds and expands on the existing views on the topic. Reform-oriented leaders opted for fast growth through economic liberalization and relaxing ideological control, yet triggering inflation and demand for political liberalization. Conservative leaders emphasized low inflation and the Party's rule, usually hurting economic growth. Conflicts between leaders, political protests, and conservative backlashes generated cycles of national reform policies, especially before 1994. Since 1994, the rise of orthodox leaders who discourage demands for political reforms has eased the cyclic change in policies. Against the backdrop of elite conflict during 1978–1992 reformists prudently adopted a zigzag approach to sustain reforms. They pushed through liberal policies when the circumstances were favorable, and retreated and gave conservatives a larger role in policies when conditions turned adverse. Once the situation became amicable, they renewed reform initiatives. Orthodox reformists also tried to find a political common ground with conservatives in order to prevent a devastating political showdown. This strategy of "two steps forward and one step back" has gradually taken China's reforms far down the road toward a market economy.

In the 1980s and much of the 1990s Chinese politics could be characterized as the rule of men. National leaders, especially members of the Politburo, the most powerful decision-making body, thus exerted considerable influence on policies. Reformists, especially Deng, clearly recognized the importance of staffing the Politburo with liberal-minded officials. Chapter 4 examines the profile of the Politburo in the 1980s and the early 1990s. Over these years the number of reformists at Politburo especially from the liberal coast was rapidly increasing, whereas that of Maoists and conservatives dwindled. New Politburo members tended to have college education and had worked at the administration, instead of only in the military or Party affairs. The technocratic leadership tended to possess college education, knowledge and administrative experience that was useful for managing the economy. In addition, Politburo members tended to have both central and local working experience, which enabled them to take a balanced stance toward central and local interests. These young technocratic reformists that Deng groomed provided a strong backing for the reforms during Deng's triumph over conservatives in 1992 and beyond Deng's life time.

Chapter 5 examines national selection of individual provinces that were opened first for international business. National leaders purposefully picked Guangdong as the vanguard in the opening. Guangdong was blessed with extensive links to the world economy through Hong Kong in the recent century, a productive agriculture, and a sizable light industry, and most importantly, open-minded cadres and population. Central leaders minimized fiscal remittance from the province, allowing it to retain most of its revenue in its experiment with reform. Reformist leaders intentionally appointed able and senior officials who were well connected with the center to govern Guangdong. This calculated and biased selection of winners through choice of location and careful political and fiscal arrangements allowed Guangdong to launch and sustain reforms and to enjoy miraculous economic growth. Guangdong's success invited liberal provinces to demand their opening, and pressured conservative provinces to adjust their policies.

On the basis of a statistical analysis on twenty-seven provinces, chapter 6 investigates the types of provinces the national government chose to open up earlier. It is found that the center appeared to have targeted its reform efforts at provinces that enjoyed sectoral support for the Open Policy, that had influential central patrons, that could enhance their fiscal remittance to the center or could reduce their reliance on central subsidies, and that might expand external trade after the opening. This finding resembles to a great extent the same criteria on which the opening of Guangdong and Fujian were based.

The next question is which type of provinces would be bolder in promoting the non-state economy. Chapter 7 addresses the question. Statistical analyses find that liberal provinces tend to be close to the coast, have a good potential for external trade, benefit from employment in non-state sectors and light industry, have considerable fiscal capacity, and have been opened up earlier.

Taking up the conclusion in chapter 7, chapter 8 compares reform policies in Shandong and Jilin Provinces from 1978 to 1994. Although sharing many economic similarities and even certain similar reform policies in the early 1980s, the two provinces had followed divergent paths of reforms since the mid-1980s. Bolder reforms in Shandong could be traced to its better fiscal conditions, its more favorable fiscal arrangements with the center, more efficient provincial bureaucracy, more liberal and provincial leadership, influence from larger non-state sectors, coastal proximity, greater potential for external trade, and earlier central opening up of this province. In contrast, Jilin's sluggish reform resulted from its constant fiscal shortfalls and barely adequate subsidies from the center that deprived the province of resources for financing liberal measures. In addition, Jilin's slow reform was caused by a larger yet inefficient bureaucracy, hardly liberal provincial leadership, influence from a predominant state sector, smaller gains from trade, and late opening up of the province.

A number of transitional and developing countries, including Russia, India, and Indonesia, appear to show strong interests in China's reform. Chapter 9 sums up many positive lessons and a few negative lessons policy makers and scholars can learn from China's reform. It suggests that success in economic transition can be greatly enhanced by leadership skills, management of elite conflict, recruitment of young leaders, favorable arrangements for advantaged localities to try out and showcase liberal policies, appointment of able leaders to head these localities, right incentive structures for localities (especially fiscal arrangement) and good governance. Lastly, the chapter also discusses the remaining political, economic, and social problems in China's reform and highlights efforts by post-Deng leadership, especially the Hu-Wen team to meet these challenges.

2

Non-State Sectors Policies, 1978 to Present

As stated, one of the most prominent features of China's reform is the liberalized entry of non-state firms to markets. Since 1978 previously prohibited enterprises of collective, private, foreign, and hybrid ownership have been allowed to enter markets and compete against SOEs. This influx of dynamic non-state firms (or private firms in the Western sense which incorporate individual- and group-owned firms) injects a new dynamics and momentum in the dormant Chinese economy and helps engineer high growth. This liberalization of entry, of course, has been done incrementally.

In tandem with liberalized entry is the gradual opening of China to the world economy. This is called the Open Policy (*kaifang zhengce*). Cities, counties, and provinces that were opened up by the center enjoyed greater jurisdiction over local economic affairs, including reform of the labor, welfare, price, and foreign trade institutions and greater leeway in procuring production inputs, raising funds, and approving investment projects.

This chapter briefly introduces the history of policies toward each of the three major non-state sectors, namely, collective enterprises, private businesses, as well as foreign enterprises and joint ventures; documents the evolution of these policies from the 1980s till the early 2000s; and reviews the expansion of these non-state sectors. In addition, the evolution of the opening of China's provinces will be outlined and a pattern will be identified. While the opening of China's provinces primarily aims to boost exports and attract foreign direct investment (FDI), it is also accompanied with economic and administrative decentralization, helping other non-state businesses to expand. Contrary to the claim in some studies (Treisman 1999), there is no substantial political decentralization in China, reflected in the fact that the higher authority still tightly controls the appointment of local officials (Huang 1996). Only deputy chiefs at the village level, namely, village chiefs, are open to election by the local population. The Party, through its township party committees, still appoints the most powerful village leaders, namely, village party secretaries.

China's policies toward private businesses are deeply influenced by official ideology and economic agenda. Influenced by Marxism, the state viewed negatively the private economy and joint ventures operated by non-communist employers (such as Western and Asian-run enterprises in China). It accused the sectors of allowing capitalists to inhumanly exploit workers.

The policies toward private and foreign ownership since the founding of the People's Republic of China underwent the following stages: (1) nationalization and collectivization in the 1950s and the Soviet assistance during 1953–1960; (2) an outright or covert prohibition from the early 1960s to the late 1970s; (3) incremental and cyclical liberalization after 1978.

After the Chinese Communists assumed power, they built the command economy in the 1950s by launching a campaign called socialist transformation. In 1952, there were 18.1 million self-employed individuals in commerce and manufacturing (mostly handicrafts) and about 160,000 private entrepreneurs. In the same year non-state firms accounted for 58 percent of the nation's gross industrial output. As a result of the state's expropriation and its promotion of production cooperatives, by 1956, 91.7 percent of the handicrafts-persons had joined the cooperatives, and 82–99 percent of private enterprises had turned into public-private joint ventures or cooperatives. By 1958 most private businesses in China had been nationalized or collectivized. The share of the non-state sectors dropped to 46 percent in 1957 and a much lower 12 percent in 1962 (SSB 1990b: 15; He et al. 1995: 108–09, 118–19).

Meanwhile, from 1953 to 1957 China implemented the first five-year plan with the financial and technological assistance from its ally the Soviet Union. The USSR provided China loans amounting to US$300 million at a low 1 percent annual interest. It also helped China to build 156 major projects. China built a rudimentary planned economy during these five years. However, as China-Soviet relations were strained, the USSR terminated all its cooperation with China in 1960 (He et al. 1995: 57, 241).

Between mid-1960s and the late 1970s, the private economy was regarded as "the tail of capitalism" and the enemy of the command economy and was strictly prohibited. Only a small number of them could operate covertly or underground. Mao cherished self-reliance and dismissed foreign aid as kowtowing to foreign influence. Virtually no foreign joint venture existed in China.

Since the late 1978, the state has very cautiously lifted its ban and widened the parameters for the operation of the private, collective, and foreign enterprises. The state's policies, however, have undergone twists and turns in the following two decades, correlating mostly with policy debates among Chinese leaders regarding urban unemployment, rural surplus labor, SOEs, as well as the strength and priority of reformist leaders.[1]

Policies toward Rural Enterprises

A Brief History

Rural enterprises refer to enterprises that are run and operated by rural residents and are based usually on the countryside. Rural enterprises can be collective and private by ownership. With a good reason, many analysts tend to view rural enterprises as collective enterprises. A larger number of rural enterprises are in industry.

Rural enterprises had been hailed until the late 1990s as the Chinese path of industrialization, the core of the Chinese economic miracle (Oi 1999), or the Chinese alternative to private ownership (Walder 1992, 1995). This characterization, as will be discussed later, turned out to be too optimistic. Nevertheless, from the early 1980s to the early 1990s rural enterprises did play a significant role in the expansion of China's non-state economy. Into the 2000s, however, the clout and competitiveness of these enterprises gradually decreased due to not-yet-clarified property rights, a lack of technology and competent management, as well as the separation of formerly collectively registered private firms.

Rural enterprises have a long and complex history of development in the People's Republic of China (PRC). They originated from the handicraft industries and small workshops in rural areas that had long existed in China. As late as 1954, over 10 million peasants worked in these businesses on a part-time basis, generating an output of 2.2 billion yuan. During the agricultural cooperative movement of 1955–1957, these businesses were incorporated into specialized sideline production teams under agricultural producer's cooperatives. During the Great Leap Forward, Mao pursued an ambitious development program urging peasants to actively industrialize the countryside through rural enterprises. As a result, in 1958 agricultural cooperatives were transformed into people's communes, and handicraft cooperatives commune and brigade enterprises (CBE). By the end of 1958, 6 million CBEs were formed. The output from rural industry grew from RMB2.29 billion in 1957 to RMB6.25 billion in 1958, and its share in national gross industrial output (NGIP) increased from 4.3 percent to 5.8 percent. With the collapse of the Great Leap Forward, rash rural industrialization was criticized, and the number and output of CBEs plummeted during 1962–1966. During the Cultural Revolution Mao suggested in his May 7 instructions that peasants could run some industries. Nevertheless, CBEs could only operate covertly; they were still prohibited officially. By 1976 CBEs produced an industrial output of RMB25.7 billion, accounting for 8 percent of the NGIP (Byrd and Lin 1990: 3–11; Chen Xuewei 1998: 235–37).

Policies in the Reform Period

Commune and Brigade Enterprises entered a new era after 1978. In the following years, despite ups and downs CBEs and their successors did enjoy increasingly greater leeway with the progress of economic reform. Now and then the state issued official announcements and regulations that protected the legal rights of CBEs and guided their institutional development.

The Third Plenum of the Eleventh Party Central Committee in late 1978 announced that CBEs "should strive for great development," granting the first official green light to the sector since 1962. In 1979, the State Council formulated the first regulations on CBEs, that is, the "State Council Regulations on Several Issues regarding Developing Commune and Brigade Enterprises." The regulations stipulated that the property and autonomy of CBEs should be respected and should not be nationalized, that CBEs should follow strict accounting rules, and that the state would provide them low-interest loans.

During economic retrenchment of 1981–1983, all domestic enterprises, especially rural enterprises, faced a harsh macroeconomic environment and had to scale down their investment and production. Rural enterprises were viewed as disruptors of macroeconomic stability and greedy grabbers of production inputs that could have been used for SOEs. In 1981 a few national ministries proposed that CBEs in a dozen sectors should be closed down in order to protect SOEs and to scale down investment. In response, the State Council promulgated in 1981 "Several Provisions regarding Implementation of the Policy of National Economic Adjustment by Commune and Brigade Enterprises." The provisions stated that CBEs affected employment and economic interests of 30 million peasants as well as supplies of necessary commodities and that CBEs constituted an important part of the rural economy. While CBEs should undergo retrenchment as other enterprises, their autonomy should be respected and retrenchment should be done on the basis of careful investigation. During the retrenchment of 1981–1983, however, CBEs did suffer a slower growth and even encountered outright prohibition and forced closure in some localities.

Following the replacement of people's communes and brigades by township and villages in 1983, the Party Central Committee and the State Council jointly issued a circular in 1984, renaming CBEs township and village enterprises (TVEs). It was also proposed that TVEs should introduce an economic responsibility system and receive the same treatment as state enterprises (Byrd and Lin 1990: 11) and that TVEs could develop into share-holding cooperative enterprises in 1985.

In 1990, the State Council promulgated "Articles on Enterprises of Township and Village Collective Ownership of the PRC." It declared that the state protected the legal rights of TVEs of collective ownership and prohibited any organization and individuals from infringing upon their property. The articles also detailed the nature, obligations, tasks, establishment, change, and rights of these enterprises, as well as relations between enterprise and the government.

During the post-Tiananmen retrenchment of reform from 1989 to 1991, however, various governmental agencies and especially localities complained that rural enterprises took away much needed raw materials, talents, and markets from SOEs and had caused many SOEs to lose money. They reduced raw materials and loans for rural enterprises, yet increased tax burdens on them. In some localities an outright ban on rural enterprises was even imposed. Rural enterprises suffered a severe setback.

This adverse situation changed after Deng's reform-promoting Southern Tour and the Party's declaration to build a market economy at the Fourteenth Party Congress in 1992. Finally in 1996 a law on TVEs, that is, Law on Township and Village Enterprises of the PRC was promulgated, granting TVEs legal protection and inducing an amiable political environment for their expansion.

Township and Village Enterprises have played a more prominent role in local economic development in the coast, especially Jiangsu, Zhejiang, Guangdong, Shandong, Fujian, and Liaoning. Jiangsu, Zhejiang, and

Guangdong each have developed their own unique models of TVEs, which are termed Sunan, Wenzhou, and Pearl River Models, respectively. The Sunnan Model centered around southern Jiangsu, especially Suzhou, Wuxi, and Changzhou. Until the mid-1990s, TVEs there tended to be owned and operated by townships and villages. They evolved as local corporations promoting collective welfare of local population. In Zhejiang, TVEs are best represented by those in Wenzhou. Originating from household business, they later evolved into private or stock-holding businesses. In the Pearl River Delta as well as coastal Fujian TVEs are a hybrid of city, township, village, private, and foreign ownership and are heavily externally oriented. They are built with the capital, technology, and management imported from Hong Kong, Macao, and Taiwan and many of their products are exported to the world market (Oi and Walder 1999: 13–17; Yang 1998: 195–205).

In comparison, TVEs in inland regions started late and developed at a lower level. In 1990, the value of gross social output in the country-side per capita amounted to RMB2,929 in the coast, but only RMB 1,382 in the central region and RMB976 in the western region (or the west). Out of this per capita rural output, TVEs contributed upto RMB1,967 in the coast, RMB695 in central China, and RMB272 in the west. Thus TVEs accounted for 82 percent of the coastal-central gap and 87 percent of the coastal-western gap in per capita gross rural social output (Chen Xuewei 1998: 249). The Party declared in the report of the Fourteenth Party Congress in 1992 that it would continue to strive for greater development of TVEs, especially in the central and western and ethnic minority regions. In 1992 the State Council promulgated "Decisions to Develop Faster TVEs in the Central and Western Regions," requiring local leaders of these regions to take responsibility to develop SOEs, agriculture, and TVEs simultaneously and to help solve major problems for TVEs. In addition to increasing loans to TVEs, the State Council also decided to allocate RMB5 billion of special loans for TVEs in these two regions. With the attention and help from the state, the gross output value of TVEs in the two regions increased from RMB690 billion in 1992 to RMB3,793 billion in 1997, growing on average 40.6 percent a year (Chen Xuewei 1998: 250–51).

The state also helped TVEs in the nation to upgrade and improve their technology and to expand their exports. In 1986, the State Science Commission launched the Spark Program (*xinghuo jihua*), aiming to introduce technology to rural enterprises and agriculture.

In the following years the state issued several regulations and programs for the same purpose, including the "Outline for Implementing the Strategy of Technological Progress at Rural Enterprises" in 1988 and "Opinions on Accelerating Technological Progress at Rural Enterprises" and the "Outline for Scientific and Technological Progress at Rural Enterprises of the Ninth Five-Year Plan" in 1996. The state offered help to rural enterprises in setting up institutions, attracting talents, beefing up research capacity, inducing innovation, and installing sound management. As a result of the state support and own initiatives, the share of technicians among employees of rural enterprises increased from 2.6 percent in 1988 to 5.9 percent in 1997 and the contribution of technological progress to growth of rural enterprises from 35 percent to 45 percent (Chen Xuewei 1998: 245–46).

Finally, the state also actively encourages rural enterprises to expand their exports. In 1985, Premier Zhao Ziyang proposed that rural enterprises on the coast could export labor-intensive products to the world market. In 1988 five ministries and two state banks set up a joint office of trade, industry, and agriculture and established bases for exporting commodities through bidding. They also provided these bases special bank loans backed by full interest payments by the central and local governments, and offered them tax reduction and exemption. In 1991, 192 bases were designated. In 1995, five ministries and the Agricultural Bank promulgated "Opinions on Accelerating the Externally-oriented Economy of TVEs," encouraging TVEs to raise their level of exports, utilize FDI, and develop internationalized corporations. By 1997 exports by TVEs already amounted to RMB695 billion, accounting for 35 percent of the national exports. A total of 1,000 TVEs had obtained export licenses. Those TVEs that were joint ventures with foreign investors totaled 29,700 in number and their investment totaled US$27 billion (Chen Xuewei 1998: 247–48).

With rapid and continuous expansion, TVEs emerged as a major player in China's economy in the 1990s. By 1996, TVEs produced 40 percent of the GNP and 55 percent of the gross industrial output value (GIOV). During 1978–1996, TVEs contributed 4.5 percent of the 17.5 percent annual average growth of the GNP and 4.4 percent of the 17.8 percent annual average growth of the GIOV of the nation (Chen Xuewei 1998: 251). TVEs were hailed as holding up half of the sky of the national economy.

In the late 1990s, especially since the Fifteenth Party Congress of 1997, together with SOEs, collective-owned TVEs have been viewed as components of public ownership and thus would enjoy the same political recognition and much of the legal status of the state sector. The Third Plenum of the Sixteenth Party Central Committee in October 2003 approved the "Decisions on Several Issues regarding Perfecting the Socialist Market Economic Structure." The Party declared that one of the primary tasks for building a market economy was to perfect an economic system that was composed mainly of public ownership and joint development of various types of ownership. Public ownership, it pointed out, could be revitalized through developing mixed ownership of state, collective, and private share holding and popularizing the share-holding system.[2]

Recent Challenges

Into the 2000s, rural enterprises, especially those of collective ownership, are facing intense competition from foreign and private enterprises and some of the well-run state enterprises. Ambiguous property rights and technological weaknesses have started to take their toll on the performance of these rural enterprises. Many struggling collective enterprises have also been privatized. By 2001, 187,698 rural enterprises had been transformed into stocking holding and stock cooperatives nationwide.[3] In southern Jiangsu Province, 93 percent of the 85,000 rural enterprises had been transformed into share-holding or private companies by the end of 2000.[4] It has been widely accepted that the Sunan Model has lost out in a long-term race to the Wenzhou Model and probably the Pearl River Model.

There is a large body of literature analyzing economic causes, institutional settings, and local government's role in expansion of TVEs, as well as development profile, operation, and economic attributes of TVEs. While the findings are complex, a few interesting findings are worth mentioning. Rural reform in the early 1980s increased agricultural outputs, cumulated funds, and freed rural labor for industrial endeavors. These factors, along with governmental permission of TVEs and greater factor mobility in the wake of reform, propelled the growth of TVEs in that period. After 1983, expansion of TVEs was sustained by legitimization of private enterprises, market demands for their goods, internal funds, and increases in urban and rural incomes (Byrd and Lin 1990: 41–42; Du 1990; Findley and Watson 2001). In the wake of fiscal decentralization local governments endeavored to expand TVEs in order to generate revenue income (Gore 1998; Oi 1999; Jin and Qian 2001; Whiting 2001). County government policies also affected the timing and scope of rural reform and shaped labor and capital mobility, and hence influenced the fate of TVEs. In addition, geography, history, access to capital and world markets conditioned the contour of the growth of TVEs (Svejna and Woo 1990; Whiting 2001). Overall, peasants, entrepreneurs, and local cadres act as locomotives for the early growth of TVEs. Arguably, local agents have played a larger role in developing TVEs than other non-state enterprises. On the other hand, central (or national) policies, as discussed above, might act as a traffic signal and a fuel supplier. This point will be detailed in chapter 8.

Policies toward Private Businesses

Evolution of State Policies

The policies toward the private economy since the founding of the People's Republic of China underwent the following periods: (1) nationalization and collectivization in the 1950s; (2) a ban from the mid-1960s to the late 1970s; (3) limited tolerance between 1978 and 1982; (4) a wait-and-see stance between 1983 and 1986; (5) active promotion during 1987 and 1988; (6) stepped-up supervision and restriction between 1989 and 1991, and (7) steadfast liberalization after 1992.[5] Local officials, possessing considerable power in interpreting and implementing policies in accordance with changing political atmosphere, significantly affected the growth of the local private economy (Young 1995: 40–44).

Between 1978 and 1982, the state lifted its ban on the private economy in order to create jobs for millions of urban laborers. In March 1978, the State Council approved and distributed a report from the national meeting of chiefs of the Bureau of Industrial and Commercial Administration (BICA), allowing for the first time since 1957 the small private sector (termed the individual economy). The BICA has hence become the primary state agency administering the private sector. In late 1979, the central Party, upon the request of six departments headed by the Department of the United Front, removed the derogatory political label of capitalist from 860,000 former business owners (Chen Xuewei 1998: 302–03). In August 1980, the state openly encouraged urban job hunters to start their own business under the guidance of the state plan.

During the retrenchment of 1981–1983 the state slowed down investment, controlled the pace of economic growth, and very cautiously undertook liberalization. Earlier in the period, private businesses encountered greater opposition by local officials and SOEs and had a difficult time in operation. However, as unemployment was rising in the wake of retrenchment, the state felt the pressure to generate jobs in private businesses in commerce and light industry that had much lower start-up costs than heavy industry. The state thus formulated a number of regulations and laws to protect and encourage the small private economy, which referred to self-employment and small private business and was termed the individual economy (Young 1995: 21–22). In March 1981, the State Council encouraged the individual economy to expand in the countryside. Two state documents in June 1981 stipulated that individual economies were components of the national economy. In July, the State Council promulgated the first special regulations on the individual economy, that is, "Several Policy Provisions regarding Urban Non-Agricultural Individual Economy," spelling out its policy stance for protecting the small private sector. The state allowed private business to employ one to three apprentices and placed the maximum allowable number of employees at five (Chen Xuewei 1998: 304–05).

In 1982, a controversy was stirred up when a peasant in Fujian hired 20 peasants at his tree farm on barren hills that he had leased. At Deng Xiaoping's request, the Politburo decided to take a neutral stance over the expansion in the size of individual private businesses (Chen Xuewei 1998: 308). In this year the amended Party constitution and the amended state constitution stipulated that the individual economy was "a necessary and beneficial complement to the socialist economy" and that the state would protect its legal rights and interests.

Between 1983 and 1986, the state adopted a wait-and-see stance toward the private economy. Originally a private firm was allowed to employ a maximum of only five employees. From early 1983 to 1984, the state maintained its neutral stance over hiring of employees by household businesses, paving the way for the growth of these firms (Chen Xuewei 1998: 309). In 1984, the Third Plenum of the Twelfth Party Central Committee promulgated the "Decisions regarding Reform of the Economic Structure," declaring that the individual economy was "a necessary and beneficial complement" to the socialist economy and that maintaining joint development of a variety of economic forms was a long-term policy of the Party, giving assurance to small private business.

In 1987 and 1988, the state adopted even more liberal policies. It permitted the larger-sized private businesses (officially termed private enterprises or privately run economy) to exist. The Seventh National

People's Congress introduced a constitutional amendment, stipulating that the state permitted the private economy to exist and develop within the law, that it was a complement to socialist public ownership, and that the state protected its legal rights and interests while guiding, supervising, and administering it. Similar stipulations were spelled out in the "Provisional Articles on Administering Urban and Rural Industrial and Commercial Individual Households" in 1987 and the "Provisional Articles on Private Enterprises" in 1988.

During the 1989–1991 retrenchment of reform, the state still rhetorically regarded the private economy as a necessary complement to the economy. However, the No. 9 Central Party Document in 1989 declared that private entrepreneurs earned their income through exploitation and should not be allowed to join the Party. Many local officials saw it as a green light for discrimination against the private economy. Party branches in some localities proposed to appropriate private businesses with compensation (as the Party did in the 1950s). In several counties, private enterprises were abolished overnight at the order of the local Party leader; in some others private entrepreneurs were arrested or were ordered to pay taxes without due justification (Chen Xuewei 1998: 313–15).

In 1992, the state finally adopted a liberal ideology and policy, greatly easing the concerns of many private entrepreneurs. The Party declared in 1992 and 1993 that it was striving to build a socialist market economy and that various ownerships should exist and prosper over a long period.[6] In 1997, Jiang defended the Party's promotion of private and foreign enterprises amidst heated criticisms by leftist ideologues and intellectuals.

In the 2000s state policies toward private businesses further liberalized. On July 1, 2001, Jiang Zemin indicated in a much-watched speech that as a measure to fulfill its new ideology of "Three Represents" the Party would recruit qualified private entrepreneurs as its members. This marked a watershed in the Party's political policies toward private entrepreneurs. Traditionally, the Party prided itself as a vanguard of the working class and a fighter against capitalists or private employers in the past decades. Over the decades the Party's concept of the working class has been gradually extended from urban workers to peasants, soldiers, and intellectuals. As recent as in August 1989, however, Jiang still had firmly ruled out the possibility of admitting private entrepreneurs into the Party. Jiang's reversal of his position in 2001 signaled to private entrepreneurs that they could obtain political representation in the Party and that they could confidently expand their business in China without having to engage in capital flight and wasteful spending.[7]

In June 2002, the National People's Congress (NPC) passed Law on Encouraging Small- and Medium-Sized Enterprises (SMSE). The law stipulated that the state should provide decent services for SMSE in financial and fiscal assistance, start-up support, taxation, technological innovation, development of markets, and social services. As most of private businesses were SMSE, this law aimed to facilitate the growth of the private sector (LWCNPC 2002).

In March 2003 the Second Session of the Tenth NPC, the Chinese legislature, approved four constitutional amendments: (1) include Jiang Zemin's "Three Represents" into the constitution; (2) regard private entrepreneurs as "socialist builders;" (3) grant protection to legal rights and interests of non-public sectors; and (4) protect lawful private property and declare "citizens' lawful private property is inviolable." These amendments will certainly give private and foreign businesses the much-needed assurance about the state's acceptance of their economic role and due protection of their assets.[8]

Nevertheless, observers notice three limits. First, the legal status of private property still falls short of that of state ownership, which is given a dominant role in the economy as well as a de-facto inviolable status. Second, the above shortfall is due to opposition forces within the Party that lament income disparities and personal wealth accumulated through corrupt dealings. Third, a constitutional amendment limits private property by stipulating that "[T]the state may, in the public interests and in accordance with law, expropriate or requisition private property for its use and shall make compensation for the private property expropriated or requisitioned."[9] Weak public supervision may allow officials to tilt the law to their benefit and infringe upon private property in the name of public interests, economic zone building, and urban development.

The Third Party Plenum of the Sixteenth Party Central Committee in mid October 2003 upgraded the status of the private sector as "important forces" for accelerating China's economic growth. It declared that the private sector should be granted the same treatment in market access, bank loan, taxation, land use, and foreign trade as had been enjoyed by enterprises of other ownership. While the Party Plenum called on non-public enterprises to pay taxes and abide by the law, it also suggested that agencies in charge should improve supervision and services to these enterprises.[10]

Growth of Private Enterprises in the Reform Era

Three types of private enterprises can be identified in today's China. First, private economy that employs a very small number of people, and in many cases, involving mainly the owners themselves or no more than seven employees, is called self-employed individuals, **individual household business** (IHB), or the **individual economy**. Second, private economy that employs a larger number of people (eight or more in the mid-1980s) is termed **private enterprises** (PEs). Third, private economy that has stock holding and yet is owned primarily by a few individuals can also be regarded as private firm. The Chinese statistics identifies mainly the first two types. Data on stock-holding private firms tend to have been collated with that of other types of stock-holding firms and are difficult to disaggregate.

The private economy has gone through ups and downs in the growth in fixed asset investment (FAI), share of total FAI, and job provision. In terms of fixed-asset investment, the private economy expanded very rapidly in the early 1980s, registering a whopping 49.8 percent growth in 1981. The annual growth rate remained at an impressive 26 percent between 1985 and 1988. During the retrenchment of 1989–1991, the growth rate declined sharply to 5.4 percent per annum. With liberal state policies, the growth rate recovered to 20 percent between 1992 and 1997. However, with a slowdown in China's economy, it dwindled to 11.15 percent between 1998 and 2001.

The share of the private economy in total fixed-asset investment also underwent an interesting or even puzzling U-turn. It started at a moderate level, registering 13.1 percent in 1981. It reached 21 percent between 1985 and 1988, and ironically, even peaked at 23.4 percent in 1989. With liberalized state policies after 1992, its share did not increase but declined to 11.3–14.6 percent between 1992 and 2001. It stood at 15 percent in 2002. Reasons for this abnormality are not entirely clear. One possible factor is that since 2000 the State Statistical Bureau has stopped collecting data on non-state enterprises below a certain size and has thus underestimated the size of the private economy. As a result, data on private businesses are incomplete and limited in the 2000s.

The private economy is generating an increasing number of jobs in the nation. In 1978, on the eve of reform, it accounted for merely 0.04 percent of the jobs. In 1985, when the sector was still in its infancy, it created only 0.9 percent of the jobs in the nation. The share increased to 3.5 percent in 1990. As the state further relaxed its control over the sector after 1992, the share of the private economy in employment jumped to 8.2 percent in 1995, and 11.6 percent in 1999 before reaching 11.1 percent in 2002.

Among the two identifiable components of the private economy, IHB has been generating more jobs than PEs. In 2002, urban and rural IHB accounted for 3.1 percent and 3.4 percent of total employment, respectively, and urban and rural PEs 2.7 percent and 1.9 percent, respectively. In the last few years, the private economy has seen its contribution to employment declining slightly. Its share in the nation's employment declined from 11.6 percent in 1999 to 10.4 percent in 2000 to finally reaching a high of 11.1 percent in 2002.[11]

In the 1980s, a majority (probably 75 percent) of the private businesses was located in the countryside. According to official statistics, the share of private businesses in the gross output value of township enterprises increased from 6.9 percent in 1984 to 27 percent in 1992 (Young 1995: 7–8). Registration of private enterprises as collective ones had been common until the mid-1990s, due to political insecurity of private enterprises and local encouragement (Young 1995: 108). A survey by the state on collective enterprises in 1995 in 16 provinces found that individuals, instead of collective entities, owned over half of the assets at 21 percent of these enterprises and that the number of collectively registered private enterprises were twice as large as that of registered private enterprises (Zhang 1999: 51). As of 1993, most private businesses were concentrated on the coast (or the eastern region), as the ratio of individual household enterprises in the eastern, central, and western regions was 5:3:2, and that for private enterprises 7:2:1 (Young 1995: 9). The provinces where private business provided the highest percentage of jobs in 2001 included Shanghai (38 percent), Liaoning (29 percent), Beijing (27 percent), Zhejiang (24 percent), Inner Mongolia (21 percent), and Tianjin (19 percent)(Lai 2004b: 12).

The private economy has become a significant player in retail sales and industry. The private economy's share in retail sales of consumer goods rose from 18.6 percent in 1989 to 38.6 percent in 1999. Its share in industrial output also followed a similar upward trend—from 4.8 percent in 1989 to 18.2 percent in 1999. Its contribution to the state's tax revenue appeared much smaller, ranging between 6 percent and 8 percent. This low share of taxes could be attributed to widespread tax evasion. However, unlike state enterprises and collectively owned firms, the private economy received scant financial and raw material inputs from the state. Therefore, its fiscal contribution is net and genuine (Lan 2001: 27; Lai 2004b: 12).

Privatization of SOEs and Stock Listing

The reform of SOEs also gives private firms the necessary impetus to expand their operation. The Fifteenth Party Congress in 1997 approved a reform program of overhauling and helping 1000 large SOEs and letting go of the small ones (*zhuada fangxiao*). Since the mid-1990s tens of thousands of small- and medium-sized SOEs have been restructured, sold off, closed down, or leased out.[12]

In the course of the reform, even the number of SOEs among large- and medium-sized enterprises (LMEs) declined, though the number of LMEs remained constant between 1994 and 1999. The share of SOEs in LMEs has declined, from over 95 percent in 1985, to 67.9 percent in 1994 and to only 50.6 percent in 1999. The average share of state-owned assets had also fallen from 69 percent in 1994 to 51 percent in 1999.[13]

To increase private stakes about 1400 SOEs are partially or totally privatized via listing in the stock markets both at home and abroad. Over 300 domestically listed companies have also seen a change in ownership since 1993.[14] However, other scholars have doubts over the actual extent of privatization of SOEs. Based on a survey of 683 SOEs in eleven cities between 1995 and 2001, Garnaut et al. (2003: 3) suggest that although 80 percent of SOEs claimed to have completed property rights reforms, the transformation from state to private ownership was rather sluggish.

In addition, only 57 private firms were listed by the end of 2001. The number remains small for two reasons. First, the state favors listing of SOEs for political reasons. Second, only a limited number of firms ranging from 70 to 90 can be listed each year. To overcome this limit, some private companies choose to take over listed SOEs.

Policies toward Foreign and Joint Ventures

Special Economic Zones and Opening of the Coastal Region

China pursued an inward-looking developmental strategy from the 1960s to the late 1970s. During the 1950s, foreign investment in China was limited to four joint enterprises with the Soviets and one joint enterprise with the Polish (Gao, Wang, and He 1993: 1412). These enterprises were respectively in petroleum, metal, aviation, ship-building, and shipping industries (ibid). The Chinese took over the four Sino-Soviet joint ventures in 1954. Between 1955 and 1978, China was nearly free of foreign direct investment (FDI) (ibid., 1412–13; Reardon 1998: 498). During this period, tensions created a rift in China's relations with the United States and with the USSR after 1960. Mass introduction of investment from the Eastern and Western blocs was politically inexpedient (Kleinberg 1990: 104–09). As a result, the Chinese turned to economic nationalism and emphasized self-reliance (Gao, Wang and He 1993: 1412–13).

Foreign loans, a politically less sensitive form of foreign capital, played a minor role in development, especially between 1960 and 1976. Between 1950 and 1960, most of China's foreign loans came from the Soviet Union, totaling 1.274 billion rubles. During the 1960s and 1970s, China's foreign capital other than direct investment was mostly down payment for sellers' credit to purchase equipment from Western Europe and Japan (ibid.).

In the late 1970s, China's leaders were strongly interested in borrowing foreign capital to finance development. In July 1979, the Central Committee of the Chinese Communist Party (CCCCP) and the State Council approved the request from Guangdong for setting up special zones in Shenzhen, Zhuhai, and Shantou and also the request from Fujian in Xiamen. In August 1980, the National People's Congress (NPC) approved "the Articles on Special Economic Zones (SEZs)." The construction for SEZs started afterward.

A preliminary institutional framework for managing FDI started to emerge. First of all, laws on FDI were promulgated. In July 1979 a Sino-Foreign Joint Venture Law went into effect, spelling out 25 percent foreign investment as a minimal criterion for foreign enterprises and guaranteeing legal protection for foreign investment. The state also promulgated laws on income tax on Sino-foreign joint ventures and on foreign enterprises, procedures on approval of Sino-foreign joint ventures, and regulations on provision of labor management at Sino-foreign enterprises (Chen Xuewei 1998: 331). Furthermore, a state agency administering FDI, that is, the State Committee for Administering Foreign Investment, was established (ibid.).

Special Economic Zones enjoyed the following special policies compared to the rest of the nation until April 1984. First, joint ventures and foreign-owned enterprises were largely prohibited outside the SEZs. Second, within the SEZs prices and distribution of goods were regulated by the market, whereas outside the zones they were regulated by central plans. Third, SEZs had broader jurisdiction in approving investment projects. They could approve projects up to RMB100 million, light-industrial projects up to RMB30 million or heavy industrial projects up to RMB50 million. Finally, enterprises especially foreign enterprises at SEZs enjoyed tax holidays and preferential treatment in imports and exports, obtaining raw materials, and using land. For example, the corporate income tax at SEZs was set at a preferential rate of 15 percent, even lower than the 18.5 percent in Hong Kong. Inputs and equipment for production of foreign enterprises were exempt from import tariffs and exporting goods of these enterprises from export tariffs (Chen Xuewei 1998: 287–88).

During the first three years of opening, FDI inflows occurred at a very timid pace. The first foreign enterprise, Beijing Aviation Food Limited Corporation, a Sino-foreign joint venture, was set up in May 1980. From 1980 to 1983, foreign enterprises in China totaled 1361 (Chen Xuewei 1998: 333–35). Foreign enterprises in China can be categorized into one of the four following forms—Sino-foreign equity joint ventures, Sino-foreign contractual joint ventures, foreign-invested companies limited by shares, and foreign-owned enterprises (or foreign-capital enterprises) (Liu and Yang 2001: 235–72).

The areas where FDI could enter were expanded gradually from SEZs to elsewhere over the decades. However, the process had been wrought with political hazards and risks. Between 1981 and 1982 and from mid- to late 1983, conservative leaders criticized SEZs and Guangdong for causing inflation, smuggling and other economic crimes, and Guangdong leaders were pressured to slow down or even halt their economic reform measures. This ordeal ended in January 1984 when Deng launched a political whirlwind that revitalized the Open Policy and reforms (Crane 1990: 93–94; Kleinberg 1990: 53; Howell 1993: 63–65). In May the Central Secretariat of the Party and the State Council granted the status of "open cities" to fourteen coastal cities—Tianjin, Shanghai, Dalian, Qinhuangdao, Yantai, Qingdao, Lianyungang, Nantong, Ningbo, Wenzhou, Fuzhou, Guangzhou, Zhanjiang, and Beihai. These cities accounted for less than 8 percent of the nation's population, 23 percent of the nation's industrial output, and 17 percent of colleges and universities. They also enjoyed the amenities of extensive railways, highways, roads and developed telecommunications as well as ocean harbours or river ports (Chen Xuewei 1998: 290–92). They helped to integrate the nation into the world economy.

These open cities were granted the following preferential policies. First, they could approve investment projects up to a considerable size.

They could approve manufacturing projects utilizing foreign capital for upgrading or beyond state planning up to an amount that varied with the cities. The limits were US$30 million for Tianjin and Shanghai, $10 million for Dalian, and $5 million for other cities. These cities could also approve manufacturing projects of any size outside the parameters of central planning. Second, foreign investment in technology—or knowledge-intensive, or energy and communications projects, or investment exceeding US$30 million could be entitled to 15 percent corporate income tax. Equipment, inputs, and commodities for production or office management were exempt from import tariffs and their exporting products from export tariffs. Finally, open cities could designate an area as an economic and technological development zone where special policies adopted by SEZs could be implemented (Chen Xuewei 1998: 291).

In February 1985, in the wake of the CCCCP's decision to build planned commodity economy and with Deng's approval, the State Council made 61 cities and counties in the Pearl River, Yangtze, and Southern Fujian Deltas "coastal open economic areas" (Howell 1993: 63–74; Chen Xuewei 1998: 292; Yang 1998, I: 265; Chen Li 2002: 80).[15]

Open economic areas benefited from expanded jurisdiction and favorable treatment for foreign-investment. First, provincial capitals and major cities and counties enjoyed a greater say over foreign business and trade; their equipment for technological upgrades, as well as seeds and equipment for export-oriented processing of husbandry and agricultural products were exempt from import tariffs and value-added taxes for a given period. Second, foreign-invested manufacturing or Research and Development (R&D) enterprises in districts of cities, counties, and satellite cities and towns were entitled to corporate income tax at 24 percent; foreign-invested enterprises in energy, transportation, harbours, and technology—or knowledge-intensive projects or above US$30 million could enjoy corporate income tax at 15 percent. In addition, equipment, raw materials, or self-used vehicles for foreign enterprises were exempt from import tariffs and unified industrial and commercial tax (Chen Xuewei 1998: 293).

New legislation and favorable policies for foreign investment were also promulgated. In April 1986, the Law on Foreign Capital Enterprises came into effect. In October, the State Council issued the "Regulations for Promoting Investment by Foreign Businesses." In the twenty clauses of the regulations the state granted foreign enterprises managerial autonomy, as well as concessions over land use fees, labor services fee, production and management arrangements. In October 1987 the State Planning Commission (SPC) issued additional regulations for accelerating the development of the externally oriented economy as well as favorable policies for Taiwan investment. In April 1988 Law on Sino-Foreign Contractual Joint Ventures was approved (Chen Xuewei 1998: 338).[16]

In early 1988 General Party Secretary Zhao Ziyang proposed the coastal development strategy, calling on the coast to integrate with the world economy and inland frontier cities to engage in extensive trade and cooperation with Eastern Europe and Russia (Howell 1993: 86–87). In March 1988 Liaodong and Jiaodong Peninsulas, as well as a number of coastal cities were also opened up. In April 1988, two years after the state's preparation, the First Session of the Seventh NPC legislated that Hainan had become a province and a SEZ. By then, the major economic areas in the coastal region, which were central economic areas in China, had opened up. The coastal open areas contained five SEZs, fourteen coastal open cities, and five open economic areas (three deltas and Liaodong and Jiaodong Peninsulas), covering 293 cities and counties, 280 million population, and 426,000 square kilometres of area (Chen Xuewei 1998: 294, 337, 295).[17]

Between 1984 and 1988, foreign enterprises developed into a visible presence in China. In 1983, the number of newly established foreign enterprises only registered 470. This number quadrupled to 1,856 in 1984, and increased rapidly to 3,073 in 1985. The number dropped to 1,498 in 1986, but recovered to 2,233 in 1987, and more than doubled to 5,945 in 1988. The amount of utilized FDI averaged about US$300 million each year during 1979–1982. It doubled to $640 million in 1983, again doubled to $1.26 billion in 1984 and grew sharply to $1.66 billion in 1985. In the following years FDI utilization increased rapidly, registering $1.87 billion in 1986, $2.3 billion in 1987, and $3.2 billion in 1988 (see table 2.1).

Post-Tiananmen Retrenchment and the Opening of Pudong

The rapid inflows of FDI in China were interrupted by conservatism in reform between 1989 and 1991. In the wake of Deng's failed price reform and hyperinflation in 1988, as well as the Tiananmen movement in 1989, Deng also stepped down from his last yet most powerful official post, namely, the Chairmanship of the Central Military Commission (CMC) in late 1989. Conservative leaders gained an

Table 2.1 China's FDI inflows and exports in the reform era, 1979–2004

Year	Number of projects	Utilized FDI ($ billion)	Exports ($ billion)
1979–1982	922	1.17	
1983	470	0.64	22.23
1984	1,856	1.26	26.14
1985	3,073	1.66	27.35
1986	1,498	1.87	30.94
1987	2,233	2.31	39.44
1988	5,945	3.19	47.52
1989	5,779	3.39	52.54
1990	7,273	3.49	62.09
1991	12,978	4.37	71.91
1992	48,764	11.01	84.94
1993	83,437	27.51	91.74
1994	47,549	33.77	121.01
1995	37,011	37.52	148.78
1996	24,556	41.73	151.05
1997	21,001	45.26	182.79
1998	19,799	45.46	183.71
1999	16,918	40.32	194.93
2000	22,347	40.72	249.20
2001	26,140	46.88	266.10
2002	34,171	52.74	325.60
2003	41,081	53.51	438.23
2004	43,664	60.63	593.37

Source: SSB 2005b: 161, 168, 169.

upper hand over politics and economic policies. They instituted macroeconomic and reform retrenchment. Conservative propagandists even questioned past economic policies during the period 1987–1991. They equated the market economy to abolition of public ownership and central planning, and juxtaposed the former and the latter as mutually exclusive embodiments of socialism and capitalism. They urged that the nation should reject everything that could be deemed capitalist, including private, foreign, and even rural collective owner-ship; they deplored the foreign-contracted development of designated pieces of land in Hainan as a sell-out of national sovereignty (Yin and Yang 2004: 127–29).

The austere measures and hostile environment led to a decline in the number of FDI projects in China, from 5,945 in 1988 to 5,779 in 1989. Meanwhile, the amount of utilized FDI grew sluggishly from $3.19 billion to $3.39 billion, representing only a 6.3 percent growth, one-sixth of the 38 percent annual growth during 1987–1988 (SSB 2005: 168–69).

Only a small number of initiatives were taken during post-Tiananmen retrenchment. First, in 1990, three other bonded zones, that is, Tianjin Harbor, Futian, and Shatoujiao Bonded Zones (the latter two were in Shenzhen), were also approved. Second, Pudong and the banking sector in Shanghai were opened up.

Third, the center granted favorable policies to Shanghai in 1990, turning the mega city into a new base for the Open Policy. This was a breakthrough in the Open Policy that Deng strove for amidst the conservative backlash (Howell 1993: 94). The opening of Pudong was proposed by Shanghai in its outline for local economic developmental strategy in 1985 and in its program for municipal planning in 1986. Both considerations won the approval of the State Council in the same year (Chen Li 2002: 125–26). It was believed that Chen Yun, who spent years as an underground communist leader in Shanghai and who regarded Shanghai as his local power base, disapproved and effectively vetoed it. Deng opened up Shanghai and made Pudong District a de facto SEZ in 1990 out of two strategic considerations. First of all, Shanghai was the most-developed province with the most-skilled labor and the strongest manufacturing and service sectors. In addition, Shanghai played a pivotal role in the Yangtze Delta and even the lower Yangtze Valley. The Yangtze Delta was well connected by good transportation with central and northern China. It was the key base for foreign businesses to enter China's domestic markets. By opening up Shanghai, the Yangtze Delta could be revitalized and economic reform could gain momentum (Yin and Yang 2004: 162). Deng's second consideration was that both Shanghai's leaders and the Party Secretary supported the opening of Shanghai. Shanghai Party Secretary and Mayor Zhu Rongji was an able and committed reformist who backed Deng's economic reforms. General Party Secretary Jiang Zemin also saw Shanghai as his local powerbase. Zhu and Jiang thus warmly supported the further opening of Shanghai.

In June 1988, Deng hinted at resurrecting Shanghai's status as China's foremost financial center by stating that mainland China would build several "Hong Kongs" (Chen Li 2002: 137). In early 1990, Deng toured Shanghai, paying special attention to the opening of the Pudong area of Shanghai. Upon returning to Beijing, Deng asked Premier Li Peng to pay heed to the opening of Pudong and the development of Shanghai. In March, he suggested to leaders of the Party and the State Council that accelerating development of Shanghai was a major measure for China's economic growth. Under Deng's clear instruction, Vice Premier Yao Yilin led State Council ministers to study the opening of Pudong. In June the State Council approved the opening and development of Pudong District. In September it approved the establishment of Waigaoqiao Bonded Zone in Pudong (Yin and Yang 2004: 163–64). Meanwhile, the People's Bank of China, China's central bank, promulgated "Methods for Managing Foreign-Invested Financial Agencies and Sino-Foreign Jointly-Invested Financial Agencies in Shanghai," giving foreign banks a green light to enter China through Shanghai. In May 1991, a Japanese bank, the first foreign bank in People's Republic of China, was opened in Shanghai. Many foreign banks set up their offices in Lujiazui Financial Trade Zone in Pudong. In December 1990, Shanghai Stock Exchange Office started its business. Seven years later its office was moved into a new office named "Shanghai Stock Building" in Lujiazui (Chen Li 2002: 51, 53, 137–46).

The fourth measure in sustaining the Open Policy is that in 1990 new laws and regulations were made to assure foreign investors that China would maintain its Open Policy and welcomed foreign investment. In April the NPC amended Law on Sino-Foreign Equity Joint Ventures. It stipulated against nationalization of foreign enterprises and required compensation and abiding by legal procedures should appropriation be needed under unusual circumstances. The revised law also revoked the stipulation against foreigners becoming board directors, opening the possibility of foreign board directors through consultation or elections through partners. The revised law gave strong assurance to foreign investors who worried about China's takeover of foreign enterprises.

In April 1991 the NPC replaced Law on Income Tax on Sino-Foreign Equity Joint Ventures in 1980 and Law on Income Tax on Foreign-owned Enterprises with Law on Income Tax on Sino-Foreign Equity Joint Ventures and Foreign-owned Enterprises. The new law reduced differences in favorable tax rates for these two types of enterprises, lowered tax rates, expanded tax reduction and exemption among manufacturing enterprises, and revoked tax concessions for non-producing enterprises (Chen Li 2002: 46–51).

With these measures and assuring policies in place, the FDI inflows in China recovered and started to grow rapidly. The number of new FDI projects initially declined from 5,945 to 5,779 in 1989. It recovered to 7,273 in 1990 and grew to 12,978 in 1991. The amount of utilized FDI, however, grew at a more modest pace, from $3.2 billion in

1988 to $3.39 billion in 1989, and to $3.49 billion in 1990. It rose to $4.37 billion in 1991 (SSB 2005: 168–69)(table 2.1).

Deng's Southern Tour and Opening of Interior Cities

Geographically, further opening during 1989–1991 was mainly restricted to primarily Pudong. Nationwide, conservatism still trumped reformism. In order to break the stalemate in reform, Deng, at the age of 88, toured Wuchang, Shenzhen, Zhuhai, Yingtan of Jiangxi, and Shanghai in early 1992. He assailed conservatism and called on the nation to adopt any technology and economic institutions that could help liberate "productive forces." His tour generated a nationwide wave of liberalism. In October 1992 the Fourteenth Party Congress declared that the state would build a "socialist market economy."

In his concluding speech at the Seventh Plenum of the Thirteenth Party Central Committee in December 1990, Jiang proposed to selectively open up a few border cities (Chen Li 2002: 99). However, this bold move was possible only after the return of economic liberalism in the wake of Deng's Southern Tour. A new round of opening was set in motion in 1992, resulting in several bold moves of opening up China's inland regions. First, the Yangtze basin became a focal point for opening. Six harbor cities along the Yangtze, namely, Wuhu, Jiujiang, Huangshi, Wuhan, Yueyang, and Chongqing, were opened up; the setup of the Yangtze Three Gorge Economic Open Region was approved. Second, thirteen frontier cities were opened up and fourteen border economic cooperation zones were approved. The frontier cities included Heihe and Xufenhe in Heilongjiang; Huichun in Jilin; Manzhouli and Erenhot in Neimenggu; Yining, Taicheng, and Bole in Xinjiang; Pinxiang and Dongxing in Guangxi; and Hekou, Wanding, and Ruili in Yunnan. The border economic cooperation zones included one in each of these above border open cities plus the Fenxuhe Border Economic Cooperation Zone. Third, eighteen provincial capital cities that were located inland were also opened up during June and July. They included Harerbin, Changchun, Hohhot, Shijiazhuang, Taiyuan, Hefei, Changsha, Nanchang, Zhengzhou, Nanning, Chengdu, Kunming, Guiyang, Xi'an, Lanzhou, Yinchuang, Xining, and Urumqi. These open frontier cities and provincial capitals enjoyed some of the preferential policies adopted in the coastal open cities (Chen Xuewei 1998: 342; Chen Li 2002: 52, 103–04).

Progress was also made in the opening-up of China's coast and banking sector. In March 1992 the State Council approved the setup of the Yangpu Economic Developmental Zone in northwestern Hainan (Chen Li 2002: 114–16). In 1993, Tianjin, Dalian, and Guangzhou became the cities where foreign banks could operate after Shanghai (Chen Li 2002: 53). The liberalization drive in 1992 also resulted in an explosion in the number of developmental zones nationwide from 117 in 1991 to 2,000 in early 1993 and unjustified seizure of land. This prompted the State Council to issue an "Announcement to Strictly Approve and Conscientiously Clean Up Various Developmental Zones" in May 1993 (Chen Li 2002: 90–92). During 1992–1994 a few prominent scholars and policy commentators questioned whether SEZs should continue to enjoy preferential policies. In June 1994, Jiang declared that SEZs should continue, ending this controversy (ibid. 187–88).

The new wave of liberalism during 1992–94 generated explosive growth in FDI inflows in China. The number of new FDI projects in China nearly quadrupled, growing from 12,978 in 1991 to 48,764 in 1992. It nearly doubled to 83,437 in 1993. The utilized FDI nearly tripled, increasing from $4.37 billion in 1991 to $11 billion in 1992. It more than doubled to $27.5 billion in 1993. When the state started to consolidate its liberal policies and clamped down on overambitious expansion of developmental zones, the FDI inflows slowed down to a lower but still impressive pace in 1994. The number of projects declined from 83,437 in 1993 to 47,549 in 1994, but the amount of utilized FDI gained significantly from $27.5 billion to $33.8 billion (SSB 2005: 168–69)(table 2.1).

Further Opening of the Interior Regions and the WTO Entry

Since 1995, China has continued to encourage FDI to enter previously restricted sectors as well as the interior regions through the state's promulgation of new regulations and China's entry to the World Trade Organization (WTO). In June 1995 the SPC, the State Economic and Trade Commission (SETC), and the Ministry of Foreign Trade and External Cooperation (MOFTEC) jointly issued "Provisional Regulations on Direction of Foreign Investment" and "A Guiding Catalogue regarding Sectors for Foreign Investment," permitting foreign business to invest in cultivation of barren hills, irrigation, local railway, microelectronics, and bio-engineering (Chen Xuewei 1998: 342). In particular, foreign investment was strongly encouraged in agricultural technology and comprehensive exploration, new or advanced technology, energy, transportation, key raw materials, renewable and recyclable energy and inputs, and pollution reduction. In addition, the state also encouraged FDI that engaged in exports and utilized human capital and natural resources to go into the central and western regions (Chen Li 2002: 224–28).

Between 1998 and 2000 the state announced a set of policies that aimed to facilitate the inflows of FDI into the interior regions. In April 1998 the Party Central Committee and the State Council issued "Several Opinions regarding Further Expanding External Opening and Raising the Level of Utilized Foreign Investment." According to the document, advantaged sectors in the interior regions that were indicated in "A Guiding Catalogue regarding Sectors for Foreign Investment" could enjoy preferential policies. In addition, a number of agricultural, irrigation, transportation, energy, raw materials, and environmental protection projects in these regions would be set aside for foreign investment. In October 2000 the State Council issued "An Announcement regarding Several Policies and Measures for Implementing Great Western Development," specifying that agriculture, irrigation, ecology, transportation, energy, municipal utilities, environmental protection, minerals, and tourism in the western region were open for foreign investment. Foreign investment could also enter on a trial basis areas of banking, commercial retails, and foreign trade in the capital cities of western provinces; foreign banks in the western region could gradually provide financial services in RMB; foreign business could invest in telecommunications, insurance, tourism, accounting and legal consultancy, engineering project design, as well as railways and highway cargo transports. Foreign investment was encouraged to take stock shares and take part in management as well as merging and acquisition of enterprises in these regions. Experiments with foreign capital in build-operate-transfer (BOT) and transfer-operate-transfer (TOT) were permitted. In December 2001, the State Council promulgated "Opinions regarding Implementing Several Policies and Measures for Great Western Development," further revising and updating policies for FDI (Chen Li 2002: 228–32; Lai 2002).

Developmental zones continue to be set up across the nation. Since 1992 China has set up 15 bonded areas, 49 national-level economic technological developmental zones, and 53 national-level new and high tech industrial developmental zones.[18]

The boldest move for China to open up its economy for foreign investment since 1992 has been its entrance to the WTO. After decades of strenuous negotiations, China and the United States concluded a landmark agreement regarding China's WTO entry in November 1999.[19] Half a year later, China and the European Union (EU) also reached an agreement on the issue. In December 2001, China became a new member of the WTO. China made this bold move of joining the WTO for a set of external and domestic reasons. They included overcoming external trade barriers (including the U.S. Congress's annual review of China's most-favored nation status) and earning a favorable external environment for China's long-term growth, stimulating inflows of FDI, forging ahead with domestic economic reform, creating norms for a market economy, forcing uncompetitive sectors to improve their performance and generating growth and jobs (Lai 2001b: 246–51).

According to the protocol for China's WTO entry, China would cut its import tariffs. More importantly, it has committed to open up its goods-producing sectors, as well as services sectors such as retail sales, stock exchange, accounting, legal consultancy, construction, and tourism. China's motor vehicles, agriculture, banking, and telecommunications may be vulnerable to foreign competition in the wake of the WTO accession (Lardy 2002: 111–19). China would have a transition period of three to five years (Chen Li 2002: 234–39, 456–62). Non-state players (including peasants, enterprises, and individual business people) would have to adapt to more intense foreign competition. China's large SOEs, such as state banks and state firms in petrochemical, steel, automobiles, aviation, and railway, have been preoccupied with strengthening themselves during the transition period ahead of full-fledged foreign competition.

The state is also under heavy pressure to adjust to the WTO entry. The first major move was to cut tariffs. In the early 1980s China's general tariff level had been reduced steadily. China's average statutory import tariff rate declined from 55.6 percent in 1982 to 43.3 percent in 1985, to 39.9 percent in 1993. China lowered its tariff level to 23 percent in 1996 and further to 17 percent in 1997 (Lardy 2002: 34). On January 1, 2001 the state reduced tariffs from 17 percent to 15.3 percent. In 2002, in meeting its obligation as a WTO member, China further cut its tariff level to 12 percent. China is prepared to reduce its tariff level to 10 percent, lower than the average level of developing countries.[20]

In addition, the national, provincial, and local leaders have been undergoing training to familiarize themselves with China's WTO accession protocol; moreover, the state is overhauling its legislation and regulations to make them WTO compatible. The NPC has been reviewing, modifying, and annulling laws; the State Council ministries and the local governments across the nation have been busy with reviewing, changing, or revoking regulations. By December 2002, the State Council had annulled 830 rules or regulations, revised 325, and overhauled 1,155. In addition, the national and local governments are publicizing formerly strictly internal documents related to trade and the economy. They also post regulations in advance of formal promulgation for feedbacks. The state has drastically scaled back the items that required administrative approval. The MOFTEC (which later became part of the Ministry of Commerce) also set up three departments to take care of issues related to China's WTO entry, that is, the Department for WTO Affairs, the China WTO Notification and Enquiry Center, and the Bureau for Fair Trade for Imports and Exports (Lai 2003: 154–58).

In the wake of China's WTO entry and growing acceptance of national treatment for all enterprises in China, a trend is emerging. First, the very favorable corporate income tax for foreign enterprises will be phased out. Instead, a uniform corporate income tax will apply to all enterprises. Second, the Chinese state will extend favorable treatment (such as granting the entry of markets for sectors) from foreign enterprises to collective-owned, private, and non-state stock-holding enterprises. However, for a few years to come foreign enterprises may still enjoy favorable treatments such as concessions from local governments over use of land, provision of electric power, and speedier administrative services.[21]

China's embrace of the world markets described above has yielded handsome economic returns. During the decade 1995–2004, despite fluctuation, FDI inflows in China were growing rapidly. The amount of utilized FDI grew steadily from $33.8 billion in 1994 to $41.7 billion in 1996 and peaked at $45.5 billion in 1998. In the wake of the Asian financial crisis, however, it declined to $40.3 billion in 1999 and $40.7 billion in 2000. China's conclusion of the WTO agreement with the United States in late 1999 and subsequent WTO accession, however, reversed this declining trend and triggered another wave of the FDI inflows. The utilized FDI grew to $46.9 billion in 2001 and to $60.6 billion in 2004 (table 2.1). For most of the 1990s China was the second largest recipient of FDI in the world (Lardy 2002: 4). Since 2003 China has become the top recipient.

Propelled by the Open Policy and foreign investors, China's foreign trade has been growing at a miraculous pace. China's exports grew from $9.75 billion in 1978 to $62.1 billion in 1990, to $249.2 billion

Table 2.2 Share of state and non-state sectors in gross industrial output (provincial total = 100) (%)

Area	1978		1994		1978–1994
	State	Non-state (Collective)	State	Non-state	Change in the size of non-state sector
National Average	77.6	22.4	37.3	62.7	40.3
Coastal region					
Beijing	82.7	17.3	44.4	55.6	38.3
Tianjin	80.7	19.3	35.3	64.7	45.4
Hebei	71.8	28.2	32.8	67.2	39.0
Liaoning	82.5	17.5	42.8	57.2	39.7
Shanghai	91.7	8.3	42.4	57.6	49.3
Jiangsu	61.4	38.6	19.9	80.1	41.5
Zhejiang	61.3	38.7	16.1	83.9	45.2
Fujian	74.1	25.9	32.0	68.0	42.1
Shandong	67.6	32.4	24.5	75.5	43.1
Guangdong	67.8	32.2	21.7	78.3	46.1
Guangxi	78.9	21.1	42.9	57.1	36.0
Hainan	82.5	17.5	50.0	50.0	32.5
Central region					
Shanxi	78.1	21.9	43.7	56.3	34.4
Neimengu (Inner Mongolia)	79.1	20.9	65.4	34.6	13.7
Jilin	78.9	21.1	62.4	37.6	16.5
Heilongjiang	83.1	16.9	69.3	30.7	13.8
Anhui	79.9	20.1	18.8	81.2	61.1
Jiangxi	78.2	21.8	37.1	62.9	41.1
Henan	74.1	25.9	34.8	65.2	39.3
Hubei	77.3	22.7	44.4	55.6	32.9
Hunan	75.0	25.0	44.4	55.6	30.6
Western region					
Sichuan	81.4	18.6	37.1	62.9	44.3
Guizhou	81.1	18.9	69.8	30.2	11.3
Yunnan	80.5	19.5	73.4	26.6	7.1
Xizang	76.5	23.5	78.6	21.4	−2.1
Shaanxi	84.2	15.8	57.9	42.1	26.3
Gansu	93.8	6.2	74.6	25.4	19.2
Qinghai	82.4	17.6	84.0	16.0	−1.6
Ningxia	83.0	17.0	70.8	29.2	12.2
Xinjiang	89.1	10.9	75.2	24.8	13.9

Sources: SSB 1990b, 1996b.

in 2000 and to $593.4 billion in 2004. Its rank of total trade volume in the world improved from the twenty-seventh in 1978, to the sixteenth in 1990, to the eighth in 1997, and to the third in 2004 (table 2.1; SSB 2005b: 161, 206). China has been transformed from a populous and underdeveloped economy to a powerhouse of exports and manufacturing in the world.

China's active promotion of non-state sectors in the reform era has changed its economic landscape beyond recognition. In 1975, on the eve of reform, the state sector accounted for 81 percent of gross industrial output value (GIOV) of the nation, and the non-state (collective) sector merely 19 percent. However, by 1993, the share of the state sector in the GIOV declined to 47 percent, that for the collective, private, and foreign and mixed sectors grew to 34 percent, 8 percent and 11 percent, respectively. For the first time, the non-state sectors dominated the GIOV. By 2004, this trend deepened, as the share of the state sector in the GIOV for enterprises up to a designated size declined further to 35.2 percent.

In recent years the collective sector has also suffered from relatively unclear property rights and poor management. Its share in the GIOV declined to 5.7 percent in 2004. Another reason is, as stated above, that many private enterprises that were previously registered as collective ones have changed their registration as business environment improves.

In 2004, private, foreign, and stock-sharing and mixed sectors grew rapidly, as their shares in the GIOV reached 16.5 percent, 31.4 percent, and 11.2 percent, respectively (table 1.2; SSB 2005: 127). This diversified and dynamic change in ownership composition has resulted in a rapid expansion of the industry, as the GIOV increased by 4 times during 1978–1993, and by 2.3 times during 1993–2004 (SSB 2005: 22). Moreover, non-state sectors took up probably an even larger share in the tertiary sector, whose size was only second to that of the industrial sector. Non-state sectors expand at highly varying paces across provinces. This is reflected in the varying changes in the share of the non-state sectors in the GIOV during 1978–1994 (table 2.2). In general, coastal provinces have witnessed more explosive growth of non-state sectors and a sharper decline of the state sector than inland regions. The regional variance in reform from 1978 to 1994, as well as the policy cycles suggested in the above analysis, will be a focus of investigation in the later chapters.

3

Managing Elite Conflict and Policy Cycles

Two outstanding issues regarding China's reforms will be examined in this chapter—policy conflict within top leadership and the progress of national reform policies during 1978–1994. Top leaders occupy central positions and wield a primary and even overriding influence in policy making. They were, however, divided into contending factions. This division affected the progress of reforms, resulting in cyclical changes of policies.

This chapter examines conflict within the top leadership over reform, reformist management of the conflict, and political business cycles. It analyzes the rise of pragmatic leadership, subsequent division between orthodox and moderate reformists and between reformists and conservatives, consequential political business cycles, and the decline of the cycles after 1994.

In explaining policy cycles, I will review existing explanations of cycles, use empirical evidence to verify these arguments, uncover the dynamics of cycles, and discuss periods of the cycles. My first argument is that reformists and conservative factions strove to meet popular demands for fast growth and low inflation, respectively, and triggered political business cycles. My second argument suggests that reformists adopted a flexible strategy that allowed them to sustain reforms. They took on favorable occasions to push through liberal policies. When the results of the policies were unfavorable and when backlashes against reforms were intense, they made tactical retreats, leaving conservatives a larger voice in policy making. Through this strategy of two steps forward one step backward, reformists, especially Deng Xiaoping, kept the marketization program alive despite repeated and even catastrophic setbacks. In addition, Deng had avoided open and violent clashes among top leaders and ensured political stability, though at the price of permitting a delay of political reform. At the end, despite cyclical change, China's economic liberalization progressed incrementally.

The rest of this chapter has the following sections. In the first and second sections I will first examine top leadership and its factions in China during the reform era, and then analyze reformist strategy of managing elite conflict. In the third section I will review the periods of cycles and cyclical changes in China's reform policies. I will then investigate the sources of cycles by examining and verifying existing arguments on the topic.

Top Leadership and Factionalism

China's political system is centralized and hierarchical. At the apex of China's power pyramid is the top leadership that had a vital say in policy making. The importance of leadership arises from the fact that the Chinese political regime is authoritarian, centralized, and Leninist. This point is stressed at times by China scholars.[1] Tang Tsou (1986), for example, argued that political elites played a very critical role in integrating China into a political community.

Until the 1990s the tremendous influence and even the rank order of top leaders was based not just from their formal positions, but more importantly, on their long careers in the political system, their seniority, their prestige, and their extensive personal connections. Strategic reform decisions were made by top leadership. According to Lieberthal and Oksenberg (1988: 35–37), top leaders in the 1980s and the early 1990s might comprise 25 to 35 leaders and could be categorized into the following four types—the paramount leader, Party elders, generalists, and functional specialists. First was the paramount leader, namely, Deng Xiaoping. Deng was a close ally of Mao since the 1930s and was highly trusted by Mao until the early 1960s and during 1973–1975 (Gao 2003). Deng had extensive experience in both the Party and the military (J. Huang 2000). He was a political commissar of one of the four field armies in the civil war and was regarded as the Eleventh Marshall who did not receive the military rank due to his civilian background (Teiwes 1995: 68). During 1954–1966, Deng was one of the top leaders of the Party, serving as a General Secretary of the Party. In the post-Mao period, Deng became the most influential leader. He took charge of most senior personnel appointments, specified ideological guidelines, and identified primary tasks for the state (Lieberthal and Oksenberg 1988: 36).

Second, there were several Party elders. The undisputable top elder (just next to Deng) was Chen Yun. Chen was the most senior leader in the post-Mao period, yet his influence was restricted to the Party and the administration. Chen was long regarded as the top expert in finance and economics in the Party and continued to dominate the State Planning Commission and the Ministry of Finance, two most powerful economic departments of the government. Thus Chen Yun competed against Deng primarily for control over economic policies. In the early 1990s, other top veterans in the rank order were Peng Zhen, Yang Shangkun, Bo Yibo, Li Xiannian, Deng Yingchao, and Wang Zhen. Deng, Chen, and these six veterans were called "eight elders" (*ba lao*) (Ren 1997: 52–54). In the early 1980s, Marshal Ye Jianying was also an influential veteran whose influence was as great as that of Deng and Chen.

Third were "generalists" who coordinated activities of the large Chinese bureaucracy and served as lieutenants of the paramount leader. They were also responsible for handling bureaucratic conflicts, managing daily state affairs, and deciding upon major policies. They included Party Secretary Hu Yaobang, Premier and late Party Secretary Zhao Zhiyang, Vice Premier Wan Li, and Premier Li Peng who succeeded Zhao.

Fourth were functional leaders who took charge of individual function areas of the state, including Party discipline and legal affairs; legislation; foreign affairs; the economy; the military; the ideology; propaganda; culture; education; and science and technology. Most of the top leaders in the third and fourth category and many of those in the second category were members of the Politburo. Their profile will be discussed in chapter 4.

China scholars widely note that Chinese politics is characterized by factional conflict. Factions are informal and flexible networks of personal relations that exchange support for resources (Dittmer 1990; Baum 1996: 9). Factions usually consist of a leader and a group of followers. Members of a faction share policy preferences that differ from those of other factions. Differing preferences often cause conflict between factions.[2] Jing Huang (2000) attributes factionalism in Chinese politics to four factors—concentration of power in the hands of individual leaders on top of the hierarchy, the Party's monopoly of legal channels for expressing diverse interests, failure to formally institutionalize the decision-making process, and frequent intervention of the military in politics. Other scholars, on the other hand, regard factionalism as a form of informal politics, a result of fusion of state and society and personal connections (*guanxi*), which is common in

East Asia. They regard informal politics as a complement to formal politics governed by formal rules and institutions, especially when the rule of law has yet to be fully adopted (Pye 1995; Fukui 2000: 1–14). The end result of these factors is that factions, sometimes fluid and complex, permeate Chinese politics (Dittmer 1995; Tsou 1995). Differing policy preferences, or political lines (*lu xian*) and ideological outlooks, separate one faction from another.[3] During 1976–1978 China's top leadership was divided into Maoists (Whateverists) and pragmatists; it fell into two clusters of reformists and conservatives during 1978–1992.[4]

Whateverists versus Pragmatists. Between 1976 and 1978 the Chinese leadership consisted of "whateverists" represented by Mao's hand-picked successor Hua Guofeng, and pragmatists, represented by Party veterans such as Chen Yun, and later Deng Xiaoping. "Whateverists" were orthodox Maoists, and were named after their adherence to whatever Mao had said. They maintained that class struggle should remain the Party's key political line and that Mao's purge of "capitalist roaders" (referring to supporters of household farming and elements of market economy) such as Deng was justified.

Hua desperately wanted economic growth in order to demonstrate his leadership abilities. Since domestic capital was insufficient for building his 120 mega projects in industry and transport, Hua turned to foreign capital. However, he obviously would not tolerate the use of foreign capital to such a large scale as to undermine China's planned economy and to upset Mao's policy of minimizing the practice of the market economy. As discussed in the following chapter, Hua thus supported the use of foreign capital in few aspects and in restricted areas. Although apparently at odds with his conservative political tone, it served his ambitious economic goals. Therefore, his version of opening might somehow resemble Ceausescu of Romania who promoted exports so as to finance foreign loans to support industrialization and who practiced personal cult and outmoded politics.

Pragmatists, including reformist Deng and conservative Chen, rejected Mao's radical politics in favor of an orthodox Party ideology and balanced economic growth. Deng, relying on an extensive power base that he cultivated during his impressive career, carefully coordinated attacks on Hua. In late 1978 Hua succumbed and lost his political influence. In 1980 Hua handed over his positions of the Party General Secretary and the Premier to Deng's protégés, Hu Yaobang and Zhao Ziyang, respectively.

The Third Plenum of the Eleventh Central Committee of the Communist Party (CCCP) in December 1978 marked the start of the reforms. The Plenum declared that the Party had shifted its focus away from Maoist ideological campaigns and toward "socialist moderniza- tion." The Plenum also decided to raise procurement prices of agricul- tural goods, lower prices of agricultural inputs, and delegate power to the localities. The first two measures were to win over the support of peasants, and the third measure was to generate growth (Tang 1998: 98–99; 88–89) as well as support for reform from provinces (Shirk 1993).

After late 1978, pragmatists occupied the political stage. Disputes over the pace and contents of reforms started to divide the pragmatist camp into two opposing factions, namely, reformists led by Deng versus conservatives led by Chen.

Orthodox and Moderate Reformists.   In the economic arena, both orthodox and moderate reformists supported progressive liberalization. They welcomed economic reform experiments and were willing to adopt ones that were successful.

Orthodox reformists, such as Deng, firmly upheld the dictatorship of the Chinese Communist Party (CCP). *Moderate* reformists, on the other hand, formally believed that some degree of political opening could help improve the governance of the CCP.[5] Their representatives were Deng's protégés, namely, Hu Yaobang during 1980–1986 and Zhao Ziyang in 1989. Deng's post-Tiananmen-movement comments regarding the dismissals of Hu and Zhao from their posts of the Party General Secretary illustrate the divergence between moderate and orthodox reformists (Tang 1998: 365):

> We did not make a mistake in selecting them as the Party General Secretary. However, they later made a mistake and fell on a fundamental issue, namely, that of four cardinal principles. The core of the four cardinal principles is the (Communist) Party leadership and socialism. The opposite of the four cardinal principles is bourgeois liberalization. For several times in each of these years, I have talked about upholding the four cardinal principles and opposing bourgeois liberalization. However, neither of them implemented what I said.

Conservatives.   The arch conservative was Chen Yun. Other leading conservatives included Li Xiannian, Peng Zhen, Bo Yibo, and, prior to 1992, Li Peng. Economically, conservatives adhered to the central role of economic planning and state ownership, and acceded to market forces a secondary position. Referring to the market as a bird and to economic planning as a cage, Chen Yun proposed that China's economy should become a bird in a cage. Chen, the leading conservative, even believed that the command economy could be saved and rationalized (Fewsmith 1994: 10). They also wanted to limit the extent of China's opening to the world economy (Lieberthal 1995: 137), though some of them did not oppose China's opening. In addition, they emphasized balanced growth and real economic results and opposed big pushes in reforms. Thus conservatives were at odds with reformists over whether China needed a full-fledged market economy.

In addition, conservatives, especially Chen, disagreed with Deng's bold strides toward economic liberalization and might even have regarded his moves as somewhat reckless. Deng tried to use rapid growth to garner popular backing for the CCP, as expressed in his talk with national leaders in 1990 during the post-Tiananmen retrenchment:

> Some countries run into problems. A fundamental reason is that their economies cannot grow, that their living standards decline, and that their people have to live a thrifty life. Why do the people support us now? It is because development has occurred in the past decade and because development is noticeable. Suppose the economy grows at four or five percent, or even two to three percent, what kind of consequence will it lead to? The consequence will not only be economic, but also essentially political (Tang 1998: 417).

Conservatives, on the other hand, were more concerned with macroeconomic stability (Dittmer and Wu 1995), the quality of growth, and inflation. Chen, the leading conservative and a top Chinese expert in the command economy, emphasized growth that balanced agriculture and heavy and light industries and stressed on low inflation. Chen's views reflected that of much of the bureaucracy and Party apparatus in charge of economic affairs and planning, where he spent most of his career. In addition, Mao's desire to create rash growth and consequential economic chaos also reinforced Chen's view on balanced growth.[6] This view led Chen to frequently stress on low inflation and macrostability. This view was also based on his experience of taming hyperinflation in large cities predominantly in coastal areas (such as Shanghai, Beijing, Tianjin, and Shenyang) between 1949 and 1950 that resulted from the nationalist government (He et al. 1995: 23–28). Chen acutely realized that public outrage over rampant inflation helped to weaken the National government and that the Chinese Communist government should avoid the inflation trap.

Conservatives, on the other hand, agreed with *orthodox* reformists regarding the CCP monopoly of power. In addition, conservatives such as Chen Yun emphasized Party discipline and honesty, and were constantly on guard against cadre corruption and decadent lifestyles (Bachman 1985: 85).[7]

The elders, especially Deng Xiaoping and Chen Yun, wielded enormous power over economic policies prior to 1994. They could initiate a policy and secure its approval at the Politburo, the Central Committee and the Congress of the Communist Party, the State Council, and the People's Congress. But usually the elders were preoccupied with fundamental economic and political decisions and major appointments at or above the ministerial or provincial level. As the most senior and the ultimate leader of the military, Deng was "the first among the equals" in the senior leadership. His profile and seniority in the Party and the administration surpassed the other Party elders, with the exception of Chen Yun. Deng, on the other hand, had built a tremendous influence and following within the military, popularity among the people, and international recognition, which Chen did not achieve (Dittmer 1995: 26). In addition, as stated, Deng had been among Mao's core group, was highly praised by Mao in his meeting with Khrushchev in the 1950s and in his recall of Deng to the office in 1973. Deng was also in active control of central Party, administrative, or military affairs prior to 1966 and during 1973–1976 (Teiwes 1995: 62–68). As stated, he also had unparalleled power in major appointments and over the propaganda machinery and benefited from a relatively polished public image (Dittmer 1995: 23–24). The latter gave him an edge over Chen.[8]

Reformist Strategy of Overcoming Opposition

Within the small circle of political elders mentioned above, however, reformists led by Deng appeared to be a minority. The paramount leader and elderly top leaders were more powerful than the generalist and functional specialist top leaders. The steadfast reformist elders among the eight elders were only Deng and Yang Shangkun. Yang's rank was even lower than those of Chen and Peng. Among the remaining elders, Chen Yun, Peng Zhen, Li Xiannian, and Bo Yibo were clearly conservative. Deng Yingchao appeared to be inactive in the debates over reforms. Therefore, given their minority position and given Chen's unparalleled reputation as the top economics expert in the Party, reformists faced an uphill battle in launching their liberal agenda.

Reformists adopted Fabian tactics in expanding marketization and overcoming conservative opposition. First, they utilized favorable occasions to push forward reforms, yet were willing to retreat and allowed conservatives to take over the policy platform whenever reforms ran into trouble. Specifically, when local initiatives yielded favorable results, and when political atmospheres and economic situation permitted liberal measures, reformists would waste no time in relaxing ideological control, calling for more local initiatives, and allowing rapid growth in local investment. When reforms led to economic problems such as inflation, economic overheat, smuggling and other economic crimes, as well as public resentments, reformists were wise to allow conservatives to speak up, take over the control of policies, and introduce retrenchment to restore macroeconomic balance. However, reformists readily seized amicable timing to take back the control of policies and rekindled liberal initiatives.

Second, in executing the Fabian tactics and forging ahead with progress in marketization, reformists tried to mobilize public support. They were keenly aware that the Chinese were tired of Maoist political campaigns and were impatient with the stagnation in their living standards. They realized that accelerated reforms could generate rapid growth as well as a quick increase in the living standard and the number of jobs. They "advertised" to the populace their reformist agenda as an effective approach to ending poverty and generating prosperity. In doing so, they did win considerable public support, especially from the countryside in the early and mid-1980s and in the coastal provinces in the reform era.

Third, reformists, especially Deng, effectively utilized their control of the military to back up their political position. At the crucial moment, Deng used the military as an important supporter in the policy debate. As stated, among the eight elders, only Deng had an indisputable command of the military. Therefore, Deng retained his chairmanship of the Central Military Commission, the top agency in charge of the military, until after the Tiananmen crackdown. Even after his retirement from that post in 1989, his loyal lieutenants still ran the military affairs on his behalf, and his generals filled the key military posts. This military backing gave Deng unparalleled influence in politics. Deng took great care not to offend the military leaders. In 1981, he rejected the draft of a Party document on assessing Mao Zedong because it was too negative on Mao. As a significant number of military leaders was loyal to Mao's ideology, if not his radicalism, accepting the draft would have cause these military leaders to resent

Deng and would have weakened his control of the military. Thus Deng wisely struck a balance between strong supporters and critiques of Mao and allowed only partial exposures of Mao's errors (Baum 1996: 134–37).

Fourth, as suggested by scholars and will be discussed in greater details in the following chapters, reformists decentralized economic power and granted favorable policies in selected provinces, encouraging provincial leaders to experiment with economic reforms. Successes and preferential policy in the pioneering provinces also prompted other provinces to demand from national leaders similar treatments. As provincial leaders made up a significant portion of the Party Central Committee (a policy body that elected the Politburo and its Standing Committee), they constituted an important constituency in the influential elite circle.

Fifth, orthodox reformists led by Deng also took pains to forge a political alliance with conservatives. Both factions shared a consensus on maintaining the Party's monopoly of power and opposing political liberalization. In doing so, Deng eased the suspicion of conservatives about reformist intention for marketization. Deng proved to his economic opponents that orthodox reformists were deeply concerned with the integrity of the Party leadership and that their liberal economic agenda aimed at strengthening the regime, instead of undermining it. By doing so, orthodox reformists offered conservatives carrots and lured them to continue their political acquiescence to Deng's position as the core of the leadership and his impulse toward marketization. However, there is a high price for this compromise—political reforms in China remain sluggish and democratization is moving only at a pace of crawls. The following discussion of policy cycles in China will underscore the first three and the fifth reformist strategies to sustain and accelerate reforms amidst setbacks and backlashes.

China's Political Business Cycles

Elite conflict over reform policies reveals itself in cyclical changes of reform policies. For example, China's Open Policy was marked by strong cycles of opening up and retraction (Crane 1990: 146–55; Kleinberg 1990: 139–41; Howell 1993: 44–124). While reformists served as an engine driving for economic liberalism, conservative leaders acted as a strong brake to keep reform from proceeding at a speed or even a direction that they deemed unsafe. China's reform, as well as its economy, has by and large gone through the following periods of cyclical change of the economy and politics. Policy fluctuation has subsided since 1994.

Expansion of 1978–1980. Mao's successor Hua Guofeng pursued high growth through launching dozens of mega projects in industry and transport, exporting a large amount of raw materials and borrowing foreign capital. His overambitious economic drive, however, raised inflation from 0.3 percent in 1976 to 2 percent in 1977 (SSB 1990b: 6), and resulted in severe undersupplies of raw materials (Naughton 1996: 67–74). Pragmatist leaders initiated economic reforms and retrenchment in 1978. This is the only period during which retrenchment went hand in hand with reforms. Wan Li, the First Party Secretary of Anhui Province and Deng's protégé, supported family farming during 1977–1979 and oversaw rapid growth in grain output. Deng threw his support behind the new initiative despite strong Maoist resistance. In addition, restrictions on rural and private enterprises were loosened. The Party also tentatively approved the establishment of four SEZs in Guangdong and Fujian Provinces.

Rising inflation (from 0.7 percent in 1978 to 2 percent in 1979) in the wake of fast growth, however, invited liberals at the Democracy Wall Movement in Beijing to criticize the Party during the winter of 1978–1979 (point A in figure 3.1). Protests against abuse of power by local officials also broke out in Beijing. Under pressure from the conservatives, Deng arrested the leading liberals and introduced "four cardinal principles" that upheld the Party leadership (Baum 1996: 77–82). In 1980, Deng renewed the reform drive by endorsing four SEZs (Tang 1998: 227–32). Lively elections of county-level legislators were held (Baum 1996: 97–100).

Contraction of Reforms of 1981–1983. Fast growth again pushed inflation up to 6 percent in 1980. Strong pushes by liberals in large cities for political opening since 1979 also alerted and displeased Deng and Party elders. Subsequent outcries by liberals and Maoists broke out. In response, conservatives proposed to combat initially "bourgeois (political) liberalization" and later "spiritual pollution" and reclaimed fiscal and administrative power from provinces. Deng approved of the two campaigns in December 1980 (point B in figure 3.1) (Baum 1996: 102–04, 110–13), but Hu Yaobang, Zhao Ziyang, and Wan Li resisted them. The only noticeable yet largely politically convenient reform measure was to relax restrictions on urban collective firms and tolerate urban private sectors in order to solve soaring

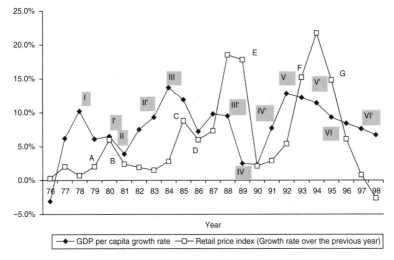

Figure 3.1   GDP per capita growth rate and inflation in China, 1976–1998.

Marked points on the inflation curve:

A. 1979. Crackdown on Democracy Wall and arrests of liberal activists
B. 1980. A campaign to oppose bourgeois liberalization
C. 1985. Five student protests; the Party's efforts to clean up bourgeois liberalism
D. 1986. Student protests in Hefei, Shanghai, and Beijing. Hu Yaobang, an open-minded Party General Secretary, was forced to resign in January 1987.
E. The Tiananmen Movement that demanded greater political opening and crackdown on official corruption
F. 1993. Start of anti-corruption campaign
G. 1995. Prosecution of at least two top provincial leaders and three provincial-level leaders for their corruption. Detention of political activists after the largest wage of calls for democracy by dissidents and intellectuals since 1989

Letters on the GNP growth rate curve:

I–I': 1978–80, expansion of reforms; II–II': 1981–83, contraction of reforms;

III–III': 1984–88, expansion of reforms; IV–IV': 1989–91, contraction of reforms; V–V': 1992–94, expansion of reforms; VI–VI': 1995- (1998 in Figure 3.1), reduced fluctuation. I, II, III, IV, V, and VI stand for the starting point of a period, and I', II', III', IV', V', and VI' the ending point of the period.

Sources: SSB 1990b: 32, 1998: 57, 301; Baum 1996.

unemployment in the cities due to retrenchment. In 1983, conservatives started to assault SEZs and other reform initiatives and violated Deng's core premise, that is, economic reforms. Deng worried that conservatives were using their control over policy agenda to sabotage his reform course and decided to stop them.

The Reform Drive of 1984–1988. Deng's change of heart and lowered inflation during retrenchment favored a number of new reform measures: Active promotion of rural enterprises, the opening of fourteen cities and key economic areas from the coast to the world economy, protection of private business, moderate reforms of state enterprises, and the state's deregulation of prices. Again, rising inflation in the course of accelerated growth triggered student protests in the second half of 1985 and early 1986 (points C and D in figure 3.1). Deng, the leading orthodox reformist, was also upset over Hu's consent to liberal Party members' calls for ending the personal cult of Deng and for his retirement (Ruan 1994: 162–68). Conservative and orthodox reformists joined force in tightening ideological controls. In the end, Zhao Ziyang replaced Hu Yaobang as the Party General Secretary (Baum 1996: 190–203). In the aftermath, conservatives clamped down on the local investment zeal.

During October–November 1987 the Thirteenth Party Congress promoted a liberal Party platform and rejuvenated reforms, especially regarding foreign investment, urban collective sectors, private business, state enterprises, and prices. A premature rush toward price reform in 1988, however, caused a buying pacnic, and inflation skyrocketed to 18.5 percent.

The Retreat of 1989–1991. Rising inflation triggered the largest prodemocracy protests in the post-Mao era during the summer of 1989 (point E in figure 3.1). Zhao tried to calm the protests by following a conciliatory approach toward the protesters. After one-and-half months of protests and well into late May scores of students continued to occupy the Tiananmen Square, the symbol of the political center in China, insisting on immediate political opening and public reversal of the negative verdict of the protests on the *People's Daily* on April 26. Zhao lost Deng's support. Deng called in the troops to crush the protests. Along with leading conservatives he picked Jiang Zemin to replace Zhao as the General Secretary of the Party. Conservatives dominated policy making by tightening the ideological clap, ferreting dissidents, slowing down growth, and protecting state enterprises at the expense of non-state business. A Party document in 1989 even declared that private entrepreneurs earned their income through exploitation and that they should not be allowed to join the Party (Chen 1998: 313–14). Many local officials blatantly discriminated against private business and rural enterprises. The state deregulated prices of major food staples and industrial inputs (Gao et al. 1993: 1708; Tang 1998: 405–08). Inflation was lowered to 2.9 percent in 1991.

Deng's Last Reform Drive of 1992–1994. Retrenchment caused the annual economic growth rate to register low—2.1–2.9 percent.

Deng hoped the 1992 Party Congress, the last one held in his lifetime, would enshrine his reformism. Otherwise, the reform course he championed since 1978 would be lost. Deng, who formally retired from all positions, used his political resources and network and made the biggest gamble of his career in order to salvage reforms. Deng toured the southern provinces, local frontrunners in marketization, and called for bolder reforms. The military and the coastal provincial leaders warmly applauded his calls. In response, national leaders actively promoted rural, private, and foreign enterprises and opened up inland provinces for foreign investment. The Fourteenth Party Congress of 1992 accepted marketization as the Party platform.

As the economy grew rapidly, inflation soared to 21.7 percent in 1994, resulting in increasing public grievances. In addition, local officials channeled funds into investment and financial speculation and failed to pay peasants for their grains. During 1993–1994, over 1,300 rural riots broke out, involving 850,000 peasants, and causing over 20 billion yuan in property losses (Baum 1996: 378). The top leaders reacted on two fronts. Economically, in June 1993 Vice Premier Zhu Rongji, the de facto premier, recentralized financial control and stepped up tax collections and payments for agricultural procurements (Gao and He 1998: 370–413; Tang 1998: 478, 488). Politically, Jiang launched an anti-corruption campaign in August 1993 and arrested a number of high-profile officials on corruption charges (point F in figure 3.1)(Tang 1998: 467).

Reduced Fluctuation since 1994. Economic reform continued to progress, yet the tolerance for calls for thorough political reforms in the 1980s had disappeared. So did nationwide movements for democratization. Economic reforms continued to proceed toward a more efficient, open, and equitable economy under sufficient central supervision. In 1994, the currency was devalued to be in line with market exchange rate, the tariff level was slashed by 7.3 percent, and a uniform national tax system and a central-provincial tax-sharing system were implemented. Since 1994, the state has introduced a set of measures to develop market mechanisms. The Party has also made efforts to overhaul state enterprises. Between 1999 and 2000, China made substantial progress by its entry to the WTO and promising to drastically open up China's markets. The Party endeavored to develop the interior regions, which culminated in its western-development drive in 2000, while the coastal provinces were urged to upgrade their technology.

Orthodox reformist leaders practiced conservative politics during 1994–1996 in response to political strains triggered by economic problems. As inflation hovered respectively to 21.7 percent in 1994 and 14.8 percent in 1995, a number of liberal activists and prominent intellectuals petitioned National People's Congress in the spring of 1995 for political opening (point G in figure 3.1). Jiang suppressed this largest protest since the Tiananmen Movement of 1989, and also arrested the Party Secretary of Beijing on corruption charges to ease public outrage over corruption. In 1996, Jiang approved the firing of missiles over Taiwan in retaliation for its leaders' pro-independence rhetoric, and issued a long Party document warning against Western political influence.

The political atmosphere relaxed in 1997, with inflation dropping to an unusually low 0.8 percent, and with the Fifteenth Party Congress announcing further reform measures. Discussion on political reforms also surfaced. In 1998, liberal euphoria grew during Clinton's visit. In 1999, however, due to growing difficulties in state enterprises, unemployment increased, and official urban unemployment hit 3 percent, up from 2.6 percent in 1993. In April, 10,000 followers of the Falun Gong sect surrounded Zhongnanhai, the office and residential compound of top Chinese leaders, in protest over the media's unfavorable coverage of the sect. Jiang reacted by hardening his fist of control, outlawing the sect in July and chilling the expectation for political opening.

Views on Sources of Cycles in Post-Mao China

Many scholars have noticed the above cyclical pattern in China's reforms between 1978 and 1994, but disagree over the exact causes. I will try to advance a systemic explanation of the cycles, employing key political and economic indexes and statistical tests to verify their conflicting arguments. I will begin by discussing *cleavages between moderate and orthodox reformist leaders*, which a number of authors had neglected. I will then highlight policy differences between conservative and reformist leaders. I argue that from 1980–1994 *the division between reformists, coupled with that between reformists and conservatives*, molded the ideological environment and fiscal policies, affected economic growth and inflation, and triggered protests or complaints against the policies. This caused *economic and political swings between 1980 and 1994*. I will also explain *why policy cycles faded away after 1994* which *most* of the existing literature fails to do.

It will be helpful to have an overview of arguments out of a scattering body of literature and their limits. China scholars have identified the following aspects of the cycles mainly *up to 1994* (Tsou 1986: 219–58; Harding 1987: chapter 4; Hamrin 1990: 4–7; Howell 1993;

Ruan 1994; Lieberthal 1995: 137–44; Dittmer and Wu 1995; Baum 1996: 5, 7–9; Shirk in Baum 1996: 5–9).

1. Conflict between liberal and conservative policy packages helped to intensify economic swings between boom and bust.
2. Reformist leaders encouraged economic liberalization, growth, and political relaxation. Economic liberalization tended to lead to destabilizing outcomes.
3. Macroeconomic and political instability induced conservative policies. Consequently, political control would be tightened, and reform and growth would slow down (Ruan 1994; Dittmer and Wu 1995; Lieberthal 1995; Baum 1996: 5, 7–9).

On the other hand, these scholars held different views regarding the subtle interaction of politics and economics, specifically, over the following three issues:

1. Regarding sources of political oscillation. Some scholars believed that political oscillation was caused by a dichotomy between reformists who favored ideological relaxation and conservatives who believed in ideological orthodoxy. Such a division resulted in liberal political atmospheres during some years, and a stern political environment in others (Dittmer and Wu 1995; Lieberthal, 1995). Other scholars (Ruan 1994 and Shirk c.f. in Baum 1996: 6–7), however, accept that Deng, a widely believed reformist, leaned toward political liberalism in certain years and toward political conservatism in others in order to appease the conservative pressure.
2. Regarding the sources of economic swings, Lieberthal (1995) as well as Dittmer and Wu (1995) attributed the alternation of boom and bust to the reformist preference for rapid growth and the opposing conservative insistence on stable and minimal growth. However, these authors tended to stress different causes of boom and bust. Lieberthal (1995: 137) argued that Beijing could propel economic prosperity through devolution of economic control to localities and that recentralized economic control could dramatically decelerate the economy. Dittmer and Wu (1995: 487–88), on the other hand, suggested that national expansionist policies triggered economic expansion and that national austere fiscal and monetary policies could suffice to cool off the overheating economy. Shirk, again according to Baum (1996: 5–7), traced the rise and fall in growth rates to China's partially planned and partially marketized economy.
3. Interaction of political and business cycles. Dittmer and Wu (1995) and Shirk in (Baum 1996: 5–7) argued that both cycles were synchronized after 1980 since political cycles went hand in hand with business cycles. Baum (1996: 7) countered that these cycles are irregular, rather than

synchronized. Shirk emphasized the effect of the business cycle on the political cycle, while Dittmer and Wu argued the opposite.

In the following section, I attempt to probe the exact sources of policy cycles. I will address two key questions most relevant to China's approach to reform—What were the key policy differences among moderate and orthodox reformists as well as conservatives? What caused the cycles?

From Elite Division to Policy Cycles

The existing literature mostly attributes the conflict among leaders as the primary cause for cyclical policies. Two versions on factional conflict, however, existed. One view suggested that Deng, standing on the side of the reformist camp, fought against the conservative camp. Another view suggested that Deng oscillated between these two camps over the years. Both views make sense, yet are not accurate in and of themselves. Deng was an orthodox reformist, liberal on economic issues, yet conservative on political ones. *Along with the moderate reformists*, including Hu Yaobang and Zhao Ziyang, *Deng fought against conservatives for comprehensive economic reform and an extensive opening up of China. Meanwhile, he also joined hands with conservatives in suppressing political liberalism advanced by radical intellectuals and tolerated by Hu and Zhao.* This point has been illustrated in my preceding analyses of leadership and factions.

I shall emphasize that the distinction of Deng as an orthodox reformist from Hu and Zhao as moderate reformists serves as a very useful tool for understanding three important aspects of the policy oscillation. *This also helps to distinguish my interpretation of the policy cycles from the existing ones.* First, this distinction helps to illustrate when, why, and over what issues Deng would ally with moderate reformists and fight against conservatives, and when, why, and over what issues Deng would ally with conservatives and fight against moderate reformists. Second, the rift between the two camps of reformists may help to explain why high-profile student protests broke out at times in the 1980s, but not in the 1990s. Ironically, Deng and the conservatives were right empirically in claiming that tolerance by moderate reformists led to the *occurrence* of student protests. As moderate reformists faded away in Chinese politics in the late 1980s, and as new orthodox reformist leaders have taken a tough stance against political protests, large student protests against governmental policies had vanished in the 1990s. Third, and finally, student protests in the 1980s were always followed by the reversal of a relaxed ideological environment and halts of the economic reform and the usual expansionary fiscal policies.

Factional Conflict and Dynamics of Cycles

As elaborated in detail, reformists, especially Deng, were obsessed with high growth (Dittmer and Wu 1995). Lieberthal (1995: 244–45) observed that Chinese leaders guided economic reform with a growth-oriented strategy in order to keep up with rapid expansion of its East Asian neighbors and create jobs for a growing population. Deng's speeches in 1982 and 1984 reveal that he desired fast growth for another reason: By quadrupling the per capita GNP between 1980 and 2000, China could potentially lift itself out of poverty, and Chinese communism could prove its economic vibrancy (Deng 1993: 10–11, 63–64, 77).

Deng's urge for rapid growth and receptiveness to markets was based on his pragmatism and his observation of the huge gap in China's underdevelopment and the achievements in mainland China's Asian neighbors including Japan, Singapore, and Hong Kong. Deng was particularly shocked by what he saw on his visit to Japan in October 1978. He was impressed with the luxurious life of a family of Japanese workers. At a Nissan auto plant, Deng was told that on average a worker could produce 94 cars each year, whereas a worker at the Changchun Auto Factory, the most advanced auto plant in China could make only one a year. Deng sighed in acknowledgement: "Now I understand what modernization means" (Yang 1998: 245). At his 1978 visit of Singapore, a small island populated initially by illiterate peasants from southern China, Deng was again deeply impressed with its rapid modernization and governance. He was determined to emulate its success in the vast China (KY Lee 2000: 714). It was out of his strong urge to take China out of underdevelopment and the Chinese out of poverty through the East Asian path of modernization that Deng promoted rapid growth and marketization.

Conservatives, on the other hand, emphasized macroeconomic stability. Chen Yun instinctively opposed any move that could generate a rapid rise in prices. He saw bold reformist pushes at marketization as steps toward hyperinflation, a loss of central control, and economic instability. Deng's reformist faction and Chen's conservative platoon thus emphasized different sets of policies. Hence the first observation (in italics) on cycles follows:

Proposition 1. Reformists preferred fast growth and pursued a high growth rate, whereas conservatives cherished stable growth and tried to maintain low inflation.

Sources of business cycles thus lie in the fundamentally different policy preferences of reformist and conservative leaders. As we shall see, both factions would mobilize resources to accomplish their policy preferences. Both factions initially fought in the ideological sphere for a number of reasons. First, as Lucian Pye (1981: ch. 1) cogently argued, real power in China was often displayed subtly. Leaders who were in ultimate control often challenged their adversaries indirectly. This is particularly true in post-Mao China (Ruan 1994). Hence Baum (1996: 12–13) argued that factional conflict was often waged in political discourse and in subtly different political terms. In the uncertain and high-stakes game of politics, ideology signalled to national and local officials the relative strengths of either faction in a given point of time.

Second, along with organization, ideology is a crucial instrument of political control and ruling in communist countries (Schurmann 1968). As Baum (1996) insightfully noted, Chen Yun emphasized ideological purity, whereas Deng stressed economic growth. Each faction tried to use the propaganda machinery to publicize policy orientation and rally political support.

Once they have an upper hand in factional conflict, reformists introduced a relaxed ideological environment. The ease in ideological control, as it related to economic initiatives such as the expansion of non-state sectors, encouraged local officials to push forward with economic reform without worrying about possible setbacks to their careers. Such an environment, along with the center's adoption or tolerance of expansionary fiscal policy, encouraged local efforts to bring about local economic boom. In contrast, once conservatives began to regain control of policy, they attempted to tighten the ideological bridle. A stern ideological atmosphere naturally dampened enthusiasm for bold economic reform efforts. National conservative leadership promoted austere fiscal policy, discouraging an increase in local investment and facilitating the arrival of local bust and lower inflation. Table 3.1 provides a snapshot of the ideological environment and coding in China. The following proposition thus arises.

Table 3.1 Coding of ideological control and fiscal policies in China: 1978–1999 (Coding: 0: conservative; 1: liberal)

Year	Coding of ideological control	Events shaping ideological environment in China	Coding of fiscal policies
1978	1	Third Plenum of Eleventh CCCCP Democracy Wall Movement	1
1979	0	Petitioners' protest in Beijing in January. Deng's four cardinal principles and his suppressing of the Democracy Wall Movement	0
1980	1	Official calls for political reforms; local elections of People's Deputies; college students' election campaigns in Beijing and Changsha	0
1981	0	Official campaign against bourgeois liberalization	0
1982	1	Twelfth PC; debate over alienation and socialist humanism	1
1983	0	Official campaign against humanism and spiritual pollution	0
1984	1	The Party's embrace of planned commodity economy; opening up of 14 coastal cities	1
1985	0	Campaign against bourgeois liberalism (from the end of 1984 to the early summer); student demonstrations in Beijing and Nanjin between September and December.	1
1986	1	Discussion of political reforms; mass student protests in Hefei, Shanghai, Nanjing, Tianjin, and Beijing in December	0
1987	0	Removal of Hu in January; Thirteenth PC, the theory of primary stage of socialism, and calls for an economic trinity of state, market, and enterprises	0
1988	1	Price reform; criticism on conservative Chinese culture on a TV series (*River Elegy*)	1
1989	0	Tiananmen democracy movement and military crackdown	0
1990	0	Tight ideological control; economic austerity and stress on the state sector	0
1991	0	The same as above	0
1992	1	Deng's southern tour; Fourteenth PC approved a Party program to build a socialist market economy	1
1993	1	The Party's call for building socialist market	1
1994	0	Attempts to strengthen the Party; anti-official-corruption campaign	0
1995	0	Stable reform stressed; arrests and harsh sentencing of political activists	0

Continued

Table 3.1   Continued

Year	Coding of ideological control	Events shaping ideological environment in China	Coding of fiscal policies
1996	0	PLA fired missiles around Taiwan. Party document urge fighting against western values	0
1997	1	Fifteenth PC and economic liberalism; 1 discussion of political reforms; call for rule of law	
1998	1	Political openness around Clinton's visit to China	1
1999	0	Suppression of Falun Gong; protests and surge of conservatism against the NATO bombing of the Chinese embassy in Belgrade	1

Note: The ideological coding for the period of 1978–1995 is based on Ruan 1994, Baum 1996, and Lieberthal 1995. Events are from Baum 1996, Ruan 1994, Tang 1998, and news on China from Lexis-Nexis. Coding of fiscal policies of 1978–1991 is from Huang 1996, 158–66. Coding for other years is based on annual growth rates of state investment in fixed assets (SSB 1993–1999).

Proposition 2. Reformists tended to ease ideological restrictions over economic liberalism and encouraged a large increase in investment; conservatives were inclined to enforce the ideological restriction, promote austere fiscal policy, and encourage a moderate growth in investment.

Finding 1 of Tests 1 and 2 summarized in Tabulation 3.1 suggests that investment and the fiscal policies were closely correlated with the ideological environment. It lends support for Proposition 2: Liberal ideological atmosphere tended to stimulate growth in investment, whereas a conservative environment tended to induce a decline.

As pointed out earlier, moderate reformists diverged from orthodox reformists on ideological liberalization. The former, represented by Hu and Zhao, not only endeavoured to propagandize economic liberalism, but also tolerated at times calls for political reforms and retirement of senile leaders. On the contrary, orthodox reformists were interested in economic reforms and growth but abhorred liberal political calls.

Heavy investment encouraged by reformist policies usually induced rapid growth. Growth generated demands for a large variety of production inputs, including raw materials, investment in fixed assets, and labor. Between 1978 and the early 1990s, China's economy still bore certain characteristics of the command economy (Shirk according to Baum 1996: 5–7). Shortage in raw material supplies was one of them (Wong 1986). In addition, as demand for labor increased during the boom period, wage bills also increased, driving up the demand for food and consumers goods. Strong demand and shortages fueled price hikes. Premature price reforms at removing the state's control over these staple items, such as grain, meat, edible oil, and clothes would

Tabulation 3.1   Statistical analysis on the dynamics of sequences (0.5 is the a critical level of high correlation)

Finding 1: Relaxed ideological control encouraged increasing investment, whereas ideological restrictions dampened investment.

Test 1: Correlation coefficient between the ratings of ideological environment (1 = liberal and 0 = conservative) and the annual growth rate of state investment between 1980 and 1999 = 0.521. The year of 1980 is chosen as the starting year for the reason detailed in the discussion.

Test 2: Correlation coefficient of indexes of ideological environment and fiscal policy during 1978–1999 = 0.633

(Ideological index: 1 = relaxed, 0 = strict; index for fiscal policy: 1 = expansionary; 0 = austere)

Finding 2: An increase in state investment induced higher growth.

Test 3: Correlation between growth rate of state investment in fixed assets and GDP per capita growth rate between 1978 and 1997 = 0.692

Finding 3: Higher growth drove up inflation and slower growth lowered inflation in the following year.

Test 4: Correlation between GDP per capita growth rate and inflation rate in the subsequent year between 1978 and 1997 = 0.582

Finding 4: Inflation caused public protests.

Test 5: Correlation coefficient between inflation rate and the frequency of social protests, 1980–1993 = 0.728 (Source: Dittmer and Wu 1995, footnote 25).

Finding 5: Ideological control would be tightened and investment would stagnate in the year following high inflation. Ideological control would be eased, and investment would go up in the year following low inflation.

Test 6: Correlation between the ratings of inflation (1 = liberal and 0 = conservative) and ideological environment in the subsequent year = −0.498 (very close to 0.5)

Test 7: Correlation between inflation and growth rate in state investment in fixed assets in the subsequent year between 1980 and 1998 = −0.572

Data Sources: SSB 1990b: 32: 1998: 57, 301; Baum 1996.

further aid the escalation in these prices in the short run (Hu 1994: 249, 264–70).

As the reformists mismanaged the economy and triggered soaring inflation in their pursuit of high growth, conservatives gained an upper hand, stepping in and calming the volatile economy. Conservatives thus tended to pursue austere fiscal programs and reduce investment in an attempt to combat inflation, cooling the overheating economy. The following hypothesis thus follows:

Proposition 3: Reformist encouragement of heavy investment did succeed at producing faster economic growth, yet also triggered soaring inflation. Conversely, conservative control of investment helped to slow down economic growth and inflation.

Findings 2–3 in tabulation 3.1 confirm this proposition. Tests 3 and 4 suggest that an increase in investment led to faster growth in per capita gross domestic product (GDP) in the same year, and that a higher per capita GDP growth rate also prompted higher inflation in the following year.

Inflation increased the production and living expenses. Higher prices in basic staples hurt urban residents (including college students) who were politically vocal and influential. Inflation thus induced protests in the cities. Political dissidents took advantage of these opportunities, as well as moderate reformists' tolerance, voiced their politically liberal opinions, and demanded changes in ideological control and increased supervision of state officials. Public discontent with the regime's policy made the population more sympathetic for these political demands. A proposition thus follows:

Proposition 4: High inflation resulted in more public protests.

Finding 4 of test 5 in tabulation 3.1 (reported in Dittmer and Wu 1995, footnote 25) provides statistical evidence for this proposition. The correlation coefficient between inflation and the frequencies of public protests during 1980–1993 reaches 0.728, well above the 0.5 level, indicating a strong correlation.

As discussed, between 1978 and 1994 moderate reformists tolerated discussion on political reform, emboldening liberal intellectuals. Relaxed political control and economic complaints, such as high inflation, combined to produce explosive protests. The regime's legitimacy and control of power were consequently challenged. In response, orthodox reformists and conservatives blamed moderate reformists for having been too lenient on dissidents and protesters. Conservatives attacked reformist policies, silenced reformists, and took over policy making. Conservative leaders tightened the Party's ideological leash on the officials, cut investment, decelerated the economy, and restrained inflation. Nevertheless, as inflation decreased to a low level, macroeconomic stability allowed room for renewed growth. Reformists would then use sluggish growth and the people's stagnant living standard to refute the conservative policy. Reformists relaxed ideological restrictions, encouraged investment, and promoted growth. Another round of cycles was initiated. The following proposition seems to capture this aspect of the cycles:

Proposition 5: The state reasserted ideological control and cut investment in the year following high inflation. The state relaxed ideological control, and encouraged investment and growth in the year following low inflation.

Finding 5 of tests 6 and 7 in tabulation 3.1 supports this proposition. At Test 6, the correlation coefficient between inflation rate and the ideological environment score in the subsequent year is nearly a negative 0.5, the benchmark of statistical significance. At Test 7, that between inflation rate and growth rate for state investment in fixed assets in the subsequent year is a negative 0.57. This suggests that factors in these two pairs are reversely associated. That is to say, the state tightened ideological control and cut investment in the year following high inflation, yet eased ideological control and increased investment in the year following low inflation.

Each cycle typically goes through the following process. When reformists dominated policy making, they loosened the Party's grip on ideology and encouraged bold economic initiatives. They pursued and tolerated expansionary fiscal policy, and oversaw a surge in investment. Extensive capital input produced high growth, igniting inflation and creating macroeconomic instability. Rising costs of living, a declining income, and moderate reformists' tolerance consequently invited public protests. Conservatives then criticized moderate reformists' political tolerance of dissidents as well as orthodox and moderate reformists' reform programs, and usually succeeded in gaining an upper hand in policy making. Conservatives imposed ideological surveillance over the society, cut investment and spending, decreased economic growth, and controlled inflation and public protests. As economic growth slowed to a crawl, the people's living standard stagnated. Reformist leaders then launched a political comeback, and criticized the conservative program. They relaxed ideological indoctrination, called for reforms and growth, boosted investment, and championed growth. High growth inevitably increased inflation, macroeconomic instability, and public grievance and protests, therefore inviting a

Reformist ideological relaxation >> expansionary policies >> surge in investment >> high growth >> inflation >> political liberalism and protests
    >> Conservative ideological control >> economic austerity >> cut in investment >> lower growth >> low inflation >> malaise >> reformists regained control over policy

Figure 3.2   Dynamics of cycles

conservative resurgence. A flow chart (figure 3.2) sums up this process, with >> representing the direction of causation.

The above analyses help to clarify the ongoing controversies and misunderstandings on cycles. First, political business cycles are rooted in the deep disagreements between reformist and conservative policy preferences, namely, pro-growth versus pro-low-inflation, and pro–ideological-relaxation versus pro–ideological-control. The cycles also originate from the division among orthodox and moderate reformists, as moderate reformists' political tolerance encouraged political protests against high inflation. Cyclical changes in politics precede those in the economy, and the latter only reinforce the former. Second, ideological relaxation or control plays an important role in the cycles, usually marking the start of a cycle. Emphases on different political phrases, such as "reforms and opening up" versus "oppose bourgeois liberalism," signaled to local leaders which faction was in control of policy and which program was to be implemented. Third, lag effects existed in the cycles. Confirming Baum's remark (Baum 1996: 5–9), political and business cycles may not synchronize. High growth tended to drive up inflation in the following year. Similarly, ideological and investment controls would be tightened *a year after* high inflation. Fourth, the legacies of the command economy and the strong state also enabled the Chinese leaders to exercise extensive and direct influence over investment and monetary policies. As the finding of Test 3 indicates, national leaders could use state investment to boost or decrease the growth rate of the national economy.

The dynamics of political business cycle of 1978–1993 described above has seemed to weaken after 1993 out of two possible reasons. First, orthodox reformist leaders have dominated policies in the post-Southern Tour era (even until the time of writing), thereby reducing swings in economic policies and politics. These leaders, especially Jiang Zemin and recently Hu Jintao, urged economic liberalization while containing inflation and suppressing calls for democratization. They embraced this orthodox reformist platform for two reasons. First is that their key patrons, that is, orthodox reformists and conservatives would converge on it. After Deng's Southern Tour of 1992, orthodox reformists have installed market-economy-oriented reform as the Party platform. Meanwhile, orthodox reformists struck a deal with conservatives by eliminating moderate reformists and readily defending the Party's monopoly of power. A second and more important reason is that the post-Tiananmen syndrome has also reinforced orthodox reformist leaders' fear that failure to stick to this orthodox reformist formula would invite another popular movement opposing the Party's monopoly of power, consequential political backlashes, and their own losses of power or influence. Their predecessors, namely Hu and Zhao, failed to abide by this orthodox reformist mix by tolerating calls for political reforms, and thus lost their posts after large student protests. As an orthodox reformist platform serves to suppress open and large-scale protests and push forward economic reforms, it has thus reduced swings in politics and the economy.

Second, between 1978 and 1993 low inflation seemed to induce leaders to pursue fast growth in the following year, whereas high inflation would encourage them to decelerate growth. This is confirmed by Test 1 in tabulation 3.2. A negative but significant coefficient above 0.5 suggests that inflation and growth in per capita GDP in the subsequent year was reversely associated and that low inflation would encourage the state to increase investment and pump up economic growth in the subsequent year. Such a relationship, however, falters into statistical insignificance after the data of 1994–1997 is included (Test 1 versus Test 2). Even though China's government pursued proactive fiscal policies in the late 1990s to accelerate the economy so as to reduce negative fallouts from the Asian Financial Crisis, economic growth slowed down. The economy seemingly does not respond to the

Tabulation 3.2 Did low inflation trigger higher growth in the following year?

Finding: *"Yes" for the period of 1978–1993 and "no" for that of 1978–1997.*

Test 1: Correlation between the growth rate of retail prices (1977–1992) (P_{t-1}) and the growth rate of GDP per capita in the subsequent year from 1978–1993 (Y_t)= −0.641

Test 2: Correlation between the growth rate of retail prices and the growth rate of GDP per capita (Y_t) in the subsequent year from 1978–1997 = −0.380

---

state's intervention as much as it did in the past, probably because it has become more marketized and responds more to market signals than before.

Features of Cycles

Given the above findings, I employ the curves of the growth rates and of the retail price index to identify and describe cycles of national policies. In particular, I will discuss the reformist management of the elite conflict and the cyclical change in policies toward the non-state economy. The cycles are depicted in figure 3.1, where several major points on the curves are marked and explained. Table 3.2 summarizes basic economic features of each period of the cycles. These periods were described in an earlier section.

Among these periods, reform expansions are characterized by high growth rates and high inflation, and periods of retraction are marked by low growth rates and low inflation (table 3.2).[9] As indicated in figure 3.1 and table 3.2, *an expansion period of reforms, with the possible exception of the first period of 1978–1980, usually started with a year after low inflation and accelerating growth, and ended with relatively lower growth and unusually high inflation.* For example, the expansion of reform during 1984–1988 was preceded by modest inflation of 1.5 percent and moderately high growth of 9.3 percent in 1983. It started with an impressive 13.7 percent growth rate in 1984, and ended after runaway inflation of 18.5 percent and a moderately lower 9.5 percent economic growth in 1988 (table 3.2).

Table 3.2   Growth rates and inflation of five periods (%)

Periods of reform		Average GNP growth	Average inflation	Growth rate (by each year)	Inflation (by each year)
1978–1980	Expansion	9.2	2.9	10.2, 6.1, 6.5	0.7, 2.0, 6.0
1981–1983	Retraction	7.9	1.9	3.9, 7.5, 9.3	2.4, 1.9, 1.5
1984–1988	Expansion	11.6	8.7	13.7, 11.9, 7.2, 9.8, 9.5	2.8, 8.8, 6.0, 7.3, 18.5
1989–1991	Retraction	5.3	7.6	2.5, 2.3, 7.7	17.8, 2.1, 2.9
1992–1994	Expansion	13.1	14.1	12.8, 12.2, 11.4	5.4, 15.2, 21.7
1995–1998	Reduced fluctuation	8.0	4.8	9.3, 8.4, 7.6, 6.7	14.8, 6.1, 0.8, −2.6

Sources: SSB 1993–1999.

In contrast, *a contraction of reforms tended to be precipitated by spiraling inflation and a significant yet decelerating growth rate in the previous years, and ended after years of low inflation.* The economic retreat of 1989–1991 followed unusually high inflation in 1988, and witnessed a dramatic slippage in the retail price level in 1990 and 1991.

Conclusion: Cycles and Reformist Approach to Elite Conflict

To summarize, national policies between 1978 and 1994 had go through cycles. Each cycle started with relaxation (or tightening) of ideological control and was followed by aggressive (or conservative) investment policy, resulting in accelerating (or declining) growth and inflation and later popular protest (or unemployment and a stagnating living standard). As a result, ideological orientation and investment policy shifted, inaugurating another cycle. After 1994, the technocratic and orthodox reformist leadership tried to contain inflation as well as calls for political reforms, successfully preempting nationwide public calls for democracy. In addition, as the economy was becoming marketized, the state's monetary policies alone could not determine economic growth or inflation. Cycles have thus subsided after 1994. This new political-business dynamics persists today.

This chapter indicates that attempts by powerful factions to meet popular demands for high growth and low inflation engineered the cyclical change in national reform policies over the period 1978–1996. Three factors helped to shape the cycles during the period 1978–1993. The first factor was the division and interaction within national leadership. The balance of power between reformists and conservatives conditioned the policy debate and changes. The second factor was the population's desire for rapid growth and low inflation, which eventually meant a substantial increase in their living standard. As explained above, Deng's reformist factions opted for fast growth, whereas the conservative faction opted for low inflation. These two popular demands, however, were often inconsistent in a growing economy: Rapid growth tended to induce inflation, whereas low inflation often required slow growth. The third factor was the state's administrative and political approach to the economy. This approach acted as a powerful accelerator as well as a strong brake for the Chinese economy, exacerbating the rise and fall of the growth rate and inflation.

From the above analysis, two features of China's reforms between 1978 and 1994 have become clear. First, factional leadership prevented radical reform, yet generated wild political and economic swings and even occasional setbacks in reform. Conservatives and even the population opposed any radical marketization out of fear of inflation and job losses. Likewise, a powerful coalition of conservatives and orthodox reformists vetoed any political liberalization favored by moderate reformists. These divergences within the leadership had generated intense conflict over policies and even led to subsequent purges of leaders in 1987 and 1989, resulting in costly economic and political cycles.

Second, given the above influence of conservative forces, reformists, especially Deng, adopted flexible tactics and displayed political persistence, allowing reforms to withstand popular discontent, conservative attacks, and temporary setbacks such as the failed price reform in 1988 and the Tiananmen crackdown and subsequent retrenchment. Deng adopted a "two step forward one step back" strategy to forge ahead reforms. When the conditions were favorable, he relaxed ideological control, promoted local reform experiments, and announced liberal policies including agricultural decollectivization, the setup of SEZs, the opening of large cities and coastal areas, and promotion of collective, private, and mixed ownership. When reforms were trapped in a quandary, such as inflation, macroeconomic imbalance, and economic crimes, Deng would step back from the helm of economic policies and allowed conservatives to take over and rectify these ills. However, once conservative policies ran into trouble and caused slow growth and unemployment, Deng would take the political front and reassert his line of liberalism. In pursuing this strategy, Deng also intentionally appealed to the popular desire for a higher living standard, provincial demands for greater economic power, and intellectual embrace for economic liberalism. In addition, Deng tried his best to hold on to his baseline of politics—never allowed his critiques to openly denounce his program of market-oriented reforms. For example, when conservatives started to sabotage SEZs and other reformist initiatives in the retrenchment of 1981–1983, Deng stopped them and the campaign altogether. In the next year (1984), Deng launched another wave of reforms.

In the wake of the traumatic Cultural Revolution, Deng tried to follow a consultative style of decision making and to avoid any major intra-Party split and violent political struggles. Thus he took pains to consult other elders before announcing major political and economic agendas. He tried to incorporate their voices into policies and political formulations. He also included a few candidates such as Li Peng and

Yao Yilin who were favored by conservatives in the Politburo to reflect their policy preferences. Partially for this very reason, Deng also avoided pushing through radical economic reforms against strong conservative opposition. Should he have been determined to overcome their opposition, he could have triggered a showdown with conservatives, a violent political conflict, an open split among the top leadership, and even open intervention of the military that he commanded. Deng refrained from this destructive style of conflict resolution.

As elaborated above, Deng adopted two tactics in managing elite conflict. First, he tried to repair ties with conservative elders by allying with them to resist political opening. Indeed, this choice has resulted in a lack of political liberalization. However, Deng earned trust from elders for his commitment to maintaining the communist regime.

Second, Deng carefully protected his status of the ultimate arbitrator of the Chinese politics. One key tactic was that he cultivated sufficient support from the military and avoided alienating himself from it. In 1992 when Deng launched his last onslaught on the conservative economic agenda, the military offered its crucial support and pledged to "patrol and safeguard the course of reforms."

Moreover, Deng would not allow his reformist agenda to be aborted just for the sake of maintaining the Party unity. When the timing was critical and the political stake was very high, he would not hesitate to thrust himself into the controversy, even against considerable political risks and opposition. A clear example is his final personal crusade for reforms in 1992. After the failure of the price reform in 1988 and the Tiananmen crackdown in 1989, Deng took a temporary hermitage from the Chinese political stage. Yet conservatives were too eager to exercise their influence on economic affairs, and Jiang, Deng's heir apparent, too eagerly toed the conservative economic line and stalled reforms. Deng, when he had officially retired and had no official title, toured the southern provinces, mobilized local and military support for reforms, and openly challenged the conservative center. Deng did realize that his gambit posed certain political risks and might be deemed illegitimate. He told people around him prior to the southern tour: "You do have good reasons in worrying. But I must take the risk. Without taking risks, you cannot expect to do anything and get anything done" (Yang 1998: 515). At that time, the top young Party leaders appeared to readily yield to the conservative agenda in the upcoming Fourteenth Party Congress that was scheduled in 1992, apparently the last Party Congress in Deng's lifetime. Deng was thus keenly aware that this was the only chance for him to salvage his reformist agenda, a course he fought hard for during the 1980s and early 1990s. Deng's bold move did pay off. It mobilized the military and provinces to support reforms and forced central leadership to accept reforms. This critical move by Deng secured the acceptance of a reformist platform in the Party at the last Party Congress before Deng, Chen, and other old guards passed away.

In sum, given that political ecology of leadership division over reforms, Deng followed a zigzag course of reform and maneuvered cleverly to ensure that the course of reforms would head in a more liberal direction toward the market economy. Should Deng have failed to compromise at key junctions, reforms in China would have run into greater trouble such as hyperinflation and would have lost much popular support. Should Deng have failed to push for marketization at critical moments, reforms would have been stalled and slow growth and economic and social malaise, instead of liberalism and high growth, would have been the norm, as China experienced in the post-Tiananmen retrenchment.[10]

In this sense, despite Deng's own limits over democratization, he has been remarkably successful in assessing *fortuna* (contingencies) and *necessita* (determinant factors) and fully exploiting his *virtu* (political strength, charisma and skills) for the course of economic reform. As scholars acutely pointed out, agile political skills and maneuvering were Deng's great political assets (Dittmer 1995: 23; Teiwes 1995). In employing mature political skills, Deng has engineered a reform that has been more successful in modernizing the Chinese economy than any previous attempt.

4

Installing Technocratic Young Leaders

Differences in policy visions among the Chinese leaders, as the previous chapter demonstrates, were largely responsible for the cyclical change of China's policies regarding economic reforms. The leadership thus played an important role in initiating reform policies in China, including policies regarding reforms in the provinces. The importance of leadership arises from the following facts: The Chinese political regime is authoritarian, centralized, Communist, much less institutionalized, and deeply shaped by its rule-by-men tradition (Lee 1991: 6–7, 387).[1] It follows that one strategy to break out of the old developmental model imposed by Mao is to place liberally minded leadership in top positions so that they could move reforms forward. This is exactly the political strategy Deng followed.

The membership at the Politburo changed considerably between the late 1970s and the early 1990s. Two events marked this change. First, around 1980, a coalition of reformists and conservatives led by Deng defeated Maoists at the Politburo, forcing the losers to exit the political stage. This was accompanied by rehabilitation of veteran cadres and purges of "three types of people," or Maoists (Lee 1991: 163–253) at various levels. Second, starting from the early 1980s and well into the 1990s, the Chinese top leaders, especially Deng, retired a large number of veteran cadres at various levels and actively promoted younger and technically more competent cadres.[2]

Deng was a key initiator in these two events of leadership change. Deng apparently understood too well the Chinese political tradition of rule by men and the significance of installing reformist leaders for his reform agenda. As early as December 1977, shortly upon returning to power from his third fall from grace, Deng told senior military leaders to carefully select and groom young successors. In July 1979, he spoke of the importance of appointing younger leaders, whom he called "successors," to carry out policies he deemed appropriate: "Once a political line has been set, it has to be concretely implemented by people, and the results will vary depending on who does the implementing, those who are in favor, those who are against, or the middle-of-the-roaders. This raises the question of what kind of people should be our successors."[3] Between August and November 1980, in preparing for the final exit of Hua, Deng also seriously contemplated retiring newly rehabilitated veteran leaders through establishing an advisory committee and called for promoting young leaders. Deng's calls earned the agreement from other influential veterans, including Marshal Ye Jianying in September 1979 and Chen Yun in 1980 (Lee 1991: 230; Xia and Gu 1999: 384).

Deng set a key tone for the Party's recruiting of young leaders and retiring of old ones. He departed from Mao's radical change of leadership, but also made moderate and tactical concessions to veteran leaders by emphasizing political qualification. In August 1980, Deng proposed a slogan of making the cadres "better educated, professionally more competent, and younger." The Party also criticized the Maoist "helicopter" appointment of young cadres into top leading positions, which bypassed the bureaucratic ladders. After listening to the complaints from the old leaders, Deng included "revolutionariness" as a criterion for young leader.[4] He also agreed to flexibly apply the age and educational requirements and to recruit young leaders more gradually. Meanwhile, he instituted an advisory committee as an intermediate approach for veteran leaders to withdraw from politics (Lee 1991: 232–34; Xia and Gu 1999, 384–85).

The implementation of reformist leadership recruitment started in early 1982. In February 1982, the Party passed a "Resolution regarding Establishing a System to Retire Veteran Leaders." The Twelfth Party Congress in 1982 elected a much younger Politburo, and approved the establishment of advisory committees at the national and provincial levels for retired leaders. In 1983, the Organizational Department of the CCCCP promulgated "Opinions regarding Establishing a System for Reserves of Provincial Cadres." In 1985, the Party Congress approved a round of change in national leaders. In 1986, the CCCCP promulgated a "Notice regarding Several Issues in Adjusting the Positions of Disqualified Leading Cadres," forcing the retirement of a number of cadres. The Thirteenth Party Congress in 1987 elected another echelon of young leaders. At the Fourteenth Party Congress in 1992 the Central Advisory Committee was finally abolished, and all key formal positions were filled by young leaders who could exercise substantial influence. Deng's aim of promoting young leaders had come to a successful conclusion.

Understandably, retirement of veteran cadres was a prerequisite for vacating key positions for the rise of younger technocratic cadres and leaders. Cadre retirements were based on age. The oldest cadres, however, tended to occupy the highest positions of the state and the Party. This constituted a conflict of interests (Manion 1993: 16). According to Manion (17), norms for retirement were instituted gradually in the following way. First, compromise was made in making cadre retirement policies. A few dozen senior leaders at the very top were exempted from retirement. Instead, special advisory commissions and positions were created for them to continue to exercise their influence from behind the scenes. As stated in chapter 3, these leaders included the eight veteran leaders. Most of the leaders below the top level, however, had been retired.

Second, middlemen who were in charge of retiring veteran cadres and young leaders who aspired for the vacated positions formed a coalition that promoted cadre retirement. The few top veteran leaders who stayed also joined this coalition. Both middlemen and especially young cadres stood to gain from retirement of veterans. However, middlemen, for the sake of winning the cooperation from veterans for retirement, also negotiated and cut a deal acceptable for veteran retirees, sometimes more generous than young and veteran leaders liked (Manion 1993).

Nevertheless, with the gradual institutionalization of cadre retirement system, an echelon of young technocratic leaders emerged to fill the positions and to run daily affairs of the state. Over major policies they did consult the few remaining top veteran leaders such as Deng and Chen. At critical junctions such as Deng's 1992 campaign for reform young technocratic leaders also joined hands with veteran reformists to consolidate the reform course. After Chen Yun, Li Xinian, Peng Zhen, Wang Zhen, and Deng passed away during 1990–1997, young technocratic leaders who Deng groomed and helped install have eventually become the dominant players in China's politics.

As the Politburo membership changed between 1977 and 1992, the ideology, experiences, and outlook of the political elites naturally would have had a profound impact on policies. The makeup and the profile of the Politburo members offer useful hints at the direction of reform policies in China in the 1980s and the early 1990s. Consequently, a fruitful discussion on the making of policies regarding reform should start with the profile of Chinese leadership, or of top power holders.

The Formation and Power of the Politburo

In the Chinese political system, the highest decision-making body is the Politburo. Within the Politburo is a Standing Committee that oversees major decisions on a regular basis. According to the Party Constitution, the Chinese Communist Party (CCP) holds its Party Congress once every five years and elects a new Central Committee. The Central Committee can be abbreviated as the CCCCP. At the First Plenum of the CCCCP that is held immediately after each Party Congress, the Central Committee elects a new Politburo and its Standing Committee. In the period this study investigates, the Eleventh Party Congress was held in 1977, the Twelfth Party Congress in 1982, the Thirteenth Party Congress 1987, and the Fourteenth Party Congress 1992. As we shall see shortly, there had been exceptions to the election of members of the Politburo and its Standing Committee between 1978 and 1992. In 1978, 1982, and 1985, a number of new members of the Politburo and its Standing Committee were chosen even at the plenum of the CCCCP other than the first plenum.

The Politburo and its Standing Committee have become the most powerful decision-making bodies for the CCP for three reasons. First, they are entrusted greater power than other bodies in the Party. The Party Constitution (1982: Article 21) grants the Politburo and its Standing Committee the right to "exercise the functions and powers of the Central Committee." Second, they meet more regularly than the CCCCP and the Party Congress. The CCCCP usually meets only once a year, and the Congress once every five years. It is impossible for either of them to formulate policies on a regular basis, or make decisions when occasions arise or call for. In contrast, the Politburo and the Standing Committee meet regularly. The Standing Committee meets probably even once a week (Lieberthal 1995: 161). In addition, both the Central Committee and the Congress are too large to be a deliberative body for decision making. The Fourteenth Central Committee had 189 full members (plus 130 alternate members), and the Fourteenth Party Congress over 2,000 delegates. It is difficult for two sizable bodies to discuss policies in details. In contrast, the Fourteenth Politburo had only 20 full members and its Standing

Committee—seven members. Their small size could facilitate discussion and effective policy making.[5]

During the time period this study covers, the CCP witnessed the Twelfth Politburo (1982), the Thirteenth Politburo (1987), and the Fourteenth Politburo (1992). The makeup of the Politburo changed quite significantly also in 1985. In these years, important reform initiatives were also introduced. The Eleventh Politburo formed in 1977, one year before the reform was launched, served as a good starting point for our observation. The profiles of the Politburo in these years are thus examined.

Details of the profile of the Politburo and its Standing Committee are summarized in tables that follow. The primary data sources are *Who's Who in the People's Republic of China* and biographic sketches of the Chinese leaders.[6] A variety of sources on the internet, especially those from official Chinese websites and in some cases postings from seasoned China observers or insiders provide useful information on individual leaders. These webs include the following: http://www.chinaoninternet.com, http://www.china.org.cn, http://www.wuhaidj.com, http://www.people.com.cn, http://www.china.com.cn/, and http://www.xjbz.gov.cn. The following features of the Politburo profile will be discussed: (1) size, generation and previous membership; (2) ideological preferences over reform; (3) functional backgrounds; and (4) provincial and regional backgrounds.

Changes in the Politburo and Implications

Size, Age, Generation and Membership. The size of the Politburo (in terms of the number of its full members) between 1977 and 1992 fluctuated between 15 and 25. Overall, it shrank slightly. In 1977, it started at 23, expanded slightly to 25 in 1982, and shrank slightly to 21 in 1985, and significantly to 15 in 1987. It went up to 20 in 1992. The age of Politburo members in 1977 averaged relatively young 65. It increased to a high 72 in 1982. It declined only slightly to 70 in 1985 and quite significantly to 63 in 1987. It further declined to 62 in 1992 (table 4.1).

The membership turnover was quite high in 1977, yet dropped considerably to a moderate level in 1982 and 1985. In 1982 and 1985, only 28–40 percent of the members were replaced each time. As a result, an average member in 1982 and 1985 had served at the Politburo for 9 to 10.5 years, similar to that in 1977. However, the turnover accelerated in 1987 and 1992, reaching 70 percent.

Table 4.1 Size, age, generation and membership of the Politburo, 1977–1992

Year	Size	Age	Average year of birth	Main political generation	Newly elected members (%)	First-time members (%)	New members since last Congress (%)	First year of Politburo membership	Years of Politburo membership
1977	23	65	1912	Long March	48	35	61	1970	6.9
1982	25	72	1910	Long March	28	24	36	1973	8.8
1985	21	70	1915	Anti-Japanese War	40	29	29	1975	10.5
1987	15	63	1924	Civil War	70	40	80	1985	1.5
1992	20	62	1930	Socialist Transformation	70	70	70	1991	1.5

Note: Data sources for tables 4.1–4.6 are those for profiles of leaders that are described in the text.

In each of these years, the share of first-time members and of members elected after the previous Party Congress roughly matched that of newly elected members. It was high in 1977, then declined in 1982 and 1985, and returned to a high level in 1987 and 1992.

Cheng Li (2001: 6–14) suggested that the following major events marked the generations of leaders—the Long March of 1934–1935, the Anti-Japanese War of 1937–1945, Socialist Transformation of 1949–1958, the Cultural Revolution of 1966–1976, and the Economic Reforms since 1978. Given that on average the leaders at the Politburo were born between 1910 and 1930, I add the Civil War of 1945–1949, and identified the following political generations: the Long March, born around 1910–1912; the Anti-Japanese War, born between 1915 and 1923; the Civil War, born around 1923; and the Socialist Transformation (or "Liberation"), born in 1930.

Average Politburo members in 1977 and 1982 were born between 1910 and 1912 and reached adulthood between 1928 and 1930. As they were usually politically active at this age, they would have participated in the Long March and can thus be regarded as the Long-March generation. An average Politburo member in 1985 would have joined the resistance against the Japanese invasion at the World War II (WWII) of 1937–1945, those in 1987 would have fought against the Nationalists in the Chinese Civil War from 1945 to 1949, and those in 1992 would have witnessed the Communist "liberation" of the nation and the founding of the People's Republic in 1949 and the socialist transformation of the nation in subsequent years. In sum, in 1977 and 1982, the Politburo was dominated by the Long March generation. In 1985, the baton was passed from the Long March old guards to

Anti-Japanese-invasion fighters. The baton was passed successively to the Civil War generation in 1987 and further down to the "Socialist Transformation" generation in 1992.[7]

In 1977, members of the Politburo had served in the body for seven years. The membership experience increased to 9–10.5 years in 1982 and 1985, but declined sharply to one year and a half in 1987 and 1992. The Politburo also underwent a significant generational shift, especially after 1982.

It appears that after triumphing over Maoists around 1980 conservatives and reformists added their own people to the Politburo. In the early and mid-1980s (between 1982 and 1986), the age of Politburo members was moderately lower. The average age of its members declined significantly in 1987, suggesting acceleration of recruitment of younger leaders. One direct effect of the rise of younger top leaders is that leaders became more energetic, more attentive to, and more able to handle technical and complicated issues; more informative of latest domestic and external development and trends; and were more susceptible to new ideas.

Ideological Orientation. Concomitant with the above generational change in the Politburo members was the significant change in their ideological outlook. This change is summarized in table 4.2. These members were categorized into six types. (1) Orthodox Maoists, or steadfast whateverists discussed earlier, who would follow strictly what Mao had prescribed. The best example is Hua Guofeng. (2) Moderate Maoists, who leaned toward whateverists, yet were somehow flexible in their stance toward economic reform. Ye Jianying fell under this category. (3) Conservatives, who supported limited market-oriented reform. The chief example is Chen Yun. (4) Orthodox reformists, who supported progressive and eventually broad market-oriented reform, yet strictly ruled out any development toward political liberalization. (5) Moderate reformists, who supported progressive and eventually broad market-oriented reform while tolerating moderate development toward political liberalization and limited overhaul of the political system. (6) Unknown, whose political stances were not known. The ideological profiles of six Politburos are summarized in table 4.2.

The Politburo in 1977 was packed with Maoists. Even after the Gang of Four, or four radical Maoists, were arrested and purged from the Politburo, over half of the members remained orthodox Maoists. This to a large extent reflected late Mao's political arrangement to

Table 4.2   Ideological orientation of Politburo members, 1977–1992

Year	Orthodox Maoist	Moderate Maoist	Conservative	Orthodox reformist	Moderate reformist	Unknown
1977	0.52	0.04	0.09	0.04	0.04	0.26
1982	0.12	0.04	0.24	0.08	0.24	0.28
1985	0.05	0.05	0.29	0.05	0.43	0.14
1987	0	0	0.33	0.13	0.53	0
1992	0	0	0	0.70	0.25	0.05

ensure that the leadership after him would observe his policies. This makeup, however, clearly hampered the initiation of reforms.

Within the months following the Third Plenum of the Eleventh CCCCP where the decision to proceed toward reform was sanctioned, crucial changes in the top leaders occurred. First, in December 1978 Chen Yun, an influential conservative leader who backed cautious and limited reform toward the market economy, was added to the Politburo Standing Committee. Meanwhile, Hu Yaobang, a moderate reformist and Deng's close follower, along with Madame Zhou Enlai and a conservative general Wang Zhen, were also added to the Politburo. Second, in September 1979 Zhao Ziyang, an accomplished governor from Sichuan and moderate reformist, along with influential conservative Peng Zhen, were added to the Politburo. Third, in February 1980, Hu Yaobang and Zhao Ziyang were elevated into the Politburo Standing Committee. Hu took over the post of Party Secretary from Hua Guofeng. Wang Dongxing, a former chief of bodyguards for Mao and Hua's key ally, lost his post at the Standing Committee. Three other Maoists were relieved of their Politburo membership. In August, Zhao replaced Hua as the Premier. During November and December, the Politburo accepted Hua's resignation of his last important post, namely, the Chairmanship of the CMC of the CCP. By then, anti-Maoist coalition of conservatives and reformists had won the battle against the Maoists.

In 1982, the Twelfth Party Congress elected another eight new members to the Politburo, including three reformists and two conservatives. This congress cemented the dominance of the anti-Maoist coalition in the leadership. The Politburo membership was also a reward for senior leaders, such as Marshal Xu Xiangqian, General Yang Dezhi, propagandist Hu Qiaomu, and veteran Xi Zhongxun, and for supporters of the anti-Maoist leadership. It also placed reformists, such as Wan Li and Yang Shangkun in key positions for pushing forward the reform course. As a result of personnel changes in the previous years and at the congress, the Maoists only made up 16 percent of the Politburo membership. In contrast, conservatives and reformists constituted 24 percent and 32 percent, or a comfortable majority of 56 percent. This pro-reform majority would permit or encourage initial efforts of liberalization.

During 1985–1987, reformists and conservatives continued to expand their influence at the Politburo, reducing the power of the Maoists. Reformist and conservative shares of the Politburo membership were respectively 48 percent and 29 percent in 1985, and 66 percent and 33 percent in 1987. The Maoist shares declined from 10 percent in 1985 to 0 percent in 1987. This change in the balance of power produced two consequences. First, it was easier to adopt reform policies than in the late 1970s and early 1980s. Second, given the new political landscape at the Politburo, the reformists would face the opposition and disagreement more frequently from conservatives, their former ally against the Maoists, than from Maoists, their defeated enemy. The focus of debate had thus shifted away from whether to reform at all, but how fast and in which direction reform should proceed.

As discussed in the previous chapter, reformist drives at times led to popular discontent or outbursts of demands for political liberalism. When this happened, powerful conservatives such as Chen Yun and orthodox reformists such as Deng Xiaoping, who were among the eight veteran leaders, would join hands to slow down economic initiatives. Conservatives were able to block certain economic reform proposals. The division among the leaders between 1977 and 1992 thus necessitated incrementalism in reform. The debate between conservatives and reformists was settled only after 1992. In 1992, reformists took a lion's share of 95 percent of the Politburo membership. Conservatives were no longer capable of mounting any serious opposition against the reformist agenda.

Functional Backgrounds

Hong Yung Lee characterized the change of leadership in China in the 1980s as from revolutionary cadres to Party technocrats. He argued that as the Party shifted its task from revolution to economic development, it found its cadres were "too old, too poorly educated, and too ossified in their thinking" for the new task. The Party recruited new leaders who were trained in narrow technical fields because they were uncritical in their ideology and likely to improve the existing system

(Lee 1994: 401–03). Lee (1994: 255–86) analyzed the work back-grounds the provincial/ministerial- or lower- level cadres in the early and mid-1980s, and Cheng Li (2001: 51–80) examined closely the educational backgrounds of national and provincial elites. This study examines the political fields where the Politburo members developed their careers. Based on the length of their work experiences in any possible fields, a field where each leader's career developed is identified. Then the number is tallied.

In Mao's era there were two major criteria for upward mobility in China's society. The first was ideological purity and correctness, or revolutionary spirit. This was termed "red," and this system of promotion was coined virtuocracy (Shirk 1982). The other was technical competence and professional knowledge (or being an "expert"). According to Shirk, during the Cultural Revolution, expertise was nearly completely ignored or even harshly criticized and only "redness" was upheld. In practice, however, the Maoist emphasis on "redness" turned out to be a disappointment for idealists believing in revolutionary and selfless devotion and for those who endorsed technical competence (or "expert"). Virtuocracy degraded into political favoritism and factional struggles, generating political cynicism in the population. Those who were promoted were technically incompetent and their management incurred considerable economic and social costs (Shirk 1982: 186).

After Deng Xiaoping returned to power, the new emphasis was placed on technical expertise even though a minimal degree of "redness" was needed. The new mixture of the two recruitment criteria was partly a reversal of Mao's virtuocracy and was also a means to fulfill Deng's new mode of governance. Deng's governance program aimed to continue to improve the Chinese living standard. Only technically qualified people could accomplish this task. Therefore, meritocracy was restored in order to promote competent talents suitable for Deng's policy. Meanwhile, minimal political acceptability was also required for recruits into political posts to conform to the Party's political ideals (Shirk 1982: 194) and support the Party as the sole ruling party. As discussed above, Deng also favored young technocratic leaders who wholeheartedly embraced his economic reform while allowing very limited political change.

Overall, the outlook and experience of Politburo members (refer to table 4.3) reflected a transition from revolutionary cadres to Party technocrats, as suggested by Lee. During 1977–1982, among seven functional fields, the largest number of leaders came to military and security field. Prior to 1982, those leaders who fought for the revolution constituted the largest plurality in the Party. This was no longer true after 1982. In the years that followed, they were gradually replaced by leaders who specialized in other non-military fields. Between 1985 and 1992, the military and security field by itself only accounted for zero to 14 percent of the leaders. In 1985, 1987, and 1992, most leaders came from two fields—(1) government, or (2) the Party and government, plus a possible third field. Among these two fields, the former overtook the latter in 1992 to become the largest field. In comparison, other cross-fields, such as the military and the Party, the military and the government, or mass organizations, legislature and the Party, produced much fewer leaders. The field of Party affairs gained importance in 1987, yet went back to its level of 1985 in 1992.

With the gradual passage and even death of leaders of the Long March generation, later generations were clearly ascending in the late 1980s and early 1990s. These new leaders tended to have experience in governmental affairs and were better educated. Politburo members

Table 4.3   Functional and educational backgrounds of the Politburo members

Year	1977 (%)	1982 (%)	1985 (%)	1987 (%)	1992 (%)
Functional Fields					
Military and security only	39	28	14	0	10
Party only	13	4	14	20	15
Government only	4	8	19	27	35
Party and government, plus a possible third field	22	28	19	40	30
Government and military	13	8	10	0	0
Party and military	4	4	5	7	0
Mass organizations, legislature and Party	4	20	19	7	10
Summary Statistics					
Broad Categories					
1) Military and security	39	28	14	0	10
2) Non pure military	61	72	86	100	90
Selected Groupings					
Government and others	39	44	48	67	65
Military and others	57	40	29	7	10
	1978	**1982**		**1988**	**1992**
Percentage of members with college education	23	32		67	86

Note: The data on educational background came from Cheng Li 2001. *China's Leaders: The New Generation*. New York: Rowman & Littlefield Publishers, Inc.: 38.

who received college education also grew into a clear majority after 1987, registering 67 percent in 1988 and 86 percent in 1992. Overall, Politburo members after 1985 tended to specialize in governmental affairs, or jointly in governmental affairs. From 1987 to 1992, around 65–67 percent of Politburo members had this background. The government, which oversaw economic and social issues, appeared to be the best place for training leaders in the era of reform. The military men or even those with military experience were phased out gradually from the political scene. Those who specialized in Party affairs, or specialized in the mass organizations (such as the Youth League and the Labor Union), or the legislature (the National People's Congress) increased in number in the mid-1980s, yet declined to a combined 25 percent only in 1992 (table 4.3). Therefore, Party technocrats appeared increasingly to be "government" technocrats as well. With this change in the leadership, the new leaders were better informed about economic and social affairs, were more competent in managing sophisticated affairs that arose from development and could make sounder reform policies with technical proficiency.

Overall, young cadres who emerged in Deng's era tended to be better educated and know better about the modern economy, trade, finance, law, and management of an evolving society than most veteran leaders. They were more capable of engineering economic modernization and reform than veterans. Finally, they were more energetic and in much better health for managing daily affairs. In contrast, many veterans were in frail health and had outdated knowledge about economic and social management. By the mid-1990s, most of them had also passed away. Therefore, their replacement by young and technocratic cadres was natural and beneficial for the Party that aimed to engineer rapid economic growth and manage an increasingly complex society.

The rise of technocrats, as a matter of fact, is not unique for China alone. As Williamson (1994) has suggested, the developing economies in East Asia and Latin America have all witnessed the ascendance of technocrats as top leaders. Their rise serves the need of these economies for grappling with an increasingly complex economy and to ensure that the nation can thrive or survive increasingly tense international economic competition.

Provincial and Regional Backgrounds

In central-local relations, Politburo members' ties with a certain province or region might considerably affect their stance over reform in the province or the region. Three types of regional backgrounds can be identified on the basis of their length of work experience after the Communists assumed power in China (in 1949 in most places and a few years earlier in a few places): (1) central, local or mixed; (2) regional backgrounds. Two types of regional backgrounds are used in China: coastal, central, or western; or north, northeast, northwest, east, south, and southwest; (3) provincial backgrounds, classified by the twenty-nine provinces that existed in mainland China at the start of reform. The central/local, regional, and provincial backgrounds of the Politburo members are summarized in tables 4.4–4.6.

First, on the basis of their length of work experience in the Communist period at the national or local agencies, Politburo members might be roughly classified as central, local, or mixed. If they had

Table 4.4   Central or local experience of the Politburo members

Year	Central (%)	Local (%)	Mixed (%)	Local/central (%)	Central/local (%)	Total (%)
1977	52	43	4			100
1982	60	20	20			100
1985	57	24	19			100
1987	27	27	47	27	20	100
1992	15	35	50	35	15	100

Table 4.5   Regional backgrounds of Politburo members

Year	1977 (%)	1982 (%)	1985 (%)	1987 (%)	1992 (%)
Coastal	**44**	**56**	**52**	**60**	**65**
Central	39	32	19	7	15
Western	17	12	29	33	20
Total	100	100	100	100	100
North	**30**	**32**	**29**	**27**	25
Northeast	4	8	5	7	20
Northwest	4	12	14	20	10
East	26	20	19	20	**30**
South	22	24	19	13	5
Southwest	13	4	14	13	10
Total	99	100	100	100	100

Notes: Percentages in bolds signify the highest shares in the given year. The total in 1977 does not add up to 100 due to rounding.

Table 4.6 Provincial backgrounds of Politburo members

Year	1977	1982	1985	1987	1992
Beijing	3	4	4	<u>4</u>	<u>3</u>
Sichuan	<u>2</u>	<u>1</u>	<u>3</u>	2	2
Guangdong	<u>1</u>	<u>4</u>	<u>3</u>	<u>2</u>	1
Liaoning	1	<u>2</u>	<u>1</u>	1	<u>3</u>
Jiangsu	2	1	1	0	1
Fujian	2	2	0	0	0
Shanghai	0	0	1	2	<u>4</u>
Shandong	0	1	1	0	1
Guangxi	1	1	0	0	0
Tianjin	0	0	0	0	1
Shanxi	2	<u>2</u>	2	0	0
Anhui	1	1	1	1	0
Hunan	<u>2</u>	0	0	0	0
Hubei	<u>1</u>	<u>1</u>	1	0	0
Henan	1	1	0	0	0
Inner Mongolia	1	1	0	0	0
Jiangxi	<u>1</u>	0	0	0	0
Heilongjiang	0	0	0	0	1
Jilin	0	0	0	0	1
Shaanxi	0	1	1	0	0
Guizhou	1	0	0	0	0
Gansu	0	0	1	<u>2</u>	<u>2</u>
Qinghai	1	1	0	0	0
Ningxia	0	0	1	<u>1</u>	0
Xinjiang	0	1	0	0	0
Total	23	25	21	15	20

Notes: Underlines indicate members of the Standing Committee and bolds suggest provinces that had the highest representations from Politburo members.

spent most (two-thirds of or more) years in the national Party, administrative, legislative, and military apparatus or national mass organizations, they are regarded as central. If they had spent most of their years in the local Party, administrative and military apparatus or local mass organizations, they are considered local. If they had spent a considerable portion of their careers in national agencies (defined as one-third) and the rest of them (between another one-third to two-thirds) in local agencies, or the other way around, they would be classified as mixed, or having substantial national and local experience.

As table 4.4 suggests, the majority (or 52–60 percent) of Politburo members in 1977, 1982, and 1985 were "centralists," namely, they spent much more time at the national agencies than in local governments after 1949. Meanwhile, the second largest group was "localists," who spent much more time working at the local governments than the national governments. They made up 20–43 percent of the Politburo seats. The mixed category was the smallest group, accounting for 4–20 percent. Centralists dropped out quickly from the Politburo after 1985, the mixed group grew into the largest group in the Politburo after 1987, and localists saw their seats at the Politburo increase and overtook the centralists in 1992. Among the mixed group, those who spent more time serving as local leaders outnumbered those who spent more time working at the central government in 1987 (27 percent versus 20 percent) and in 1992 (35 percent versus 15 percent). The rise of the mixed group, especially the group members who spent more time in localities than at the center, as well as localists, helped to account for China's economic decentralization in 1987 and 1992, when economic reform was in full swing.

The strong presence of the centralists in the early and mid-1980s seems to contradict the decentralization trend in China at that time. However, three factors explained this gap. First of all, the leading Maoist Hua Guofeng was a "localist," and partially for this reason, also supported some sort of decentralization (such as the establishment of a SEZ in Shenzhen). Second, the ideological preferences of the leaders probably mattered more than their central/local background at that time. In general, conservatives and especially reformists supported decentralization more strongly than Maoists, and reformists more strongly than conservatives. In 1982 a pro-reform coalition of conservatives and reformists controlled the majority of the Politburo. In particular, reformists controlled nearly one-third of the seats, outnumbering the other two major groups (the conservatives with 24 percent and the Maoists with 16 percent)(table 4.2). As some of the Maoists and conservatives might also support decentralization due to their long local experience, decentralization would have gained enough support at the Politburo. Third, as localists increased their share of the seats in 1987 and 1992, decentralization went further than in the early and mid-1980s.

Politburo members' provincial background is coded on the basis of the province where they had served for the longest time after the founding of the People's Republic. The underlying assumption is that work ties and political connections a leader cultivated in a province remained more or less stable in the post-1949 period, or at least much more stable than during the Long March, the Anti-Japanese War, and the Civil War.

Let us first look at the regional backgrounds of the leaders (table 4.5). Among the coastal, central, and western regions, the coast produced the most number of Politburo members. Nevertheless, before 1982, less than half of the Politburo members had worked in the coastal region. After 1982, more than half of them did. In 1987 and 1992, a clear majority of them (60–65 percent) had served in the coastal provinces. Prior to 1985, more leaders came from the central region than from the western region. After 1985, however, the situation reversed, and more leaders had worked in western provinces.

This change was broadly in line with the political influences of the three regions. In the 1970s the national government still favored the inland regions over the coastal provinces. Between the 1960s and the early 1970s, national leaders, apparently led by a majority who had worked in the inland provinces, favored heavier investment in the central and western regions than in the coastal provinces.[8] For example, the national government invested billions of yuan to build the Third Front to prepare for possible war against the Soviet Union.[9] Starting from the early 1980s, however, leaders with coastal background gained a majority at the Politburo. As a result, the national government shifted its developmental efforts away from the interior and toward the coast. This coast-oriented policy was epitomized by the opening of the coast to the world economy and the "coastal developmental strategy" in 1988, announced by Zhao Ziyang. In 1992 when Deng himself toured southern coastal provinces to promote reform and opening, the coastal leaders gained unprecedented ascendance at the Politburo and pushed for another wave of coastal development.[10]

The nation can also be divided into six regions, namely, North, Northeast, Northwest, East, South, and Southwest. In most of the years, the North contributed the greatest number of seats at the Politburo, followed by the East, and then by the South (table 4.5). The Northeast produced the lowest number of national leaders. The year of 1992 appeared to be a year of change, when the East overtook the North to become the region that produced most of the leaders, the seats of the Northeast also increased, yet those of the South declined steeply. This reflected the prominence of the leaders from Shanghai (part of the Eastern Region), the rise of leaders from Liaoning, and the declining influence of leaders who had worked in Guangdong.

Finally, when we look at the provincial backgrounds of leaders (table 4.6), overall the Beijing Municipal Party Committee and Government were the place where most leaders had ever worked.

The next provinces were Sichuan, Guangdong, and Liaoning. The other noticeable provinces were Shanghai, which contributed the most leaders in 1992, Shanxi, which produced two leaders each in 1977, 1982, and 1985, and Gansu, where two leaders each in 1987 and 1992 (including Hu Jintao and Wen Jiabao) achieved political ascendance. The prominence of Guangdong, Shanghai, and to some extent, Sichuan and Beijing, went hand in hand with their pioneering role in China's economic liberalization. Guangdong was the most glaring example. As suggested in table 4.6, in 1982, 1985, and 1987, it had 2 to 4 leaders with previous work ties with it, and importantly, at least one of them served at the Politburo Standing Committee. Likely because of the strong endorsement from the central leaders, it became the earliest province to be opened up and experiment with bold urban and external trade reform initiatives. Guangdong's luck, however, seemed to come to an end in 1992, when its central representation was overtaken by Shanghai. In that year, four Politburo members were originally local leaders from Shanghai, including the Party Secretary Jiang Zemin and the de-facto Premier Zhu Rongji. Therefore, it became the center of gravity for the nation's regional development and reform. Sichuan, on the other hand, was a pioneer of reforms in the late 1970s and the early 1980s, thanks partially to its national representatives. Beijing, on the other hand, enjoyed relatively more freedom in local development and certain reform initiatives in the 1980s and the early 1990s (especially under Chen Xitong). It appears that national leaders who had worked in these few provinces might have helped them to gain particular treatment. Nevertheless, before a thorough nationwide analysis, we cannot be sure whether the same thing can be said about other provinces in China. This analysis would be taken up later.

Conclusion

In China, a country with long tradition of rule by man, leadership plays a key role in initiating changes in policies and launching economic reforms. China's reformist leaders, especially Deng Xiaoping, took this point to heart and tried to ensure that men in power would follow his reforms agenda. Using his own status as the paramount leader in the post-Mao era, Deng actively pushed for retirement for, first, Maoists and then most of veteran leaders except for a handful of top veterans including himself, and for promotion of young and knowledgeable leaders. The profile of the Politburo members between

1977 and 1992 suggested that reformists gradually dominated the leadership. A growing percentage of them had work experience in the government (and to a lesser extent the Party) at both national and local levels, familiar with economic, social, and local affairs, and had graduated from colleges. An overwhelming percentage of young leaders worked in the coastal region and hence might inevitably favor coastal development. The North that consistently appeared to have produced more national leaders than the rest of the nation, was only surpassed by the East in 1992. Specifically, prior to 1992, Beijing, Guangdong, and Sichuan produced more powerful national leaders than the other provinces. In 1992, they were replaced by Shanghai. Therefore, national patrons might have helped the faster development in Guangdong and Beijing in the 1980s and Shanghai after the early 1990s.

Overall, technocratic young leaders helped manage the opening and liberalization in the 1980s, rescue economic reform in the early 1990s, and sustain marketization after Deng's death. While the presence of conservative leaders necessitated incrementalism in reform in the 1980–1992 period, reformist young leaders, especially Hu Yaobang, Zhao Ziyang, Wan Li, Qiao Shi, Li Ruanhuan, and Zhu Rongji, successively helped Deng to coordinate and design economic reforms. Zhao, for example, supervised the opening of the coast in the 1980s, the expansion of rural enterprises, and the boom of private businesses. He also proposed the coastal development strategy in 1988. In 1992, young technocratic leaders, such as Qiao Shi, Li Ruihuan, and Zhong Rongji, rallied to Deng's calls for reform and helped secure the Party's acceptance of a marketization program. They thus played a significant role in the critical triumph of reformists over conservatives. Since then and even after Deng's death in 1997, they have been maintaining the trend of economic reform. Deng's grooming of technocratic, reformist, and young leaders did pay off politically during and beyond his life time.

5

Selective and Showcase Liberalization

After Deng's strategies of managing elite conflict and grooming pro-reform young leaders are reviewed, it is time to zero in on his efforts to put into action liberal measures in opening up the nation. Among major reform initiatives introduced by post-Mao leaders, few have caught as much attention as the opening of China. Thus in examining national reform policies, the Open Policy is chosen as the case study. Whether or not to open up China's economy to the outside world was a highly controversial and sensitive issue concerning national pride among the elites and the populace. The forced opening of China after its defeat in the Opium War in the mid-nineteenth century, called the Open Door Policy, is different from the Open Policy engineered by Deng Xiaoping. The Open Door Policy has been viewed by the Chinese as a national disgrace as well as an imperialist imposition of trade preferences on a sovereign country. Communists came to power in 1949 with a strong anti-imperialist tone that deeply influenced the Chinese for the coming decades. For fervent nationalists, the nation's opening in any form resembled a sell-out of national economic interests to foreign intruders and abandoning of decades-old hard-line policy against the West. When I was on a field research trip in Tumen, Jilin in 1982, a veteran Chinese soldier who fought the United States in Korea in the 1950s vented his disappointment in the Open Policy to me: "How can the government do business with Americans who fought against us in Korea and have been our enemy for the past three decades?"

The opening also challenged the command economy and self-reliance that China had cherished for decades. In the 1960s and the late 1970s, the Chinese economy centered around economic planning with a particularly strong emphasis on self-reliance. It was thought that throwing wide open the Chinese door to foreign business people would erode this orthodox mode of development.

The fact that Chinese leaders overcame tremendous political opposition is thus no simple feat. In this chapter I examine the leadership's strategy in introducing the Open Policy in the first two provinces. Mainland China had a population of 963 million and twenty-nine provinces under its jurisdiction in 1978. An average province had a population of 33 million and an area of 330,000 square kilometers, equivalent to a medium-sized country. Provinces naturally assumed an important role in administering a population of such a considerable size as well as policy implementation. The center also gave provincial leaders discretion in local administration because of large regional diversities. Provincial discretion has increased in the wake of decentralization in the reform's era. Provinces serve as a key link between the national and local governments. Among representatives of localities, provincial leaders are the primary ones that could bargain with, and influence policy making of the central government. No major national policies could thus be implemented without going through the provincial layer. That is why it is necessary to examine the start of the Open Policy by looking at the first two provinces where it was tried out.

This chapter suggests that national reformists selected provinces with the greatest propensities to open up first to experiment with the Open Policy. They also tried every means necessary to ensure that these pilot experiments would be economically successful and appealing to other provinces. Guangdong and Fujian were close to Hong Kong and Taiwan, respectively. They had strong social and family links with overseas business people and had a long recent history of external and domestic commerce. Local cadres and populations in the provinces, especially in Guangdong, were quick to embrace the Open Policy. National reformists staffed these provinces with committed liberals and seasoned politicians. Extensive connections of leaders in Guangdong with central leadership provided political insurance for the reform course in the province. National reformists and leaders in Guangdong skillfully navigated reforms through changing political and ideological storms and made needed retreats when facing strong conservative backlashes and adverse macroeconomic conditions. Over the years the Open Policy produced shining successes, especially in Shenzhen of Guangdong. This prevented conservatives from attacking it on economic grounds. Other provinces were impressed with

Guangdong's economic achievements and were jealous of its special policies and economic discretionary power. They requested similar policies from the center. This triggered competitive liberalization across the provinces, pressuring central leaders for greater opening in the mid-1980s.

The Early Years of the Open Policy

The idea of an export processing zone was first proposed by central officials in 1978. Under the instruction of Vice Premier Gu Mu, the SPC and the Ministry of External Economy and Trade (MOEET) sent in April two inspection teams to survey Hong Kong and Macao, as well as Western countries, respectively. The Hong Kong-Macao inspection team reported on June 3 to central leaders, suggesting that Bao'an and Zhuhai in Guangdong Province be turned into bases for export production, processing, and tourism for Hong Kong and Macao Chinese within three to five years. Hua Guofeng listened to the report. Eager to use foreign capital to fund his ambitious, mega state-run projects, he approved the general idea (Vogel 1989: 130–32; Yang 1998: 246). The exact reasons for his approval of the proposal will be elaborated.

Meanwhile, Yuan Geng, the Standing Deputy Board Director of China Merchants Steam Navigation Company (CMSN), Ltd., a subsidiary of the Ministry of Communications in Hong Kong, consulted with Liu Tianfu, the vice director of the Revolutionary Committee of Guangdong, the province's ruling body at that time, regarding setting up an export processing zone in Bao'an. Liu agreed immediately. Minister of Transportation Ye Fei and Deputy Minister Zeng Sheng also traveled to Guangzhou to discuss the matter. They reached a consensus with Guangdong.

In early January 1979, the Guangdong authority and the Ministry of Communications jointly submitted a report to the State Council and Vice Premier Li Xiannian, who might share Hua's enthusiasm to borrow foreign capital to fund state-dominated developments. The former proposed that the CMSN invest in sectors related to naval navigation in the area in Bao'an neighboring Hong Kong. In late January, soon after the Chinese new year, Li Xiannian and Gu Mu met with Peng Deqing, the Minister of Communications and Yuan Geng. Li approved the report, designated the zone in the Shekou Peninsular, and requested that Gu coordinate the work on the issue.

In early February, Gu convened a meeting on the issue, attended by the SPC, the State Construction Bank, the Ministry of Foreign Trade

(MFT), the People's Bank, and the Ministries of Finance and Communications. Gu announced Deng Xiaoping's proposal for Guangdong and Fujian to implement some sort of opening. The meeting worked out the arrangement for the zone.

From early 1979 onward, Guangdong leaders played a more active role in pushing for greater opening of the province, beyond the initial export processing zone in Bao'an. In late February, Guangdong Party Secretary Wu Nansheng lobbied for more flexible policies for Shantou and obtained the agreement from Guangdong First Party Secretary and Governor Xi Zhongxun. When attending the Central Work Conference in April 1979, Xi Zhongxun asked the Politburo for flexible policies and special institutional arrangement for Guangdong. With Deng, the paramount leader at that time showing interest in the proposal, Hua, who was formally the Party Chairman yet in fact had no power, agreed to Xi's request. Xi also requested that overseas Chinese and certain foreign business people be allowed to invest in the province. A vice premier immediately barked at the idea. Deng, however, voiced his support for the idea. After Xi's report, Deng talked to Xi in private and named the trade cooperation zones that Xi proposed as special zones.

In the following months, Gu Mu led a team to survey Guangdong and Fujian regarding special exporting zones. In July, the CCCCP and the State Council issued No. 50 Document. It approved the requests from the two provinces for special policies and flexible measures and for setting up zones in Shenzhen, Zhuhai, and Shantou of Guangdong and Xiamen of Fujian. In March 1980, the CCCCP renamed special exporting zones special economic zones (SEZs). In the second half of 1980, the NPC approved the Articles on SEZs, and the construction for SEZs started afterward.[1]

Existing Explanations of the Open Policy

For the purpose of this research, the opening is also intellectually fascinating because it reveals much about central-local relations in the reform era. The existing literature on China's opening up till the 1990s falls under three categories—studies on particular provinces or areas (Jao and Leung 1986; Yeung and Chu 1998, Yeung and Chu 2000; Cheung et al. 1998; Vogel 1989); studies on the Open Policy as a whole (Crane 1990; Kleinberg 1990; Howell 1993; Shirk 1994; Zweig 2002), and studies on a topical issue, such as foreign invested firms (Pearson 1991).

The first stream of the existing literature focused on one of the following three levels of analyses, that is, local, national, or international, and discussed the relative importance of these levels. Some of them, for example, emphasize local interests in obtaining foreign business. For example, it has been shown that provincial leadership played a significant role in ushering in reforms and opening up (Cheung et al. 1998; Cheung 1998b). It was also suggested that the Xiamen government would ignore central political restrictions on Taiwanese capitalists because their capital was much needed (Kuo 1992). A number of scholars, on the other hand, contend that the national authority and its preferences largely shaped China's opening. Kleinberg (1990), for example, showed that the Chinese authority pursued mercantlist policies and could exercise control over foreign investment already made in China. Solinger (1991) and Fewsmith (1994), and to some extent Vogel (1989), echoing Wade's (2004) argument of an East Asian developmental state, proposed that the Chinese state was autonomous enough to steer the direction of development and was far sighted enough to promote the course of modernization. Another group of scholars maintained that China's Open Policy was dictated by international forces. In his study of China's textile, silk and shipbuilding industries, Moore (2002) suggested that the extent of international competition was a primary cause for the state's decision to liberalize a sector. As early as 1991, Townsend (1991) suggested that foreign parties had exercised their influence to keep China open. Lardy (1992) shared this view in arguing that international market forces drove China's opening and its process. In parallel, Pearson (1991) argued that in the wake of China's Open Policy, competition among governmental elites and foreign lobbying weakened the state's control of foreign investment. Lever-Tracy, Ip, and Tracy (1996), Lilley and Hart (1997), and Wang (2001) highlighted the significant and even primary role of overseas Chinese in FDI in China as well as their business operation and networks. It has also been suggested that villagers' pursuit of foreign business was conditioned by whether or not they received money from overseas relatives (Woon 1990). In recent years China scholars also argued that international economic organizations such as the WTO, the IMF, and the World Bank also imposed economic rules on China while providing it with expertise, assistance, and information, facilitating China's opening (Economy and Oksenberg 1999).

A second group of scholars emphasizes the interaction between actions at the same or different levels (Howell 1993; Shirk 1994;

Yang 1997; Pearson 2001) or between politics and economics (Howell 1993; Zweig 2002). Howell, for example, explained the cycles in China's opening by referring to the opening-enhancing forces consisting of central deregulation and provincial pursuit of foreign resources as well as the opening-obstructing forces of provincial excessive external demands, inflation, and central intervention to restore stability. Shirk (1994), examining the political dynamics of reform, argued that national leaders courted support for reforms from coastal leaders through particularistic contracting with them. Yang (1997), on the other hand, explained how the opening spread nationwide through a process called competitive liberalization. Localities, according to him, bided against each other in offering investors more liberal policies in order to attract investment and stimulate local growth. Pearson (2001) found that international players, national leaders' learning about international rules and trade, and domestic constituents combined to affect China's stance toward General Agreement on Tariffs and Trade (GATT)/WTO accession. Zweig (2002) criticized the above studies while recognizing their contributions. He advanced a complex model integrating domestic and external forces and accepting their circular interaction and different levels of analyses. He acknowledged the central role, yet pointed to its limits after the Open Policy was initiated. He postulated a division among bureaucrats toward opening based on their prospective gains, yet argued that over time they would move toward opening. He argued that provinces would compete for the center's varying regulations toward localities and that these regulations in turn helped foster competitive advantage of localities and condition how individuals in the localities respond to the opening. Lastly, while internationalization shaped growth and inequality, localities either demanded greater opening or evaded established restraints. In response, the state might impose control, and this cycle might replay.

The ongoing debate suggests a number of useful perspectives on the opening, especially on the role of actors or forces at each level. International factors, including market forces, overseas Chinese investors, superior economic performance in the West, especially the East Asian Newly Industrialized Economies (NIEs), exerted pressure on China to open up and helped sustain its opening afterward. In addition, the Chinese national authority and local government bargained and interacted, each seeking to enhance their own positions and enriching their political or economic resources in the process of opening up and continuing opening. Local and individual players, such as some well-connected villagers and overseas Chinese investors, also acted in their interests to facilitate the opening. Lastly, these actors interacted. Provinces competed for better policies from the center and against each other for foreign capital. Overseas Chinese, Asian, and Western investors also competed against each other in lobbying China for greater opening.

Despite these insights from the existing studies on a variety of factors in the opening, we have yet to fully understand the complex role of national leaders, their political and economic considerations, and national patronage of provincial reforms. These factors arguably underpinned China's other economic reform policies. For example, despite decades or years of international pressures, China failed to open up prior to the 1980s. This demonstrated that leadership and its preferences mattered. The above literature, including that employing multilevel and multifactor interaction, has its noticeable limits. The stimulating models of central-local bargaining (or central catering to the provinces) and competitive liberalization may also have their large analytical "blind spots." Zweig (2002: 15–16) argues that China opened first the coastal provinces despite provincial lobbying for the policy as suggested by competitive liberalization. This illustrates both the role of national authority and the comparative advantage of the coast. For this reason, Zweig rejected Shirk's argument about the center's buying off the coast by arguing that the coast would automatically line up for reform in their own interests. Only through an in-depth empirical analysis can we tell whether this critique is sensible or not.

Considerable analytical and theoretic efforts have been made to explain the *event* of the opening of China. However, in comparison, there have been fewer efforts to shed light on the *policy-making process* of the opening. In addition, with probable exceptions of Shirk (1994), few researchers ponder over the practical question of reform management. Few ask how national reformists strategized the opening process in a way that helped them to overcome centuries-old aversion to accommodating to foreign economic interests. In addition, available information on China's reform history suggests that leaders from Guangdong, not other provinces, were the primary proponents for opening in the late 1970s. Several interesting questions thus beg our answers. Why did national leaders decide on selective opening rather than nationwide opening at the beginning? What explained the timing of the opening as well as the provinces that national leaders selected for the earliest opening? How did national leaders manage to turn other provinces (including coastal and inland provinces) into active seekers of the opening? Reformist strategies and information on reform policy making can help solve the puzzle.

This chapter utilizes recently published Chinese materials revealing the decision-making process of the opening. In the past decades, some of these materials, deemed sensitive by the Chinese authority, were kept away from the public. In the recent five years, with the consolidation of the Open Policy, these materials are published in the form of histories on the provinces or major economic events. They profoundly enrich our understanding of the politics of the Open Policy and also throw doubts on some of the existing explanations or conjectures about the policy. In addition, this chapter also draws on China scholars' research on Guangdong and the Open Policy. It investigates national leaders' consideration in opening up and selecting the early places for opening, provincial leaders' lobbying in the case of Guangdong, the possible roles of overseas investors, and competition among provinces. Furthermore, the study also benefits from the author's intimate knowledge about Guangdong. Born and having grown up in the province, the author has extensive first-hand experience with the economy and society in the province.

In addition and importantly, this study examines political and economic explanations proposed by China scholars and students on economic policies in the light of the nationwide pattern of opening of provinces. This study would assess the roles of reformist strategies, provincial lobbying, national patronage, political control, and economic considerations in China's Open Policy. Few empirical studies of the policy systemically survey and evaluate these factors. The available new information allows us to undertake this task with greater ease.

Environment, Initiatives, Patronage, and Strategy

Briefly stated, the decision to open up and to choose the locations were triggered by a host of factors. International opportunities, reflected in abundant foreign capital and price gap in factors across the border, were present. At that time, central leaders were also looking around for foreign capital to finance modernization. But more significantly, China's political environment improved as a result of the rise of pragmatic leadership in the post-Mao era. Local and provincial leaders were emboldened to demand opening, and national leaders were open-minded to accept it for the sake of achieving their growth targets. As far as the opening of Guangdong is concerned, both local and central leaders valued their regional, personal, and political bonds, especially the place of their birth and childhood, or where they served for a considerable period in their career. Finally but very importantly, the contour of the reform policies was conditioned by central leaders' strategic consideration. Central leaders cared very much about the success of their policies. Reformists wanted to set a glaring example of success for the Open Policy. Guangdong, especially Shenzhen, became a favorite choice for its location, external linkages, local political liberalism, and entrepreneurship. It thus became the place that national reformers favored for earliest opening and where liberalization had the greatest chance for success. These factors will be examined closely in the following paragraphs.

Pressure for Change: Differences in Factor Prices

Economists distinguish several types of factors in production. With the simplest categorization, three factors, namely, capital, land, and labor can be identified. Frieden and Rogowski (1996) theorize that international market forces, through gap in prices in the same factor across border and the lobbying of owners of surplus factors for production, exert influence on national policies and facilitate economic internationalization. On the other hand, Shirk (1996) countered that an authoritarian and strong Chinese state prevented price signals from changing domestic prices and hence national policies. Interestingly enough, both views have their merits, which depend on the political leadership and national policy atmosphere.

In China's case, it had at least two opportunities for accessing relatively less expensive foreign capital. First, in the mid-1950s, as is to be elaborated, Hong Kong was suddenly showered with a large amount of capital and could use it at low interests. Second, in the late 1970s, Hong Kong firms found prices for local land and wages for local workers escalating. They were looking for cheaper land and labor. So in the mid-1950s and the late 1970s, price for capital was relatively cheaper in Hong Kong than in Guangdong. In the late 1970s, prices for land and labor (the latter in the form of wages) were lower in Guangdong. In both periods, Guangdong provided a convenient destination for investors from Hong Kong.

National Policy Atmosphere

National policy atmosphere conditions the effect of forces for internationalization on economic policies. Policy atmosphere directly hinges on the policy orientation of the paramount leader as well as the balance of power of major factions among the leadership. As Shirk (1996) suggested, price gaps in factors had to filter through political institutions in China before relevant policies were enacted. In Mao's era, top leaders especially Mao himself ignored changes in relative prices and precious external resources in economic policy making. Mao cherished self-reliance and was reluctant to use foreign capital. In the Cultural Revolution of 1966–1976, radical Maoism even prevailed. Its key advocates, including Mao's successor Lin Biao and then the Gang of Four, openly condemned advocates of foreign capital as Western slaves and political capitulationists.

In the mid-1950s Guangdong leaders were eager to take advantage of international market forces. At that time, businessmen in Southeast Asia moved their capital out of the region to Hong Kong to avoid the surging nationalist movement. The Hong Kong economy was benefiting from the sudden inflow of low-interest loans. When Mao Zedong was inspecting the province in 1956, Guangdong First Party Secretary Tao Zhu proposed to him that Guangdong be allowed to take advantage of Hong Kong capital to develop industries and agriculture in the province. Mao took Tao's proposal with him back to Beijing, but gave no reply (Yang 1998: 241–42). In the mid-1960s Tao even fell from grace and was condemned as a "capitalist roader" by the Red Guards, and any efforts to promote FDI in the nation were be harshly attacked.

As a result of this blatant neglect of international market forces and signals for internationalization, China's economy remained backward by the late 1970s. In the 1940s and 1950s the living standard of Hong Kong was not too far apart from that in Guangzhou, or even from those of neighboring areas in Guangdong. Between the 1950s and 1970s, Hong Kong embarked on rapid industrialization and was emerging as a world-class free port. In contrast, the economy in Guangdong initially stumbled in the reckless Great Leap Forward in the late 1950s and then in the ensuing zealous political campaigns. At the end of the 1970s, the living standard in the Pearl River Delta lagged behind that of Hong Kong by decades.

Since the late 1970s, however, the policy environment in China started to change. In 1977 Mao's successor Hua Guofeng announced ambitious developmental goals. He intended to use economic success to consolidate his fragile power position (Yang 1998: 108–10). He proposed to raise the ratio of agricultural mechanization from under 10 percent to over 70 percent in 1980 and build 120 mega projects in manufacturing, including 10 mega steel mills and 10 mega chemical plants. Hungry for capital and confronting limited funds at home, central leaders were compelled to use foreign capital (Naughton 1996: 59–95; Yang 1998). It was in this context that the SPC and the MOEET sent an inspection team to Hong Kong and Macao in April 1978 and that Hua approved, in June, the team's recommendation to utilize foreign capital to build export-processing zones in Guangdong. This willingness to use foreign capital and technology was a small leap forward from radical Maoism. Hua's "Importing Leap Forward" (*yang yaojin*), however, went into a string of problems—overambitious targets could not be fulfilled, production and exports of petroleum, a crucial material, fell short, foreign loans and purchases had to be cancelled, and macroeconomic imbalance was severe (Naughton 1996).

Deng Xiaoping, the paramount leader in China since December 1978, viewed foreign business with even greater enthusiasm. During a CCCCP work conference in November and December 1978, Hua was sternly criticized for his Maoist ideology by veteran yet influential Party leaders, including Chen Yun. Hua's position as a core leader was replaced by Deng Xiaoping (Yang 1998: 136–42). The ensuing Third Plenum of the Eleventh CCCCP cemented Deng's position and policies promoted by him and Chen. The plenum announced that the Party had shifted its main work away from class struggle to economic development. In order to facilitate national development, the plenum decentralized economic authority to the provinces and localities, encouraged external economic cooperation, and promoted the use of advanced technology from abroad (He et al. 1995: 444). This relatively liberal economic platform encouraged Guangdong authority and the Ministry of Communications to jointly propose to build an export-processing base in early January 1979. In the midst of this relaxed economic atmosphere it was easy for Vice Premiers Li Xiannian and Gu Mu to support the proposal.

It was also in this context that Xi, the top Guangdong leader, proposed in April 1979 to central leaders to allow greater economic autonomy for Guangdong. Xi's seniority in the Party also gave considerable weight to his request (Yang 1998: 251). Deng, the paramount leader at that time, gave his support. Hua, who supported an earlier proposal by the SPC and the MOEET to set up an export-processing base in June 1978, felt obliged to give his approval.

An intriguing issue would be the differences between Hua's and Deng's views of opening up. As discussed earlier, Hua's support for use of foreign capital in certain places definitely placed him apart from his former opponents, namely, radical Maoists represented by the Gang of Four. He was willing to use foreign loans in order to serve his ambitious economic goals of building his 120 mega projects in industry and transport and show off his leadership skills. However, he obviously would not tolerate a massive inflow of FDI that would challenge China's SOEs-dominated planned economy. Therefore, his version of opening was severely limited. Deng, on the other hand, would tolerate not only the use of foreign capital, but also imports of Western management, economics, and market institutions. Contrary to Hua, Ye, and conservative leaders who might support limited opening, Deng would not mind that foreign capital and international market forces upset and transformed China's command economy. Deng's open support for the opening and his status as a paramount leader pressured Hua and conservatives to oblige. Howell (1993: 48) describes as follows the difference between Hua and Deng over the opening:

> Compared to the traditional policies of the 1950s, Hua Guofeng was prepared to tolerate a higher level of foreign borrowing, in part for reasons of economic expediency and in part because of the growing influence of leaders such as Deng Xiaoping. However, there was still considerable controversy over foreign borrowing, linked partly to the issue of self-reliance. This was reflected in the contradictory statements of leaders in 1977 and 1978. Whilst the reformers were pressing for greater amounts of and more diverse forms of credit, supporters of Hua Guofeng wanted only a moderate increase in foreign loans, if any.

In short, different political ideology and policy preferences gave rise to different calculus in economic policies and produced distinct stances over factor price gaps in China for the past three decades. Mao and radical Maoists perceived the gaps as capitalist forces that served to undermine the communist regime and would ruthlessly resist them. Hua would employ foreign capital on a limited scale to achieve his ambitious plans, consolidate his own political power, and eventually maintain his political orthodoxy and the command economy. Deng would use foreign capital, know-how, management and economic institutions to transform China's backward economy and would not hesitate to upset the planned economy.

Local Agents for Change

Reformists also skillfully used their appointment of provincial leaders to advance liberalism. Deng, for example, appointed Xi Zhongxun and Yang Shangkun around the late 1970s—two reformists and veteran national officials, as top leaders in Guangdong. He wanted them to rehabilitate local leaders purged by radical Maoists, install reformists in key positions, and prepare the province for economic reforms. Around 1980, he appointed Ren Zhongyi, a reformist and a skillful provincial leader as the Party Secretary of Guangdong, and appointed the open-minded Liang Lingguang as the Guangdong Governor. Both teams effectively promoted, designed, and safeguarded reforms of agriculture, industry, and foreign trade in the province. Through promoting reformist and technocratic young leaders, central leaders ensured the adoption and expansion of liberal economic policies in Guangdong. This confirms the argument in chapter 4.

Officials and leaders in Guangdong felt most strongly the price gaps in capital, land, and labor between Hong Kong and Guangdong in the late 1970s. Geography and local culture are probably some of the important reasons. Hong Kong was only a hill or just a few miles of water away from Guangdong. Residents across the border shared the same dialect, cuisine, traditional cultural habits, and in some cases, the same ancestors. When the People's Republic of China was founded, the living standard of Guangdong was once at a par with that in Hong Kong. By the late 1970s, however, it was only a fraction of that in Hong Kong that was on the other side of the border. It was thus difficult for Guangdong residents to attribute the developmental gap to the people in Hong Kong and believe in the officially touted superiority of communism. As a result, human smuggling and illegal border crossing constantly occurred, and southern Guangdong was even flooded with potential illegal immigrants from other provinces. This created political and social problems for Guangdong. Guangdong leaders wished to improve the living standard of the province, reduce popular dissatisfaction with the government, and contain illegal border crossing. The remedy, however, required economic liberalization, support from national leaders, and favorable national policy atmosphere.

Immediately adjacent to Hong Kong was Bao'an County in Guangdong, which later became Shenzhen, the eventual location for the first SEZ. Between January and November 1978 alone, 13,800 native Bao'an residents attempted to flee the county for Hong Kong, and 7,000 (about half) of them succeeded. In addition, the county also intercepted another 39,000 illegal border crossers in 1978 alone, including many from outside the country. From 1976 to 1981, nearly half a million people (mostly illegal immigrants) moved from China to Hong Kong (Kleinberg 1990: 49). Hundreds of illegal border crossers were killed in crossing the sea and scaling steep slopes and barbed wire entanglements (Yang 1998: 249–50). What motivated them to risk being detained, subsequent political and social stigmas, and even their lives was the price gap in labor.[2] In Hong Kong, they each could make 2,000 yuan a month (Yang 1998: 249–50). In Guangdong, they could only make 20 yuan. In 1977, an average villager in Luofang in Shenzhen earned only 134 yuan a year. Across the border, villagers in Luofang in the New Territories, who illegally immigrated from Shenzhen, each made an equivalent of 13,000 yuan a year (www.researchchinese.com, posted on September 1, 2000). In addition, the considerable chance for successful illegal border crossing, especially in the case of local residents in Bao'an County, also encouraged people to take the risks. As stated, between January and November 1978, 51 percent of the 13,800 residents in Bao'an who attempted illegal border crossing succeeded (Yang 1998: 249).

Mass illegal immigration was a profound embarrassment for the state (Kleinberg 1990: 51). Following several mass flights of immigrants across the border in 1977, Guangdong Party Secretary Wu Nansheng conducted a field trip to Shenzhen. He was shocked to find out the above stark contrast in wages across the border. Later, he became a strong supporter for SEZs. Guangdong First Party Secretary Xi Zhongxun also inspected the county. Initially, he declared illegal border crossing a classical issue in "class struggle." Then a local party cadre countered his view by asking him how socialism could be superior when locals lived a desperately poor life after laboring day to night all year long, but could live a decent life overnight by crossing the border. An enraged Xi threatened to relieve the outspoken cadre of his post. After days of field investigation, Xi realized that China's restriction on the use of foreign capital was the main source for the huge gap in living standards. He publicly retracted his criticism of the outspoken cadre and even aired a self-criticism (Yang 1998: 251). He was also determined to ask central leaders for a liberal policy in Guangdong. The relaxed policy atmosphere at that time also encouraged him to seek a reversal of the restrictive policy. During the Cultural Revolution, as suggested above, he would have risked his political career and even his life for making such a request.

Local leaders thus have an incentive to channel price gaps into a source of local development. Once local economic conditions improve, they could take political credits, earn positive remarks from their superiors, and have greater chance for promotion. However, they would need to evaluate their policy option in the context of the national policy atmosphere. Only when their policy option accords with the national political atmosphere would they actively propose it. Reformists, especially Guangdong leaders and their patrons, understood all too well the first move advantages in implementing the Open Policy. In a China which was characterized by autarky and underdevelopment, the first province that opened up could attract most of the FDI to the nation and become a primary base in the nation's exports. It could also stimulate reforms and growth of the province. Therefore, Yuan Geng, as well as Guangdong leaders such as Xi, also requested central leaders that Guangdong be made the only starter in the opening up (Ye 2001: 1768–75).

Personal connections or career-related geographic links also played a role in the initiation of the Open Policy. Several leaders of Guangdong who requested greater economic laxity from central leaders were either natives of the province, or veteran Party cadres or leaders in the province (table 5.1). Wu Nansheng, a Deputy Party Secretary between October 1977 and September 1980, was born and grew up in Shantou, Guangdong. He served as a Party cadre in Shantou between 1936 and 1944. From then to the late 1970s, he had been serving as a local leader or senior Party official in the province. He was still emotionally attached to his home town. In early 1979, when the Party was calling for economic development, Wu was shocked by the miserable living conditions of residents in his home town, and realized that the situation resembled that under the KMT that motivated him to join the Party. Eager to take advantage of central willingness to promote local development, he proposed an export-processing zone in Shantou. Xi took up his idea and called on central leaders to grant the whole province flexible measures at a national work conference. After the center decided to build a SEZ in Shenzhen, Wu assumed the post of Shenzhen Mayor between September 1980 and March 1981, overseeing its early development. Wu was succeeded by open-minded and able Liang Xiang, a native of Guangdong. Between 1978 and 1980, other senior provincial leaders who supported the opening, such as Liu Tianfu, who had also either joined the guerrilla in Guangdong during the WWII and the Civil War, or had served as a senior official in Guangdong for a long time. These provincial leaders developed political ties, social connections, and emotional bonds in or with Guangdong and would support the province's modernization. In addition, as is to be elaborated shortly, other leaders such as Xi, Yang, and later Ren Zhongyi were very open-minded. They were receptive to local calls for greater economic autonomy and would make these proposals in front of top leaders (table 5.1).

Table 5.1 Leaders in Guangdong: Regional backgrounds

Name	Position in Guangdong between 1978 and 1980 (year.month or year- year in parenteses)	Policy stance toward Guangdong	Previous personal or career links with Guangdong
Xi Zhongxun	Party Secretary (1978.12–1980.11)	Rehabilitated purged cadres; proposed the opening and reforms	
Yang Shangkun	Second Provincial Party Secretary (1978.12–1979.3); First Party Secretary of Guangzhou (1979.4–1981.6)	Supported reforms and the opening	
Liu Tianfu	(Deputy) Party Secretary and Vice Governor (1978.12–1981.3); Governor (1981.3–1983.4)	Supported economic reforms and the opening	Party leader and guerrilla commissar in western or central Guangdong (1939– 1945); prefectural party leader and bureau chief in Guangdong (1949–1978)
Wu Nansheng	(Deputy) Provincial Party Secretary (1977.10–1980.9); Shenzhen Mayor (1980.9–1981.3); Guangdong CPPCC Chairman (1985–1995)	Proposed an industrial zone in Shantou in February 1979 and supported the opening	Birth and childhood in Shantou, Guangdong; Party cadre in Shantou (1936–1944); deputy Party Secretary of Shantou and Hainan, Guangdong Party Propaganda Chief; Guangdong Party Secretary (1950–1979)
Ren Zhongyi	Party Secretary (1980.11–1985.7)	Pushed forward reforms and the opening	
Liang Lingguang	Governor (1983.5–1985.7)	Pushed forward reforms and the opening	Guangzhou First Party Secretary (1980.11–1983.5)
Ye Xuanping	Governor (1985.8–1991.5)	Continued reforms and the opening	Birth in Guangdong. Vice Governor of Guangdong (1980.8–1983.4); Guangzhou Mayor (1983.5–1985.8)
Lin Ruo	Party Secretary (1985.7–1991.1)	Continued reforms and the opening	Born in Chao'an, Guangdong. Graduated from Zhongshan University; joined the Party and the guerrilla (1945–1947); served as local leader in Guangdong (1949–1982); Deputy Guangdong Party Secretary (1983.9–1985.7)

Sources: Refer to data sources on leadership profiles in chapter 4.

In addition, the status of provincial leaders also played a role in their calls for new policies. Xi Zhongxun, the First Party Secretary of Guangdong, was a veteran Party official. In 1934 he was the head of the Shaanganbian Soviet Government, supervising the Party branch in Shaanxi and Gansu, which later became part of the primary base for the Red Army during World War II. He served as Vice Premier between 1959 and 1962. After the fall of the Gang of Four, he was appointed the Second Party Secretary and then the First Party Secretary in Guangdong and was in charge of rehabilitating cadres purged by Maoists. Xi was an outspoken reformist leader. He favored economic reforms as well as the reversal of Mao's radicalism in the late 1970s. He also opposed conservatives' attacks on Hu Yaobang in 1987 as well as the eventual removal of Hu from his position as the Party Secretary. Yang Shangkun, who served as the Second Party Secretary of Guangdong and then First Party Secretary of Guangzhou between late 1978 and late 1981, was also a veteran Party official. He served for years as the Director of the Office of the CCCCP after 1948. He was a moderate reformist. When serving in Guangdong, Xi and Yang promoted economic liberalization. When they returned to the center, they continued to support the devolution of power to Guangdong and gave reforms in Guangdong considerable political backing.[3]

National Agents for Change: Patronage and Ideology

National leaders were the ultimate gate keepers in the channeling of factor price gaps into final policies. As stated, radical Maoist leadership would prevent international market forces from transforming the radical ideology and the command economy. In the post-Mao era, Hua and Li, supported the use of foreign capital. Deng, on the other hand, was more open-minded about the capitalist economy and was ready to accept imports of Western economic institutions and market practices. Also importantly, a number of open-minded central officials, some of who came from Guangdong, pushed for initiatives that led to the eventual opening (see table 5.2).

Deng, Marshall Ye Jianying, Yang Shangkun, Zhao Ziyang, and a few other senior central leaders were personally aware of the factor price gaps that harassed leaders in Guangdong, especially Bao'an. In November 1977, upon returning to power, Deng paid a visit outside Beijing. He toured Guangdong, along with Marshall Ye Jianying, the

Table 5.2 Central leaders and officials with close ties with Guangdong

Name	Central position	Policy views toward Guangdong	Positions and tenure in Guangdong	Other links with Guangdong
Ye Jianying	Vice Chairman of CMC; Defense Minister; Politburo Standing Committee Member (PSCM) from 1973–1986	Supported rehabilitation of purged leaders; supported economic development and industrial zones in Guangdong	Revolutionary activities in Guangdong from 1924–1927; military and government leader of Guangdong from 1949–1954	Birth and childhood in Mei County, Guangdong
Zhao Ziyang	Sichuan Party Secretary and Vice Premier in 1979; PSCM Premier from 1980–1989;	Supported reforms in and the opening of Guangdong	Guangdong local leader from 1951–1955; Guangdong Party Secretary from 1955–1967 and from 1971–1975	Guangdong wa the province where he serve the longest
Xi Zhongxun	Politburo member from 1982–1987	Rehabilitated cadres purged by radical Maoists; proposed the opening of Guangdong and supported reforms	Guangdong Second Party Secretary and then First Party Secretary from 1978–1980; Guangdong Governor from 1979–1980	
Yang Shangkun	Politburo member from 1982–1992; Secretary General or Vice Chairman of CMC from 1981–1992.	Supported reforms in and encouraged the opening of Guangdong	Second Party Secretary of Guangdong and then First Party Secretary of Guangzhou from 1978–1980	
Wei Guoqing	Politburo member from 1977–1982; Director of General Political Department of PLA in 1977.	Unable or unwilling to purge radical Maoists and correct their policies between 1976 and 1978	First Commissar of Guangzhou Military Region from 1973–1977; Guangdong First Party Secretary from 1976–1977	
Yuan Geng	Director of External Affairs Bureau, Ministry of Communications from 1975–1978; Vice Standing Board Director, CMSNs (Ministry of Communications) from 1978–1992	Proposed an export processing zone in Bao'an, Guangdong in January 1979; directed the first SEZ in Shekou District, Shenzhen, China in subsequent years	A Dongjiang Guerrilla in Guangdong during WWII; a communist negotiator in Hong Kong in 1945 and a founder of an agency that became the top Chinese political liaison in Hong Kong.	Birth in Bao'ar Guangdong
Zeng Sheng	Deputy Minister and Minister of Communications	Supported Yuan's proposal to build an export processing zone in Bao'an.	Local guerrilla leader in Guangdong from 1938–1942; Commander of the Dongjiang Guerrillas from 1943–1946; Deputy Commander of Guangdong Military Region; Vice Governor of Guangdong; Guangzhou Mayor for years after 1949	Birth in Huiya (adjacent to Shenzhen), Guangdong

Sources: Refer to data sources in chapter 4.

Chairman of the Chinese legislature. In reporting provincial work to Deng and Ye, Guangdong leaders mentioned mass illegal border crossing to Hong Kong in Shenzhen, a town with less than 30,000 residents at that time. Deng made two comments on the issue: That was because our policies had problems; even troops could not stop it (www.researchchinese.com, posted on September 1, 2000). Clearly, Deng was well aware that the main causes for mass flights of immigrants were the factor price gaps, the contrast in the living standards across the border, and Maoist autarky and rejection of market forces.

Among the central leaders and officials who strongly backed Guangdong's request for greater autonomy, seven of them had personal or career bonds with Guangdong (table 5.2). Marshal Ye Jianying was a native of Guangdong who had commanded the military takeover of the province from the KMT troops. Afterward, he also served for a few years to establish the civilian government in Guangdong and restored order.[4] Zhao Ziyang, a member of the Politburo from 1979 to 1989 and Premier between 1980 and 1987, served in Guangdong for twenty years. Guangdong was indeed the province he was most familiar with and had the closest bond. After serving in Guangdong for several years, Wei Guoqing, Xi Zhongxun, and Yang Shangkun returned to Beijing between late 1970s and the early 1980s and became Politburo members. Xi and Yang especially favored further economic liberalization of the province. Yuan Geng, though a mid-level cadre, played a special role in Guangdong's opening. While serving as a deputy head of a large subsidiary for the Ministry of Communications, he made one of the earliest proposals for an export processing zone in Guangdong. He was a native of Bao'an, the location for the zone. He fought alongside the Dongjiang Guerrillas in Guangdong during WWII. In 1945, he was a communist negotiator in Hong Kong, and founded an agency that became the Chinese political liaison in Hong Kong. In proposing the export processing zone, he also gained support from his superior Zeng Sheng. Zeng was a native of Huiyang in Guangdong which is adjacent to Shenzhen. He was a Commander of the Dongjiang Guerrillas between 1943 and 1946. Since 1949, he had served as Deputy Commander of the Guangdong Military Region, as Vice Governor of Guangdong, and as Guangzhou Mayor. Therefore, he had extensive personal and political connections with the province. He, too, enthusiastically supported the SEZ (Vogel 1989: 131–32).

Politics of Selecting the First Open Areas

Demonstration Effects of Successful Trial Experiments

Central leaders, especially Deng, also appeared to be calculative in choosing Guangdong as the starter. Seasoned statesmen like Deng Xiaoping knew quite well that an initial success mattered very much in launching and popularizing a new and controversial policy (Vogel 1989: 83). For any advocate of a new and bold policy, one of the priorities is to ensure its initial success. A good start could quiet vocal critics. More importantly, it could create a demonstration effect nationwide, encourage imitation or bandwagoning by other provincial leaders, and create a powerful trend of transplanting of the successful policy in other localities. On the contrary, blatant initial failure of a new policy would lead to overwhelming rejection of the policy, weaken potential support, and reduce significantly the chance for it to be accepted by other provinces.

Deng first spelled out two tactics for incremental reforms in his concluding speech at the central work conference in December 1978, where he had just emerged as the new paramount leader. He stressed that a small trial experiment should be carried out to test new economic measures including external cooperation. Through experiments, lessons could be learned, effective measures uncovered and adopted, and ineffective ones found and discarded. Afterward successful measures would be applied nationwide. He said:

> We must learn to manage the economy by economic means. If we ourselves don't know about advanced methods of management, we should learn from those who do, either at home or abroad. These methods should be applied not only in the operation of enterprises with newly imported technology and equipment, but also in the technical transformation of existing enterprises. Pending the introduction of a unified national program of modern management, we can begin with limited spheres, say, a particular region or a given trade, and then spread the methods gradually to others. The central government departments concerned should encourage such experiments. Contradictions of all kinds will crop up in the process and we should discover and overcome them in good time. That will speed up our progress.[5]

He also suggested that demonstration effects could be used in spreading reforms from a few regions, certain enterprises, and some strata to others. Thus if a carefully designed trial experiment turned out to be successful, it would encourage other areas to follow suit. He announced his visionary approach to starting reform as follows:

> In economic policy, I think we should allow some regions and enter-prises and some workers and peasants to earn more and enjoy more benefits sooner than others, in accordance with their hard work and greater contributions to society. If the standard of living of some people is raised first, this will inevitably be an impressive example to their "neighbours," and people in other regions and units will want to learn from them. This will help the whole national economy to advance wave upon wave and help the people of all our nationalities to become prosperous in a comparatively short period.[6]

At the very beginning, reformists had two choices in implementing the Open Policy: opening up all provinces at the same time, or opening up a few selected places first. Central leaders dismissed the first option as "spreading pepper powder on noodles." As valuable foreign capital was spread thinly across the nation, strongly positive effects could be hardly seen. In some places the Open Policy could even turn out to be a failure because they had poor local investment environment for for-eign business and because foreign competition in the wake of the opening might hurt local producers and sectors. Therefore, for national reformists the best choice for advocates of the Open Policy was to target a few places with favorable conditions. This was exactly the logic behind the opening of Guangdong and Fujian. Central leaders opted for the opening of selected areas in these two provinces first because of their advantageous conditions and the need to avoid widespread failure and negative political fallouts.[7] This point will be elaborated further.

Guangdong and Fujian, as well as the initial four SEZs in the provinces, enjoyed a number of geographical, economic, historical, and political advantages over other provinces. First, they were located adjacent to Hong Kong and Taiwan, respectively, which were devel-oped economies where the majority of the population was Chinese. For Chinese leaders, overseas Chinese have been known for their strong bonds with their motherland. In the past, they had actively par-ticipated in activities for overthrowing the late Qing Dynasty, aiding the Nationalist Revolution in the early twentieth century, and partici-pating in economic development of China in the 1950s. In addition, by the late 1970s, many overseas Chinese business people in Hong Kong,

Taiwan, and to a lesser extent Macao and Southeast Asia had cumulated large amounts of capital and were looking for cheaper land and labor for reinvestment. Guangdong and Fujian could provide exactly what they wanted. Once overseas Chinese investors reaped profits in their ventures in China, it could create demonstration effects. Japanese, Korean, and Western investors would be anxious to follow suit. The four SEZs were chosen largely because of their geographic proximity to neighboring advanced economies. All of them were coastal cities. Shenzhen was adjacent to Hong Kong, Zhuhai was connected to Macao by land, and Xiamen was close to Taiwan and the offshore islands controlled by the Republic of China based in Taiwan. Shantou was located between Hong Kong and Taiwan.

Second, many overseas Chinese originally came from Guangdong and Fujian, and they had strong entrepreneurship. They maintain strong bonds with their home towns in these provinces and many families in the provinces had overseas relatives. Therefore, the provinces could be ideal places for attracting overseas Chinese investment (Chen 1998: 284–85; Vogel 1989: 125–31; Yeung and Chu 1998: 4–6). As stated, many residents in Shenzhen fled to Hong Kong in the previous years, and Shantou was known as the hometown of the most successful entrepreneurs among the overseas Chinese, including Lee Ka Sing, the richest Hong Kong tycoon.

Third, both provinces have a historical tradition in trade and entrepreneurship (Howell 1993: 20). For the last thousand years (from the Song Dynasty onward), Fujian, and especially Guangdong had experienced growth in foreign trade. Some of the cities, such as Guangzhou, Shantou, Quanzhou, Fuzhou, and Xiamen were once important sea ports of the nation. Guangdong led the nation in foreign trade and manufacturing in the Qing Dynasty, and its merchants had traveled around the nation and overseas.[8] As a result, residents in the two provinces were receptive to foreign business and external cooperation.

Fourth, as documented by many studies and the above analysis, Guangdong leaders since the late 1970s had been quite liberal minded, and rather forward- and outward-looking in their attitudes toward local development and utilizing foreign capital (Vogel 1989; Howell 1993: 21; Cheung 1998a, 1998b). In fact, leaders from Guangdong were the first among the provinces to ask for the opening and foreign investment (Yang 1998). Fujian leaders did not act as early as did leaders of Guangdong. After Deng supported the SEZs in Shenzhen and Shantou in April 1979, Fujian leaders expressed their interests in having a SEZ, and submitted a report to the State Council. Fujian leaders simply followed Guangdong's push for opening, though they were thus receptive and welcomed the central decision.[9]

Therefore, for central leaders, both provinces had the access to external capital (from Hong Kong and Taiwan), convenient ocean harbors, entrepreneurship, open mentality receptive to foreign economic practice, and liberal cadres who supported foreign ventures and the transformation of the command economy. All these factors bode well for SEZs in Guangdong and Fujian. They thus became the best candidates for testing out the Open Policy.

Consolidating the Open Policy

The Open Policy was unfolding smoothly between 1978 and 1980, when influential central leaders favored an expansion in reform. In mid-July 1979, the CCCCP and the State Council jointly approved reports by Guangdong and Fujian regarding SEZs as well as "special policies and flexible measures" for reforms in the provinces. Dubbed as the No. 50 central document, it laid out the comprehensive institutional arrangements for the opening of and complementary reforms in the two provinces. Nevertheless, in October 1979, following the Fourth Plenum of the Eleventh CCCCP, the center rolled out policies of adjustment and overhaul, aiming to cool down an overheating economy and correct macroeconomic imbalances. In talking with provincial leaders, however, Deng declared the two provinces, especially Guangdong, should boldly open up and reform while trying to comply with the adjustment decision. Deng's statement helped the provinces to proceed with the ground work for setting up SEZs and jump-starting local reforms.

Between late 1980 and 1983, however, central policies shifted to retrenchment, Guangdong was under stronger pressure to curtail its opening and slow down its reforms. Provincial leadership stepped in to ease the pressure and encourage local leaders to proceed with the opening and liberal measures. In December 1980 central leaders, especially conservatives, were alerted by relatively high inflation, which registered 6 percent, compared with an annual rate at the range of -5.9–1 percent for all but three years from 1955 to 1976. Chen Yun declared that prices should be frozen for at least six months. Zhao Ziyang and Hu Yaobang were pressured to call for a slowdown in reforms, especially in Guangdong. Even though Deng stressed that the reform policy of the Third Plenum of the Eleventh CCCCP remained unchanged, he also wanted provincial leaders to "be realistic" in their work. Under this national atmosphere for retrenchment, criticisms for reforms and the opening up were mounting. Attendants at a central work conference in mid-December 1980 even questioned whether SEZs were no different at all from extra-legal territories that imperial powers imposed upon China in the previous century.

Under intensified pressure, Guangdong leaders, led by Ren Zhongyi, defended SEZs against their critics. He asked local leaders in Guangdong to play a dualist strategy: steadfastly implementing what the center demanded in order to avoid macroeconomic imbalances, yet continuing with economic liberalization. He also called for cadres to guard against the Maoist or conservative (leftist) orthodoxy. At a work conference on Guangdong, Fujian, and SEZs hosted by the State Council in July 1981, leaders from Guangdong and Fujian complained loudly that central ministries failed to follow through their promises to grant the provinces special policies and flexible measures. With the support from Vice Premier Gu Mu, the CCCCP and the State Council agreed to devolve economic power to the provinces (Ye 2001: 1778–1815).

In 1982, however, the center again stepped up its pressures on Guangdong to slow down its opening. In mid-December 1981, Deng Xiaoping was unhappy with the continuing spread of smuggling activities in Guangdong and Fujian despite central orders for crackdown in February. He suggested that the Party Central Commission for Discipline Inspection sent teams to enforce the crackdown.[10] Concurring with Deng, Chen Yun demanded a swift and tough crackdown on smuggling as well as punishment of responsible cadres, especially in Guangdong.

Chen, an arch conservative, however, took advantage of Deng's support for crackdown on smuggling in the open provinces to attack the SEZs. Chen told the SPC to reject all demands from other provinces to set up new SEZs in order to prevent illegal smuggling and speculative trade from spreading.[11] Under Chen's heavy pressure, Hu, Zhao and Gu demanded Guangdong and Fujian to tighten its reform policies, including those regarding the SEZs. Peng Zhen, a conservative leader in charge of legal affairs, might have spearheaded legal investigation of economic crimes (Howell 1993: 57–58). Instructed by Chen and conservative propagandist Hu Qiaomu, the General Office of the CCCCP distributed a document on the extralegal territories in China prior to 1949, reminding them of the danger of allowing the SEZs to degrade into extralegal territories. Ren, the Guangdong Party Secretary, was forced to make a written self-criticism to the CCCCP. Due to the conservative's pressure, Deng also told cadres throughout the nation to apply swift action and severe punishment in order to stop the wave of economic crimes, including smuggling (Yang 1998: 253–56; Ye 2001: 1820–24).

Local cadres were quite sensitive to changes in central policies. In many other provinces, goods, salespersons, and cadres from Guangdong were suspected of being related to smuggling and were discriminated against. The image of Guangdong was tarnished in the nation.

Guangdong leaders tried their best to safeguard the reform course. They told local leaders in the province to stick with the dualist strategy stated above. Ren even told them that he and other provincial leaders, not all local leaders, were to be blamed for the past errors. Nevertheless, he halted economic decentralization in the province given mounting political pressure.

The first ordeal for SEZs and the Open Policy ended in October 1982. In that month, Guangdong leaders submitted a report summarizing their efforts to clean up economic crimes in the SEZs and the province. Chen Yun expressed his satisfaction with the efforts. One month later, in the presence of Chen and Li Xiannian, the Central Secretariat of the CCCCP declared that Guangdong and Fujian had already rectified their problems (Ye 2001: 1819–28).

The second ordeal for the SEZs started in the middle of 1983. Peng Zhen, a conservative, became the head of the NPC. He urged a crack down on economic crimes. In the second half of the year, Peng joined efforts with Li Xiannian, Chen Yun, and chief conservative theoretician Deng Liqun to launch a campaign attacking spiritual pollution, which referred to political liberalization as well as decadent (or "bourgeois") life style and entertainment (Howell 1993: 61–63). Deng supported the campaign in October partly to appease the growing conservative influence and partly to curb political liberalization. Deng Liqun, however, went so far in the campaign that he lamented that Shenzhen was trying to be like Hong Kong and having nothing "socialist except for its five-starred red flag flying in the sky." Both foreign investors and Chinese cadres became concerned with the fate of the Open Policy (Howell 1993: 62–63).

Deng Xiaoping eventually stepped out and halted the campaign. He did so probably out of three reasons. First, Deng worried that if he failed to put a stop to the escalating conservative attack, the Open Policy and reforms would eventually become the victim of such railing and his vision for a prosperous China would be derailed. Deng Liqun's attacks on the SEZs in the name of anti-spiritual pollution particularly worried and even angered Deng Xiaoping. Because of this Deng Liqun almost lost his Directorship of the Department of Propaganda of the Party (Baum 1996: 156–62).

Second, key SEZs and the Open Policy had achieved their initial success. Before 1978, foreign capital and FDI in China were quite limited in scale. After 1978, they had been growing rapidly. Utilized foreign capital in China grew from US$263 million in 1978 to US$2 billion in 1983 (including $640 million in FDI), and exports in the nation rose from US$9.8 billion to US$22 billion. Guangdong and Fujian witnessed rapid growth in foreign capital, investment and trade and continued to account for a significant share of the national total (Gao, Wang, and He 1993: 1704; SSB 1996b: 152). For example, utilized foreign capital in Guangdong grew from US$91 million in 1979, to US$407 million in 1983, and exports from US$1.7 billion to 2.4 billion. Shenzhen and Zhuhai, the cities that hosted the two most important SEZs due to their proximity to Hong Kong and Macao, performed even much better. In Shenzhen, utilized foreign capital surged exponentially from US$15 million to US$144 million, and exports from US$9 million to US$62 million. Zhuhai's performance, even though it lagged slightly behind that of Shenzhen, far outperformed Guangdong and the nation. As a result of reform and opening, provincial and national economy grew much faster. National income in China grew annually at 5 percent between 1974 and 1978, but at a much faster 7 percent from 1979 to 1983. These rates were faster in Guangdong, at 7 percent and 9 percent, respectively. The annual growth rates reached astounding levels in SEZs, registering 44 percent during the 1979–1983 period in Shenzhen and 28 percent in Zhuhai. In the initial period of reforms, fiscal revenue income at national and local levels started to grow. Between 1979 and 1984, national fiscal revenue income grew moderately from 110 billion yuan to 125 billion yuan, a growth of 13.6 percent. Meanwhile, fiscal revenue in Guangdong grew much faster, from 3.4 billion to 4.2 billion, an increase of 23.5 percent. Fiscal revenue even tripled in Zhuhai and grew by eight times in Shenzhen (table 5.3). Equally important, mass illegal immigration from China to Hong Kong had ceased to be a major issue by 1982 as the living standard of Shenzhen had grown to a comfortable level. Some immigrants even returned (Crane 1990: 37–38).

Third, economic autonomy and the initial success of Guangdong also invited other provinces to demand opening up and establishment of their own SEZs. Dali Yang (1997: 44–46) coherently argued that late liberalizers would lose in fiscal terms to early liberalizers and

Table 5.3   Exports, FDI, and GDP growth after the Open Policy

	China	Guangdong	Shenzhen	Zhuhai
Utilized Foreign Capital (million US$), 1979	449	91	15	9
Utilized Foreign Capital (million US$), 1983	1,981	407	144	21
Exports (million US$), 1979	13,660	1,702	9	4
Exports (million US$), 1983	22,230	2,385	62	29
Fiscal Revenue Income (million yuan), 1979	110,330	3,428	17	24
Fiscal Revenue Income (million yuan), 1983	124,900	4,228	156	89
Annual Growth of National Income, 1974–1978 (%)	5.2	7.3		
Annual Growth of National Income, 1979–1983 (%)	7.3	9.2	44.4*	28.4*

* GDP growth rate.
Sources: SSB 1996b, 1990b; Guangdong People's Government and Guangdong Statistical Bureau 1999.

that as a result, all provinces would compete for liberalization when the choice was available. In a similar vein, early liberalizers enjoyed first-move advantages of more efficient economic institutions and could outperform the provinces that have not liberalized. As table 5.3 suggested, the open provinces and SEZs experienced phenomenal growth in GDP and fiscal revenue income. Their successes provided enormous incentives for other provinces to emulate. Otherwise, the latter would continue to lose out. Guangdong's positive records thus had great demonstration effects to the rest of the nation. Provincial leaders realized that opening up could help their provinces to rapidly expand their economies and fiscal revenue and earn valuable foreign hard currencies. They also believed that SEZs were an attractive way to develop the local economy. In addition, as Shirk (1994: 33–41) argues, other provinces were jealous of the special privileges Guangdong and Fujian had in revenue and foreign exchange retention, as well as economic benefits from exports and FDI as well as freedom from the central plan. Thus as early as in 1982, other provinces also asked the central government for their own SEZs and similar privileges (Yang 1998: 255). In December 1984, Gu Mu implicitly implied in an interview that inland provinces also wanted to open up. Between March and September 1985 several articles on leading newspapers and magazines in China also made similar appeals (Howell 1993: 68, 70, 80).

In the above context, in January 1984, Deng launched a counteroffensive against the conservatives and renewed the Open Policy and reforms. Accompanied by Yang Shangkun and Wang Zhen, he visited the SEZs in Shenzhen and Zhuhai, as well as a model township enterprise in Shunde in the Pearl River Delta. He was gratified by rapid urbanization and industrialization in these cities as well as economic achievements of the SEZs. He inscribed his comments, one praising the Zhuhai SEZ, and the other for the Shenzhen SEZ affirming the central decision to build the SEZs. In February, he inspected the Xiamen SEZ and inscribed that the SEZ be better managed.[12]

Upon his return to Beijing, Deng talked to the leaders in charge of the CCCCP and the State Council, presumably Hu Yaobang and Zhao Ziyang, and explicitly told them that the policy of setting up SEZs and opening up should continue and expand to several sea ports, including Dalian and Qingdao (Yang 1998: 257–58). In late March the Central Secretariat of the Party and the State Council held a talk with ninety leaders of fourteen coastal cities, who were all enthusiastic about the opening. In May, these cities were declared open cities (Ye 2001: 1835–37).

In October 1984, the Third Plenum of the Twelfth CCCCP approved "A Decision Regarding Reform of Economic Structure," stipulating that China would build planned commodity economy based on public ownership (Yin and Yang 2004: 100). After the plenum, the leaders of the State Council and central ministries headed by Zhao Ziyang surveyed the Pearl River and Yangtze Deltas and proposed to the CCCCP to open up these two deltas and Liaodong and Jiaodong Peninsulas so that the open areas would become adjacent to each other in the coast. Deng fully approved the proposal (Chen 1998: 292).

In January 1985, Deng met with Gu Mu to discuss the opening of the Pearl River and Yangtze Deltas. Gu suggested to also include the southern Fujian delta, and Deng agreed.[13] In February, the State Council made 61 cities and counties in these three deltas coastal open economic zones (Howell 1993: 63–74; Yang 1998: 265). Leaders and people in these three deltas warmly welcomed liberalization. By then, the major economic areas in the coastal region, China's economic center, had opened up. The Open Policy was consolidated.

As we have seen, even a moderate change in central leaders' tone of the policy debate would send a shock wave across the country and produce a magnifying effect in the nation. Many local leaders and cadres would capitalize on the new policy atmosphere, undermine policies that central leaders cast doubts on, and would promote policies that conformed to the prevailing ideology.[14] We thus should not dismiss ideological differences over reforms between reformists and conservatives as minor. Indeed, both of them agreed on the need for Party discipline and political order. However, their approaches to these issues were largely conditioned by their clashing views over reforms, especially over whether China needs a fully developed market economy.[15] Deng wanted to crack down on economic crimes in 1982 in order to clean up abnormalities that tarnished the reputation of the Open Policy and to pave the way for further opening and the rise of an unbridled and dynamic economy. Chen, on the other hand, wanted to use the crackdown not only to maintain Party discipline, but also to dismiss liberal cadres and to arrest the trend for greater opening that he deemed detrimental.

An illustrating case is of Xiang Nan, the Party Secretary of Fujian. He was a strong advocate for opening and proposed to turn Xianmen into a free harbor like Hong Kong. Central conservatives, however, accused him of degrading Xianmen into a colony. They disliked his liberal economic view and his close association with Hu Yaobang, an equally honest, liberal, and outspoken central leader. In the mid-1980s, Xiang Nan reported to central leaders that a model rural enterprise in Fujian produced fraudulent medicine. Chen and a few conservative veterans played up the issue and accused Xiang of committing a severe error for awarding the enterprise in the past. They relieved him of his post, called him back to Beijing, and forced him to semi-retire. Fujian residents, however, viewed Xiang as the best leader the province ever had since 1949. They liked him for his consideration for people's daily life and his upright and honest life style. When he left Fujian for Beijing, he took the exact meager personal belongings that he brought with him years ago.[16] When he returned to his home town upon retirement, people in his hometown spontaneously lined up on the streets to welcome him. If conservatives were truly concerned with the integrity and the popular image of the Party, Xiang should have been promoted and the case of the enterprise should not have been blamed on him. Obviously, conservative leaders were more interested in defending their conservative economic policies and guarding their political influence than protecting and rewarding upright, honest, and dedicated officials. Party discipline became a tool for them to remove liberal cadres and halt China's opening.

Conclusion

A Chinese saying well captures the challenge of policy making: The beginning is the most difficult part of any project (*wan shi kai tou nan*). Two proverbs in English also tell a similar axiom: Nothing succeeds like success; a good start is half. A clever choice of areas for liberalization experiment meant a good start of the reforms course. Wise selection of trial reform sites, clever appointment of able liberals in the pioneering provinces, and a strong commitment yet flexible tactics of national reformists helped the Open Policy to start and be sustained. The keys to the smooth start and progress of China's Open Policy and reforms are the following. First, as demonstrated above, central reformists opened up first provinces with the greatest advantages. Guangdong and Fujian were close to Hong Kong and Taiwan, respectively, had a large number of families whose relatives lived and worked as overseas business people. These two provinces had also a long recent history of foreign economic contact and domestic commerce. Finally, these two provinces, especially Guangdong, had relatively more open-minded local leaders and a population who would be receptive to the Open Policy.

Second, national reformists were also politically shrewd in staffing the local bridgehead of reforms, namely Guangdong with committed liberals and experienced politicians. They also appointed different provincial leaders for distinct purposes. Between late 1978 and the late 1980, Deng sent two liberal leaders with considerable central profiles, namely Xi Zhongxun and Yang Shangkun, to take charge of cleansing the Maoist influence and followings in Guangdong. Being outspoken and not afraid to name cadres who toed the Maoist line, Xi's straightforward style suited his task. As the cleanup mission was over, Deng recalled Xi back to Beijing and sent a reserved, experienced, yet open-minded Ren Zhongyi to launch reforms and opening in Guangdong between 1981 and mid-1985. Ren's moderate and consultative style enabled him to mix well with local cadres, spurt the liberal local initiatives, and provide covert protection for local reforms against central conservatives without offending the latter. After Ren Zhongyi, Ye Xuanping, a Guangdong native and a son of Marshal Ye Jianying, emerged as a key Guangdong leader. His extensive political connections and liberal orientation enabled reforms and internationalization in Guangdong to progress despite heated debates among central leaders over reforms between mid-1985 and 1990. These clever appointments helped reforms and the Open Policy to take off in the first province and become a powerful showcase of the liberal program for the rest of the nation.

As suggested in this chapter and in chapter 2, the opening up of localities in China to the world economy resulted from local initiatives and national decisions. The exact weight of these factors might vary from case to case. In the opening and reforms in these two provinces, Guangdong leaders played a very significant role, much more than those of Fujian. Chapter 2 suggests, however, that Shanghai's request for greater opening by making Pudong District a special area in the mid-1980s failed to materialize. A key cause might be the opposition by an arch conservative Chen Yun. Only in 1990, with the strong push from Deng Xiaoping and Shanghai leaders especially Zhu Rongji, as well as firm support from General Party Secretary Jiang Zemin, a special and very open Pudong District eventually became a reality.

It thus becomes apparent that statesmanship helped secure the survival of SEZs and the Open Policy. In pursuing the Open Policy national and local reformists skillfully and carefully navigated through changing political and ideological currents, including the shifting balance of power of reformists versus conservatives and fluctuating macroeconomic conditions. Deng, along with other reformists, such as Hu, Zhao, Gu, and Yang, made concessions when the political situation called for it. Provincial reformists, especially Guangdong leaders, such as Ren Zhongyi, Liang Lingguang, Ye Xuanping, and Lin Ruo, skillfully and courageously resisted conservative backlashes against problems that arose in the course of opening (such as smuggling) and protected the enthusiasm of local cadres in liberalization. When the situation became amicable, they renewed reform drives. With their protection and efforts the Open Policy produced initial success, a growing number of provinces requested the center for their own opening and obtained it. Through local competitive liberalization, the Open Policy was accepted across the nation.

In allowing Guangdong and Fujian to set up the first four SEZs, the center also granted them privileges in economic reform. First, as stated in chapter 2, until April 1984 SEZs enjoyed the right to host foreign enterprises, preferential treatment in imports and exports, raw materials procurement, and land use for foreign enterprises, as well as regulation of prices and distribution of goods by the market instead of the state plan (Chen Xuewei 1998: 287–88). Second, both provinces, especially Guangdong enjoyed unparalleled leeway in reforming prices, labor, and circulation of goods through markets. Third, Guangdong and Fujian were allowed to retain most of its local revenue income. The actual portion of revenue income both provinces remitted to the center, that is, remittance rates, provided telling examples. Guangdong's remittance rate was 22 percent in 1980. It was cut to 20 percent in 1982, sharply down to 11 percent in 1985, and further to 9 percent in 1986. It was raised slightly to 12 percent in 1988. Fujian, on the other hand, received a net subsidy from the center, equivalent to 10 percent of its revenue income in 1980. This ratio was increased to 11 percent in 1982, and decreased moderately to 8 percent in 1986. Only in the 1988–1991 period did the ratio decline to about 1 percent. The generous remittance arrangements in Guangdong and Fujian stood in sharp contrast to Shanghai, whose remittance rate started at a whopping 91 percent in 1980 and stayed at a high range of 74–90 percent between 1982 and 1986.

All these "particularistic concessions" were to provide policy space and fiscal incentives and insurance for reform experiments in the two provinces. Equally important, they helped to ensure that these experiments would succeed there, thereby becoming a national showcase for reform. Nevertheless, as Guangdong emerged as the largest provincial economy in China, the center required it to increase its fiscal contribution to the country by sharply raising its remittance rate to about 51 percent in 1994.[17]

Lastly, Guangdong rapidly ascended in its national ranking of economic indicators, thanks to its bold, steadfast, and pragmatic reform and opening. Its GDP was ranked only the sixth nationwide in 1980, the year when the SEZ was established. Its ranking, however, was soaring afterward with the deepening of its reform, to the fourth in 1985, the second in 1990 and the first in 1995. In 1995, the province accounted for 6.1 percent of local revenue income, 9.4 percent of GDP, 33.3 percent of the imports and exports, 25 percent of the utilized foreign capital of the nation (SSB 1996b: 1–216). Guangdong's meteoric rise demonstrates to all the other provinces that reform and opening did pay off, inviting them to follow suit.

6

Extending the Open Policy

The previous chapter outlines the politics of the Open Policy in the earlier years, especially between 1978 and 1985. It focuses on reformists' political and economic considerations in their selecting the SEZs in Guangdong and Fujian as well as the reformist strategy of generating competitive liberalization for opening among the other provinces. Two questions naturally arise—how can we account for the opening of all provinces between 1978 and 1994? Do any possible factors underline the pattern of the nationwide opening of the provinces? This chapter addresses these questions. Using the central government's selection of open areas in the provinces during 1978–1993 as an example, I test the relevancy of possible factors which, according to the existing literature, shaped national policies toward reforms in the provinces.

I find that the center opened up faster those provinces that had patrons among the top leadership, where non-state sectors were providing numerous jobs, that either contributed heavily to the center, or depended heavily on central subsidies, and to some extent, those that had a certain potential for developing trade with nearby external economies. Overall, support from labor force from the existing non-state sectors, central patronage, means to strengthen provincial fiscal capacities, access to sea ports and proximity to the coast, as well as trade potential apparently helped to account for the center's opening of the provinces. The central government acted on multiple motives instead of a single one—patron-clientelism, fiscal revenue, social support, and economic efficiency.

To recap the discussion in chapters 2 and 5, the opening of China's provinces between 1978 and 1994 went through five periods. First, during 1978–1984, four SEZs, three in Guangdong and one in Fujian, were opened to external investors and the international business community. Second, in 1984 fourteen coastal cities were declared open cities for foreign business. Third, in 1985 the State Council made sixty-one cities and counties in three deltas coastal open economic zones (Howell 1993: 63–74; Yang 1998: 265). Fourth, in 1990 the Pudong District in Shanghai gained a status similar to the SEZ. Fifth, in 1992 the state opened up most of the provincial capitals as well as major cities in the inland regions. By then, all provinces enjoyed varying extents of opening.

On the surface, the rationale of opening up Guangdong described in chapter 5 might appear to explain why the coastal region was opened up ahead of the inland regions. Let us call it "the-most-able-reform-first." The coast enjoyed much better political and geoeconomic conditions for opening. The region was close to the advanced economies in Asia and in North America. It had ocean harbors. It had a relatively developed industrial base. It had a history of dealing with foreign business in the recent centuries. Therefore, the Open Policy would have gained greater political support from provincial leaders, pro-market sectors and employees, and even population. It would have a greater chance for success there. The coastal success would pressure the inland regions to follow suit.

Nevertheless, we should be cautious in applying the explanation of opening up of Guangdong and Fujian to the rest of the nation for several reasons. First, we have yet to be sure this explanation applies to the opening of provinces at a national level. While opening varied between the coastal and inland regions, it also varied among coastal provinces as well as inland provinces. Some coastal provinces were opened up earlier than other provinces; some inland provinces enjoyed greater opening than others. This variation in regional opening demands sophisticated answers and careful analyses. Second, other factors may also have played a role in the varying pace of opening of the provinces. The existing literature suggests a wide range of alternative ones. Only nationwide statistical tests will give us a systemic survey of the opening and a convincing test for the "most-able-reform-first" explanation as well as other existing explanations.

A carefully evaluation of these explanations will help us to better understand the political strategy of China's reforms as well as its operation and implementation, which are the core issues in this book. On the basis of the examination of available explanations can we be sure what might have driven national leaders' decisions to open up provinces nationwide from 1978–1993, what facilitated and constrained local reforms, and how central leaders utilized local catalysts and overcame local constraints in sustaining the reform momentum.

In order to verify explanations for opening, a ready and operational indicator of provincial opening is needed. I measure provincial opening by *the share of open cities and counties in provincial population*. The higher the share, the greater the province was open to the world economy. The calculation of this index is quite labor-intensive, for a coastal province could have scores of open cities and counties after 1985. Therefore, only indexes in selected instead of all years between 1979 and 1994 are computed. As stated in chapter 3, China's reform followed a cyclic pattern of surge and retraction. Specifically, the policies were characterized by the following of an interplay of liberalism and conservatism—expansion 1978–1980, retraction of 1981–1983, expansion of 1984–1988, retraction of 1989–1991, and expansion of 1992–1994. I choose 1980, 1982, 1986, 1990, and 1993 as years to represent this period of 1979–1994. Except for 1980, the selected years were the mid-point year of each period. The year 1980, instead of 1979, for the period of 1978–1980 was selected because of two reasons: (1) The statistics on many counties, cities, and provinces in 1979 were not available; (2) the reform started in November and December 1978, and as a result, the choice of 1979 or 1980 did not matter a great deal. This index will be correlated with relevant indicators in order to test the validity of given explanations.

Existing Explanations

Fiscal Explanation

One of the explanations for provincial opening given by scholars and analysts is fiscal. Levi (1989) demonstrates persuasively the importance of fiscal revenue for the state. As Wang (1995: 91–92) stated vividly, just like no human being can survive without blood, no state can function without revenue. Central-local fiscal relations could be characterized as follows: The local government plays a dual role of collecting taxes from local tax-payers and paying taxes to the center. The center's capacity to extract revenue is conditioned by its bargaining power vis-à-vis localities and by its calculation of costs and benefits of actions (Wang 1995: 91–92).

As China scholars and officials suggest, central leaders, in deciding on policies toward reforms in provinces, needed to consider two effects of reform—the effect of provincial reform on central fiscal income, and that of fiscal arrangements on provincial incentives for reforms (Wong, Heady, and Woo 1995; Wong 1997). Taken together, however, they give us incomplete clues about how fiscal arrangements would affect the central decision to open the provinces.

First, central officials would weigh very carefully fiscal implications of opening a province, especially fiscally enhancing effects versus fiscally disrupting effects of opening up a province. In terms of their net fiscal remittance to the central government, provinces could be categorized into three types: large contributors to the central coffer, small contributors, and beneficiaries of central coffers (or subsidized provinces).[1] Effects of opening for provincial fiscal revenue appeared uncertain in the earlier years. When it succeeded, it could expand revenue income of a province, permitting it to remit a greater sum to the center or receive smaller subsidies from the center. When reforms failed, however, revenue income of a province would be undermined, reducing their fiscal remittance to the center or increasing their dependence on central subsidies. If the center was confident that the Open Policy would succeed, it would use the opening of provinces to compel provinces to improve their fiscal capacity. It would urge large fiscal contributors to open up more and increase their fiscal revenue and remittance to the center; it would compel less-developed provinces to improve their fiscal health and reduce their dependence on the center. If, however, the center was risk averse and was much worried about the disrupting effects of the opening, it would try to minimize fiscal disruption. It could permit only limited opening of heavily remitting provinces so as to prevent their revenue from being undermined by the opening.[2] It could allow only slight opening of heavily subsidized provinces so that they would not become more dependent on central subsides. It could open up drastically lightly remitting provinces since they entailed the lowest fiscal risk for the center. These provinces had certain capacity to generate revenue. Even if their fiscal income was reduced after the opening, they would not disrupt the overall pattern of central fiscal income.

Second, scholars suggest that fiscal arrangements could affect provincial incentives for reforms. Provinces would be motivated to promote reforms only when they could retain a large portion of the fiscal increase, as a reward for their reform efforts. Otherwise, it did not pay fiscally for provinces to make extra efforts to open up their economy.[3] In Oi's term, localities needed to obtain the rights to residual (Oi 1999). Invariably, the center needed to increase marginal retention rates for provinces in order to stimulate local reform efforts (Wong, Heady, and Woo 1995: 86). As stated earlier, lower fiscal remittance from large contributing provinces, however, could severely undermine central fiscal strength. Significant central fiscal concessions to small contributors, on the other hand, could have desirable effects of motivating these provinces.[4] However, scholars do not discuss what kind of fiscal incentives would have motivated heavily subsidized provinces to pursue reforms. We thus do not know the overall relationship fiscal arrangements had with central preferences for local reforms.

If the center was fiscally risk-averse it would have opened up heavily subsidized provinces last in order to prevent failed reform from deepening their dependence on central subsidies. If this is true, we should expect an inverted U-pattern between fiscal remittance rate and provincial opening. That is to say, provinces which remitted a moderate share of their revenue to the center or those which were moderately subsidized by the center were opened up much faster than provinces that transferred most of their revenue to the center, or those that were heavily subsidized by central revenue.

To investigate the relationship between provincial fiscal retention and provincial opening, I plot the index of provincial opening on the average share of the provincial fiscal revenue remitted by the province (or provincial remittance rates) from 1980–1993 (figure 6.1).[5] We do observe a curvilinear pattern, or a U-curve, instead of an inverted U-curve. Namely, provinces that had a high remittance rate (large contributors) or very high negative rates (heavily subsidized provinces) would have higher indexes of opening. Large contributors were opened up to a greater extent than subsidized provinces.

A more rigorous statistical analysis further confirms that provincial opening was in a U-shaped relation with fiscal arrangements. Regression results yield the following formula about the relationship between the index of provincial opening (provincial opening) and provincial remittance rate (RemitRate)(tabulation 6.1). The dependent variable (provincial opening in this case) is equivalent to the coefficient of the independent variable (remittance rate), plus a coefficient to the squared of the independent variable, and plus a negative coefficient to the power of four of the independent variable. In mathematical terms this function is a typical curvilinear one (U-shaped pattern). T score of the coefficients in parentheses underneath the coefficients in tabulation 6.1 suggests statistically significant results. The formula as a whole is statistically highly significant (at 7.32623×10^{-6}), and it

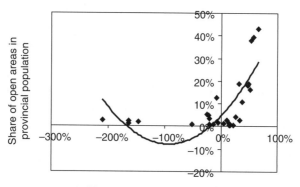

% of Local revenue remitted to the center

Figure 6.1   Revenue remittance and opening of provinces, 1980–1993.

Tabulation 6.1 Equation on relationship between the remittance rate and provincial opening

Provincial opening = 0.03 + 0.27 RemitRate + 0.252 (RemitRate)^2 −0.029 (RemitRate)^4
                    (1.52) (6.56)   (4.39)   (−2.17)
Adjusted R square = 0.66, significance level = 0.0000007, and F = 15.7.

can account for a considerable degree (66 percent) of variation in provincial opening (see adjusted R square).

This unusual U-shaped pattern demands an explanation. Obviously the central government was not as fiscally risk-averse as one line of the above analyses suggests. Why were large contributors and heavily subsidized provinces opened up faster than provinces that received a moderate amount of subsidies from the center? Two possible factors might be responsible. First, the central government was making bold moves to bolster its fiscal health. It opened up first provinces that contributed heavily to the center likely out of the hope that fiscally able provinces would generate greater fiscal capacity after opening. The center also opened up earlier and to a lesser extent provinces that depended heavily on central subsidies. By doing so, the center might pressure fiscally dependent provinces to improve their fiscal abilities after opening. A possible account for this central optimism in the Open Policy might be that central leaders were impressed by the successes of Guangdong and Fujian that had undergone the pilot projects of opening up. They inferred from the experience of the two provinces that opening could also enhance the fiscal status of both remitting and subsidized provinces.

Second, economic geography mattered. Provinces remitting heavily to the center tended to locate along the coast and were closer to developed economies in the Asia-Pacific. Heavily subsidized provinces tended to locate along the border in China's southwest, northwest, north and northeast, which were close to other neighboring countries that could be potential trading and investment partners. Both types of provinces had a geoeconomic advantage in opening up first. In contrast, provinces receiving moderate amount of subsidies from the center tended to locate in the central region. They were close neither to developed economies in the Asia-Pacific, nor to those in Southeast Asia, South Asia, Central Asia, and Russia. Therefore, they were opened later. As is to be elaborated shortly, economic geography played a marginally relevant role in provincial opening. Therefore, the second explanation carries some but not much weight.

Distance from Beijing

It has been proposed that a province's distance from Beijing conditioned its leeway in carrying out economic reform. Vogel (1989: 83), for example, suggested that Guangdong was picked as a pioneer in the Open Policy because it was far away from Beijing and that failure in its reform would produce small political risk for the central government. Yang (1996) made the most systemic and eloquent case for geographic and political distance from Beijing. He argued that the farther a province was away from Beijing, the more likely it engaged in rural reform and broke away from the People's Commune between 1979 and 1981 (Yang 1996: 136–38). He found a statistically significant relation between provincial rural reform and distance from Beijing.

Taking up this argument, I also try to examine whether distance from Beijing influenced the opening of a province. I correlate the index of provincial opening with the distance of the provincial capital from Beijing. The data on distance from Beijing was taken from Yang's study (Yang 1996: 132–33). The data for Hainan is added in by summing the lengths of the Guangzhou-Beijing rail, the Guangzhou-Zhanjiang rail distance, and the Zhanjiang-Haikou sea lane. The correlation coefficient was −0.33. The sign was indeed negative, yet the correlation is much lower than the −0.50 benchmark.[6] In addition, a graphic display of a plot of the two variables (figure 6.2) shows no clear statistical correlation. Thus we can conclude that in the case of provincial opening no relationship exists between opening and distance from Beijing at the national level. This finding is surprising.

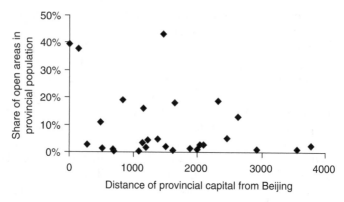

Figure 6.2 Distance from Beijing and opening of provinces, 1980–1993.

What accounted for this lack of strong correlation? One possible explanation is as follows. Some coastal and inland provinces were close to Beijing. But only those on the coast were opened up, and those in the inland regions were not. Similarly, some coastal, central, and western provinces were far away from Beijing, yet only those on the coast benefited from the Open Policy in the earlier years. This may be why we do not observe any connection between long distance from Beijing and propensities for being opened by the center.

Provincial Leadership

A popular view in the studies of provincial reforms holds that provincial liberal measures were largely a result of provincial leadership. If a province's leaders had a liberal attitude toward economic reforms, they would demand that central leaders accord permission for liberal initiatives in the provinces, resist central restrictions on reforms, protect local reform initiatives, and push forward meaningful policies in the province.[7] Provincial leadership over reforms could have also affected provincial opening. Reformist provincial leaders could have actively lobbied central leaders for earlier opening and earned favorable treatment and policies. On the other hand, conservative provincial leaders might oppose central efforts to open up their provinces.

To examine the effect of provincial leadership on provincial opening, I correlate the data on provincial leadership in reforms to the provincial index of opening. Several edited volumes on provincial leadership and provincial profiles as well as analyses on individual provinces provide us with useful information on political orientation and efforts by leaders in eighteen provinces in reform.[8] I code provincial leadership in selected years (1980, 1982, 1986, 1990, and 1993) in three levels—(1) for conservative, (2) for weak support for reform or a neutral stance over reform, and (3) for being reformist. The coding of (2) corresponds somehow to "bandwagoning" used in the existing literature, describing opportunistic behavior or no solid commitment on the part of provincial leaders toward reforms. The data are shown in table 6.1. I correlate the index of provincial leadership with the provincial opening index in these *individual* years. The correlation coefficient is 0.455, lower than the 0.5 benchmark. A plot of averages of the two sets of variables (shown in figure 6.3) also suggests a lack of strong and clear relationship between provincial leadership and provincial opening. Therefore, even though provincial lobbying played a key role in the opening of a few provinces, especially Guangdong, at the national level the relation between provincial

Table 6.1   Coding of provincial leadership in reforms and provincial opening index

Provinces	1980	1982	1986	1990	1993	Average	Average Opening Index (%)
Beijing	2	2	3	3	3	2.6	39
Tianjin	2	3	3	2	2	2.4	38
Liaoning	1	1	1	3	3	1.8	19
Shanghai	1	1	3	3	3	2.2	43
Jiangsu	1	1	1	1	1	1	16
Zhejiang	1	1	1	1	1	1	18
Fujian	1	1	3	2	3	2	13
Shandong	2	2	3	3	3	2.6	11
Guangdong	3	3	3	3	3	3	19
Guangxi	1	1	3	3	3	2.2	5
Shanxi	1	1	2	2	3	1.8	1
Anhui	3	1	1	3	3	2.2	0
Jiangxi	1	1	3	3	3	2.2	1
Henan	1	1	1	3	3	1.8	0
Hunan	1	1	1	1	1	1	1
Sichuan	3	2	2	2	2	2.2	3
Shaanxi	1	1	1	1	1	1	2

Notes: Opening index is the share of open areas in provincial industrial output. Coding of leadership is as follows: 1 for conservative, 2 for cautious, neutral, or bandwagoning on national trends, and 3 for reformists.

Sources: Data sources for provincial leadership: Cheung, Chung, and Lin 1998, Goodman 1997, Hendrischke and Feng 1999, and Fitzgerald 2002. Specific data sources for individual provinces are listed in endnote 8. Data sources for provincial opening index are listed at the end of the book.

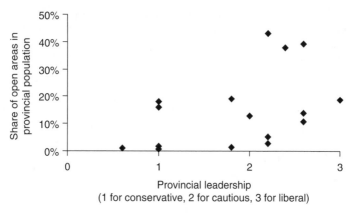

Figure 6.3   Provincial leadership and opening of provinces, 1980–1993.

leadership and provincial opening is not strong, though their relation is clearly a positive correlation.

Other Explanations

National Patrons for the Provinces

English and Chinese studies on Guangdong discussed in the previous chapter imply that provincial reforms might benefit from national patrons. In other words, the luck of a province might also rest on its connection with the central leaders. Specifically, national leaders who had strong ties with a given province could make institutional arrangements favorable for reforms in the province. One question that naturally arises is that whether this applies to the other provinces. Should this be true for the provinces in general, we should expect that the more national patrons a province had, the greater freedom it should have enjoyed in reforms, and the greater extent of opening it should have experienced.

Politburo members and the eight powerful elders mentioned in chapters 2 and 3 were the most influential national patrons for provinces. Chapter 3 also discusses the regional background of the Politburo members. The coding and data of national patrons for provinces are detailed in table 6.2. It is very likely that Politburo members and the eight elders mentioned in chapter 3 would serve as patrons for the province where they worked for the longest time in the post-1949 period. The underlying reason is as follows. While a leader

Table 6.2 National patrons of provinces, 1980–1993

	1980	1982	1986	1990	1991	1992	1993
Total	21	26	25	18	18	26	26
Beijing	3	4	4	4	4	4	4
Tianjin		1	1	1	1	1	1
Hebei							
Liaoning	1	2	1	2	2	4	4
Shanghai			1	1	1	4	4
Jiangsu	2	1	1			1	1
Zhejiang							
Fujian	2	2	2				
Shandong		1	1			1	1
Guangdong	1	4	3	1	1	2	2
Guangxi	1	1					
Hainan							
Shanxi	2	2	2	1	1	1	1
Neimenggu	1	1					
Jilin						1	1
Heilongjiang						1	1
Anhui	1	1	1	1	1		
Jiangxi							
Henan							
Hubei	1	1	1	1	1		
Hunan	2						
Sichuan	2	2	2	3	3	3	3
Guizhou	1						
Yunnan							
Xizang							
Shaanxi		1	1				
Gansu		1		2	2	2	2
Qinghai	1	1	1				
Ningxia			1				
Xinjiang		1	1	1	1	1	1

Notes: Data sources are provided in chapter 4. National patrons included Politburo members in these years, as well as the eight elders when they served at the Politburo or in key positions, or were alive afterward. The province for which they provided patronage was the province where they served the longest in the post-1949 period. If a leader had not served in any province in the post-1949 period, the province where s/he served the longest in the pre-1949 period, or his/her home province would be taken instead. Reasons for this coding are elaborated in the text of the chapter.

was working in a province, s/he would have established a political base there. Even after taking up a national position, existing connections would be strengthened by promoting central treatment that is favorable toward the provinces. A good example is that of Jiang Zemin. Shanghai is the province where he worked for the longest time

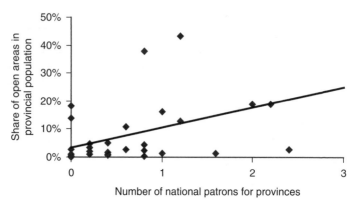

Figure 6.4   National patrons and opening of provinces, 1980–1993.

and cultivated an extensive network. After he became the General Secretary of the CCP, he promoted many of his former associates from Shanghai into central positions. He also favored further opening of and preferential policies for Shanghai.

The data readily available on national patrons are in regard to 1980, 1982, 1986, 1990 and 1992, the years when the provincial opening index is available. I correlate the average provincial opening index with the averaged number of national patrons in these years. The correlation coefficient is 0.522, above the statistical significant level of 0.50. A plot of the number of national patrons and the provincial opening index (figure 6.4) demonstrates a moderate level of correlation between them. Thus the hypothesis that provinces enjoyed a privilege of being opened up earlier because of support from national patrons receives support at the national level. National patronage apparently facilitated not only opening of Guangdong, but also that of other provinces.

Trade Potential

One purpose for the central government to open up the provinces was to promote trade and attract foreign capital (Howell 1993). It followed that central leaders would have paid attention to the appeal of individual provinces to foreign business and investment. Studies of trade of China's provinces suggested that provinces varied in their potential in developing trade, largely due to their locations and proximity to nearby advanced economies, such as Hong Kong, Taiwan, Japan, and South Korea. For example, it has been widely acknowledged that the first SEZ in China, namely Shenzhen and later on many areas in Guangdong were opened up primarily because of Guangdong's proximity to Hong Kong and differences in factor prices in these two places. Hong Kong businessmen found in Guangdong cheaper labor, easy transportation between the two places, convenient coastal access to overseas markets, and linguistic and dietary affinity (Goodman and Feng 1994; Cheung 1998b; Vogel 1989). Similarly, Fujian had an appeal to Taiwanese investors who resided across the strait and many of whom had family lineage back in Fujian (Chen 1998: 284–85; Yeung and Chu 1998: 4–6). In a similar vein, Womack and Zhao (1994) distinguished three types of provinces in terms of their location and trade potential—coastal provinces that favored internationalization, border provinces that were interested in relations with a neighboring country, and inland provinces that gained less from internationalization.

Two economic geographic factors affect a province's trade potential. First, the province's nearest primary potential trade partner and the distance between them; second, the size of this trade partner's economy and more importantly, the volume of imports of this closest trade partner. For example, for Guangdong, Hong Kong was a potential partner and was very close to Guangdong. In addition, as an international entrepôt, Hong Kong imported a large volume of goods despite its relatively small economic size. Thus the trade potential between Guangdong and Hong Kong could be very large.

Economists suggest that the trade between two economies is in a positive relation with trade potential (Tp) between two economies, but in a reverse relation with distance between them (D). Economists depict trade potential as the product of their economic sizes (S1 x S2). I suggest that the actual trade volume of neighboring economies is a better indicator of trade potential for the following reasons. First, the Chinese leaders were interested in following the trade-led growth path paved by Japan, Hong Kong, Singapore, and Taiwan. Therefore, trade from neighboring economies matters more than their size. Second, the actual trade volume of the nearby economy is a more reliable indicator for its trade potential with any given province than the size of their economies. Some potential large trade partners, especially Hong Kong, Taiwan, South Korea, and to a lesser extent Japan, depend more heavily on trade (measured in share of trade in GNP) than do many other economies (including Western countries and communist nations). In addition, the developmental level in many Chinese provinces in the early years of reforms was low, but it was growing rapidly during the reform. For these reasons the product of size of two economies (such as the mediocre size of Guangdong's economy and trade and the relatively small size of Hong Kong's economy) proposed by trade economists underestimates the trade potential between the Chinese provinces and their neighboring economies.

I construct the index for provinces' trade potential by dividing the trade volume of a province's nearby major economy by the province's distance from the economy (table 6.3). The distance is measured in terms of that between the province's primary port to the nearby port of this economy. For the sake of simplicity, one closest and large potential trading partner is identified. For example, Hong Kong is identified for Guangdong, and Taiwan for Fujian. Guangdong's trade potential is the trade volume of Hong Kong divided by its distance from Hong Kong. In some cases (such as a few provinces in the north) decisions are carefully deliberated in choosing the nearby major economy.[9] To get a quick cut of the data, I choose a meaningful year for the period 1979–1994. The year of 1985 is chosen for the following reasons. It was the year when China's coastal region was open to the outside world. The State Council declared sixty-one cities and counties in three deltas coastal open economic areas. In the previous year, the fourteen coastal cities were declared open cities for foreign business. The index for trade potential for each province in 1985 is constructed (table 6.3).

In the analysis, the average index of opening of a province between 1980 and 1994 is correlated with the index of the province's trade potential in 1985.[10] The correlated coefficient is 0.482, slightly falling short of the 0.5 benchmark. It suggested a marginal but not yet strong correlation between these two variables. A plot (figure 6.5) confirms that they are weakly related. This finding suggests that central leaders to some extent considered economic returns of the Open Policy. They had a slight tendency to open up earlier provinces that were located close to large trading economies and that had a great potential for trading with these neighbors.

Province's Distance from the Coast

Scholars outside and inside China widely note that the coast was opened up much earlier than were the inland regions for foreign business and that the central government gave the coast greater leeway and more preferential economic policies (Howell 1993; Yang 1997: 15–39; Wei 2000; Zweig 2002: 49–106). Other than possessing a more developed industrial base, an important reason is that the coast had sea

Table 6.3   Trade potential of provinces with nearby economies in 1985

Provinces	Nearby major economy (NME)	Trade volume (TV) of NME, (million US$)	Distance from NME (km)	Distance route	Trade potential (TV/distance)
Beijing	Japan	306,346	2,519	Beijing-Tianjin-Yokohama	121.6
Tianjin	Japan	306,346	2,382	Tianjin-Yokohama	128.6
Hebei	Japan	306,346	2,290	Qinhuangdao-Yokohama	133.8
Liaoning	Japan	306,346	2,031	Dalian-Yokohama	150.8
Shanghai	Japan	306,346	1,930	Shanghai-Yokohama	158.7
Jiangsu	Japan	306,346	2,156	Lianyungang-Yokohama	142.1
Zhejiang	Taiwan	50,820	6,99	Ningbo-Xiamen- Kaohsiung	72.7
Fujian	Taiwan	50,820	3,06	Xiamen-Kaohsiung	166.1
Shandong	South Korea	61,412	8,90	Yantai-Pusan	69.0
Guangdong	Hong Kong	59,889	182	Guangzhou-Kowloon (rail)	329.1
Guangxi	Vietnam	2,707	296	Beihai-Hei Phong	9.1
Hainan	Hong Kong	59,889	306	Haikou-Hong Kong	195.7
Shanxi	Japan	306,346	3,090	Taiyuan-Jinan-Yantai-Yohokama	99.1
Neimenggu	Soviet Union	169,797	3,680	Erlianhaote-Novosibirsk	46.1
Jilin	Japan	306,346	3,003	Changchun-Dalian-Yokohama	102.0
Heilongjiang	Soviet Union	169,797	4,270	Harbin-Novosibirsk	39.8
Anhui	Japan	306,346	2,545	Hefei-Shanghai-Yokohama	120.4
Jiangxi	Japan	306,346	2,767	Nanchang-Shanghai-Yokohama	110.7
Henan	Japan	306,346	2,728	Zhengzhou-Xuzhou-Lianyungang-Yokohama	112.3
Hubei	Hong Kong	59,889	2,649	Hankou (river)-Shanghai-Hong Kong	22.6
Hunan	Hong Kong	59,889	888	Changsha-Guangzhou-Kowloon	67.4
Sichuan	Hong Kong	59,889	3,923	Chongqing (river)-Shanghai-Hong Kong	15.3
Guizhou	Hong Kong	59,889	1,742	Guiyang-Guangzhou-Kowloon	34.4
Yunnan	Thailand	16,331	2,820	Kunming- Bangkok	5.8
Xizang	India	24,868	1,000	Lhasa-Calcutta	24.9
Shaanxi	Japan	306,346	3,239	Xian-Xuzhou-Lianyungang-Yokohama	94.6
Gansu	Japan	306,346	3,915	Lanzhou-Xuzhou-Lianyungang-Yokohama	78.2
Qinghai	Japan	306,346	4,131	Xining-Xuzhou-Lianyungang-Yokohama	74.2
Ningxia	Japan	306,346	3,862	Yinchuan-Tianjin-Yokohama	79.3
Xinjiang	Soviet Union	169,797	1,740	Urumqi-Novosibirsk	97.6

Sources: Trade data comes from Word Bank,1987. Distance routes and distance come from *Zhongguo Jiaotong Yunying Linchengtu (Mileage Charts of China's Transportation in Operation)*, 1991. Beijing: Remin Jiaotong Chubanshe; *Quanguo Tianlu Lüke Lieche Shikebiao (National Passenger Train Timetable)*. Beijing: Zhongguo Tiedao Chubanshe; *Zuixin Shiyong Zhongguo Dituce (An Updated Practical Map Book of China)*, 1992. Beijing: Zhongguo Ditu Chubanshe, as well as internet sources.

ports and enjoyed easy access to the world market as well as low costs in transporting commodities and products. As a result, we should expect that the central government would open up earlier provinces close to sea ports. A province's distance from the a sea port can be measured by the distance by railway from the provincial capital to the

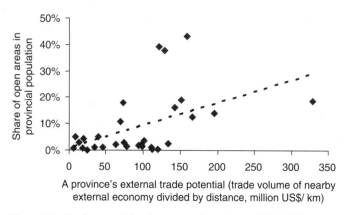

Figure 6.5   Trade potential and opening of provinces, 1980–1993.

closest sea port in China. If a province had its own sea port, the distance is coded as zero. The data on the distances come from Jin and Chen 1996: 134. The correlation between the provincial opening index and provincial distance from a sea port registers −0.553, reaching a level of statistical significance. Hence the two variables are in a significantly reverse relationship. This is confirmed by figure 6.6. This is to say, the closer a province was to the coast and a major sea port, the more likely the central government opened it up earlier. Obviously, the center was taking advantage of the coastal access to sea ports and the world markets in implementing its Open Policy.

Provincial Pro-reform Groups

Another possible factor that was responsible for the central decision to open up a province was the strength of pro-reform groups in the province. Among the major economic sectors, light industry might benefit more from opening than heavy industry, and the non-state economy clearly would benefit more from the opening than would the state sector. China's development in Mao's era followed to a large extent the Soviet model in the following ways: Personal consumption was depressed, and heavy industry was expanded excessively in order to propel rapid industrialization. In the reforms period, as the state's cap on personal consumption was lifted, demands for consumer goods and hence light industrial goods would expand. More importantly, as China was opened up, foreign investors would take advantage of China's cheap labor and land to produce labor-intensive goods which

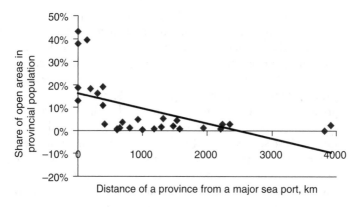

Figure 6.6 Distance from sea port and opening of provinces, 1980–1993.

were usually related to light industry. Therefore, after the opening, China's light industry would experience expansion. In contrast, heavy industry would see its monopoly on heavy industrial products (such as heavy machinery) undermined by imports (Shirk 1985: 207). Therefore, provinces with large heavy industry might resist opening and those with sizable light industry might support it. As Shirk (1985) demonstrates, interest groups, such as heavy industry, could influence governmental policies through controlling a considerable amount of resources and through representation in governmental agencies (such as the Bureau of Metallurgical Industry). Light industry, which stood to benefit from reforms and opening, might also influence policies through its representative governmental agencies (such as Ministry of Light Industry).

A large body of literature in political science provides theoretical underpinning for effects of interest groups in public policies. One strand of political-economic literature suggests that the influences of interest groups come from two factors. First, their relative smaller size compared to the general population makes it easier for these groups to organize and persuade officials. Second, these groups share a clearer set of interests compared to the population. Thus, they can feel more intensively the benefits of taking a common stance as well as the harms of failing to do so (Olson 1971, 1982; Mueller 1989: 307–319). Another strand of political sociological literature emphasizes the institutional expansion and governmental access of interest groups (Bentley 1908; Truman 1971).

In China non-state sectors and light industry appeared to enjoy these three prerequisites for influence on policies. First of all, they were significantly smaller than the population and were thus more likely to share similar interests and act together to influence governmental policies. Although they were limited in size, they were growing rapidly due to their efficiency and agility in responding to the markets. With growing employment and resources, they had an increasingly large clout in shaping the government's policies. Second and more importantly, these sectors would feel strongly the benefits and costs of policy alternatives. They would benefit greatly from the Open Policy because the opening will stimulate exports of light industrial goods and allow the market and non-state businesses to play a greater role in the economy. Conversely, they would feel intensely the harms of continuing autarky and the command economy that restricted exports and marketized enterprises. Third, they possessed certain institutional access to the government, and could shape governmental policies through their respective supervising governmental agencies. Between 1981 and 1988, at the provincial level these agencies included the Bureaus of Light Industry, Textile Industry, Food Industry, Agriculture, Agricultural Cultivation, Grain, Forestry, Hydropower and Water, Commerce, External Trade, External Economic Liaison, and Foreign Experts; the Administration of Handicraft, the State Administration of Computer and Industry, the Agricultural Commission; the Administrations of Aquatic Product, Industry and Commerce, and Imported and Exported Goods Inspection; the Administrative Commissions of Foreign Investment and Imports and Exports, the Supply and Marketing Cooperation, and the Customs Office (table 6.4). These sectors would voice their concerns to the government through these agencies, as well as many local governments that were eager to stimulate local economic growth.

China's economy can be categorized into two main sectors by ownership, namely, the state sector and non-state sectors. The former refers mainly to state-owned enterprises. As in other communist countries, state enterprises were marked by ambiguous property rights and a lack of supervision of the management, inefficiency, slow technological innovation, poorly designed products, and inadequate incentives for workers, technicians, engineers and managers. As a result, the Chinese state gradually lifted its restrictions on non-state sectors in the reforms period. Understandably, employees in the state sector would fear losing their jobs and income and would thus be reluctant to support reforms. Those in non-state sectors, on the other hand, would

Table 6.4 National economic ministries (bureaus at the provincial level), 1981–1993

Related sectors	Governmental agencies between 1981 and 1988	Governmental agencies between 1988 and 1993
Pro-reform Sectors Light industry	Total: 22 Ministries of Light Industry, Textile Industry, and Food Industry, Central Administration of Handicraft, and State Administration of Computer and Industry (5)	Total: 11 Ministries of Light Industry and Textile Industry (2)
Agriculture and rural enterprises	State Agricultural Commission, Ministries of Agriculture, Agricultural Cultivation, Grain, Forestry, Hydropower and Water Resources; State Administration of Aquatic Product (7)	Ministries of Agriculture, Forestry, and Hydropower and Water Resources (3)
Foreign and private enterprises	Central Administration of Industry and Commerce; Bureau of Foreign Experts (2).	Central Administration of Industry and Commerce; Office of Special Economic Zones (2)
Trade and markets	State Administrative Commissions of Foreign Investment and Imports and Exports; Ministries of Commerce, External Trade, and External Economic Liaison; State Supply and Marketing Cooperation, General Customs Office, State Administration of Imported and Exported Goods Inspection (8)	State Economic Structure Reform Commission; Ministries of Commerce and External Trade and Economic Work; General Customs Office (4)
Reform-resistant Sectors Heavy industry	Total: 35 Ministries of Metallurgical Industry, Chemical Industry, First, Second, Third, Fourth, Fifth, Sixth, Seventh, and Agricultural Machinery Industry, Building Materials, Coal Industry, Petrochemical Industry, and Electric Power; State Administrations of Whole Sets of Machinery and Equipment, Nonferrous Metal Industry, and Instrument and Meter Industry (17)	Total: 19 Ministries of Metallurgical Industry, Geology and Minerals, Chemical Industry, Machinery and Electronic Industry, Energy, and Aviation and Space Industry; State Administration of Building Construction (7)

Continued

Table 6.4   Continued

Related sectors	Governmental agencies between 1981 and 1988	Governmental agencies between 1988 and 1993
State planning and state enterprises	State Planning Commission, State Economic Commission, State Commissions of Basic Construction, Machinery Industry, and Energy; Ministries of Railway, Communications, and Post and Telecommunications; State Administrations of Labor, Materials, Prices, Civil Aviation, Drug, Foreign Currencies, Broadcast and Television Industry, Personnel, Scientific and Technological Cadres, and Urban Construction Projects (18).	State Planning Commission; Ministries of Materials, Labor, Personnel, Railway, Communications, Post and Telecommunications, as well as Broadcast, Television and Films; State Administrations of Prices, Civil Aviation, Land, and Drug (12).

Source: Zhao Libo 1998: 58–59.

benefit from the expansion of the sectors and a rapid increase in their income and would thus support reforms and opening up. When the state was opening up the provinces in the late 1970s, the size of light industry and non-state sectors varied widely across provinces. Such a regional variation persisted in the reform era. Some provinces had a much larger labor force employed in these two sectors and thus would have a stronger popular backing for reforms.

The correlation coefficient between the proportion of labor force in state and collective-owned urban sectors working in light industry in 1990 and the subsequent extent of the national opening of the province in 1993 is 0.42. The relation is statistically not significant. Figure 6.7, a plot of two variables, confirms a lack of close relation. Figure 6.8, however, suggests a close relation between the proportion of labor force in non-state sectors and the extent of provincial opening between 1980 and 1993. The correlation coefficient between the two variables is significantly very high at 0.81. The center apparently favored the opening of provinces with sizable and influential pro-reform sectors, namely, a large share of non-state sectors in employment.

The last provincial group that had a stake in reforms and could have significantly affected national policies toward provincial reforms was employees in provincial governmental agencies and public institutions. They were in charge of regulating economic sectors, trade, and

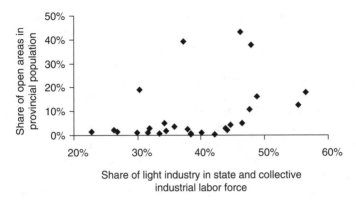

Figure 6.7   Employment in light industry and opening of provinces, 1980–1993.

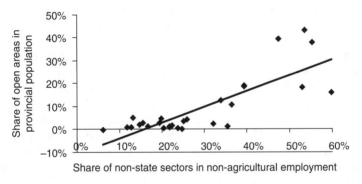

Figure 6.8   Employment in non-state sectors and opening of provinces, 1980–1993.

markets, economic planning, allocation of critical resources such as minerals, water, and land, as well as provision of essential services, such as power, telecommunications, and transport. Some of them supervised enterprises in a given sector. China's administrative structure experienced significant changes in 1981, 1988, and 1993. The effects of governmental restructuring in 1993 would probably be felt in 1994 the earliest. Since this study examines reforms during 1978–1993, it thus focuses on restructuring of the government in 1981 and 1988. All the governmental agencies (ministries at the national level and bureaus or departments at the provincial level) can be distinguished roughly into two types, following Shirk's suggestion (1985). One set is related to sectors that would benefit from market-oriented reforms in the 1980s and early 1990s, including light industry, agriculture, trade, and foreign sectors. The other set is associated with sectors that would decline in their size, significance, and clout over the course of economic reforms. They included heavy industry, state enterprises, and state planning. Between 1981 and 1988, twenty-two national ministries and vice-ministry-level bureaus were related to reform-enhanced sectors, and thirty-six reform-withered sectors. Between 1988 and 1993, eleven national ministries and bureaus were associated with reform-oriented sectors whereas eighteen were associated with reform-resistant sectors (table 6.4). At the provincial level, usually there would be an agency corresponding to that at the national level. Therefore, in terms of number of provincial bureaus and departments, this balance of power for and against reform would be similar. On the whole, the administrative bureaucracy at the national and provincial levels thus tended to be conservative, because the number of agencies representing sectors that would be hurt by reforms outnumbered agencies supervising sectors that stood to benefit from them.

On the basis of this observation, we can infer that the larger the provincial bureaucracy, the greater the resistance to reforms in the provinces, and the greater the difficulties that the national government would encounter in opening up the province. Due to the different sizes of labor force across the provinces, a good measure of the size of provincial bureaucracy is the number of bureaucrats weighed by the size of its labor force. Only data on the number of employees in provincial governmental agencies and public institutions are available. Public institutions are closely related to the government, for they are established by the Party-state and receive their budget from the government. Many of them provisioned public goods and services, such as education, R&D, publication, media, and other urban and rural public services (Zhao 1998: 273–291). Any shrinking in the size of the government would eventually affect the revenue and survival of these public institutions. For this reason, public institutions may be inclined to resist economic reforms because reforms would undermine their own clout and resources.

The correlation between the share of government and public institutions in labor force in 1990 in a province on the one hand and national opening of the province in 1993 on the other was 0.38, well below 0.5, the benchmark of significant correlation. In addition, the positive sign suggests a positive correlation between the size of provincial government and national opening of the provinces, contradicting the hypothesized conservatism of provincial bureaucracy.

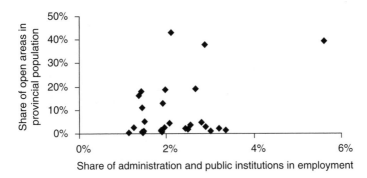

Figure 6.9   Size of provincial bureaucracy and opening of provinces, 1980–1993.

As demonstrated also by figure 6.9, provincial bureaucrats did not seem to significantly affect national opening of the provinces. It is also likely that the center did not need to be concerned with the stance of provincial bureaucracy in announcing its policies to promote reforms in the provinces.

Conclusion

This chapter investigates the possible causes of national policies regarding reforms in the provinces. Table 6.5 summarizes the results. The national selection of open areas in the provinces is chosen as an example. According to the existing literature, factors such as distance from Beijing, provincial leadership, and size and weight of light industry would have been relevant for national policies toward reforms in the provinces. However, they turn out to be unable to account for differentiating national policies toward provinces. One factor that is not considered carefully in the literature, namely, the size of provincial government, also did not seem to affect national opening of provinces.

Apparently, the national government took into careful account the size of pro-reforms sectors (especially labor force in non-state sectors), national patronage for provinces, coastal proximity, and to some extent trade potential in opening up the provinces. It thus appeared to have acted both as a rational and patron-clientelist decision maker and was concerned with both political and economic implications of its policies. On the political front, the center also would like to see its policy accepted by the sectors and labor force directly involved in the

Table 6.5   Correlation coefficients of national opening of provinces with likely factors

Independent variables (IV)	Measure of IV	Correlation with national opening of provinces (share of open areas in provincial population)
Provincial distance from Beijing	Distance of provincial capital from Beijing by rail (if N.A., waterway and highway)	−0.33
Distance from a Sea Port	Distance of a province from a major sea port	**−0.553**
Potential for trade with nearby external economies, 1985	Nearby foreign trade partner (NFTP)'s foreign trade volume/ distance from NFTP, 1985	*0.482*
Fiscal arrangements	Share of remittance to the center of provincial revenue	**A curvilinear relation (U-curved, statistically significant)**
Provincial leadership	Coding of leadership—1 conservative and 3 reformists	0.455
National patrons	Number of patrons for a province in central leadership	**0.522**
Bureaucracy	Share of government agencies and political associations (including parties) in labor force	0.38
Labor in Light Industry	Share of light industry in employment in state and collective industrial enterprises	0.42
Labor in non-state sectors	Share of non-state sectors in non-agricultural labor	**0.81**

Note: Bolds stand for statistical significant correlation and bold italics nearly statistical significant correlation.

economic process of open-up. It wanted to win new constituencies in opening up the provinces. Understandably, when the leaders at the national level and relevant sectors in the provinces strongly supported the Open Policy, resistance against the opening would be significantly reduced, and the chance for social acceptance of the opening and its success would be higher.

The center would like to satisfy national patrons for the provinces by opening up their favorite provinces earlier. National patrons might readily reach out to help when open provinces ran into difficulties. This would help guarantee the success of the opening of their "client" provinces. On the economic side, the center to some extent wanted its Open Policy to utilize the coastal access to sea ports and the world market and realize the trade potential of the provinces and generate rapid growth in China's exports to advanced or neighboring economies.

This strategy of opening up the nation is similar with that of earlier opening of Guangdong in three regards. First, national leaders realized that existing liberally oriented local economic sectors were a key asset in sustaining the Open Policy in the province. In opening up the nation, the national leader favored provinces with a sizable sector that stood to benefit from opening, namely, non-state sectors with large employment. In addition, compared to other pro-reform forces, such as provincial leadership, non-state sectors may be more endurable. Therefore, by opening up more provinces in greater pro-reforms sectors, the center appeared pragmatic and clever in rallying and building social support for reform policies. This would ensure that reforms in a province permitted by the center would have cooperation of potential winners and a good chance to succeed and that populace in the province would not aggressively oppose the opening.

Second, just as in the case of Guangdong, national patrons appeared to have facilitated the opening of other provinces. Earlier opening of a province was viewed as preferential treatment because the province would be granted considerable authority over foreign investment, resources, and policies. Top leaders appeared to have granted these privileges mostly to the provinces with which they were politically connected.

Third, apparently national leaders also wanted the opened provinces to achieve economic success. In opening up the first province, national leaders allowed Guangdong to establish the first SEZ because of its proximity and external linkages with Hong Kong, local political liberalism, and entrepreneurship. These characteristics gave Guangdong the most favorable conditions for successful liberalization in the nation. In opening up the provinces across the nation, the central government allowed provinces located near the coast and sea ports and with greater potential for external trade to be opened up first and to experience rapid growth in foreign trade. This also aimed at generating noticeable economic outcomes for national opening.

However, even though the two provinces the center opened up earliest (namely, Guangdong and Fujian), enjoyed low fiscal remittance to the center, nationwide the provinces that were opened up faster did not benefit from this special treatment. In fact the pattern suggested that the center opened up the quickest the coastal provinces that were required to remit the largest shares of their revenue to the center. A few heavily subsidized provinces enjoyed an intermediate level of opening probably because they shared borders with neighboring economies and potential trade partners. The provinces that had experienced the lowest degree of opening were those that were moderately subsidized by the center and that tended to cluster in the central region. By pushing hard revenue remitting and subsidy-receiving provinces toward the world market the national government appeared to be interested in generating greater remittances from the former and reducing subsidies to the latter through reform and opening.

7

Provincial Reform Initiatives

National strategies of opening the first two provinces and opening up the rest of the nation have been discussed. Questions concerning reform initiatives naturally arise—did provinces carry out reform at a similar pace? Why or why not? What helped to account for possible provincial differences in reform? According to the existing literature and views, provincial reform efforts could have been conditioned by a number of institutional factors—distance from Beijing, distance from a sea port, central-local fiscal arrangements, provincial leadership, influence and size of labor in non-state sectors, the size of the provincial bureaucracy, as well as national promotion of reforms through its opening up of provinces. In this chapter I will examine closely the correlation of the measure of provincial reform with these factors.

Findings of statistical analyses suggest that provinces would push forward faster reforms when they were located near a sea port and had a great potential for developing trade with neighboring external economies, when pro-reforms sectors such as light industry and non-state enterprises created substantial employment in the province, and when the province was in good fiscal conditions. Finally, central policies such as the national opening of provinces also conditioned the pace of provincial reforms.

Significance of Provinces and Provincial Differences in Policies

There is a popular saying in China: The superior issues policies, and the subordinate adopts counter-policies (*shang you zhengce, xia you duice*). This saying illustrates well the relationship between the national and provincial governments. When the center announces a reform policy, it is up to the provinces to decide how to implement it.

Both Chinese scholars and provincial leaders have acknowledged that reform policies differed in provinces. Even provincial leaders admitted that some provinces, especially the southern coastal provinces, pushed for bold reform whereas the others acted cautiously.[1] For example, the Party Secretary of Jilin, an interior and northwestern Province, stated at a meeting of provincial leaders in November 1992: "Over many issues regarding reform and development we have lacked the courage and boldness. Instead, we sought stability and avoided trouble. While other (provinces) had acted, we were still hesitating and debating. While other provinces had succeeded, we were still waiting and looking on. Due to the hindrance of (conservative) ideas we could not even implement the good methods and experience which we initiated" (*Jilin Yearbook* 1993: 2). In contrast, a number of the provinces took advantage of the center's relaxation and implemented reforms as fast as the center could tolerate. As a result, even though the center promoted reforms among provinces, the provinces responded in various ways.

Provinces are significant implementers of central policies for the following reasons. First, an average province in China had a population of 38 million in 1990 and was equivalent to a medium-sized country. This large size of provinces further complicates the national government's task of monitoring and ensuring implementation of national policies. Second, development of China's thirty provinces as of 1988–1997 was highly unequal, and its regional disparity in the poverty indices was worse than that of Brazil and India (UN 1997: 23). Around 1995, the ratio of per capita income of rural residents in the coastal, central, and western regions was 2.3: 1.3: 1, and the ratio of per capita income of urban residents was 1.44: 0.98: 1. Regional disparity might encourage localities to implement rules differently and might complicate national coordination and supervision of local observation of national reform policies. In many cases, the national government chose to entrust provincial government with the power to formulate guidelines for implementing many national policies during 1978–1994.

Third and importantly, the provinces have reserved power in appointing the Party Secretary and the chief from the prefectural down to the county level even in the period of reforms.[2] Through the nomenklatura system, Party committees at provincial, municipal/county and township levels largely determined careers of officials at their own levels. Since the Communist Party was the sole ruling party in China, clean political record and strong Party endorsement were prerequisites for bureaucratic and political advancement. Local Party committees could blemish political records of local officials who refused to go along with the organ's economic policies. Local Party committees are also given authority to supervise Party members who are governmental officials regulating the local economy, as well as Party members who manage large state enterprises and even other local firms (such as township enterprises)(Shirk 1993; Huang 1996). Therefore, provincial Party leaders (including the governor who is usually Deputy Party Secretary) can control provincial bureaus and departments in charge of the economy as well as leaders of cities and counties. City and county leaders in turn control local Party committees and bureaus (including those regulating the economy)(Huang 1996).[3]

Fourth, China's provincial governments reserve considerable power in law enforcement, market regulations, and economic management,[4] thanks to dominance of the Party at each level and economic decentralization, as well as legacies of state interference into the economy and weak rule of law. Economic decentralization has also empowered local governments. Since the late 1970s, the national government has decentralized economic power, allowing local governments to implement national economic policies as they deem appropriate in local settings. As a result, local governments have an important role in local development and regulations of the economy. The primary criterion for cadres' performance has also shifted from ideological confirmation to economic growth; and local economic wealth has become a main source of bureaucratic prestige and even cadres' material benefits (Whiting 2001). Furthermore, through economic decentralization, the national government also passes down numerous administrative tasks to local governments. For example, the national government requires local government to be responsible for schooling children, providing unemployment benefits and health care for workers of state enterprises and governmental institutions, and in the central and coastal provinces until recent years, building local roads. But it gives them little money. In order to finance these unfunded mandates, local governments are pressed to resort to administrative interferences to generate local economic growth, expand local tax bases and even impose irregular fees in order to generate revenue. As local governments depended much on local revenue, local officials valued and exercised considerable discretion in collecting and reducing taxes and fees (Lai 2003; Goodman 1994; Walder 1995).

Furthermore, the legacies of a strong state, the command economy, and weak rule of law result in extensive ties between local governments and local firms and give local governments considerable power to interfere in the local economy. A considerable number of local enterprises have close ties with local governments. Local governments have fiscal and political stakes in the health of these enterprises. They are not subject to effective checks of local legislature, media, or the court. They may thus resort to illegal means to protect local enterprises from external competition (Huang 1990).

Local governmental offices reserve considerable power over the survival and operation of enterprises under their jurisdiction. Local governmental offices control firm registrations. Governmental utilities offices also oversee state firms producing water, gas, and electricity. These agencies are under weak public supervision. They could thus pressure these firms to meet their demands. With weak legal, legislative, and media oversight, even local Party and administrative leaders can pressure officials in charge of economic affairs to toe their line and implement policies that violate national laws. Other than their power as a superior, local leaders possess an extensive administrative network. They can even affect the promotion and welfare of family members of local officials in charge of economic affairs, as well as the education of their children. They can thus use these supplies and resources to force local officials to serve local interest at the expense of national interests and laws (Huang 1996; Lai 2003).

In this context, it is not surprising to find that provincial governments were able to use a number of instruments to promote or stall the growth of non-state businesses—the most dynamic component of the post-Mao economy—and hence set the pace for provincial reforms. Until the early 1990s, as suggested by Huang (1996) and confirmed by Whiting (2001), local governments were able to arrange bank loans and set effective tax rates for non-state sectors, thus shaping the course of development of these sectors.[5] Whiting's (2001: 72, 93–96; 99) study of several counties in coastal China suggested that tax evasion by local governments was common.

Local officials were motivated to stimulate economic growth even at the expense of efficiency. Performance of local officials in China is evaluated in terms of the economic growth and provision of public goods and not efficiency. Take townships for example. Rapid growth of collective enterprises, especially in the coastal provinces with favorable conditions, was the key to fulfil these tasks. Thus township officials were motivated to get bank loans for these enterprises. In the Chinese political system township leaders also supervised the Party affairs of agricultural bank branches at the township. Therefore, they could use this leverage to squeeze bank loans for rural enterprises from the bank regardless of the efficiency of these enterprises (Whiting 2001: 234–35).

As all levels of local government shared similar institutional arrangements with the central government, they all had similar incentives for evading taxes and pumping money to support local firms. Therefore, Whiting's argument also applies to provincial governments. In other words, the provincial government also manipulated loans and tax collection in order to generate economic growth.[6]

The most apparent outcome of varying provincial reform efforts is that non-state sectors grew at a highly differentiated pace across provinces. The change of the size of non-state sectors in the reforms era thus constitutes a straightforward and direct measure of provincial reforms efforts at promoting non-state sectors. Available data only provide the breakdown of provincial industrial output by ownership in the early and coming years of reforms, but not the breakdown of provincial GDP by ownership. Therefore, a convenient measure of provincial efforts at stimulating the growth of non-state sectors is the change in the share of non-state sectors in provincial industrial output between 1978, the starting year of reforms, and 1993, the ending of the first phrase of reforms that this project examines. Table 7.1 gives us a glimpse of the share of non-state sectors in industrial output in 1978 and 1993 as well as the change between the two years. Negative percentages indicate a decline in the share of non-state sectors. The smaller the change in the share between 1978 and 1993, the less reforms a province undertook to stimulate the growth of the non-state sectors.

These varying reform efforts at the provincial level prompt two questions. The first is "What factor helps to explain the above reform efforts by these provinces that affected the growth of the non-state sectors?" The second is "To what extent did the Center's policies shape the provincial reform policies?" To answer the first question, I will first test the change of non-state sectors in the context of the existing explanations on local reforms in China. I will also thus assess the effect of national opening of provinces on the provincial reforms.

Table 7.1   Measure of the provincial policies toward non-state industry: change in share of non-state sectors in provincial industrial output (%)

Provinces	Share in 1978	Share in 1993	Change in share from 1978 to 1993
Beijing	17	47	30
Tianjin	19	55	36
Hebei	28	60	32
Liaoning	18	44	26
Shanghai	8	51	43
Jiangsu	39	77	38
Zhejiang	39	79	40
Fujian	26	72	46
Shandong	32	64	32
Guangdong	32	72	40
Guangxi	21	45	24
Hainan	17	42	25
Shanxi	22	51	29
Neimengu	21	28	7
Jilin	21	35	14
Heilongjiang	17	24	7
Anhui	20	55	35
Jiangxi	22	53	31
Henan	26	58	32
Hubei	23	43	20
Hunan	25	50	25
Sichuan	19	50	31
Guizhou	19	28	9
Yunnan	19	25	6
Xizang	23	34	11
Shaanxi	16	37	21
Gansu	6	26	20
Qinghai	18	16	−1
Ningxia	17	23	6
Xinjiang	11	21	11
National	22	53	31

Sources: SSB 1990b, 1996b: various pages.
Note: Data have been rounded after computation.

Possible Explanations

Distance from Beijing

As Vogel (1989: 83) suggested in his study of Guangdong and as Yang (1996) also proposed in his investigation of provincial launch of rural reform in the late 1970s, a province's distance from Beijing affected its

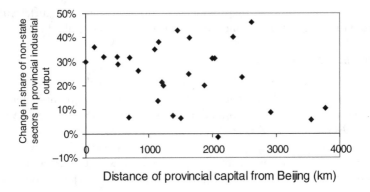

Figure 7.1   Distance from Beijing and provincial reforms, 1978–1993.

proclivity toward economic reform. The farther a province is away from Beijing, the less pressure it would feel from Beijing, the greater freedom it might enjoy in charting its own reforms course, and the smaller the political risk in attempting to break with the past practice. Following this geopolitical hypothesis, one might expect a close yet negative relation between the change in size of the non-state economy (as a measure of provincial reform efforts) and the distance of the province from Beijing. Again, Yang's data on distance from Beijing was used (Yang 1996: 132–33), and the data for Hainan is added in. The correlation between the distance of provincial capitals from Beijing on the one hand, and measure of provincial reforms on the other is -0.302 (table 7.2). It is below the 0.5 benchmark of statistical significance. It appears that provincial promotion of non-state sectors was not influenced by provinces' geographic distance from the national capital. This point is visibly captured in the plots of the measure of provincial reforms on provincial distance from Beijing in figure 7.1.

Why there is no correlation between provincial reforms and distance from Beijing? There may be a possible explanation. Suppose that geographic distance from Beijing matters, that is, distance might give a province greater leeway to pursue its own policies. The province might use this freedom to implement more conservative policies than national leaders expected. It could also pursue more liberal policies than the center preferred. For example, Guangdong and Guangxi were at roughly the same distance from Beijing, 2,324, and 2,465 kilometers by rail, respectively. While Guangdong was a national vanguard in opening and experimental reforms, Guangxi remained a backwater in economic liberalization in the 1980s and 1990s. Therefore, distance from Beijing would allow provinces to adopt policies more differently from than the national policy, but not necessarily more liberal policies.

Distance from a Sea Port

Scholars outside and inside China widely note that the coast obtained more favorable policies from the central government and implemented faster reforms than the inland regions (Howell 1993; Yang 1997: 15–39; Wei 2000; Zweig 2002: 49–106). Other than possessing a more developed industrial base, an important reason is that the coast had sea ports and low costs in importing and exporting commodities and products. This reduced the transportation and transaction costs for doing business in the coast and helped the coastal region to attract foreign and domestic investment. In addition, non-state players in the coast could enjoy easy access to the world market. We can expect that the closer a province is from the coast, the greater efforts the provincial government would make to facilitate the expansion of non-state sectors. Thus the measure of provincial reforms may be negatively correlated with the province's distance from a sea port. A province's distance from a sea port can be measured by the distance by railway from the provincial capital to the closest sea port in China. If a province had its own sea port, the distance is coded as zero. The data on the distances comes from Jin and Chen 1996: 134.

The correlation between the provincial reform index and provincial distance from a sea port registers −0.665, reaching a level of statistical significance. Hence the two variables are in a significantly reverse relationship. This is confirmed by figure 7.2. That is to say, the closer

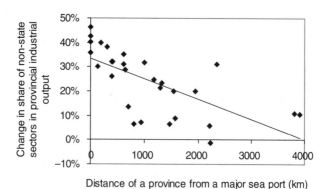

Figure 7.2   Distance from sea port and provincial reform, 1980–1993.

a province was to the coast and a major sea port, the more favorable policies the provincial government would introduce to help the growth of non-state sectors so that they could utilize the provincial access to the world market.

Trade Potential

Policies of the provincial government might also depend on the province's potential to expand trade and attract foreign capital in the course of trade (Howell 1993). The greater the potential, the more steadfastly a province would pursue fast growth of non-state sectors. It followed that provincial leaders would have paid attention to the appeal of their provinces to foreign business and investment. China's provinces varied in their potential in developing trade, largely due to their locations and proximity to nearby advanced economies, such as Hong Kong, Taiwan, Japan, and South Korea (Vogel 1989; Goodman and Feng 1994; Cheung 1998b). As stated in the previous chapter, two economic geographic factors affect a province's trade potential. First, the province's nearest primary potential trade partner and the distance between them; second, the size of this trade partner's economy and more importantly, the volume of imports of this closest trade partner.

I construct the index for provinces' trade potential in the way described in detail in chapter 6 (table 6.3). In the analysis, the index in 1985 is correlated with the measure of provincial reforms (change in the share of non-state sectors in provincial industrial output) between 1978 and 1993. The correlated coefficient is a significantly high 0.585, noticeably above the 0.5 benchmark. It suggested a strong correlation between these two variables. A plot (figure 7.3) confirms that they are indeed related. This finding suggests that a province's trade potential did affect provincial efforts to develop non-state sectors. Provincial government did anticipate the potential external economic returns before introducing reform policies.

Fiscal Arrangements

Scholars suggest that fiscal arrangements could affect provincial incentives for reforms. If fiscal arrangements permitted a province to retain a large portion of the increased fiscal revenue after reforms, the province would actively liberalize and energize the local economy. As the provincial economy expanded rapidly, so did the provincial revenue base. As a result of favorable fiscal arrangements, a province

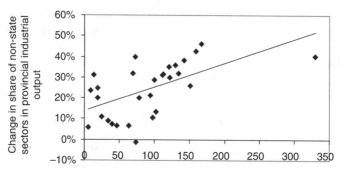

Figure 7.3   Trade potential and provincial reforms, 1978–1993.

could keep a significant portion of soaring revenue income for itself. Hence provincial efforts to promote reforms would be handsomely rewarded. In Oi's term, localities wanted to obtain the rights to residual in order to reap the benefits from reforms (Oi 1999). The center solved this problem of incentives by allowing provinces to share more of revenue income. In the 1980s and 1990s, the central government had reduced its control over budget from 37 percent of national income in 1978 to 22 percent in 1991. In the 1980s, the center introduced successive regimes of dividing revenue with the provinces and increased provincial retention rates. These arrangements stimulated local reform efforts, sometimes even resulting in zealous local efforts to expand the local tax base (Wong, Heady, and Woo 1995: 86; 127–131). Whiting (2001) documented the effects of fiscal arrangements on local reform efforts in townships in the coastal provinces such as Shanghai and Zhejiang. These two provinces, especially Shanghai, were among the main contributors to the central coffer. She suggested that the fiscal arrangement required local governments to be self-financing and led to strong and robust local governmental efforts to promote the expansion of rural non-state enterprises, even including administrative intervention in taxation and bank lending.

Central-local fiscal arrangements, however, varied widely across provinces. As Wei (2000: 47–56) documented, provincial revenue-retention rates differed considerably across provinces between 1980 and 1991. Thus, fiscal incentives for provinces to implement reforms varied. According to the above logic, lower fiscal remittance usually could provide strong incentives for these provinces to pursue reforms, expand their own fiscal resources, and retain much of their revenue income. In contrast, high remittance would dampen a province's incentives for liberalization and reduce resources at its own disposal to finance local reforms, as in the case of Shanghai in the 1980s (Wong, Heady, and Woo 1995: 128). Some scholars may assume that a high remittance rate automatically led to few local efforts to expand non-state sectors (or weaker provincial incentives for reforms). As we shall see, this is not the case.

The above scholars say little about how fiscal arrangements might affect the incentives for subsidized and usually backward provinces to pursue reforms. Even though central subsidies might alleviate the fears of these provinces about fiscal uncertainty after reforms, whether or not central subsidies were sufficient to cover expenses for their basic administrative operation and launch reform initiatives was another matter. Unfortunately, this issue was inadequately explored in the existing literature. Theoretically, central subsidies to backward provinces would work both ways, either by providing fiscal security to the provinces so as to encourage them to liberalize their economy, or increasing their fiscal dependence on the national government and suffocating their reform efforts. We could only tell from the empirical data which scenario was closer to the reality.

In order to examine the relations between fiscal arrangements and provincial reform efforts, I first correlate the measure of provincial reform with provincial revenue remittance rates. Negative remittance rates imply subsidies to provinces from the central government. The correlation coefficient registers a very high 0.771. The plot of the two variables also suggests a very close correlation between the two variables (figure 7.4). It thus appears evident that provinces with high fiscal remittance tended to be liberal in promoting non-state enterprises. Provinces remitting much less or even receiving subsidies from the center were conservative in helping out the non-state economy.

This pattern is surprising and contradicts much of the existing arguments and intuition discussed above. Nevertheless, upon closer analysis, it makes sense in the context of economic conditions. First, provinces that were obliged to remit a large portion of their revenue to the center had to collect a large amount of revenue from their enterprises, including non-state ones. A large and expanding fiscal base would have helped the provinces to achieve this end comfortably. A large non-state economy can satisfy these provinces' need for an expanding tax base. Therefore, heavily remitting provinces were under heavier pressure to push forth the growth of non-state sectors. On the

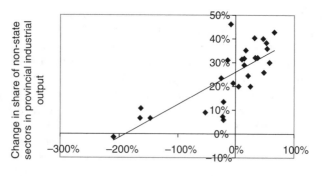

Figure 7.4   Revenue remittance and provincial reforms, 1978–1993.

contrary, provinces remitting a small part of their revenue or receiving central subsidies had no hard quota for remittance and were thus under less pressure to raise revenue. They could simply reply on and use most of their own revenue, and in the case of backward provinces, depended on central subsidies. Second, ironically but understandably, heavily remitting provinces tended to have a strong and dynamic economy, a sizable and expanding tax base, as well as a developed infrastructure, larger markets, and better environment for business. Blessed with greater fiscal income, these provinces were more capable of financing initiatives to help the non-state economy to boom. In contrast, lightly remitting and subsidized provinces tended to have an underdeveloped infrastructure, smaller markets, and less favorable investment and business environment. These provinces also lacked adequate fiscal resources to execute favorable treatment of non-state enterprises. They had limited incentives to break away from the planned economy, promote still small and fragile non-state businesses, and face fiscal uncertainties and possibly grave fiscal consequences. It is likely out of these two reasons that we observe a surprising correlation between provincial remittance rates and provincial reform efforts.

Provincial Leadership

Another possible factor in provincial reform efforts emphasized by the existing literature is provincial leadership. Provincial leaders may be regarded as "hinge leaders" interacting between central and local power networks and exerting influence on local reforms (White 1998a).

Reformist provincial leaders could have actively lobbied central leaders for favorable treatment and policies and to allow bold yet controversial reform policies to go on covertly. On the other hand, conservative provincial leaders might have blocked central efforts to liberalize the provincial economy and could have stifled local reform initiatives (Vogel 1989; Goodman 1997; Cheung 1998b; Cheung, Chung, and Lin 1998; Hendrischke and Feng 1999; Shieh 2000; Tan 2002; Fitzgerald 2002).

To examine the effect of provincial leadership on provincial opening, I correlate the coding on provincial leadership in reforms with the measure of provincial reforms. Again, my coding on eighteen provinces in 1986, 1990, and 1993 is based on available edited volumes on provincial leadership and provincial profiles. They contain useful descriptions of the propensity of provincial leaders toward reforms. As in chapter 6, provincial leadership in these selected years is coded at three levels—1 for conservative, 2 for support for cautious reform or remaining neutral over reform (or bandwagoning), and 3 for being reformist.

Plots are also made to visually present the relation between the change in the share of non-state enterprises in industrial output (the measure of provincial reforms) and provincial leadership (figure 7.5). The correlation coefficient between the average coding of provincial leadership in 1986 and 1990 with the measure of provincial reforms during 1978–1993 was 0.442, somewhat below the benchmark of statistical significance. Nationwide reformist provincial leadership thus had a positive yet insignificant effect on provincial reforms efforts.

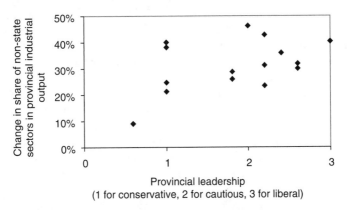

Figure 7.5   Provincial leadership and reform in provinces, 1978–1993.

National Patronage

Studies in English and Chinese on China's provinces, discussed in the previous chapters, suggest that ties between provincial leaders and national leaders could provide the former a sense of political security in pursuing reforms. Clientele relations or political connections play an important role in Chinese politics for a variety of reasons: An official's formal base gives no reliable defense for one's career (Dittmer 1995: 12); the Chinese political environment engendered psychological insecurity (Pye 1995); constant factional conflicts occurred even in the reforms era and ended with unpredictable outcomes (Baum 1996); the rules and norms are inadequately institutionalized, leaving traditions and personal ties a prominent role in politics (Dittmer 2000; Fukui 2000). It follows that personal connections with central leaders gave provincial leaders political security to pursue their course of reforms without risking their political careers. Should political troubles arise, their national patrons would come to their aid. Thus, the more national patrons a province had, the greater political security it had in pursuing its own course of reforms, and the more liberal it would be in promoting non-state enterprises.[7]

Using the data on the provincial working experience of the Politburo members and the "eight elders" discussed in chapters 3 and 4, I construct a data base on national patrons for provinces. As in chapter 6, I identify the province where a member of the Politburo or the "eight elders" had worked for the longest time as the province for which s/he served as a patron. Given the prominence of personal ties in Chinese politics suggested in the literature on Chinese leaders, a national leader might use the province as a local political base to support his national status and might be obliged to serve to a varying extent the interests of the province. Table 6.2 lists the number of national patrons each province had.

I correlate the measure of provincial reform during 1978–1993 with the number of national patrons between 1987 and 1993. The correlation coefficient was 0.365. Although it is positive, it is statistically insignificant. Figure 7.6 also depicts a weak relationship between the two variables. Thus national patrons merely weakly encouraged provincial efforts to promote non-state enterprises. This may suggest that national patrons fail to dictate provincial reforms throughout the nation, though they might exert an important role in opening up the provinces. This finding runs parallel to that of an extensive study of mobility of provincial leadership during 1949–1998. Bo (2002: 111–12; 123–24) found that provincial leaders with central connections were

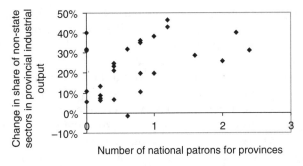

Figure 7.6   National patrons and provincial reforms, 1978–1993.

just more likely to be transferred, instead of being promoted. This career mobility might have prevented them from pursuing a stable policy.

Provincial Bureaucracy and Sectors with Stakes in Reforms

Employees in the bureaucracy, light industry, and non-state sectors might have particular interests and influence over provincial reforms. They will be generally referred to as three sectors or clusters. As to be elaborated below, reforms directly affected jobs and revenue of these three clusters; these clusters possessed considerable clouts; they generated employment, controlled economic or fiscal resources, and possessed access to the government. Thus they could influence policy making.

Employees in government and political associations (that is, parties and mass organizations) were the most influential segments. Serving in the government and associations that were involved in policy making, they could voice their preferences easily in the policy-making process and could hinder or obstruct policies. One could also hypothesize that many officials owed their careers to the continuing survival of state enterprises and to slow reform. Many officials directly supervised SOEs, or worked in associations (such as labor unions) affiliated with SOEs. Should these enterprises go bankrupt, run heavy losses, and be even shut down, officials would lose their jobs. In addition, an increasingly marketized economy might necessitate reform of the government, including streamlining of agencies, as well as replacement of inadequately educated and close-minded officials with young, well-educated and open-minded officials. Bureaucrats might thus want reforms to proceed slowly in order to protect their jobs.

As stated in chapter 6 and summarized in table 6.4, out of the fifty-seven bureaus between 1981 and 1988, thirty-five bureaus would prefer slower reforms partly because they were related to sectors and industries that would suffer from reforms. The other twenty-two bureaus supervised sectors that would benefit from accelerated reforms. These provincial bureaus would support liberal measures. Between 1988 and 1993, the conservatively oriented agencies totaled nineteen, and those that would benefit from reforms amounted to eleven. Reform-resisting bureaus outnumbered reform-supporting ones. Administrative and Party bureaucracies also varied in size across provinces. In provinces with a large bureaucracy, officials would have a stake in the existing economic arrangement, and would be more reluctant to support quick dismantling of the command economy. Therefore, we could expect these provinces to adopt more restrictive policies toward non-state enterprises.

Other than officials, two other sets of sectors, namely, light industry versus heavy industry and SOEs versus non-state enterprises, would also have a heavy stake in reforms. A province's industry can be categorized in two ways. First, it can be divided into light versus heavy industry. Second, it can be categorized into state and non-state sectors. When one sector in either set was sizable, the size of the other sector in the same set would then be limited. For example, if light industry was relatively large in a province, heavy industry would be relatively small. The same thing can be said of the state sector vis-à-vis non-state ones.

As stated in chapter 6, with the progress of reforms, the previously overexpanded heavy industry would be reduced, and the manufacturing of previously depressed labor-intensive light industrial goods in China would grow (Shirk 1985: 207). Meanwhile, benefiting from stronger enforcement of property rights, greater incentives for managers and employees, and greater flexibility in employment and responding to market signals, non-state sectors would do better than the state sector after reform. The former would support reform whereas the latter would resist it. These sectors could find official representatives at related bureaus. As indicated in table 6.4, between 1981 and 1988, seventeen bureaus supervised and represented heavy industry. Between 1988 and 1993, the number of bureaus was reduced to seven. In these two periods, the number of bureaus representing state planning apparatus and SOEs totaled eighteen and twelve, respectively. In these two periods, the bureaus overseeing economic reforms, trade, and markets and representing non-state enterprises totaled seventeen and nine, respectively. These sectors had the resources and institutional channels to influence provincial reforms. Therefore, provinces with large heavy industry or a large state sector might pursue slower reforms and those with sizable light industry or large non-state sectors might embrace faster reforms.

To test the effects of these sectors in provincial reforms, I correlate the measure of provincial reforms between 1978 and 1993 with indicators of strengths of the size of the bureaucracy, light industry, and non-state sectors. The size of the bureaucracy is measured by the average share of government agencies and political associations in labor force in 1987, 1989, and 1991; the size of light industry is measured by the share of light industry in labor force in state and collective industry of 1991; the size of non-state sectors is measured by the share of non-state sectors in non-agricultural labor force in 1987. It is worthwhile to note that the size of light industry and non-state sectors is measured by *labor force* in one year and that provincial reforms are measured by *the change* in the share of non-state sectors in provincial *industrial output* between 1978 and 1993. *Therefore, these two measures do not automatically correlate with each other.*

In order to capture the causal relation from a sector's strength to provincial policies toward non-state enterprises, data of a sector's strength usually come from years earlier than that of provincial reform (which ended in 1993 in this study). Again, 0.5 is a benchmark of statistical significance. The results are presented in table 7.2 and figures 7.7–7.9.

The correlation coefficient of the bureaucracy with provincial reforms only registers −0.251, far below the 0.5 benchmark. Thus, despite that the negative sign implies that a smaller bureaucracy led to more reforms, the correlation between the size of bureaucracy and provincial reforms is statistically insignificant. The size of bureaucracy did not have a noticeable effect on provincial reforms. This is also confirmed in figure 7.7. An exception is the case of Beijing that has the largest bureaucracy in the country, which accounted for about 6 percent of the employment. Beijing could be regarded as an outlier. After Beijing is excluded, the correlation of the bureaucracy with provincial reforms rises to 0.448, yet still noticeably below the 0.5 benchmark.

The correlation coefficient between the share of light industry in industrial labor force and provincial reform reaches 0.67; that between the share of non-state sectors in non-agricultural labor and provincial reform amounts to an even higher 0.733. Both coefficients are much higher than the 0.5 benchmark. Figures 7.8–7.9 demonstrate that

Table 7.2 Correlation coefficients of provincial reform with likely factors

Independent Variables (IV)	Measure of IV	Correlation with provincial reform (change in non-state sectors)
Provincial distance from Beijing	Distance of provincial capital from Beijing by rail (if N.A., waterway and highway)	−0.302
Distance from a sea port	Distance of a province from a major sea port	**−0.665**
Potential for trade with nearby external economies, 1985	Nearby foreign trade partner (NFTP)'s foreign trade volume/ Distance from NFTP, 1985	**0.585**
Fiscal arrangements	Share of remittance to the center of provincial revenue	**0.771**
Provincial leadership	Coding of leadership—1 conservative, 2 cautious, and 3 reformist	0.442
National patrons	Number of patrons for a province in central leadership	0.365
Bureaucracy	Share of government agencies and political associations (including parties) in labor force	−0.251
Labor in light industry	Share of light industry in employment in state and collective industrial enterprises	**0.67**
Labor in non-state sectors	Share of non-state sectors in non-agricultural labor	**0.733**
Size of non-state sectors in 1978	Share of non-state sectors in industrial output in 1978	0.419
National opening of the province	Share of open areas in provincial population	**0.535**

Note: Bolds stand for statistical significant correlation.

indeed the correlations are apparently strong. Specifically, the above data analyses suggest the following finding. Larger employment in light industry and non-state sectors did seem to induce more liberal provincial policies toward the non-state economy (table 7.2 and figures 7.8 and 7.9). Provincial leaders and officials apparently took into account the size of light industry and non-state sectors in employment and acted in accordance with the interests of employees in these sectors.

This pattern of provincial reform has some parallel with the national government's promotion of provincial reforms. The national leader

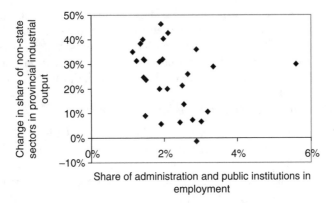

Figure 7.7 Size of provincial bureaucracy and provincial reforms, 1978–1993.

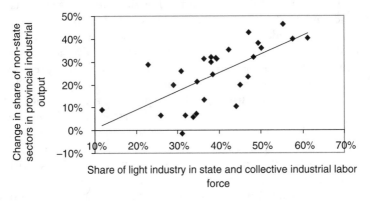

Figure 7.8 Employment in light industry and provincial reforms, 1978–1993.

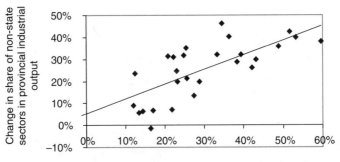

Figure 7.9 Employment in non-state sectors and provincial reforms, 1978–1993.

opened up earlier the provinces with larger non-state sectors that would benefit from opening. The center tried to rally support for liberal policies from sectoral groups in opening up the provinces. When provincial government implemented reform policies, they paid attention not only to the influence of non-state sectors, but also to that of light industry.

Path Dependency of Non-State Sectors

It has been suggested that reforms in liberal areas in China followed a trajectory of path dependence. For example, Wuxi, Shanghai, and Wenzhou inherited political and economic resources as well as forms of property rights from the commune era. Approaches to property rights and economic reform in these areas bore birthmarks of the past era (Whiting 2001: 270–73). In a similar vein, one may postulate that China's provincial reform is path dependent in the sense that a province endowed with larger non-state sectors at the beginning of the reforms would adopt liberal policies, helping non-state sectors to expand much faster and grow larger. In a way this hypothesis assumes that the dynamics of development of non-state sectors in pre-reform years could somehow carry its momentum in the reform era.

In order to test this path-dependent hypothesis, the size of non-state sectors in 1978 (measured by the share of non-state sectors in provincial industrial output) is correlated with the change in the size of non-state sectors in the subsequent fifteen years (1978–1993). The correlation coefficient is 0.419. Although carrying a positive sign, the coefficient is statistically insignificant. This finding is confirmed by figure 7.10. Therefore, provincial promotion of non-state sectors at the national level apparently did not follow a path-dependent trajectory.

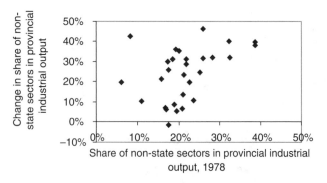

Figure 7.10   Pre-reform size of non-state sectors and provincial reforms, 1978–1993.

Effects of National Policies on the Provincial Policies

A question that naturally follows from these test findings is "Did the national policies affect the provincial policies?" Provinces might have also adopted these policies because the center directed them to do so. Given the highly centralized power structure in China, the center could have acted as an "umpire" of major provincial policies and could have pressured the provinces to adopt particular policies. On the other hand, the center's supervision of the provincial policies, however, might have been complicated by the complexity and difficulty of policing thirty provinces, determining actual provincial policies, and identifying and imposing penalty on the provincial leaders and officials who deviated from central directives.

I choose the national government's opening of the provinces to the world economy, which has been analyzed, as a measure of national policies toward individual provinces. This measure is employed and described in chapter 6. It could demonstrate the variation in the center's handling of individual provinces. In addition, the national selection of open areas could affect a wide range of provincial reform initiatives, including those regarding foreign, private, and collective firms. The higher the value of the measure, the greater the extent of opening the center bestowed upon the province. The measure of national opening of provinces is correlated with that of provincial reforms. The correlation coefficient is 0.535, suggesting a statistically significant correlation. Figure 7.11 also indicates a positive correlation.

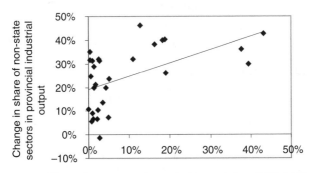

Figure 7.11   National opening of provinces and provincial reforms, 1978–1993.

National designation of open areas in the provinces seems to have led to *more liberal provincial policies toward non-state sectors.* Therefore, by discretely opening up provinces the central government helped to set the pace for provincial reform.

Conclusion

Provincial reform efforts were conditioned by a number of economic geographic, sectoral and political factors. These factors include coastal access, potential for trade with nearby external economies, fiscal conditions and pressures for remittances, employment in sectors that would benefit from reforms, namely light industry and non-state sectors, as well as national opening of provinces.

Proximity to the coast, good access to sea ports, and proximity to large external trading economies obviously invited provinces to undertake initiatives favorable for non-state sectors. These favorable geoeconomic endowments reduced transportation costs, helped to strengthen a province's link with the world market and overseas business community, and were conducive to handsome returns from provincial reforms. Therefore, provincial governments apparently were conscious about provinces' endowments and their consequential effects on the growth of non-state sectors. Their efforts to promote these sectors were contingent on these geoeconomic endowments.

Furthermore, fiscal conditions of a province also affected its efforts to expand non-state sectors. Provinces with abundant fiscal resources, which usually were major fiscal contributors to the center, were more proactive in supporting the expansion of the dynamic non-state economy. They also had sufficient revenue to undertake measures paving the way for non-state economic activities, such as bank lending, tax exemption, low fees for land usage, and administrative services. They could also undertake infrastructural construction to reduce transportation costs for non-state business. On the contrary, provinces with fiscal difficulties were usually those that remitted lightly to the center or even received subsidies from the center. These provinces lacked the necessary fiscal resources to undertake the above mentioned favorable measures for non-state sectors.

In addition and ironically, as rich provinces were assigned considerable fiscal remittance tasks, these provinces were probably under greater pressure to expand their fiscal base and to promote non-state sectors. With light remittance tasks and even central subsidies, poor provinces did not feel an intense pressure to create new tax bases and to promote new sectors. This finding seems to contradict scholars' heavy emphasis on low remittance as an incentive for local reforms. Under the Chinese political system, national leaders can decide upon the promotion and demotion of provincial leaders single-handedly without going through open public elections. According to a comprehensive study, fiscal remittance was one of the two most important factors in determining provincial leaders' upward mobility (Bo 1996). National leaders hold provincial leaders responsible for the fiscal remittance of their provinces. Thus leaders of rich provinces would naturally see to it that provincial remittance task be dutifully fulfilled in order to secure their careers and advancement.

Surprisingly, reformist provincial leadership as defined in the existing literature was found to have an insignificant effect on provincial reform nationwide. Nor did national patrons for a province affect provincial reform orientation. In addition, the size of bureaucracy also neither helped nor obstructed the expansion of non-state sectors.

The employment in light industry and non-state sectors that would benefit from economic liberalization seems to induce provincial reforms. It is likely that provinces adopted liberal policies in order to satisfy the demand from labor in these liberal sectors and create employment opportunities in these sectors for numerous job hunters. However, the size of non-state sectors at the beginning of the period of reforms does not affect provincial reforms in the subsequent years. Therefore, provincial reforms seemed not to be noticeably path-dependent.

Finally, national policies did shape provincial reforms. By introducing the Open Policy, the central authority could motivate provinces to act to promote the non-state economy. National opening of the provinces increased external resources and opportunities that provinces could utilize in promoting their market-oriented non-state enterprises. Provincial areas designated by the center as open to external business were usually given greater authority to approve foreign business up to a certain size. These areas would have greater leverage in attracting foreign investment, promoting external trade, and even conducting local reforms.

In sum, some of the variables that are believed to have affected provincial reforms, such as distance from Beijing, central fiscal concession, provincial leadership, and national patrons for provinces, did not appear to have contributed to provincial reforms nationwide. Coastal access, trade potential, size and probably influence of pro-reform sectors, and the national opening of the provinces appear to have exerted significant influence over provincial reform efforts. The logic of provincial reforms is multifaceted, involving central policies, fiscal pressures, local sectoral support for reforms, as well as potential economic gains conditioned by geography and local economic circumstances.

8

Divergent Reform Paths in Two Provinces

Our understanding of the actual process of reforms in China's provinces can be enhanced by an in-depth case study of selected provinces. This chapter compares the evolution of reform policies in Shandong and Jilin provinces during 1978–1994. Although sharing many similar economic conditions prior to 1978, the two provinces witnessed divergent reform policies after the mid-1980s. This chapter finds that fiscal resources and arrangements, the provincial bureaucracy, provincial leadership, the size of non-state sectors, coastal access, external trade potential, and national opening of the provinces accounted for their divergence. This chapter will first discuss the strategy for the comparative case study, introduce the profiles of Jilin and Shandong Provinces, and then compare policies toward non-state sectors in the two provinces. Finally, it will examine in detail the causes of their divergent reform policies.

Methodology for Comparative Studies

Strengths of hypothesis testing are obvious when the number of cases is relatively large. Sound statistical analyses can reap the benefits of rigorous theoretical reasoning, unbiased case selection, and a solid conclusion based on a complete set of data. The tests in the previous chapter help pinpoint main political-economic causes for differences in reforms in the twenty-eight provinces between 1978 and 1994. Hypothesis tests may have their weaknesses, especially a lack of information on the empirical process (Leamer 1983: 38–39). In this case, the hypothesis test in chapters 6 and 7 have not told us enough about how responsible factors generated divergent reforms in the provinces. Careful empirical studies can address unanswered questions about the empirical process (Rogowski 1995).

Although discussed long ago by classical writers such as John Stuart Mill, controlled comparison is relatively new in comparative politics. Until one or two decades ago political comparative scholars (including China scholars) still ignored controlled comparison and even preferred to study cases of a similar dependent variable. For example, scholars of revolution only investigate countries where revolution had broken out. This selection bias leads to either underestimating of the effect of the explanatory variable, or overestimating of the significance and generality of the findings (Geddes 1990; King, Keohane, and Verba 1993: chapter 4; Collier and Mahoney 1996: 88). For this reason, this chapter includes a case where the observed event (fast reforms in Shangdong) occurred, as well as an instance where the event failed to occur despite several similar conditions (slow reforms in Jilin).

Provinces for Comparison

Shandong was a populous coastal province in northern China, south of Beijing and Hebei. Jilin is an inland province in Northeast (Manchuria), bordering with North Korea and Siberia of Russia on the east.

Shandong and Jilin shared a number of similar conditions. At the very beginning of reforms, both provinces adopted similar loan and tax policies toward *the primary non-state industry (NSI)*, namely, rural or urban collective industry. They are reflected in similar income tax rates on collective sectors between 1980 and 1986 and very similar shares of rural enterprises and collective industry in the loans from the Agricultural Banks and Rural Credit Cooperatives from 1980–1982 (table 8.1 and figures 8.1–8.2).

With the passage of time, especially after the mid-1980s, reforms in Shandong started to outpace that in Jilin. The share of collective sectors in the loans in its agricultural banking system in Shandong had risen above that in the country and well above that in Jilin since 1985 (figure 8.1) and continued through to 1994. From the mid-1980s onward, Shandong also started to reduce taxes on the collective sector much further than did Jilin (table 8.1 and figure 8.2). Shandong had also adopted more favorable taxation policies toward private and foreign enterprises than that in Jilin since the early 1980s (figure 8.3).

Surprisingly, in the early years of the reforms, with the exception of coastal access, Shandong did not enjoy better conditions than Jilin

Table 8.1 Tax rates on major types of non-state enterprises in Shandong and Jilin

Year	1985 (%)	1986 (%)	1990 (%)	1993 (%)
Tax rates on rural industry (Ratio of national, provincial, and local taxes to output of rural industry)				
Nationwide	5.6	5.4	5.4	4.3
Shandong	4.2	4.3	3.5	3.1
Jilin	5.6	5.6	5.9	5.6

Year	1980 (%)	1985 (%)	1990 (%)	1993 (%)
Income tax rates on the collective sector (Ratio of taxes to output of collective-owned industry)				
Nationwide	4.3	4.3	1.3	0.5
Shandong	3.5	3.0	0.6	0.2
Jilin	2.6	3.3	1.8	0.8

Year		1990 (%)	1993 (%)
Income tax rates on the private sector (Ratio of taxes to sales of individual- or private-owned industry)			
Nationwide		0.9	0.7
Shandong		0.2	0.1
Jilin		0.7	0.3

Year		1990 (%)	1993 (%)
Income tax rates on the foreign sector (Ratio of taxes to the amount of foreign investment)			
Nationwide		5.6	1.4
Shandong		1.5	0.4
Jilin		2.9	0.8

Source: Database on political economy of Chinese provinces. See data sources and bibliography for details.

(figures 8.4–8.5). Jilin possessed higher levels of industrialization and income, a better infrastructure (reflected in a higher density of roads, railroads, and waterway), a more literate labor force, and a smaller population. In 1987, Jilin had the fifth largest amount of arable land per capita and the highest grain yield per capita in China, far surpassing those of Shandong (Wang 1989: 424–25).

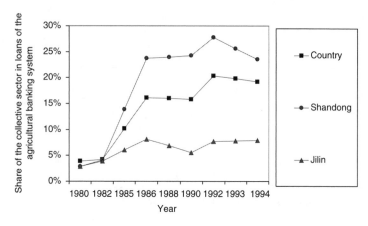

Figure 8.1   Bank loans to the collective sector in Shandong, Jilin, and the country.

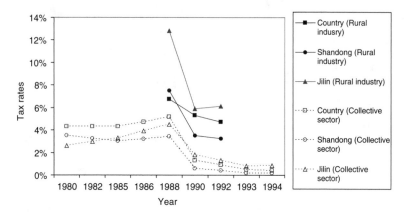

Figure 8.2   Total tax rates on rural industry and income tax rates on the collective sectors in Shandong, Jilin, and the country.

Neither province possessed any clear advantage in other aspects. Both had considerable natural resources for industrialization, including minerals for producing construction materials like marble and graphite, agricultural resources for light industry, as well as energy resources such as reserve of oil shale, oil fields, and coal mines, though Shandong had a slight edge in this aspect (Wang 1989: 5–14, 46–8; Shi and Hao 1990: 197–267).

The relative strengths of both provinces in other sectors do not explain the contrast in their reforms either. Jilin had a productive

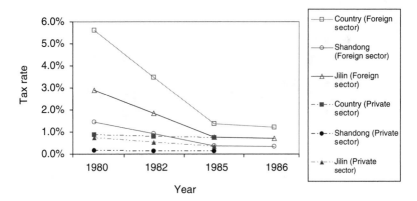

Figure 8.3 Income tax rates on the private and foreign sectors in Shandong, Jilin, and the country.

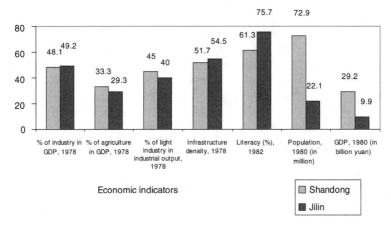

Figure 8.4 Economic conditions of Shandong and Jilin.

agriculture, as well as several nationally prominent industrial sectors, such as transportation equipment, petroleum chemicals, lumber processing, paper-making, coal-mining, grape-wine-making, and food-processing. Leading industrial products in Shandong, on the other hand, included petroleum chemicals, coal, automobiles, locomotives, tractors, watches, wine, paper, machinery, food processing, and textile (Wang 1989: 48, 210–17; Shi and Hao 1990: 201–67; Fu et al. 1992: 31–32, 55–56).

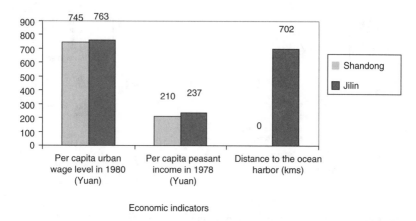

Figure 8.5   Additional economic conditions in Shandong and Jilin.

Shandong's obvious advantage was its harbors, including Qingdao and Yantai. Jilin would have to use a large harbor in Dalian of Liaoning, which was 702 kilometers by railway from Changchun, the capital of Jilin. Therefore, the sources of differing reforms in Jilin and Shandong may largely lie elsewhere. As table 8.2 suggests, several factors that explain varying reforms across the provinces in chapter 7 might have caused faster reform in Shandong than in Jilin. They included fiscal resources and arrangements, provincial bureaucracy, the size of non-state sectors, coastal proximity, and national opening of the provinces. Unlike the findings of chapter 7, provincial leadership also played a role in varying reform efforts in Shandong and Jilin.

Focus and Data

The following sections will investigate the evolution of policies promulgated by the provincial government as well as the execution of these policies in Shandong and Jilin regarding each non-state sector—rural enterprises, foreign and joint ventures, urban collective enterprises, and the private sector. Information for the case study comes from the following sources: my interviews in 1998 with the officials in Shandong and Jilin who were informed about reform policies, documents by provincial governmental agencies, publications on these provinces written by provincial officials or policy specialists, and official yearbooks of the provinces. Most of the statistics come from *Statistical Yearbook of China, A Collection of Historical Statistics of*

Table 8.2 Possible factors in Shandong's and Jilin's reform policies

Year	1982	1985	1990	1992
Central-provincial fiscal arrangement (share of provincial remittance to or central subsidies (negative data) in provincial revenue; percentages)				
Shandong	51.1	38.8	2.6	1.5
Jilin	−25.1	−18.3	−2.1	−1.9
Nationwide	−25.5	−14.3	−3.4	−2.2

Year	1980	1986	1990	1993
Governmental revenue balance (million yuan)(Share of revenue income in parentheses)				
Shandong	1804 (37.5%)	−579 (−9.3%)	−1474 (−13.5%)	604 (3.1%)
Jilin	−293 (−20.4%)	−2060 (−69.8%)	−2099 (−41.4%)	−2329 (−29.2%)
Nationwide	−6890 (−5.9%)	−8290 (−3.9%)	−14649 (−5.0%)	−29335 (−6.7%)

Year	1985	1987	1990	1992
Size of provincial bureaucracy (share in provincial labor force; percentages)				
Shandong	1.2	1.4	1.4	1.6
Jilin	2.2	2.3	2.5	2.7
Nationwide	1.6	1.8	1.9	1.9

Year	1980	1985	1989	1992
Size of non-state sectors (share in non-agricultural employment)				
Shandong	16.5	35.1	36	36.9
Jilin	20.2	26.4	24.3	24
Distance from the ocean harbor (kms)				
Shandong	0			
Jilin	702			

Year	1980	1986	1990	1994
Nationally selected open areas (their shares in provincial industrial output; percentage)				
Shandong	0	13.7	55.4	68.1
Jilin	0	0	23.3	32.7
Nationwide	0.5	18.6	30.2	39.4

Year	1980	1984	1989	1992
Number of big cities declared open by the center				
Shandong	0	2	6	7
Jilin	0	0	1	3

Source: Database on political economy of Chinese provinces. See data sources and bibliography for details.

China's Provinces, China's Regional Economy, and *Shandong Yearbook, Jilin Yearbook,* as well as statistical yearbooks of the two provinces. It was difficult to interview officials in charge of non-state sectors at the early stage of reforms, for many of them had retired, or had been transferred to other departments. Whenever interviews do not supply adequate information, inferences will be drawn from local published sources. They are the best methods available.

Evolution of Policies toward Non-State Sectors in Shandong and Jilin

Policies toward Rural Enterprises

In the 1978–1980 period both Shandong and Jilin conformed to the center's policies by declaring the expansion of rural enterprises an important task (ECLAJP 1992: 3–4). In 1979, local governments in Jilin helped rural enterprises to obtain 80 million yuan for investment, an increase by 80 percent from the previous year (ibid.: 191). In 1978, the People's Bank in Shandong started to lend to rural enterprises on a regular basis. In March 1979, the Shandong authority exempted new rural enterprises from taxes for three years, except for those producing cigarettes, wine, and cotton yarns (ECLASP 1996: 597–98).

From 1981–1983 Jilin and Shandong also followed closely the center's order to curb the growth of the enterprises and Jilin acted more eagerly. In Jilin the state industrial sector even openly accused rural enterprises of drawing raw materials, energy, and funds away. In response, governmental agencies in Jilin barred rural enterprises from obtaining urban construction projects, processing agricultural goods, opening business outside the county of their origin, and even obtaining a license. Investment funds for rural enterprises shrank, or grew modestly at best (Du 1993: 5; interviews). A number of localities even shut down many of their rural enterprises. In contrast, Shandong imposed moderate restrictions on rural enterprises. Tax exemption was rescinded, high taxes were imposed on enterprises that produced consumer goods in strong demand, and bank lending was tightened (ECLASP 1996: 153–54).

After 1984 the gap in the reform policies in the two provinces widened. In early 1984, the center called for renewed growth of these enterprises. In response, the Jilin Provincial Government (JPG) moderately increased bank loans, facilitated recruitment of personnel by rural enterprises, and cut taxes on the enterprises. In 1986, provincial leaders called for a doubling of the output of rural enterprises by 1990, and relaxed control over their entry into the markets. Local governments stepped up assistance for rural enterprises (Du ibid.). Considerable entry barriers, however, still existed.

Shandong went a large step further. Bank lending had become much more generous and taxes had been kept much lower in Shandong than in Jilin. Shandong officials tried to expand rural enterprises also through promoting exports of rural enterprises and cooperation between these and other enterprises, as well as provisioning substantial governmental services in labor training, information, research and technological upgrading, and developmental planning. In 1986, Shandong leaders signified a fundamental shift in their developmental policies by declaring the expansion of rural enterprises a key development strategy (*China Rural Enterprise Yearbook* 1988–1995; Wang 1989: 111–17, 185–94, 409; SSB 1990b, 1996b; ECLASP 1997: 424–29).

These dramatic changes that occurred in Shandong had much to do with reformist leadership. In 1984, Shandong leaders realized that their conservative policies during the 1981–1983 retrenchment eroded the advantageous position of Shandong's rural industry in the nation. Jiangsu Province had the most developed rural enterprises in China at the beginning of reforms. In 1978, rural enterprises in Jiangsu and Shandong employed 3.25 and 3.23 million peasants and generated 6.29 and 4.85 billion yuan in 1980 prices, respectively. The ratios of employment and revenue income of rural enterprises in Shandong and Jiangsu in 1978 were respectively, 0.994 : 1 and 0.771 : 1, indicating that Shandong was not far behind of the national champion. By 1983, after Shandong closely toed the center's retrenchment policies between 1981 and 1983, the ratio dropped to 0.878 : 1 and 0.593 : 1, respectively (Wang 1989: 186–87; SSB 1990b). Disappointed with the results, Shandong leaders decided to keep a step ahead of the country in reforms in the following years while implementing the center's directives.

Between 1989 and 1991 policies toward non-state sectors in the two provinces were in a sharper contrast. Shandong adopted positive retrenchment only in 1990 by improving the sectoral composition and management of TVEs. Shandong leaders used this "stone" of retrenchment to "kill two birds"—show its compliance with the center's policies while positioning rural enterprises for further expansion. In 1991 Shandong leaders decisively expanded rural enterprises and improved their property rights. Jilin, in contrast, pursued retrenchment closely between 1989 and 1991. In 1991, widespread hostility toward rural industry even caused deficiencies in production inputs for rural firms throughout the province (Du 1993: 7). As Jilin joined the national reform expansion between 1992 and 1994 by rekindling favorable treatment of rural enterprises, Shandong furthered its assistance to TVEs in upgrading their management and technology.

Policies toward Foreign Direct Investment

The first joint venture in Jilin was established in 1984. Jilin made two noticeable drives to attract FDI in 1986 and 1988. In 1986, Jilin held trade talks and sent 78 delegations abroad to initiate trade or gather trade information. In 1988, a new Provincial Party Secretary called for "all-directional opening." As a result, five open economic zones were established. After a sharp downturn in 1989, Jilin leaders reaffirmed their commitment to the introduction of FDI during 1990–1991, and set up another developmental zone for FDI in 1991. In a reform drive during 1992–1994, Jilin modified its guideline for FDI by introducing a series of initiatives. The foreign sector was declared one of the four major forms of ownership. A large area that covered the most important cities was designated as an open region. Jilin leaders stressed improving the official mindset about opening and infrastructure, and called for an innovative program of cooperation with South Korea, Mongolia, Russia, and North Korea along the borders.

A number of factors, however, obstructed these initiatives of the Open Policy. They included a prevalently bureaucratic work style, fledgling rural firms that could not play an active role in absorbing FDI and exporting goods, the fact that many state enterprises, with the exception of the automobile industry, were indifferent to and unattractive for FDI, and the center's late selection of open cities in Jilin in 1992.

Shandong did benefit from the center's early selection of open cities in the provinces. In 1984, the center granted two harbor cities in Shandong a status of "coastal open cities." In late 1987, the State Council was reported to make Shandong the primary province to handle nongovernmental and economic contact with South Korea (Chung 1998: 272). Similar to Jilin, Shandong authority has started to make systemic efforts to introduce FDI since 1986. Shandong Government promulgated an impressive set of favorable regulations toward FDI in 1986 and 1988. In 1987 and 1988 Shandong leaders called for further opening and a greater inflow of FDI with a sense of urgency (*Shandong Yearbook* 1988: 322, 1989: 383; Chung 1998: 266).

In each year between 1989 and 1994, Shandong continued to announce favorable policies toward foreign investors, improve the infrastructure, and hold trade fairs or trade talks. Shandong differed substantially from Jilin in several major aspects, especially after 1988. First, Shandong was *more consistent* in its policies. Unlike Jilin, Shandong did not retract from its embrace of foreign capital, even in 1989 and 1990. Second, Shandong took earlier and more effective measures to combat the bureaucratic work style, liberalize officials' mentality, and materialize announced policies regarding foreign enterprises. As early as 1986, Shandong formed a coordinating agency to speed up the approval of FDI projects. In each year between 1988 and 1994, Shandong leaders emphasized improving the work of the management office of open economic zones. In contrast, Jilin's bureaucracy was proportionally much larger than that in Shandong, and more assertive in maintaining its old-style and redundant procedures and protecting state enterprises in order to ensure its existence and revenue base, namely, state enterprises.

Policies toward the Urban Collective Sector (UCS)

The UCS was relatively larger in Jilin than in Shandong. Around 1986, it accounted for 14.9 percent of total industrial output and 70.4 percent of collective industrial output in Jilin (*Jilin Yearbook* 1987: 380; SSB 1996b: 375), and 11.6 percent and 43.8 percent in Shandong, respectively (*Shandong Yearbook* 1989: 482; SSB 1996b: 559). Most of the UCS was in light industry.

During 1978–1985, the development of urban collective firms in both provinces had run into stumbling blocks (Jin 1985; Cheng et al. 1989). The primary obstacle for urban collective enterprises (UCEs) in Jilin was short-sighted imitation of management in state enterprises, and the secondary obstacle was the conversion of these enterprises from light into heavy industrial production. The largest detriment for the growth of UCEs in Shandong was forceful take-over by local governments.

The pre-reform system accorded state ownership and heavy industry a central economic role and provided them with relatively abundant material, human, and financial resources. Employees in state-owned heavy industry enjoyed higher incomes, greater job security, and higher reputation than did those of collective light industrial firms. This was especially true in Jilin where state enterprises were much larger (Jin 1985).

The state sector was smaller in Shandong. The conception of superiority of state enterprises was also less prevalent. On the contrary, urban collective light industrial firms were more productive in Shandong than those in Jilin, as an employee produced an output averaging 13,144 yuan in Shandong in 1986, compared to 7,875 yuan in Jilin. The firms in Shandong also earned a large amount of hard currency through exports. Local governments in Shandong preyed on them in order to expand their revenue base.

In the following years, both provinces coped with their respective problems. To enforce property rights of UCEs, Shandong Provincial Government (SPG) surveyed the property of UCEs in 1987 and certified the property in the following years. Between 1987 and 1994 the SPG also helped UCEs to improve management, upgrade products and technology, train employees, and increase exports (*Shandong Yearbook* 1986: 293–94, 1987: 408). In nationwide post-Tiananmen retrenchment of 1989–1991 Shandong leaders declared their commitment to liberalization, boosting the confidence of officials as well as managers and employees of UCEs in expanding the UCS. As a result, the annual growth of the output of the USC accelerated from 7.1 percent in the 1981–1985 period, to 19.9 percent in the 1986–1991 period, and 21.7 percent from 1992–1994 (ibid. 1986–1995).

Jilin Province took smaller steps in fostering the growth of the UCS. It introduced the contractual system in UCEs in 1986, and promoted other incentive mechanisms in UCEs in the following years. In 1992, Jilin leaders combined the bureaus that supervised, respectively, state and collective light industries in order to reduce redundant officials and factory facilities and increase the scale of production. Not until 1994 and seven years after Shandong did Jilin survey collective property.

Several obstacles continued to obstruct the growth of the UCS in Jilin. First, state banks viewed state enterprises as their main clients, and refused to lend to collective firms because of a lack of the state's sponsorship, as well as these enterprises' apparently outdated equipment and facilities and low profile (interviews in September 1998). Second, managers of UCEs still upheld the pre-reform developmental strategy of producing most accessories in their own firms and disregarding specialization and economies of scale (*Jilin Yearbook* 1991: 298). Employees in the collective sector still admired those of state enterprises and were not motivated. Third, Jilin leaders followed in close step the center's retrenchment between 1989 and 1991, and clamped down on the growth of the UCS. Fourth, after the two bureaus of light industry were combined, efficient UCEs had to live with inefficient state enterprises and had fewer incentives for growth and efficiency (ibid. 1994: 288). As a result, light industrial output grew at a decent annual rate of 8.4 percent between 1981 and 1989. This growth rate, however, dropped to below 6 percent between 1990 and 1991 and fluctuated around 2.5–6.5 percent between 1992 and 1994.

Policies toward the Private Sector

The initial years (1978–1983). Private business was negligibly small in both provinces, yet was slightly larger in Shandong than in Jilin. In 1978, private business accounted for 0.96 percent of GDP in Shandong and 0.82 percent in Jilin (*Shandong Yearbook* 1987: 249; SSB 1996: 546). Overall, Shandong acted earlier and more consistently than did Jilin in reversing the Maoist prohibition of private business. As the center relaxed its control over the economy in 1978, unemployment soared to 6.9 percent in 1978 and 5.8 percent in 1980, greatly troubling cities in Jilin. Concerned with the problem, governmental agencies in Jilin thus adopted flexible regulations toward the private sector in 1980 (ECLAJP 1991: 109; SSB 1996b: 132). When the private sector was winning their competition against state enterprises in 1981, most localities turned against further expansion of IHEs, and cut off their supplies of grain, edible oil, and business sites for private business. State commercial enterprises also reduced their supplies of goods. Only after the center intervened directly did private business halt its decline (ECLAJP 1991: 109–10) in Jilin.

In 1979, Shandong declared its protection of private enterprises in industry and commerce, and relaxed its restriction on trade in food and small manufactured goods (ROPCCCPS 1985: 544–48; ROPCCCPS 1988: 103). Since 1980, Shandong also had been constructing urban and rural marketplaces for private business (ROPCCCPS 1985: 544–48), a measure Jilin did not conscientiously undertake until 1988 which private business needs in usually congested cities in China (ECLAJP 1991: 533).

The following years (1984–1988). Private business encountered greater discrimination in Jilin than in Shandong, though the Bureau of Industrial and Commercial Administration (BICA) in both provinces in charge of regulating private enterprises had further relaxed its restrictions over the private sector. Jilin allowed private business to engage in a range of sectors and permitted peasants to set up business in cities, while Shandong authorized peasants to enter a large variety of sectors and issued license to unregistered yet operating IHEs (*Jilin Yearbook* 1987: 500, 1988: 424–25; *Shandong Yearbook* 1987: 257, 1988: 420; ECLAJP 1991: 111–14). Nevertheless, 51,569 IHEs in Jilin closed down partly because of heavy fees, excessive sanitary requirements, inadequate marketplaces, and removal of business sites by governmental agencies in the name of making streets orderly. The number of IHEs in Jilin increased by a meager 1256 (ECLAJP 1991: 115).

Retrenchment of 1989–1991. People in Jilin and Shandong expressed their displeasure over tax evasion and subtle forms of bribes by private business. People in Jilin had a greater respect for state enterprises for their job security, and their generous income and welfare measures.[1] In 1989 many officials imposed new restrictions on private enterprises, and twenty governmental agencies charged forty illicit fees (*Jilin Yearbook* 1990: 279).

Shandong BICA publicly assured private business of its favorable treatment in August 1989, eight months earlier than did its counterpart in Jilin. While Jilin also educated private business people to abide by tax laws in order to ease public anger, Shandong Government declared its readiness to punish any transgressor of their rights (*Jilin Yearbook* 1991: 229; *Shandong Yearbook* 1991: 376).

The boom period of 1992–1994. Realizing that inconsistent promotion of private business had led to its stagnation, the Jilin Party Secretary called on officials to change their conservative mindset and boldly promote the sector (*Jilin Yearbook* 1993: 1–5). In response, the BICA of Jilin lowered requirements for registration of private enterprises, simplified its regulations on seals and receipts, and reduced taxes and fees on them. It also encouraged peasants to set up private business and rent or purchase small state enterprises (Ibid. 1995: 195–96). Jilin Government also constructed an unprecedentedly large number of marketplaces for private business (ibid.).

Shandong Government upgraded its favorable policies into a comprehensive promotion package. It honored law-abiding private business, streamlined regulations, reduced illegal governmental charges, and arranged investment funds for the private sector. It also provided technological assistance, information services and legal protection, and helped private business to improve their product quality (*Shandong Yearbook* 1993: 358, 1994: 370, 359, 1995: 188–89).

Causes of Divergence in Reform Policies

Fiscal Resources and Arrangements

Significance of Fiscal Arrangements and Resources

Revenue supports the operation of the state.[2] As stated earlier, provincial reform might be affected by two fiscal factors. First, fiscal capacity might determine the range and extent of liberal initiatives a province could pursue. The more revenue a province could generate on its own, the more liberal policy it could finance. Second, central-local fiscal arrangements could also affect local incentives for reform. The more revenue a province could retain, the greater fiscal security the center conferred on the province, and greater the incentives a province would have in undertaking new reforms.

Shandong's Fiscal Arrangements and Conditions

Between 1980 and 1984 the central government introduced nation-wide a fiscal arrangement called "dividing revenues and expenditure, and multilevel contracting" (*huafen shouzhi, fenji baogan*). Between 1985 and 1987, the central government rolled out a slightly modified arrangement. It was called "dividing tax categories, verifying revenues and expenditures, and multilevel contracting" (*huafen shuizhong, heding shou zhi, fenji baogan*). Between 1987 and 1993, the central-local fiscal arrangements were further revised.

The fiscal arrangements during these years all contained the three following components. First, distinction of provinces into remitting and subsidized provinces. Shandong was categorized as a remitting province due to its robust fiscal conditions, and Jilin a subsidized one due to its fiscal difficulties. Second, division of revenue sources into three categories, namely, central fixed, local fixed, and central-local fixed-rate shared. Their definitions were modified over the years. In 1987 Qingdao in Shandong Province was made a line-item city and the city's fiscal revenue was subject to the control of the center, instead of the province (Pang et al. 1996: 1021–24). Third, setting of the amount of provincial remittance to the center or subsidies from the center. In 1987, the center shifted from a fiscal sharing scheme to that of fixed remittance. Their amounts might vary from year to year, but were usually set in advance. From 1980–1984, for example, the Ministry of Finance (MOF) set the amount of Shandong's remittance at 1.03 billion yuan, or 25 percent of Shandong's estimated base-fixed revenue income.

Shandong's actual retention rate, the share of its retained revenue in total provincial revenue income and fiscal remittance, best portrays the actual state of the fiscal arrangements. Overall, Shandong's actual retention rate closely paralleled the scheduled rate and steadily increased from 1978–1993. In 1980 and 1981, Shandong retained 49 percent of its revenue income. The retention rate improved from 52 to 55 percent between 1982 and 1984. It soared to 79 percent in 1986. Between 1987 and 1993, the rate grew from 79 percent to 86 percent (table 8.3).

Jilin's Fiscal Arrangement and Conditions
In contrast, even prior to reforms, Jilin's public finance was already in disarray. The Cultural Revolution dealt Jilin's public finance a severe blow. Failing to fulfill the fiscal revenue target set by the central government between 1972 and 1976, Jilin degraded from a remitting province to a subsidized province (PDCCPJP 1989: 72). Categorized as a subsidized province between 1980 and 1984, Jilin was allowed to retain all local revenue and received a fixed amount of subsidies from the center. Each year the central government set Jilin's base revenue income and the base expenditure figure (at 1,338 million and 1,544 million yuan in 1980, respectively). It granted Jilin a fixed amount of subsidies (486 million yuan in 1980) to help make up for the latter's financial shortfalls (206 million yuan in 1980). These figures were adjusted upward between 1981 and 1984 (table 8.3)(ECLAJP 1991: 706–15).

Between 1985 and 1987, Jilin and fifteen provinces, whose revenues approved by the center exceeded their expenditures, would receive a fixed amount of subsidies from the center (*Jilin Nianjian* 1987: 275–76, 1988: 271; PDCCPJP 1989: 72; ECLAJP 1991: 706–15). In 1988, the center reduced its subsidies to Jilin from 2,204 million yuan in 1987 to 1,826 million yuan in 1988, and further down to 448 million yuan in 1989. In 1993, with improved fiscal conditions, the center increased its subsidies to the province to 2,503 million yuan, surpassing the previous peak amount of 2,204 million yuan in 1987 (table 8.3)(*Jilin Nianjian* 1988: 271, 1989: 325, 29–34, 1994: 231–32; PDCCPJP 1989: 72).

Jilin thus confronted two severe fiscal problems. First, fiscal deficits prior to central subsidies rose to a significant level from the mid-1980s to the early 1990s. Actual deficits started at 487 million yuan in 1980, equivalent to 31 percent of the revenue prior to central subsidies. In 1982, they increased rapidly to 746 million yuan, or 57 percent of the

Table 8.3 Shandong's and Jilin's fiscal arrangements with the center, 1980–1993 (milllion yuan)

Year	Shandong remittance to center	Shandong revenue income	Shandong actual retention rate (%)	Shandong scheduled retention rate (%)	Central subsidies to Jilin	Jilin's remittance to the center	Jilin's total revenue before subsidies	Jilin's deficits before subsidies	Jilin's deficits target	Jilin's net subsidies to revenue ratio (%)	Jilin's deficits to revenue ratio (%)
1980	2459	4811	49	25	486	49.8	1571	−487	−206	31	−31
1981	2616	5119	49	49	616	307.1	1414	−617	−5	44	−44
1982	2347	4929	52	53	746	180.4	1317	−746	−463	57	−57
1983	2288	5041	55	56	745	66.2	1565	−745	−599	48	−48
1984	2533	5360	53	56	1003	129.9	1836	−1042	−723	55	−57
1985	2662	6753	61	59	1509	26.4	2545	−1512	−1169	59	−59
1986	1322	6215	79	79	2118	29.3	3492	−1995	−499	61	−57
1987	1501	7279	79	76	2204	350.9	4323	−1365	−2695	51	−32
1988	1808	9427	81	75	1826	50.5	5188	−1811	−2819	35	−35
1989	1818	11166	84	75	448	—	5570	−2170	−343	8	−39
1990	1950	11950	84	69	—	—	—	−7678	−315	—	—
1991	2230	14300	84	75	—	—	—	−8506	−161	—	—
1992	2500	15900	84	75	—	—	—	−8001	−2489	—	—
1993	2720	19440	86	75	2503	158	8559	−2477	−3193	29	−29

Notes: The actual fiscal retention rate for Shandong is calculated on the basis of Shandong's actual remittance and revenue. The scheduled fiscal retention rate for Shandong is based on MOF-arranged fiscal retention rate and the approved base revenue income for Shandong. Shandong's scheduled rates incorporate those of Qingdao, which was a line item city during 1987–1993. The ratio of Jilin's net subsidies from the center to its revenue income was the central subsidies minus Jilin's remittance and loans to the center, divided by Jilin's pre-subsidies revenue income. No detailed fiscal data for Jilin during 1990–1992 are available.

Data sources: Pang, Lin, Wang et al. 1996: 1009–25; ECLAJP 1991: 706–18; *Jilin Nianjian (Jilin Yearbook)* 1987–1993.

pre-subsidy revenue. For the period 1980–1993 Jilin shouldered sizable pre-subsidies budgetary deficits equivalent to 31–59 percent of its budgetary income. Large deficits exerted considerable fiscal constraints on Jilin's economic and reform policies (*Jilin Nianjian* 1987: 275–76, 1988: 271, 1989: 325, 29–34, 1990: 289–90, 1991: 237–39, 1992: 250–53, 1993: 185, 1994: 231–32; ECLAJP 1991: 706–15). In contrast, during these years Shandong either enjoyed a fiscal surplus, such as in 1980 and 1993, or ran much smaller fiscal deficits. For example, its deficits accounted for only 9.3 percent of its revenue income in 1985 and 13.5 percent in 1990 (table 8.2).

Second, actual deficits far exceeded scheduled ones for most of the years after the reforms, creating a grave fiscal squeeze on the provincial government. In 1980, the Ministry of Finance (MOF) set the deficit target for Jilin at 206 million yuan, yet the actual figure more than doubled, reaching 487 million yuan. In 1986 they were 499 million versus 1,995 million yuan, respectively. From 1989–1991, actual deficits were 6 to 53 times of the target deficits (table 8.3). Third, as stated above, the amount of central subsidies declined drastically in 1988 and 1989, aggravating Jilin's fiscal shortfalls (table 8.3; *Jilin Nianjian* 1987: 275–76, 1988: 271, 1989: 325, 29–34, 1990: 289–90, 1991: 237–39, 1992: 250–53, 1993: 185, 1994: 231–32; ECLAJP 1991: 706–15).

Fiscal Health and Arrangements and Reform Policies

Overall Shandong enjoyed much better fiscal conditions than Jilin and had more resources and greater incentives for carrying out more rapid reforms. As stated, Shandong was enjoying a steadily increasing fiscal retention rate. Its fiscal conditions were in a good shape. Experts from the Shandong Provincial Planning Commission and Financial Bureau as well as Shandong University agreed that fiscal arrangements during 1980–1993 had given the province tremendous incentives for reforms and that expanding fiscal revenue income allowed the province to finance economic reforms and the Open Policy (Pang et al. 1996: 986). In contrast, the Research Office of the Jilin Party Committee admitted as early as 1986 that in the 1981–1986 period the province confronted severe fiscal shortages and lacked the funds to finance many tasks for reviving the economy (ROJPPC 1986: 32).

Specifically, Shandong could finance a low-tax policy that financially stressed Jilin could not afford, such as tax reduction, low fees, recruitment and good pays for officials to pre-empt them from preying on investors. In addition, Shandong and Jilin could also use other means to affect the growth of non-state enterprises, such as bank lending and building of business sites for non-state enterprises. These instruments might require fiscal support, or might have been negatively affected by shortages in resources.

Shandong was fiscally more motivated to promote non-state enterprises because of its high fiscal retention rate described above. As lower tax stimulated the expansion of dynamic non-state enterprises and helped expand the tax base, Shandong would keep more of revenue income for itself.

In contrast, Jilin was hard pressed to collect taxes from enterprises in order to maintain fiscal balance. The tax burden in Jilin was thus much heavier, especially after the mid-1980s. Between 1980 and 1985, the ratio of industrial and commercial taxes to industrial output in Jilin ranged from 8.6–10.9 percent, lower than Shandong's range of 9.9–13.6 percent. As its retention rate increased, Shandong could afford to lower the rate sharply to 6.3–6.8 percent between 1988 and 1990 and further to 3.3–5 percent from 1991–1993. Confronting chronic fiscal shortfalls Jilin did the exact opposite. Its tax rate stayed at a much higher range of 8–10.9 percent and remained in a relatively high range of 6.8–7.7 percent in the latter two periods, respectively (*China Tax Statistics 1950–1994*: 74, 78).

Similar things can be said about the tax burden on non-state enterprises in the two provinces. Shandong's corporate income tax to industrial output ratio for collective enterprises declined from 3.5 percent in 1980 to 3.0 percent in 1985. With Shandong's retention rate soaring, this tax rate fell sharply to 0.6 percent in 1990 and a negligible 0.2 percent in 1993 (Ibid.: 129–30). Although Jilin's tax rate started at a lower 2.6 percent in 1980, it reached 3.3 percent in 1985, surpassing that of Shandong. It declined to 1.8 percent in 1990 and to 0.8 percent in 1993, still three to four times as much as that of Shandong. Similarly, Shandong's tax burden on private and foreign enterprises was only one-third to half of that in Jilin between 1990 and 1993 (table 8.1).[3] Lower tax rates in Shandong would thus stimulate faster growth in collective, private, and foreign enterprises in the province. The province might still enjoy a steady inflow of revenue simply because of an expanding tax base created by the booming non-state enterprises.

Efficient and Supportive Bureaucracy

The political and economic roles of bureaucracy in provincial reforms can never be underestimated. The Chinese authoritarian regime precluded popular election of officials and prevented the legislature from closely monitoring bureaucrats. As a result, bureaucracy at all levels virtually becomes an influential power holder, probably only next to leaders at the same level.

Chinese bureaucrats also directly affected the formulation and implementation of reform policies in the provinces that eventually affected the development of the local market economy. They supplied information to provincial leaders necessary for decision making and participated in policy making. After policies were made, they were also responsible for carrying them out. They also directly determined the quality of governmental services for enterprises, regulated the entry of non-state firms into the market, collected taxes, and drafted and enforced regulations of enterprises. They could thus deeply shape the business environment for non-state enterprises.

The tremendous economic clout of the bureaucracy was also enhanced by the legacy of the command economy. Prior to the reforms bureaucrats acted as intermediate agents between the state and enterprises (or quasi-market agents) in the economy as well as de facto representatives of the owner of the SOEs. They determined production targets and employment quota and even sales outlets of the SOEs.

The emerging market economy in China required noninterventionist and supportive bureaucracy. It demanded bureaucrats to hand over managerial and operational decisions to enterprises and entrepreneurs. It also required bureaucrats as well as the court to help draft and enforce economic rules and contracts, ensure fair competition, and protect property rights and legitimate interests of enterprises.

Overall, the bureaucracy in Shandong was relatively much smaller, more efficient, and more open-minded than that in Jilin. As a result, it provided better services and introduced amicable policies toward non-state sectors. In contrast, bureaucracy in Jilin had been larger and more conservative. It was quick to embrace central conservative orders to protect SOEs and restrain the non-state economy. It was eager to defend their jurisdiction and cumbersome procedures, thereby encouraging gridlock, inefficiency, and rent seeking. Let us examine contrasts in the two provinces point by point.

First of all, the bureaucracy in Shandong was leaner than that in Jilin. In 1987, officials at state offices and institutions in Shandong totaled 526,000 and those in Jilin 235,000. In 1992, these numbers increased to 684,000 and 330,000, respectively. The ratio of officials to labor force was 1.4 : 100 in Shandong and 2.3 : 100 in Jilin in 1987, suggesting that Jilin's bureaucracy was 1.68 times of that in Shandong.

In 1992, both ratios increased to 1.6 : 100 and 2.7 : 100, respectively, and the latter was 1.74 times of the former. While the ratio in Shandong had been noticeably below that of the nation which registered 1.8 percent in 1987 and 1.9 percent in 1992, that in Jilin was far higher than national (table 8.4).

In addition to officials, public employees who received salaries from the government's payroll also included employees in health care, sports, social welfare, education, culture, arts, radio, film, television, as well as scientific research services. The ratio of public employees to labor force in Shandong was 4.9 : 100; that in Jilin was 7.9 : 100 in 1987. These ratios increased to 5.1 : 100 and 8 : 100 in 1992, respectively. The ratio in Jilin was 1.61 times of that in Shandong in 1987 and was 1.57 times in 1992. Jilin clearly had proportionally more public employees than did Shandong (table 8.4).

In a similar vein, Jilin's Provincial Government also had more departments than that in Shandong, even though the former had a much smaller population in its jurisdiction (i.e., 23 million versus 76 million in 1983). In 1982, Jilin's provincial government had 76 departments, compared to 66 in Shandong. After a restructuring in 1984, that in Jilin was reduced to 45, still more than the 40 departments in Shandong (ECLAJP 1994: 533–38; ECLASP 1995: 1399–1400).

Table 8.4 Public employees and officials in Shandong and Jilin (1000)

	1987			1992		
	National	Shandong	Jilin	National	Shandong	Jilin
Officials/ labor force	1.8%	1.4%	2.3%	1.9%	1.6%	2.7%
Public employees/ labor force	5.6%	4.9%	7.9%	5.7%	5.1%	8.0%
Labor force	527,830	38,501	10,238	594,315	44,051	12,245
Total public employees	29,540	1,877	807	34,159	2,228	974
By public sectors						
Officials in state agencies and institutions	9,250	526	235	11,480	684	330
Health care, sports, and social welfare	4,960	376	138	5,644	425	160
Education, culture, arts, radio, film, and TV	13,750	922	398	15,207	1,050	439
Scientific research and polytechnic services	1,580	53	36	1,828	69	45

Sources: SSB 1988: 159; SSB 1993: 103.

In general, the bureaucracy in Shandong was more efficient than that in Jilin. Jilin's large bureaucracy usually tended to be preoccupied with maintaining their pervasive control over the economy and society. It also stubbornly resisted attempts to restructuring the departments. These repulsive traits of behavior, however, were based on self-interests and their intention to keep their jobs, advance their careers, and collect rents.

Provincial officials in charge of developmental zones in Jilin frankly admitted as late as 1998 that bureaucrats there tended to emphasize strict, elaborate, and time-consuming procedures. Non-state enterprises were often required to win the approval of dozens of agencies before they could open their business, or accomplish any major task (Bao and Li 1996: 206; SSB 1996b: 367). In contrast, officials in the Yantai Developmental Zone in Shandong stressed their quick turnarounds in handling requests from foreign investors.[4]

Officials and governmental departments in Jilin also invested a lot of time and resources on defending their scope of jurisdiction and aborting any attempts to streamline the government in order to safeguard their jobs. The most telling example is a sharp contrast in the office that administered foreign investment in the two provinces. Jilin Government granted offices of developmental zones provincial-level jurisdiction over a variety of economic matters, so that they could handle various affairs regarding the zones. Fearing a loss of resources and authority, however, former governmental agencies in charge of related affairs, such as tax, banking, environment, and industrial bureaus, refused to allow offices of developmental zones to run the business in their areas (CJ 1996: 3, 5, 72).[5] In order to streamline the process of approving FDI projects, Jilin Provincial Government established in 1992 the Foreign Economic Bureau to coordinate work related to foreign investment. The bureau coordinated offices in charge of imports of technology, technological cooperation, promotion of international business, and the approval of foreign-invested enterprises (*Jilin Yearbook* 1993: 342). Provincial leaders hoped that potential international investment projects would need only the approval of this bureau, instead of dozens of agencies (interview in Jilin, September 1998). However, an effective bureau would mean a great loss of power and resources for these related governmental agencies. The latter thus refused to pass their authority to the offices of developmental zones.

In 1996, acknowledging that the bureau failed to coordinate the work on FDI, Jilin leaders were forced to replace the bureau with the

Provincial Leading Small Group (LSG) of Utilizing Foreign Investment in 1996 (unpublished document). The LSG was housed in the Economic Planning Commission, the most powerful economic department. Each of the eight related governmental departments sent two officials as representatives to the group. These departments still did not budge. They sent poorly informed officials to the LSG, and work on foreign investment still needed approval from each relevant department (interviews). In exchange for transferal of their authority to these new agencies, these departments often demanded compensations from the Provincial Office of Developmental Zones, or favors from foreign business.

The red tape in Jilin's bureaucracy contrasted sharply with the unity and efficiency in Shandong. In Shandong an intra-bureaucratic fight regarding regulations of foreign business was subdued much earlier. Between 1984 and 1986, foreign trade and investment was supervised by three agencies—namely, the State Planning Commission (SPC), and the Ministry of Foreign Trade (which was later renamed the Ministry of Foreign Economic Relations and Trade, or the MOFERT in short), and the Import, Export and Trade Commission (abbreviated as the ImExCom) under the Shandong Government. In 1987, the ImExComIn was renamed the Foreign Economic Commission (FEC), a territorial agency under the provincial government and in charge of supervising foreign trade corporations. However, the FEC soon entered into a serious conflict with another overlapping provincial agency, the Foreign Trade Commission (FTC) formerly under the functional leadership of the MOFERT. In 1990, Jiang Chunyun, the Shandong Party Secretary, merged the FEC and the FTC into the Foreign Economic and Trade Commission (FETC) in order to end the infighting between the two agencies. The heads of the FEC and the FTC were transferred to other units and an outsider was appointed to head the newly merged agency. As a result, the infighting of these two agencies stopped, and the efficiency of the new agency improved (Chung 1998: 278–79). Shandong was thereafter free of the bickering quarrels among bureaus regarding jurisdiction over foreign business.

Jilin's larger and cumbersome bureaucracy was slow to implement favorable policies toward non-state businesses announced by the province. In its attempts to attract foreign investors, Jilin Government announced thirty-four provincial-level economic privileges and thirty-eight favorable policies for foreign business in "Regulations Regarding Several Issues Concerning Provincial-Level Economic Developmental Zones" in 1992 and "Several Stipulations Regarding

Further Extending Opening Up to the Outside World and Outward-Oriented Development" in 1994. The stonewalling by department agencies successfully blocked the implementation of these laws and policies. By 1996 only two of the above seventy-two policies were well in place, three of them were unsatisfactorily implemented, and sixty-seven of them were not adopted at all (CJ 1996: 4). Even many provincial officials in charge of developmental zones were reluctant to adopt reforms announced by the Jilin Provincial Government (JPG). Favorable policies regarding developmental zones were fully implemented in merely two out of the sixteen zones, namely, Changchun New and High Technology Industrial Developmental Zone (Changchun NHTIDZ) and Huichun Borderline Economic Cooperation Zone (CJ 1996: 71–72).

Rent-seeking and incompetent officials also created unnecessary burdens on non-state sectors in Jilin and contributed to an unfavorable business environment. In order to generate extra revenue, officials imposed onerous charges and fees on a variety of non-state enterprises, causing many private sectors to terminate their business in 1989. Quite a number of the staff members at the offices of developmental zones in Jilin were not qualified either. In addition, laws regarding developmental zones remained poorly specified, and respect for laws was deficient in Jilin. Violations of proper procedures or processes by these offices occurred frequently (CJ 1996: 72). As late as the late 1990s, only one developmental zone in Changchun had an attractive business environment for foreign investors and was booming (interview in Jilin in 1998).

Bureaucrats in Jilin were more ready than their Shandong counterparts to embrace central conservative directives to restrict the growth of rural enterprises and private business during national retrenchment. During the first national retrenchment between 1981 and 1983, official media in Jilin criticized rural enterprises for their diverting resources and profits away from SOEs; governmental agencies prohibited rural enterprises from engaging in certain projects operating outside their county of origin, and from even getting a license (Du 1993: 5). In 1981, local governments used administrative obstacles, such as strict sanitary standards and removal of business sites to slow down the growth of private business, and state-owned commercial business refused to supply private business wholesale goods (Jin 1985; Cheng et al. 1989). The JPG even emulated the Soviet heavy-industry-led growth model by converting a large number of light industrial enterprises, many of which were non-state firms, into heavy industrial ones (*Jilin Yearbook* 1987: 380).

During the retrenchment of 1989–1991, Jilin officials followed closely central orders to restrict and overhaul collective and private sectors in cities and the countryside. In 1991, hostility became so widespread that rural enterprises and private enterprises could not find sufficient production inputs and their growth was severely interrupted (Du 1993: 7).

Between 1978 and 1980 Shandong officials were modestly more tolerant of non-state sectors than was their Jilin counterpart. Whereas Jilin imposed outright prohibitions of business in certain projects and outside local areas, Shandong adopted only moderate economic restrictions on rural enterprises, such as repealing its tax exemption, imposing high taxes on consumer goods in strong demand, and tightening bank lending (ECLASP 1996: 153–54). Shandong officials implemented these measures largely to show their compliance with the national policy, whereas Jilin agencies embraced draconian measures in revenge to maintain the status of state firms.

During the second national retrenchment between 1989 and 1991, the SPG acted earlier and more firmly than did the Jilin counterpart in reassuring non-state investors of no change in reform policies. It respected more openly the rights of non-state businesses, and did more to promote efficient management in non-state sectors than did Jilin.

Provincial Leadership and Governance

At the national level, no statistical correlation is found between provincial liberal leadership and provincial reforms. However in the pair of Shandong and Jilin, provincial leadership played a role in their divergent reform policies. Prior to 1986, Shandong's leaders were termed bandwagoners. They would not dare to be a front-runner in reforms. Instead, they would wait for clear central directives before launching full-scale reforms. Between 1986 and 1993, Shandong's leaders were liberal, or "pioneers." They pushed forth liberal measures and only gave minimal attention to central policy preferences (Chung 1998). In contrast, Jilin's leaders were conservative before 1988 and were slow to implement liberal policies announced by the center and sluggish in introducing their own reform measures. Between mid-1988 and 1991, Jilin's leaders could be characterized as bandwagoning. Although they made some efforts to promote the growth of non-state sectors, they were still focusing on SOEs.[6]

Most importantly, leaders of Shandong and Jilin pursued differing styles of governance and different approaches to reforming bureaucracy.

In the developmental literature, good governance was regarded as a key institutional factor for economic growth. Good governance is based on a responsible, efficient, transparent, and institutionalized (or rule-based) government.[7] In this chapter good governance is limited to primarily the regulation and management of the economy. Differing efforts to build an efficient and business-friendly bureaucracy led to varying performance of bureaucracy in Shandong and Jilin. The Shandong Provincial Government (SPG) endeavored earlier and harder to institutionalize bureaucracy and pressure officials to serve the public in a more responsible, efficient, and transparent manner. Their efforts helped produce a bureaucracy receptive to non-state businesses and conducive to economic growth.

First of all, Shandong was more determined in downsizing its bureaucracy and making it more efficient. In 1983 and 1984, the State Council organized a nationwide restructuring of the government. The SPG made greater progress in downsizing itself than its Jilin counterpart. The number of provincial officials in Shandong was reduced from 8,670 to 4,873 (by 43.8 percent), and that in Jilin from 4,285 to 3,221, a decline by a much smaller rate at 25 percent (ECLAJP 1994: 533–38; ECLASP 1995: 1399–1400).

Meanwhile, the SPG made earlier and more carefully conceived efforts to improve its efficiency and further institutionalization. Shandong clearly stated that the objectives of the restructuring were to clarify the division of labor among departments and cadres and reduce layers and stops in the bureaucracy. To achieve these goals, the Shandong Government streamlined agencies and personnel, clarified duties and introduced agency responsibility system, and promulgated a series of regulations on official duties, meetings, leadership, documents, and publications. It also retrained officials and provided veteran cadres with good political rewards and material treats to reduce veterans' opposition to promoting young and educated officials (ECLASP 1995: 1399–1400).

In contrast, Jilin's governmental restructuring lacked a clear and deserving vision. Jilin leaders treated restructuring merely as a task passed down by the center. In January 1983, Jilin leaders claimed that Jilin's restructuring would follow central policies and guidelines and would proceed according to conditions in Jilin and according to the needs for "socialist modernization." The measures Jilin emphasized were unimaginative and conventional—removing overlapping agencies, reducing layers of the government, and downsizing personnel (ECLAJP 1994: 533–38). Only in launching the restructuring of county and municipal governments in October 1983 did the Jilin Government propose that key goals were to overcome bureaucratism, improve efficiency, and strengthen the Party's leadership. Nevertheless, no stress was laid on standardizing procedures, clarifying official duties, and enforcing official responsibilities (Ibid. 540–41).

In following years, Shandong continued to strive for a lean, efficient, responsible, and institutionalized government. In 1987, under the leadership of Acting Governor Jiang Chunyun, Shandong Government passed "Regulations on Institutions of Provincial Government Meetings and Leading Cadres' Work." It specified the duties, authority, and responsibilities of the governor and vice governors and advisers for the province and required leading cadres to spend one-third of their time on surveying grass-root conditions (*Shandong Nianjian 1989*: 235–36). In 1988, the SPG promulgated documents to institutionalize governmental procedures, responsibilities, and efficiency. "Regulations on Organizational Work for Provincial Governmental Meetings," for example, listed requirements prior to these meetings, one of them being that relevant departments be consulted before any issue was submitted to these meetings for deliberation. The regulations also laid down strict requirements to make meetings productive— (1) Each participant spoke for no more than 10 minutes; (2) no participant be allowed to read other documents and discuss privately other issues among themselves; (3) nonparticipants were not allowed to be present; (4) no telephone calls would be transmitted; and (5) no private records of meetings were allowed to be publicized (*Shandong Nianjian 1989*: 268).

Shandong devoted more energy in earlier years to transform bureaucracy from a control-oriented one into a services-oriented one. In 1988 the SPG issued "Several Regulations for Improving Management Efficiency at Provincial Governmental Agencies." The document introduced the director responsibility system at each department, and instituted working style and efficiency as important components in evaluating officials' performances. It required that each unit should not spend more than three days in replying so that inquiries from localities could be replied within fifteen days. Departments in the SPG were required to streamline their administration and decentralize their power, strengthen their sense of services for groups and individuals, and improve their macromanagement (*Shandong Nianjian 1989*: 271–72).

In 1989, the Shandong Provincial Government established its press conferences. It aimed to step up transparency in its work and enhance media supervision. The SPG also required local governments and governmental departments to set up their press conferences and incorporated press and public supervision into their daily work (*Shandong Nianjian 1990*: 265–66).

In 1992, the SPG introduced another round of downsizing, aiming to simplify governmental functions, decentralize power, and create a leaner and friendlier government for businesses. It was implemented in 1,367 townships within 79 counties, cities, and large municipal districts. At the end, 6,802 administrative and institutional agencies were abolished, 56,034 employees of these agencies were released off their duties, and 119.7 million yuan of operational expenses were saved. The excessive governmental control of the society and economy was curtailed. For example, 174 items of management authority were passed down from eighty-seven agencies of the provincial government to enterprises, and large projects would be approved by one coordinating agency, or a few departments, instead of a dozen agencies as in the past (*Shandong Nianjian 1993*: 278).

In contrast, Jilin's efforts at governance were belated and timid. In 1986, three years after Shandong launched the responsibility system in the provincial government, Jilin introduced the institution. Between 1987 and 1989, Jilin was preoccupied with containing the rapid growth of its bureaucracy and paid little attention toward improving governance. Only in 1990, three years after Shandong leaders institutionalized governmental procedures and enforced efficiency did a new Jilin Governor (namely, Wang Zhongyu) call on officials to become more efficient and observe disciplines. However, without the backup by the "teeth" of hard rules and clear stipulations (*Jilin Nianjian 1991*: 123–26), these calls appeared to be just words falling on the dead ears of bureaucrats. In 1991, three years after Shandong, Jilin Governor Wang Zhongyu devolved power from governmental agencies to large- and medium-size enterprises. But only 50 enterprises were selected for this experiment (*Jilin Nianjian 1992*: 121–22).

In 1992, riding on a reform wave unleashed by the central government, Jilin sent delegations to study provinces that were pioneers in reforms, including Shandong, Jiangsu, Zhejiang, Shanghai, and Fujian (*Jilin Nianjian 1993*: 51–52). Finally in 1992, four years later than Shandong, the Jilin Provincial Government (JPG) made substantial moves to improve its governance. In 1992, JPG announced to pass down 452 items of authority to enterprises and localities concerning a wide range of functional areas, including external trade and business, finance, fiscal, price, registration and regulations of non-state enterprises. In addition, the JPG took dramatic steps to cut the number of meetings from 223 to 146, a decline by one third (*Jilin Nianjian* 1994: 75–76). Nevertheless, few attempts were made to institutionalize procedures. Jilin's eventual measures to build good governance thus still fell short of those in Shandong.

Influence of State versus Non-State Sectors

The size and influence of non-state sectors appear to be a factor that underpinned both sharp and subtle differences in policies toward the four major non-state sectors in Shandong and Jilin, especially after the mid-1980s. Non-state sectors produced 32 percent of gross industrial output in 1978 in Shandong and 21 percent in Jilin (table 8.5). In terms of employment outside the agricultural sector, non-state sectors in Shandong was not larger than that in Jilin in the early 1980s. In 1980, non-state sectors employed 16.5 percent of nonagricultural labor force in Shandong, smaller than the 20.2 percent in Jilin. As non-state sectors did not play a significant role in creating employment in Shandong and Jilin, neither province made great efforts to promote these sectors. This help to explain why reform policies in two provinces were similar until the mid-1980s.

However, after years of expansion, the role of non-state sectors in creating employment in Shandong expanded quickly. By 1985 non-state sectors in Shandong had accounted for 45 percent of industrial output and over one-third of the nonagricultural jobs in Shandong, but merely 28 percent of industrial output and 26.5 percent of the jobs in Jilin (table 8.5). Understandably, non-state sectors in Shandong could exert some pressure on the provincial government to adopt

Table 8.5   Size of non-state sectors in Shandong and Jilin

Year	Percentage of non-state sectors in nonagricultural labor force in Shandong	Percentage of non-state sectors in nonagricultural labour force in Jilin	Percentage of non-state sectors in provincial industrial output in Shandong	Percentage of non-state sectors in provincial industrial output in Jilin
1980	16.5	20.2	32.4	21.4
1985	35.1	26.5	45.4	27.8
1989	36	24.3	58.6 (1990)	29.6 (1990)
1991	34	23.4	64.4 (1993)	34.6 (1993)

Sources: SSB 1990b: 246, 258–259, 493, 506, 1996b: 375, 559; *Zhongguo Laodong Tongji Nianjian (China Labor Statistical Yearbook)* 1992: 16, 33–34.

more liberal policies. In contrast, these sectors were much less influential in Jilin and could hardly obtain favorable policies from the government.

During the second national retrenchment between 1989 and 1991, Shandong acted earlier and more firmly than Jilin to reassure the non-state investors of no change in reform policies, respect the rights of non-state sectors, and promote efficient management in these sectors. Again, one underlying reason is that non-state sectors had just grown into one of the largest components of Shandong's economy (generating 36 percent of nonagricultural jobs and 54 percent of gross industrial output), whereas these sectors remained a strictly secondary element of Jilin's economy (provisioning 23–24 percent of nonagricultural jobs and producing about 29 percent of gross industrial output).

The state and non-state sectors seemed to affect provincial reform policies in the following five ways. First, they could have considerable resources to pressure local governments for favorable treatment. This is the case of non-state sectors in Shandong in the 1984–1988 period. In contrast, Jilin continued to have a larger state sector that would have more resources than non-state sectors in lobbying the provincial government for favorable treatment at the expense of these sectors.

Second and in a similar vein, leaders and officials of a province with larger and expanding non-state sectors would see the sectors as an increasingly important source of economic growth and jobs as well as an economic base of their power and careers. They would subtly block the center's directives against these sectors in order to sustain high economic growth. In Shandong non-state sectors were posing to become the dominant ownership in economy after 1986. Failure to promote these sectors would have meant a neglect of the need of powerful constituents, a poor developmental record, few career advancement chances, and even grave economic, social, and political consequences. Leaders in Shandong thus adopted progressive reforms to help out these dynamic sectors. Meanwhile, more governmental agencies and local officials in the province had developed a stake in the well-being of non-state sectors and would treat them in a friendly manner.

Larger state sector in Jilin, on the contrary, invited Jilin leaders to listen carefully to the state sector and the center. In Jilin the state sector played a larger economic role. The leading and large state firms had close ties with the ministries in Beijing. Therefore, leaders of Jilin tended to pay more attention to the directives from the center and were cautious in adopting reform measures.

Third, when the state sector loomed large in the economy, numerous governmental agencies were needed to supervise state enterprises. A large bureaucracy revolving on state enterprises tended to function slowly and maintain cumbersome bureaucratic procedures of approving and supervising projects. Such a bureaucracy would dampen the growth of non-state enterprises. As stated above, this was very evident in Jilin.

Fourth, a large state sector tended to breed among the population greater contempt and hostility toward non-state sectors, creating unfavorable public opinion and social environment for non-state sectors. When the state sector dominated the economy, the prevalent ideology and public opinion tended to value state sectors and debase non-state enterprises. During the retrenchment of 1989–1991, for example, a charge surfaced in the media in Jilin that non-state sectors were undermining state sectors and thus the command economy. In Shandong the population did not share this view. People there valued the economic contribution from the private sector. They merely disliked the sector's tax evasion, false registration status, kickbacks in business dealings, and its active role in protests of 1989 which, in their view, had disrupted their daily lives.

Even though China started to move away from the command economy in late 1978, elements of economic planning still lingered. Well into the early 1990s raw materials and energy were in constant shortage. Rural and private enterprises consumed these resources and reduced resources available for state industry, causing resentment from the state sector. State industry lodged this complaint to the provincial government or through news media and demanded restrictions on rural enterprises.

Fifth, the state sector was less attractive for foreign investors than non-state ones, and therefore tended to be less enthusiastic about the Open Policy. When state enterprises had an interest in using foreign capital to revitalize their performance, they often lacked matching funds to materialize their projects. Thus inland provinces such as Jilin where the state sector was predominant turned indifferent or even hostile toward foreign business.

The Center's Policies, Coastal Proximity, and Trade Potential

National policies regarding the opening of China to the world economy could affect provincial reforms in two ways. First, the center's Open Policy did experience a cyclical change. Central conservative leaders threw cold water on the Open Policy in the 1981–1983 period. Between 1984 and 1988 the central government opened up major coastal economic regions. The Open Policy, however, suffered a setback during the retrenchment of 1989–1991. Only after Deng's Southern Tour did it get a strong boost between 1992 and 1994. Central leaders' oscillation over the Open Policy could exert pressure on reform policies in the provinces. Between 1978 and 1994, as stated, Jilin was more responsive to the center's conservative policies than was Shandong. Second, specific national policies could also have affected provincial reforms. In particular, the national government opened up coastal provinces including Shandong much earlier than did interior provinces including Jilin. This differentiated treatment could have indeed influenced provincial reforms.

In this regard, Shandong's reform did benefit from its coastal location, great potential for developing trade with South Korea, and national opening of the province. As a coastal province, Shandong had good ocean harbors in Qingdao and Yantai, which provided the shortest ocean lanes to South Korea for China. The potential for external trade for Shandong, calculated by dividing its nearby foreign trade partner (NFTP)'s foreign trade volume by Shandong's distance from NFTP in 1985, registered 69 million US$ /km. This is much higher than the 49 million US$ /km for Jilin's external trade potential. It is thus not surprising that the center favored Shandong in its Open Policy.

The national government declared in 1984 Qingdao and Yantai, two coastal and economically important cities in Shandong, open to international business. In March 1988, the State Council declared another four cities and their adjunct counties in Shandong as "open areas." By then, the Shandong Peninsula with six prefecture-level cities and twenty-six counties or county-level cities and with a population of 26 million had been opened up. It accounted for nearly one-third of provincial area and population (*Shandong Nianjian* 1987: 249, 1989: 283–84, 382). In 1990, the provincial capital Ji'nan and counties under its jurisdiction were included into the open area. By then, the open area in Shandong had a population of 32 million, or 40 percent of the provincial total (Pang et al. 1996: 645). In March 1993, the State Council opened up Dongying, extending Shandong's open area to eight of its seventeen prefectural-level cities (Chung 1998: 280).

Shandong was also blessed with two edges over interior provinces like Jilin. First, in 1988 Premier Zhao announced the coastal developmental strategy, granting Shandong and other coastal provinces a preferential status in promoting external trade and attracting foreign investment (*Shandong Nianjian* 1988: 383). Second, in late 1987, the State Council made Shandong the primary province to handle non-governmental and economic contact with South Korea (Chung 1998: 272). In 1992, China and South Korea established diplomatic ties. As over 90 percent of the 20,000 overseas Chinese in Korea came from Shandong and as Shandong was among the closest Chinese provinces geographically to South Korea, South Korea became a natural potential trade partner and a primary source of investment. By 1994, it ranked just after Hong Kong and Taiwan as a leading export destination and a destination for external investors (Chung 1998: 280).

In contrast, not until 1989 did the center select Changchun as the first open city in Jilin, followed by Tumen and Huichun in 1992. In 1990, the year following the center's selection of the first open city in Jilin, the open area produced only 23.3 percent of industrial output (*Database on Political Economy of Chinese Provinces*). In comparison, open cities produced 13.7 percent of industrial output in Shandong in 1986. The share jumped to 55.4 percent in 1990 and 68.1 percent in 1994.

However, provincial authorities and bureaucracy, as described above, did play a significant role in deciding how closely they should toe national policy guidelines. Shandong authority made more consistent and systemic efforts than did its counterpart in Jilin in introducing FDI since 1986. These efforts included holding trade fairs, helping cities to find sister cites abroad, organizing trade-promotion visits abroad, and calling for greater opening.

Shandong also made earlier and greater efforts than Jilin to formulate major policies and regulations, helping to institutionalize the Open Policy and to create a favorable environment for foreign business. During 1986–1996, Shandong promulgated ten laws and regulations regarding foreign business and a number of policy documents regarding developmental and technological zones, including "Shandong Province's Preferential Measures for Encouraging Foreign Business and Investment" in October 1986, four sets of regulations in 1988 and two policy documents in 1990 (*Shandong Nianjian* 1987: 239–48; *Shandong Nianjian* 1989: 385–90; Liu, Le, and Zhao, 1993: 348–60).

In contrast, belated opening of Jilin also resulted in late announcement of policies to attract foreign investment. In October 1992, JPG issued a major policy document regarding foreign business—"Jilin Province's Preferential Methods for Encouraging Foreign Investment." No major new regulations were announced until 1996. In 1996 Jilin formed the Foreign Investment Utilization Work Leading Small Group to step up governmental efforts to attract foreign business. In the following years, a series of new regulations were rolled out ("A Report on the Work on Utilizing Foreign Investment in Jilin Province," unpublished governmental report, 1998).

Shandong was also *more consistent* in adhering to the Open Policy than Jilin. In each year between 1987 and 1994, even during the post-Tiananmen retrenchment, Shandong continued to announce favorable policies toward foreign investors, improved the infrastructure, held trade fairs or trade talks and expanded exports of rural enterprises. Shandong took earlier and more effective measures to combat the bureaucratic work style, liberalize officials' mentality, and implement its favorable treatment of foreign enterprises (*Shandong Yearbook* 1988: 322, 1989: 383; Chung 1998: 266).

Not only did Jilin formulate fewer major policies and regulations to attract foreign investment; as stated above, officials in Jilin also did not faithfully implement these policies as well as minor measures promulgated by the provincial authority.

Leaders of Jilin did not start to pay attention to exports of rural enterprises until 1989 (ECLASP 1997: 435–36, 443, 447; *Jilin Nianjian* 1987–1992). As a result, the share of exports in the output of rural enterprises was higher in Shandong, registering 2.3 percent in 1987 and 7.2 percent in 1994, compared to 0.54 percent and 2.2 percent in Jilin, respectively. Jilin had a greater share of international capital in the investment in rural enterprises than Shandong in 1987 (i.e., 3.8 percent versus 3.2 percent). However, thanks to its stronger efforts, Shandong raised its share to 6.5 percent in 1994, while the share in Jilin crawled up to merely 4.1 percent.

Conclusion

Jilin and Shandong adopted somewhat similar reform policies prior to 1987, reflected in comparable tax rates on rural industry and collective enterprises. However, since 1987, both had diverged sharply in their reform efforts. Shandong had become more liberal and more persistent in promoting non-state businesses.

One of the responsible factors in this divergence in reforms was the fiscal resources and central-local fiscal arrangements. Shandong had a stronger fiscal capacity and experienced more rapid growth in its revenue income than did Jilin. It could thus finance liberal initiatives that paved the way for the development of non-state sectors, such as tax exemption, construction of business sites, and low service charges. Equally importantly, with the center's fiscal concessions, Shandong raised its fiscal retention rate to an impressive 61 percent in 1985 and an amazing 79 percent in 1986 (table 8.3). It was thus strongly motivated to shift to a high gear in its reform drive in the following years. For Shandong, liberalizing the entry of non-state enterprises would generate higher growth and greater revenue income, allowing the province to keep a lion's share of fiscal returns. Even if liberalization reduced fiscal income in the short run, Shandong, with a robust economy, would have considerable resources to cope with unexpected fiscal shortfalls.

In contrast, Jilin was in a gloomy situation. It had been receiving subsidies prior to reforms and remained so after the reforms. Even with subsidies from the center it faced chronic and in some years severe fiscal deficits. It was thus in a difficult position to support fiscally expensive liberal policies, such as tax cuts, building of business sites, and low service fees. In addition, the center reduced its subsidies relative to Jilin's revenue income in 1983, 1987, 1988, and 1989. As Jilin's non-state economy was relatively small prior to reforms, the province relied heavily on the state sector for revenue income. A convenient and politically safe option for Jilin's leaders was thus to keep the status quo, gradually and slowly expand non-state businesses and try hard to revive SOEs. This could minimize the risk of explosion of fiscal deficits due to unpredictable outcomes of liberalization.

The other important factor responsible for differing reforms in Shandong and Jilin was bureaucracy. Shandong was blessed with a leaner, efficient, and liberal government, which provided relatively efficient services for foreign business. In contrast, the administration in Jilin had been much larger and more cumbersome and bureaucratic. It even succeeded at aborting provincial attempts to streamline agencies in charge of foreign business and stalling most of the favorable provincial policies for foreign business.

Shandong's officials were also resistant to central orders to restrict the expansion of non-state enterprises during retrenchment. Shandong officials, in observing central directives during retrenchment, were more tolerant of non-state businesses. In contrast, officials in Jilin were very responsive to the calls from the center to slow down the growth of non-state enterprises.

Here provincial leadership could make a difference in reforming bureaucracy and thereby affecting the expansion of non-state sectors. Shandong leaders after 1986 could be squarely characterized as liberals or reformists, where their Jilin counterparts were mostly conservatives or "bandwagoners" who wavered depending on political circumstances. Shandong leaders made earlier and systemic efforts to make the administration responsible, efficient, transparent, and service-friendly over economic matters. Jilin did not make these moves until three years later. Therefore, Jilin leaders' efforts to build good economic governance were belated and timid, resulting in rampant red tape and conservatism of bureaucracy.

Furthermore, larger non-state sectors also helped push forward faster reform in Shandong than in Jilin. Since the mid-1980s non-state sectors, especially rural enterprises, had emerged as one of the main sources of economic output and a significant supplier of jobs in Shandong. They would have considerable leverage to affect the local government's policies. Shandong leaders and officials promoted them as an engine of growth. In Jilin the state sector continued to dominate the economic scene. Therefore, Jilin's leaders and officials were catering to SOEs and prevented non-state sectors from taking away raw materials, manpower, and markets from the state sector.

Finally, coastal proximity, potential for external trade, and the center's opening of provincial areas also conditioned, albeit did not determine the pace of provincial reforms. As early as 1984, Shandong's key economic cities and sea ports, namely, Qingdao and Yantai, were declared open cities. Jilin's first major city was opened up only five years later. In 1988, Shandong's core economic area, namely, Shandong Peninsula, was opened up. In Jilin, however, only three cities were opened by 1992.

Meanwhile, Shandong made a stronger push to introduce favorable policies to attract foreign business by formulating ten relevant laws and regulations in the decade of 1986–1996. In contrast, by 1992 Jilin had only one major regulation, although it announced numerous minor favorable measures. Shandong officials, as stated, implemented rather faithfully these laws and regulations, while Jilin officials by and large succeeded in deferring the policies and measures announced.

Policy Effects on the Non-State Economy and the Population

The above divergence in reforms in the two provinces had real and substantial effects on the non-state economy. Overall, non-state enterprises benefited tremendously from liberal policies in Shandong, but expanded rather slowly under frequent illiberal treatment in Jilin. In 1978, the year when reforms started, SOEs accounted for 68 percent of gross industrial output in Shandong. By 1993, their share fell sharply to only 36 percent. The share of collective, private, foreign and mix ownership rose robustly from 32 percent in 1978 to 64 percent in 1993. In Jilin SOEs accounted for a larger share (79 percent) of gross industrial output in 1978. The decline of their share was rather moderate in the following fifteen years. By 1993, their share registered 65 percent, a decline by merely 14 percent, compared to the 32 percent in Shandong. The share of non-state enterprises rose sluggishly from 21 percent in 1978 to 35 percent in 1993 (table 8.6).

Provincial policies also helped to various extents the expansion of collective enterprises, a primary form of non-state ownership in the 1978–1993 period in China. As a result of Shandong Provincial Government's active promotion, rural enterprises grew rapidly. It accounted for 26 percent of gross industrial output in 1978, but this share rose to 42 percent in 1993. In Jilin, the size of the collective

Table 8.6   Industrial output by ownership in Shandong and Jilin (billion yuan)

	Gross output	Growth: 1978 = 1	Gross Output (%)	State sector (%)	Collective sector (%)	Individual and Private (%)	Foreign and Mixed (%)
Shandong							
1978	29.68	1	100	68	26		6
1980	34.03	1.17	100	68	27		6
1982	39.32	1.28	100	67	26		8
1986	78.43	2.12	100	53	30		17
1988	145.52	3.07	100	46	49	5	0
1990	220.09	3.60	100	41	30		29
1993	471.35	6.99	100	36	42	16	6
Change:							
1978–1993		+599%		−32	+16		+16
Jilin							
1978	11.3	1	100	79	21	0	
1980	13.5	1.16	100	79	21	0	0
1982	14.9	1.22	100	71	22	7	0
1986	28.2	1.77	100	73	24	3	0
1988	45.4	2.62	100	71	24	5	0
1990	55.2	2.50	100	70	23	7	0
1993	103.3	3.63	100	65	20	7	7
Change:							
1978–1993		+263%		−14	−1	+7	+7

Source: SSB 1996b: 375, 559.

Table 8.7   Reform policies and economic conditions in Shandong and Jilin (Data in parentheses stand for rank in the nation.)

	Year			
	1980	1985	1990	1995
GDP Per Capita				
Shandong	402 (12)	887 (10)	1815 (9)	5758 (9)
Jilin	445 (11)	868 (11)	1746 (12)	4414 (14)
Indices of GDP Per Capita (1978 = 100)				
Shandong	117.5	194.7	263.3	556.7
Jilin	107.9	172.6	243.7	394.2
Average Annual Wage Per Staff Member and Worker				
Shandong	745 (18)	1110 (16)	2150 (13)	
Jilin	763 (14)	1081 (19)	1888 (25)	
Average Annual Net Income Per Peasant				
Shandong	210 (10)	408 (10)	680 (13)	1715 (10)
Jilin	237 (6)	414 (9)	804 (7)	1610 (12)

Source: Database on political economy of Chinese provinces. See data sources and bibliography for details.

sector remained almost unchanged, as its share of gross industrial output was 21 percent in 1978 and stayed at 20 percent in 1993.[8]

More steadfast and bolder reforms resulted in larger non-state sectors and faster economic growth in Shandong than Jilin. In Shandong, the output expanded from 30 billion yuan in 1978 to 417 billion yuan in current price in 1993. The growth was 600 percent. In Jilin the gross industrial output expanded from 11 billion yuan in current price in 1978 to 103 billion in 1993. It grew by 263 percent (table 8.6).

Finally, the other most important results of differing reforms is that Shandong's levels of development and living standard caught up with and even surpassed those in Jilin (table 8.7). In 1980 per capita GDP in Shandong was 402 yuan, ranked twelfth in the nation, lower than the 445 yuan and the eleventh rank of Jilin. In 1995, Shandong's per capita GDP amounted to 5,758 yuan, ranked ninth in the nation, far higher than the 4,414 yuan in Jilin and ahead of Jilin's fourteenth rank. Average net rural income was apparently lower in Shandong than in Jilin in 1978. Average urban wages in Shandong was also behind that in Jilin in 1980. By 1990, the average urban wage level in

Shandong surpassed that in Jilin. In 1994, the average rural income in Shandong also surpassed that in Jilin (table 8.7). More determined and consistent reforms in Shandong had thus led to much faster improvement in the populace's living standard than in Jilin and brought residents substantial economic benefits.

9

How China's Leaders Made Reforms Happen

Many post-communist economies where reforms were introduced have witnessed economic decline, and soaring unemployment. Even when some of these economies have started to recover, their unemployment has remained at an uncomfortably high level, and deteriorating public health and urban infrastructure continue to raise concerns.[1] In the aftermath of economic setbacks, economic liberalization in Russia, the former Soviet republics in Central Asia, and Southeastern European countries moved forward only sluggishly. There the economy is dominated by oligopolies run by former state bureaucrats and managers of state enterprises. In contrast, China took an incremental path to reforms. Although many Western analysts, economists, and even political scientists doubted in the 1980s and early 1990s that this path would succeed, it did eventually. Into the 2000s and with hindsight, a comprehensive and well-researched survey published in the United States on the literature on post-communist reforms concluded, however, that the Chinese incremental reform could be regarded as the most successful (Roland 2000). The success of China's economic reform has important implications for other post-communist economies as well as other developing nations that contemplate economic liberalization.

The Chinese economic success has attracted considerable attention from many other developing nations, especially from Russia, India, Indonesia, and Egypt. Russian President Putin, for example, was very interested in Deng's management of reforms. A columnist commented on Putin's trip to China in 2000, "a man as astute as Putin is likely to have gone to China not only to earn the right to speak for them at the G-8 summit, but to learn from China's success relative to the Soviet model. The GNP in China is three times that of Russia. Among the many interests that may have pushed Moscow toward a renewal of relations with Beijing is a certain fascination with the Chinese model for development."[2] Putin met and talked with Deng's daughter at the release of the Russian version of her memoir about Deng. Along with many members in the political and intellectual circle in Russia, Putin admires China's economic achievements in the past two-and-a-half decades. India, another upcoming economic giant, looks to China both as its rival as well as a reference point. In the early 1990s it followed the Chinese path of opening up its long-closed markets. It tried to emulate the Chinese SEZ by setting up its own version of special economic zones to attract foreign investment. Indonesia, the most populous country in Southeast Asia, has been hurt severely by the Asian financial crisis in 1997 and its growth hindered by severe corruption and political instability. There, intellectuals are showing their fascination with China. A leading China scholar in Indonesia has published a book entitled *Learning from China*, calling on his troubled nation to draw useful lessons from the Chinese reform experience.[3] The question that follows is how the Chinese achieved it and what their glowing successes and glaring failures are. To answer this question, we have to come up with a balance sheet of China's reform strategies.

China's Reform Strategies

Economic Strategy—Dual Track System and Liberalized Market Entry (Growing Out of the State Sector)

A crucial element of successful politics is prudent and fitting skills and strategies. Chinese reformist leaders headed by Deng adopted pragmatic reform strategies to push forward their liberal economic agenda, withstood all economic and political adversities, took China down the path of marketization, and engineered high growth for over two-and-a-half decades. China's reform strategies comprise strategies for managing economic transition, leadership conflict, and central-local relations.

On the economic side, China's leaders needed to reform two pillars of the command economy. First, prices were fixed by the state, instead of the market. As a result, they were highly distorted and gave wrong signals to producers and consumers. For example, exaggerated prices in heavy machinery relative to raw materials and agricultural goods encouraged the flow of capital from agriculture and extraction industry to heavy industry. They also led to the underdevelopment of agriculture, extraction industry and manufacturing of consumer goods and overexpansion of heavy machinery in Mao's era. To remove the state prices, Chinese leaders chose an incremental approach called a dual-track system. In the 1980s, there were two types of prices— (1) state-fixed prices for goods allocated within state economic plans; and (2) market prices for goods circulated and sold outside state plans. The government gradually reduced the amount of goods regulated by state plans and expanded those governed by the markets. Market prices played an increasingly large role in the pricing system. Through this strategy, China allowed the market to set prices while allowing economic planning to withdraw from the economy step by step (McMillan and Naughton 1993; Qian 2003). Some China scholars characterize this strategy as "growing out of the plan" (Naughton 1996). By doing so, Chinese leaders avoided the nightmarish consequences of overnight liberalization of all prices, the so-called shock therapy approach to price reform. This radical approach led to a sudden macroeconomic shock, hyperinflation, depressed demand, a collapse in growth, and a long delay in economic recovery (Berg and Blanchard 1994). In contrast, China's growing-out-of-the-plan approach to price reform enabled the economy to expand while undergoing gradual adjustment of prices.

Second, under the planning system the economy was dominated by state enterprises. They were notorious for ambiguous ownership, weak enforcement and protection of property rights, poor management and lack of entrepreneurship, ineffectual incentives for employees, rigid employment arrangement, and soft budget constraints. All these defects have led to waste and overexpansion of SOEs. These state enterprises were also accustomed to state-fixed prices and tended not to be responsive to market prices. A predominance of poorly performing enterprises was certain to result in a fragile and unproductive economy. To cope with this problem, the Chinese state has adopted a strategy that I term "grow out of the state sector." It encourages the growth of competitive and efficient non-state enterprises and pressures state enterprises to become more competitive. In doing so, China's leaders opted also for a gradual approach. They lifted the ban on non-state enterprises, gradually expanded the entry for these enterprises in markets, and offered administrative, legal, financial, and fiscal support for non-state enterprises. Meanwhile, they tried to restructure and financially help out SOEs and prevent their widespread bankruptcy. As a result, many SOEs, especially large ones survived the reforms. They prevent a surge in unemployment and collapses in demands. In competing against non-state enterprises, a number of SOEs are forced to improve their performance. Meanwhile, with liberalized entry to markets and China's Open Policy, non-state enterprises, including collective, private, and foreign enterprises rapidly expand, intensifying competition in China's economy (Gelb, Jefferson, and Singh 1993; McMillan and Naughton 1993). Since the early 1990s they have even become the primary sources of growth (Qian 2003). In contrast, in Eastern Europe new entry remained limited and substantial competition was hardly developed even years after reform (Gelb, Jefferson, and Singh 1993: 127).

This strategy of new entry to markets even enabled leaders to accomplish price reform. Deregulating price control had been difficult as the command economy was characterized by chronic shortage in production inputs and consumer goods (Kornai 1980). The main reason was that SOEs, under soft budget constraints, tended to hoard inputs to avoid uncertainty in delivery. In addition, depressed prices for inputs discouraged production of these inputs. Due to their low degree of marketization and problematic management, SOEs did not respond well to consumers' demands and were also poorly motivated to produce goods that could meet households' demands. Therefore, in an economy where shortages and dominance of SOEs prevail, any lift in price control would lead to hyperinflation and popular opposition to reforms. However, as non-state enterprises rapidly grew to become the dominant producer, they were quick to respond to consumers' demands and provide their supplies. Higher prices would only encourage them to expand their production. Thus by 1992, when non-sate businesses accounted for nearly half of the nation's industrial output, supplies of consumers' goods had become abundant. Deregulating price control would no longer lead to price fluctuation. Price reform in the early and mid-1990s became smooth and was accepted by the populace.

The absence of massive exits of state enterprises typical of many Eastern European post-communist economies allowed China to maintain a high level of employment and a steady growth of urban demand for consumers' goods and to sustain economic expansion. This book reveals how China's leaders have succeeded in implementing this "growing out of the state sector" strategy. It examines reformists' strategies of managing their policy disputes with conservatives and for implementing reforms across the provinces by opening up provinces and promoting the growth of collective, private, and foreign enterprises. It also reveals how reform was carried out in the provinces.

Leadership Conflict Management Strategy

Two Steps Forward, One Step Back

All major reform policies in the nation had to win the approval from China's national leadership. However, in the reform period of 1978–1993, national leadership was divided. Initially, it was divided into Maoists and pragmatists. Later, especially since 1980, pragmatists fell into two factions. These factions fought intensely and continuously over the pace of economic reforms and opening. The reformist faction headed by Deng Xiaoping had to manage their relations with the opponents, namely, conservatives, in order to roll out major reforms. Here, Deng displayed his adroit political skills. As examined in chapter 3, Deng advanced his liberal agenda whenever circumstances permitted. When reforms led to macroeconomic instability and imbalance as well as popular resentment, Deng did not hesitate to retreat and allow conservatives to dominate economic policies for the time being. Meanwhile, Deng alertly watched for opportunities to strike back at conservatives. When retrenchment from reforms caused economic stagnation and rising unemployment, Deng would step forth and call for liberal policies. New rounds of reforms led to immediate economic recovery. This strategy of two steps forward and one step back allowed China's reforms to sail through the political storms. By 1992, the reforms agenda had gained overwhelming support from the provinces and from within the Party.

Finding a Common Ground with Opponents

Meanwhile, Deng was quick to find strong common ground with conservatives and maintain it. He allied with conservatives in maintaining the Party's leadership. This position earned Deng the ultimate support from the veterans for his leadership, if not for all of his policies. They saw Deng as a reliable leader for ensuring the survival of the political regime in which they had invested their lifetime. Admittedly, this choice had one grave consequence, namely, the delay of political reform.

Controlling the Military

As stated in chapter 3, Deng controlled the military throughout the reform period. The military would give him a crucial backing in the event of a critical political struggle within the Party. In 1992 when he launched the final political offensive on conservative policies in his lifetime, he called on the military to make a public stance on his behalf. The military pledged to "patrol for and safeguard the course of reforms," sending a strong signal to wavering national leaders in charge of daily decision making to follow suit. The military's backing enabled Deng to eventually triumph over conservatives in a protracted and constant battle over marketization.

Utilizing the Appointment of Cadres

Deng exercised his control of personnel in a manner that helped advance his reform agenda. This strategy is closely analyzed in chapter 4. Due to his predominant status in the Party, the administration, and the military, Deng had an ultimate say over who could enter the Politburo, the top Party organ. Deng keenly recognized that reformist leaders in key posts would help implement his reform agenda. This is particularly so as China has remained, as of today, a country of rule of man, instead of rule of law. Deng thus wasted no time in purging Maoists in the late 1970s. To build up a large reserve of young leaders who backed his liberal platform during and after his lifetime, Deng had been actively promoting young technocrats since the start of reforms. Older and poorly educated leaders as well as leaders with primarily military backgrounds were persuaded to leave the Politburo. A compromise was also reached between the veteran and young leaders where a dozen top veteran leaders retained their power over critical policies and appointments to leading Party and government posts and continued to advise and supervise young frontline leaders from behind.

Nevertheless, Deng still managed to quickly drop conservatives from the Politburo and staffed it with leaders from his own faction. Since 1985, reformists had become the largest group in the Politburo. Younger and better educated leaders as well as leaders with governmental work experience made up the majority of the Politburo membership since the mid-1980s. The majority of them had worked in the coastal provinces which leaned strongly toward reforms. These young technocrats were more open-minded than those with only military, Party and inland regional working experience. They were in charge of daily policy making. They not only supported marketization, but also knew about economic management. Young and pro-reform leaders, such as Hu Yaobang and Zhao Ziyang in the 1980s and Qiao Shi, Li Ruihuan, and Zhu Rongji after 1988, helped Deng to manage and execute reforms in daily affairs and sided with Deng in consolidating the reform platform at critical junctures, such as in 1992.

Heeding National Patrons of Provinces

As shown in chapter 6, in opening up areas to foreign business, national reformists favored provinces with patrons who served as the

Politburo members or among the eight elders. This was to ensure political support from the most influential leaders for the implementation of the Open Policy in the provinces and to maximize the likelihood of success in the provinces.

Strategy for Managing Central–Local Relations

In a large and populous country like China, national leaders can be sure that their policies are implemented when provincial leaders faithfully carry them out. One of the major political blocks within China's political polity is provincial leaders. They took up a significant portion of seats at the Central Committee of the Party, an important national political body that selects national leaders. Deng and reformist leaders also made strenuous efforts to court them. Their strategy, as Shirk (1993) put it, was to decentralize economic authority for the political support from the provinces. More importantly, provincial leaders were in charge of actual policies in the provinces. However, how reformist leaders managed central–local relations and furthered reforms still deserves close examination.

Selecting Likely Winners to Reform First and Creating Demonstration Effects

As the outcome of the earliest reform in the provinces could mean life or death for the liberal course, reformist leaders carefully selected the provinces for the earliest experiment. In general, they allowed the provinces with political and social propensities for economic liberalization and the greatest economic potential for subsequent economic growth to embark on reforms first. For example, in implementing the Open Policy, they asked Guangdong and Fujian to become the pioneers. Guangdong and Fujian enjoyed geographic proximity and strong social linkage with Hong Kong and Taiwan, respectively. They have also a long history of foreign economic contact and domestic commerce. These two provinces, especially Guangdong, have the most open-minded local leaders and population who are enterprising and receptive to liberal economic policies.

Obviously, this choice of the earliest location for reforms is by no means "unbiased." From the policy maker point of view, the optimal choice has to be selective and preferential. This designed "bias" in political experiments is necessary for ensuring successes in the policy and for generating the demonstration effect for the rest of the nation. Apparently, reformists achieved their ends. The Open Policy was an astounding success in Guangdong, generating strong economic growth, and enabling the province to take up 20 percent of the FDI of the nation and 11 percent of China's exports in 1983, two to three years after the establishment of the SEZs. These shares increased to a much higher level in the coming years. In addition, Guangdong's fiscal revenue rapidly expanded. As stated in chapter 5, Guangdong even improved its rank of the provincial economic size in the nation from the sixth in 1980 to No. 1 in 1995. Guangdong's success triggered a process of competitive liberalization across the nation, as other provinces rushed to demand the central government for opening and greater authority in local economic decision making. Reformist leaders thus stimulated local pressure for reforms and opening up and were able to use the local block to fight against or circumvent central conservatives.

Generating Sectoral Support and Economic Returns in Reforms
As stated, in initiating the opening up of Guangdong and Fujian, reformist leaders wanted to create a showcase for the Open Policy. When opening up the other provinces, they had two things in mind—sectoral support and economic returns. Again, the opening of China at the second stage after Guangdong was still carefully controlled and managed. National leaders wanted to open up provinces where sectoral support would be strong, namely, where non-state sectors were sizable and could benefit substantially from the opening, and would strongly support the Open Policy. In addition, they wanted to open up provinces close to the coast, with easy access to sea ports, and to some extent, with great trade potential with the neighboring economies. Again, reformist leaders wanted to see that expanded reform would generate social support and economic success and would not simply become "goodies" tossed to any locality which asked for it. This strategic consideration would place reforms on a solid footing and enable them to take root in the economy and society.

Appointing Able Liberals to Adopt Reforms In
Targeted Provinces
An important instrument that national leaders possessed was their power to select leading officials, including Politburo members and provincial leaders. Until today central Party leadership reserves the power to appoint and dismiss provincial leaders, especially the No. 1 provincial leader, namely, the Provincial Party Secretary. In many cases, the approval of governor and vice governors by the provincial

legislature continue to be a formality, despite some exceptions. Huang (1996) detailed the central management of provincial leadership and rightly attributed this to China's continued national political unity. In the provinces where reformist leaders wanted reforms to be tested out first, Deng and his lieutenants took great care to make sure that reformist, skillful, and resourceful leaders would take charge. These leaders, such as Ren Zhongyi and Ye Xuanping in Guangdong, skillfully resisted conservative opposition to reforms in the provinces and took personal initiatives and even risks to protect local enthusiasm for reforms. They thus played a key role in designing and maintaining the reform drive in the provinces and in generating economic successes.

As stated, Deng carefully selected as Politburo members young technocrats from pro-reform coastal provinces where reforms had a greater chance of success. In addition, Deng conscientiously favored leaders with both central and local working experience and reduced the representation of those who had only central working experience at the Politburo. These young leaders could play a dual role at the Politburo—ensuring that national authority would be respected while provincial enthusiasm in economic liberalization would be duly protected. In the early 1980s, leaders who worked in the provinces that were conducting the earliest reforms, especially Guangdong took up a significant number of seats at the Politburo. Their seats would help reforms in these provinces.

Promoting Officials Who Best Generated Growth and Revenue Through Reform

As documented by China scholars (Whiting, 2001: 270–73; Bo 2002: 111–12, 123–24) and widely accepted by China analysts (Lai 2005a: 59–63, 212–224), local leaders who had embarked on bold and effective reforms, engineered rapid transformation of the local economy, and generated handsome revenue returns were rewarded with promotion. This primary emphasis on economic and fiscal growth in promoting officials gave them very strong incentives to pursue reform, attract investment, and stimulate the expansion of the non-state and state sectors. This also helped reduce local resistance to reform.

Balancing Efficiency With Equity

During Mao's era, the central government controlled many policy initiatives and uses of funds. Provincial fiscal revenue was also supervised carefully by the MOF. This rigid institution stifled local initiatives for engineering economic development. The central government also put a large portion of investment in the unproductive interior provinces and left productive coastal provinces an inadequate amount of investment (D. Yang 1990). While this strategy helped to reduce regional inequality, it came with a hefty price—the most productive coast was deprived of a good chance to grow much faster economically. Much of the population was also in poverty and poorly motivated to generate wealth.

In starting reforms, Deng proposed two famous slogans. (1) At the initial stage of development, the state should allow some people to get rich first (*rang yibufen ren xian fu qilai*). (2) At a later stage, all people should get rich together (*gongtong fuyu*). The period of 1978–1998 can be regarded as the initial stage. As stated, Deng gave preferential treatment to the coastal provinces which had the best economic potential for growth and asked interior provinces to accept a less privileged status in national development. Even in the coastal region, Deng selected some provinces to try out reforms first and raised their fiscal retention rate faster than others. These provinces include Guangdong, Fujian, and Shandong. They had a certain capacity for generating revenue, yet were not the largest contributors to the central coffer in the 1980s. After these provinces succeeded in their reforms and were expanding their economy, especially after the early 1990s, the central government started to ask them to make greater contribution to central fiscal revenue. Starting from the early 1990s, national leaders also allowed the heavy revenue-remitting provinces, especially Shanghai to retain a larger share of its fiscal revenue and to enjoy preferential policies in domestic reform and opening up. By granting Shanghai control over a greater fiscal surplus, it gave the province a great stimulant for faster reform and helped to turn the Yangtze Delta centering around Shanghai into a new region for high growth after the Pearl River Delta based in Guangdong.

Even though the coastal provinces were allowed to "get rich first," central leaders also wanted to maintain a minimal level of support for the underachieving provinces in the reforms. As described above, the central government continued to subsidize provinces like Jilin which fell into fiscal difficulties. Despite cuts in subsidies in some years its amount of subsidies grew over the years, even though it might account for a smaller share of the subsidized provinces' growing revenue. In 1993, as reform and development in the coast had consolidated, the center extracted more fiscal remittance from the coastal provinces. It also drastically increased its subsidies to Jilin, easing its fiscal deficits accumulated in the past few years. These subsidies could be regarded as a form of side-payment for reversing the Maoist preferential treatment for the interior provinces. Although sometimes the central funding was barely adequate for these provinces, it helped these provinces considerably to ease fiscal hardship and maintain their allegiance to the central government and acquiescence to reforms in the nation.

Local Reform Strategy

Reforms can succeed only when they really occur at the local level and when they are embraced by local leaders, officials, and population. It is worthwhile for us to have an overview of the local strategy for reform discussed in the previous chapter on Shandong and Jilin. Once we better understand local behavior during reforms, we can draw useful implications and have a better idea about what type of national strategy for reform would have a better chance of succeeding.

Responding to Fiscal Incentives

In both Shandong and Jilin, fiscal arrangements and conditions played an important part in kindling local reform efforts. When a province (such as Shandong) had certain fiscal capacity, higher retention rates would certainly send a strong and positive signal to local leaders to liberalize the economy. For provincial leaders, a higher retention rate means a greater residual surplus and a handsome reward for their reform efforts. The harder they promoted non-state enterprises, the faster these enterprises grew, and the more revenue provinces could generate and retain. However, when a province (such as Jilin) faced chronic fiscal deficits, its primary concern was fiscal subsistence (or survival). It would have neither the enterprising spirit to run the fiscal risk of liberalizing the economy for the hope of generating strong growth, nor the resources to offer tax reduction and exemption and to provide an amicable environment for business. It is thus difficult, though not impossible to motivate these provinces to embark on new liberal policies and face fiscal uncertainties.

Considering National Atmospheres for Reforms

As national leaders controlled the appointment of provincial leaders, provinces naturally would heed and weigh carefully national political atmospheres and central preferences for liberalization or retrenchment. However, provinces may respond differently to central directives. Shandong did not rely on central subsidies and could also retain most of its revenue. Therefore, Shandong achieved quasi fiscal independence from the center. Faster reform would allow Shandong's fiscal base to expand and permit it to retain a greater amount of revenue. In addition, Shandong's top leaders since the mid-1980s were native Shandongese. They had an extensive network and local backing. Last but not least, Shandong leaders since 1986 have been committed reformists. They had the courage to keep a distance from post-Tiananmen central directives to retreat from reforms during the 1989–1991 period. Deng tolerated this deviance and was even quietly pleased with Shandong's liberal recalcitrance. Shandong was also widely believed to have actively lobbied central ministries in the late 1980s and the 1990s for favorable policies.

Jilin, on the other hand, was fiscally dependent on the center. It relied on central subsidies to ease its chronic fiscal deficits. Leaders of the provinces were conservative prior to 1988, bandwagoners from 1988–1991, and reformists only after 1991. Therefore, the provincial leaders were inclined to minimize any possible confrontation with the central government. Whenever central leaders announced major retrenchment of reforms in the period of 1978–1991, Jilin leaders were careful to voice openly their support and did not institute any local policies that obviously contravened the center's directives.

Restructuring Bureaucracy and Building Good Governance to Improve the Business Environment

The contrast in reforms in Shandong and Jilin suggested that a lean, efficient, and friendly bureaucracy was central to the implementation of liberal economic policies decided by provincial leaders. However, such a bureaucracy usually did not exist in the first place. It takes strenuous efforts and years of persistent and well-conceived efforts by provincial leaders to build a bureaucracy conducive to economic reforms. Such a bureaucracy is the key to good economic governance, which requires the bureaucracy to act responsibly, efficiently, transparently, and be friendly, in providing services for the business community. Since the mid-1980s Shandong leaders had been consistent in downsizing the bureaucracy, introducing a set of regulations to simplify and institutionalize bureaucratic procedures, and requiring efficient and friendly services from officials. They also embraced some form of transparency and public supervision. As a result of these efforts, Shandong officials were accustomed to provide timely and good services for non-state enterprises. In contrast, efforts of this kind were few and belated in Jilin. Bureaucracy in Jilin was bloated, inefficient, and resistant to restructuring. It was keen to maintain its authority through keeping redundant personnel and departments and red tape. It was quick to support central conservative policies that allowed them to use their power to restrict activities of non-state enterprises. It was also powerful enough to stall provincial reform policies until the mid-1990s.

Flaws in China's Reform Strategies

So far I have been highlighting the bright side of China's reform strategy. There is no denying that China's reforms have failed to address a number of issues which will continue to harass China's economic development. This chapter will only discuss the most out-standing ones. These defects are partly intentional, a choice by China's leaders. They have chosen to delay the resolution of the most daunting issues that would entail tremendous economic dislocation and a possible end to the Party's monopoly of power—(1) democratization and genuine rule of law that would challenge the Party's monopoly of power, (2) drastic reform of SOEs that would lead to a sudden surge in unemployment, as well as the state's loss of control over strategic economic sectors, and (3) a complete overhaul of the banking system that could have grave effects on the financial market and the economy.

Political Reforms Lagging Behind Economic Liberalization
China's top leaders did contemplate limited political reforms in the late 1980s, such as separating the Party from the administration and enterprise management as well as expanding the role of the legislature. However, the Tiananmen protests frightened conservative and orthodox reformist leadership and caused them to worry about a possible collapse of the regime. During the Tiananmen movement, Deng ousted open-minded reformists such as the Party Secretary Zhao Zhiyang who was soft toward popular demands for political opening. Deng called in the military to crack down on the long-lasting and unyielding protests. The end of the Communist regime in the former Soviet Union and Eastern Europe and the disintegration of the USSR in the early 1990s only reinforced the Chinese leadership's fears about democratization. Since then Chinese leaders have been haunted by the post-Tiananmen syndrome. They worry that fast democratization would only cause the Party to lose its power and China to disintegrate. They have placed a hold on rapid political reforms.

Today the Party still retains its firm control over major state apparatus, including the administration, the legislature, the court, the police, the military, and the public media at all levels. Open elections are allowed only at the village level. No other political parties are allowed to compete against the Party's candidates at any level. Even the Party's leading posts at most levels are filled without competitive elections. The state has been actively ferreting out dissents. It is also restraining their expression of vocal political opinions and criticisms of top provincial and national leaders and penalizing transgressors through relieving them of their public posts and even detaining and jailing them.

Only after the new leadership headed by Hu Jintao and Wen Jiabao assumed power in 2003 did Chinese leaders start to reassess the necessity to gradually kick off the process of political liberalization. However, so far the pace of democratization has been timid. The current emphasis on political reform the current leadership has laid since the late 1990s, if any, is on tactical improvements of political mechanisms—cadres' responsibility is enhanced and enforced, corruption is cracked down, and law making in the economic sphere is strengthened. Since 2003, new leaders headed by Hu Jintao have been also holding officials accountable for major errors. They also have increased the transparency on major public policy issues including public health, catastrophes, employment, and peasants' income. In addition, they want to enhance the role of law in governmental work as well as legal protection of private property. The most dramatic move on democratization may be experiments in several localities to enlarge the role of the Party committee and congress at the national and local levels and step up their supervision of Party leaders at these levels. Entry of other parties in the political market and political competition in the form of open elections of public posts above the village level, however, are not within policy makers' horizon. Citizens' freedom to choose leaders, assemble for political purposes, speak out in public against the Party-state, and even publicly protest against official abuse of power and violation of their own interests continues to be very limited.

Many SOEs Continuing to be Inefficient

Despite efforts in the past two decades of reforms, SOEs have not fundamentally reversed their disadvantageous position in competition against non-state enterprises. Since the late 1970s, the state has initiated several rounds of SOEs reforms. First, it adjusted partially distorted prices and forced SOEs to pay interest for their capital borrowed from the bank. Second, after the mid-1980s, it introduced long-term contracts between enterprises and bureaucratic supervisors and granted managers greater autonomy in making decisions. Third, after 1993, it attempted to introduce a modern enterprise system in SOEs (Naughton 1996: 97–136, 200–243; Hannan 1998; Lardy 1998: 21–24). It accelerated the reform of SOEs after 1997 by selling out and leasing out small SOEs and restructuring and helping out medium- and large-sized SOEs. It also outsourced the social welfare function of SOEs, turned SOEs into limited liability companies, introduced boards of directors, raised pays for CEOs and managers, allowed SOEs to be listed at the stock markets, and reduced their debts and taxes.[4]

However, the reform has not yet achieved its goals of making SOEs efficient firms. SOEs witness a decline in their abnormal profits that they enjoyed in the 1980s. They are also burdened by excessive wage payments, redundant employees, and staggering expenditures on social welfare. Facing declining profitability, a significant number of SOEs rely heavily on funds raised at the stock market, heavy fiscal subsidies from the state and the state banks for "blood"-transfusion (Lardy 1998: 25–58).

Severe issues have held up the reform of SOEs. They still suffer from weak enforcement of property rights. This allows their managerial staff to engage in asset stripping. The most serious problem with SOEs is the lack of good corporate governance. There is still inadequate internal effective supervision of managers and a lack of able and responsible boards of directors. Furthermore, corporate decisions, uses of funds, and accounting often do not follow proper procedures. In addition, the necessary information is not disclosed, or the disclosed information is inaccurate and inadequate, preventing investors and regulators from effectively and timely assessing the performance of SOEs and exerting pressure on them. A number of managers of SOEs are not qualified to manage but are still appointed by the Party. Despite some recent adjustments in pays, these managers are still lowly paid compared with those of non-state enterprises. Or, they are perversely motivated to embezzle corporate funds and assets to make up for their inadequate wages. They are thus poorly motivated and hardly capable of doing a good job. In addition, although employment practice has liberalized, it is still restrained by the state's fear that mass layoffs will lead to protests and political instability. The state also requires SOEs to finance pensions for their retirees; SOEs thus need to shoulder various welfare expenses.

State Banks Overloaded with Bad Loans

Incomplete and unsuccessful reform of SOEs leads to staggering non-performing loans (NPLs). The SOEs rely on banks for financing, most of which are state controlled. The state is determined to ensure the survival of medium- and large-sized SOEs. But as the profitability of these SOEs declines, the loans they borrowed from state banks cannot be paid in time, or even recovered at all. By 2002, China's NPLs had reached an alarming level. The official estimate is that NPLs accounted for 26 percent of the total loan portfolio, yet international financial agencies placed the ratio at much higher levels, ranging from Moody's 40 percent to Standard & Poor's 50 percent.[5]

The problems with China's financial systems are graver than those in other emerging markets. First, China's NPL ratio has far surpassed the 19 percent that South Korea registered in 1997 when the Asian Financial Crisis hit. Second, China's financial system is dominated by banks, whose share of financial intermediation reach nearly 90 percent, higher than virtually most other Asian countries. Third, almost all banks in China (at least those which are allowed to operate legally and openly) are state owned (Lardy 1998: 16). Fourth, even though non-state enterprises now account for most of the economic output and activities, they, especially domestic small ones, cannot obtain adequate financing from banks. Instead, most of the bank loans are channeled to SOEs.

As China is opening up its financial markets in the wake of the WTO entry, its banks will be forced to become more competitive. However, financial opening could entail considerable risks (Lardy 2002: 128–31; C. Chen 2003). State banks may have a difficult time in competing with foreign banks that are allowed to enter China. One of the most troublesome consequences of competition is the brain drain from state to foreign banks. In the recent years many able former state bank clerks have accepted jobs at foreign banks operating in China for higher pay and a better working environment, bringing with them their networks with clients as well as insiders' knowledge about strengths and weaknesses of state banks.[6]

Major Problems in the Wake of High Growth and Remedies

In addition to the above defects of China's economic reform, China now confronts a number of serious political, economic, and social problems. They include income inequalities, an underdeveloped social safety net, resources- and inputs-intensive growth, and corruption and abuse of power. It should be noted at the outset that China is far from being alone in confronting these problems. Many transitional economies as well as developing countries also suffer from these problems. Even some developed economies also confront some of these problems. For example, income inequalities are significant challenges for the United States, Singapore, and Hong Kong. It is worth noting that China's new leaders headed by President Hu Jintao and Premier Wen Jiabao treated inequalities, social security, inefficient growth, and corruption as top priorities of their governance and have introduced a number of measures. Given limited space, only a brief overview of these problems and emerging remedial measures can be presented here.

Income Inequalities and Social Instability

In pushing for China's economic reform in the early 1980s, Deng stated that some people and regions should be allowed to get rich first. This move aimed at breaking Mao's egalitarian economic program that stifled incentives for advantaged individuals to work harder in order to earn more and for well-endowed regions to grow faster. These differentiated growth policies have helped to engineer rapid growth in the 1980s and the 1990s in China. Between 1978 and 2002 China's per capita GDP grew by 5.4 times, per capita rural income grew by 4.3 times, and per capita urban income by 3.7 times. By 2002 China's per capita GDP reached US$940, higher than that of India (US$480), Sri Lanka (US$840), and Indonesia (US$710)(SSB 2003; World Bank 2003).

Nevertheless, the state has yet to reach its ultimate goal of economic reform of enriching all the people. Residents of large cities and the coastal region are the primary beneficiaries of reform as most of them have indeed become well off. The other strata, including inland peasants and low-skilled and laid-off workers of the cities, have yet to attain a comfortable life.

Urban-rural, inter-regional and inter-strata income gaps have increased in the reform era, especially since the late 1980s. In 1978, an average rural resident's consumption was equivalent to 34.1 percent that of an average urban resident. It improved to 43.3 percent in 1985 with the success of agrarian reform, but decreased by nearly 10 percent to 33.9 percent in 1990 and to an alarming 27.8 percent in 2001. In contrast, in many other countries the rural income level was equivalent to two-thirds of the urban level. Moreover, growth varied markedly among regions. Per capita resident income in the interior region in 1985 was 67 percent that of the coastal region. This ratio declined to 55.8 percent in 1995 and reached a much lower 46.5 percent in 2001. Finally, the income gap of different strata has enlarged, as levels of skills of labor vary and wage differentials widen. The urban Gini coefficient rose from 0.16 in 1978, to 0.27 in 1993 and to 0.33 in 2001; the Gini coefficient in the countryside grew from 0.21 in 1978, to 0.32 in 1993 and to 0.42 in 2000 (Lai 2005b: 4–6).

Inequality breeds instability in China. A national survey of 15,000 urban residents in thirty-one provinces in 2002 suggested that unemployment, corruption, income disparities, and poverty were top concerns. All these concerns except corruption relate directly to rising inequality (Lai 2005b: 6). Collective disturbances have increased dramatically from 8,700 in 1993 to 58,500 in 2003 according to Chinese governmental statistics.

Upon coming to power in March 2003, President Hu Jintao and Premier Wen Jiabao viewed income inequalities as a primary social concern for the state. Arguably, they have made the most efforts to contain growing economic gaps. Subsidies and financial inputs for grain production have been increased, agricultural taxes and fees are lowered, and governmental enforcement of timely payment and respect of rights for migrant workers in the cities has been stepped up. These measures have increased peasants' income. In addition, the state has not only maintained the western developmental program, but has also launched programs to revive the rust-belt northeast and the grain-producing central region. These regional policies aim to contain rising inter-regional gaps. Finally, the state has increased its financial support for low-income groups in the cities, aiming to reduce intra-strata income gaps.

An Underdeveloped Social Safety Net

As China's economy is increasingly marketized, a social safety net can provide the labor force the best protection from brute forces of markets, including laid-off and loss of income-earning capacity due to illness and aging. Unfortunately, China's social security is still at a stage of early development. By 2003, only 36 percent of urban labor force were covered by health care and 51 percent covered by pension programs (*China Labor Statistical Yearbook* 2004: 204, 527, 571). Most of rural residents were not even covered. Therefore, the task for providing comprehensive social-security coverage for the population is daunting. The Hu-Wen leadership is striving to increase the coverage of both urban and rural population. It has increased fiscal support for health care, pension, and unemployment programs in the cities. It has also designed programs to extend health care coverage for residents in the countryside as well as migrant peasant workers in the cities. It encourages localities to build up its social security programs for its rural residents.

An "Extensive" Mode of Growth

The Hu-Wen leadership is keenly aware that China's high growth in the past decades is based partly on heavy inputs of capital as well as raw materials and energy. This extensive mode of growth has aggravated environmental degradation in China and can hardly be sustained in the coming decades. New leaders call on cadres and provinces to shift to a lighter yet intensive mode of economic growth. President Hu proposed a scientific concept of development in 2003, urging cadres to consider social and environmental costs of development in addition to economic ones. At the Fifth Plenum of the Sixteenth Party Central Committee in October 2005, the leadership incorporated this notion into its guideline for the Eleventh Five-year Plan. It proposed that new, indigenously developed and energy- and resources-saving technology should be a driving force for China's future economic growth and that local governments should make investment decisions on the basis of comprehensive costs and benefits and with sound economic rationale.

Corruption and Abuse of Power

One of the most damaging political side-effects in the reform era is rampant corruption and wide spread abuse of power of cadres in China. For example, from 1997–2002 846,000 Party members and 98 provincial or ministerial level officials were disciplined due to corruption, up by 26 percent from 1992–1997. At the grass-root levels abuse of power by officials, such as illegal demolition of housing of urban residents and illicit seizure of land from peasants, is often reported.

In order to contain corruption and abuse of power, the Hu-Wen leadership has taken a number of reactive and institutional measures. A significant number of senior corrupt officials have been exposed, including full ministers and provincial Party secretaries. In addition, the power and independence of the most powerful corruption-fighting organ, namely, the Party Disciplinary Commission (PDC) has been enhanced. Now the head of the commission at the provincial level is appointed by the central Party, instead of provincial Party committees. The center dispatches commissioners to check on provinces. The State Audit Bureau has also conducted audits of provincial agencies annually, exposing local financial and even banking irregularities. These measures help to restrain rapid expansion of corruption. The new leadership also allows for experiment of intra-Party democracy, such as permanent representation of delegates of the local Party congress, aiming to supervise the most-powerful local Party bosses.

Nevertheless, the Party continues to be above the law or behind the law enforcement. Media reports of corruption cases are closely censored. The PDC is still not fully independent at the local level. Most importantly, democracy is still lacking at the local level, as local legislators are not freely elected, elections are restricted to villages and have not been held at higher levels, and the Party and the government still muddle in law enforcement at the local levels.[7]

Lingering Restrictions on the Non-state Economy

As the non-state business is playing a significant role in China's economy, many local governments and even the national government provide generous support for large, successful, and well-known non-state firms, especially foreign ones.[8] Nevertheless, other non-state firms do not enjoy the same treatment. The Hu-Wen leadership realizes that non-state sectors have yet to enjoy favorable policies for expansion as does the state sector and that domestic non-state sectors have yet to enjoy the same favorable treatment as the foreign ones. In particular, in the following areas restrictions on these sectors remain and these sectors deserve better services and treatment. First, more sectors need to be opened to the non-state firms. In particular, those sectors that have been opened for foreign enterprises can also be opened for domestic non-state firms. Second, banks should increase its lending for these sectors, instead of focusing merely on SOEs. Third, the government should improve its services for these sectors, facilitating their expansion and generation of jobs.

In order to address these issues, the State Council promulgated in February 2005 "Several Opinions regarding Encouraging, Supporting and Guiding Development of Individuals, Privately Managed and Other Non-Public Economy" (the No. 3 State Council Document of 2005). This landmark policy document stipulates three significant measures. First of all, it declares that these domestic non-state sectors are allowed to enter sectors of natural monopoly (such as electric power, telecommunications, railway, aviation, and petroleum), public utility and infrastructure (such as water, gas, public bus, and garbage disposal), social services (including education, research, health, culture and sports), financial services, national defense industry, overhaul and restructuring of SOEs, and regional development schemes such as western development, northeast revival, and the development of the central region. Second and related to the first measure, the domestic non-state sectors would enjoy the same treatment as do those of other ownership. Finally, the state would step up support for these sectors in fiscal matters, finance and credit, financial services, direct funding-raising, credit guarantee, intermediate social services (such as information services), entrepreneurship, employee training, technological innovation, market exploration, expansion of firms, industrial specialization and sectoral agglomeration, protection of property rights and employee rights and welfare, social security for employees, and labor unions. The state would also supervise these sectors over their observation of laws and regulations, corporate management, improvement in enterprise operation and quality of managers, and labor-management relations. The government would improve its services and supervision of these sectors, such as fair fees, transparent supervision rules, and improvement in the quality of officials regulating these sectors. This document signals the Chinese state's stride toward providing for an amicable environment for domestic non-state firms. However, it will take considerable efforts and time before these new policies are faithfully implemented.

China has attained phenomenal high growth in the past quarter of a century by following a pragmatic and prudent economic reforms strategy. Its leadership skillfully maneuvers to bypass political and economic obstacles in sustaining the course of marketization. It has also wisely promoted the non-state sectors and enabled them to become a key pillar in China's high growth. In order to address existing problems, however, China needs to adjust its reform strategy by addressing economic disparities, reducing environmental damage, improving technology, introducing democracy and rule of law especially at the local levels, and sustaining the healthy growth of the non-state economy. These tasks may determine whether China can stay on a course of stable and high growth in the coming decades.

Notes

1 Economic Transition and the Case of China

1. The differences between the two models including the four economic attitudes were highlighted in Roland 2000: 330–31.

2. This view is implicit in the writings of leading big bang advocates. Refer to Lipton and Sachs 1990, Sachs 1996, Wolf 1991. A few works (such as Kornai 1990) have been viewed by some (Roland 2000; Kornai 2003) as a mixture of calls for both incremental and radical reforms.

3. For an excellent discussion on the division between the two schools over irreversibility of reform, partial reform, and the role of the state, refer to Roland 2000: 31–48, 329–32, 335, 341.

4. The center (*zhongyang* in Chinese) refers to the "State Council and its commissions, ministries, and leadership small groups in Beijing as well as the party Politburo, Secretariat, and the organs of the Central Committee." This term can be used interchangeably with the central or national government/authority for the sake of simplicity. The term "province" or "provincial government" refers to provincial Party and administrative authorities. See Lieberthal and Oksenberg 1988: 138; Cheung, Chung and Lin 1998: 3.

5. The literature on the post-Mao central-local relations is rich. Other primary but nonexclusive examples include Wong 1986; 1997; Zweig 2002; Unger 1987; Li and Bachman 1989; Lieberthal and Oksenberg 1988; Tong 1989; White 1998a; 1998b; Lieberthal and Lampton 1992; Oksenberg and Tong 1991; Howell 1993; Jia and Lin 1994; Goodman and Segal 1994; Fan 1995; Wong, Heady, and Woo 1995; Goodman 1997; Hendrischke and Feng 1999; Wei 2000; Whiting 2001; Fitzgerald 2002.

6. One exception is Susan Shirk (1993; 1994: 27–33). She attributed the success of China's reform to three factors, namely, gradualism, administrative decentralization, and particularistic contracting. However, her brief discussion can be strengthened by empirical analyses of the political tactics of managing elite conflict and promoting young leaders, as well as varying central fiscal contracts with provinces.

7. Treisman (1999) analyzes the differing effects of decentralization in Russia, Yugoslavia, and China. His innovative arguments can be strengthened by distinguishing economic decentralization that can lead to economic gains, as practiced in China, from political decentralization which can threaten national unity.

8. In this book I define strategies broadly as *conscious choices* for managing reforms. A key point is that Chinese reformist leaders consciously managed reforms in a certain way and rejected other alternatives. Their choices could be made for political convenience and could vary according to phases or tasks of reforms, but have turned out to be fruitful over the years. But their choices were often made after weighing the high costs of alternative options. For example, Deng supported marketization but opposed democratization. He feared that the latter would generate chaos, weaken the state's governing capacity, undermine the Party's power, and derail China's economic development. In addition, he opted for compromises with conservatives when his reforms met severe setbacks, instead of resorting to Mao's all-out attack at his opponents during the Cultural Revolution, or Gorbachev's style of democratization in order to crush conservatives. Deng believed these two alternatives had undesirably large political costs and conscientiously refrained from doing so. Incremental reforms, which are *not* a focus in this book, can also be regarded as a conscientious, albeit not carefully planned reform strategy. The Chinese leaders intentionally favored experiments, constant adjustment, and incrementalism, and rejected shock therapies.

9. Roland (2000: 36–37) modeled gradualist reform as an outcome of strategic compromise by reformists and conservatives. Reformers are optimistic about the outcomes of reform, whereas conservatives are more pessimistic. Reformers prefer radical reforms (liberal measures in the Chinese case) and conservative status quo. Reformers may have the power to propose reforms, but conservatives may veto the proposal. At the end, reformers settle for gradual reforms in order to win the support from conservatives; conservatives also favor gradualism in order to reduce deviation from the status quo and instill pessimism among reformers. As Shirk suggested (1994: 29), this political division largely predetermines that China's reforms would be incremental and that any shock therapy would be opposed and vetoed by conservatives.

10. Interviews with municipal and provincial officials in Guangdong on official performance evaluation in Deng's era, December 2003. This study will only briefly refer to the making of political entrepreneurs as it has been extensively discussed in the literature. Samples of the literature include Gore 1998 and Whiting 2001.

11. Information supplied by a vice minister in charge of SOEs at a talk at East Asian Institute, National University of Singapore, May 7, 2004. Data for figure 1.1 are based on the author's own computation using statistics in SSB 1997, table 13-3; SSB 2000: 409.

12. A recent study (Lai 2005c) suggests that the state sector and reform initiatives in the subnational units, entrenchment of central planning, the size of the defence industry, policy choice and the historical context help explain the differences in Soviet and Chinese reforms. In particular, a predominant state sector in the former Soviet republics had stifled local reform initiatives. Gorbachev resorted to democratization to generate popular support for marketization, yet resulting in the breakup of the nation and destabilization of the economy. In China, some provinces had sizable non-state sectors and were inclined toward marketization. Reform resulted in expanding non-state sectors, generating high growth.

13. For discussion on case selection, refer to Collier and Mahoney 1996; Geddes 1990; King, Keohane, and Verba 1993: Chapter 4; Rogowski 1995. Chung (1995) notes similar methodological shortcomings in the studies of central-provincial relations in China in his review of the literature.

2   Non-State Sectors Policies, 1978 to Present

1. For a detailed account of policy measures, institutions, and agencies regarding private business as well as the growth of private business between the 1950s and the 1980s, refer to Solinger 1984, Young 1995, Kraus 1991, and Lai 2004a.
2. "Full Text of the Communique of the Third Plenum of the Sixteenth Central Committee of the Chinese Communist Party," posted at http:// www. chinanews.com.cn/n/2003-10-14/26/356787.html on October 14, 2003.
3. Rural Enterprise Bureau of Ministry of Agriculture, "An Overview of Development of Rural Enterprises in 2001," *Zhongguo Xiangzhen Qiye Nianjian (China Rural Enterprise Yearbook) 2002*, Beijing: Zhongguo Nongye Chubanshe, p. 4.
4. Chen Lisheng, "Mainland Economic and Trade Microwaves," *Zhangyang Daily*, posted at http://www.cdn.com.tw/daily/2001/07/07/text/90070717.htm.
5. For a historical analysis of the policies between 1949 and 1980, refer to Solinger 1984, 157–295; Kraus 1991: 49–59.
6. For a collection of the policies, refer to Zhang, Liu and Zhu 1985.
7. For a discussion on the relations between the state and private entrepreneurs, refer to LAI Hongyi, "Jiang Attempts to Revive Party Ideology," *EAI Bulletin*, September 2001, vol. 3, no. 2: p. 4; Wibowo 2001; Dickson 2003.
8. "Congress Hails Constitutional Changes" and "Amendments to the Constitution," *China Daily (Hong Kong Edition)*, March 15, 2004: 1–2. See the PRC Constitution posted at http://english.peopledaily.com.cn/ constitution/constitution.html.
9. Charles Hutzler, "Equality Still Eludes China Private Property," *The Asian Wall Street Journal*, December 24–28, 2003 A1, A4.
10. "A Decision concerning Several Issues Related to Perfecting Socialist Market Economic Structure," posted and accessed at http://news.xinhuanet.com on October 21, 2003.
11. For a discussion of economic features of rural private enterprises and the effects of these enterprises on income distribution in the 1980s, refer to Odgaard 1992. For studies on the growth of private businesses in the 1980s, refer to Young 1995: 91–117; Kraus 1991: 62–141.
12. *Zhongguo Jingji Nianjian (China Economic Yearbook) 1997*, pp. 709–10; Stephen Green, "Two-thirds Privatisation: How It Happens," *Chatham House Briefing Note*, London: Royal Institute of International Affairs, December 2003: 2.
13. Jefferson, Hu, Guan, and Yu, 2003: 94, 95, 97.
14. Green, "Two-thirds Privatisation: How It Happens," p. 2; Sun Qian, "China's Bourses Are Looking Up," *Business Times*, February 3, 2004.

15. For a detailed analysis of the SEZs and the Open Policy between 1978 and 1985, refer to chapter 5.

16. "Devotion to Reform and Opening Up," posted at http://big5.xinhuanet.com/gate/ on August 19, 2003, accessed on November 1, 2003. For a detailed analysis of China's laws and regulations on joint ventures from 1979 to 1988, refer to Kleinberg 1990: 167–217; Pearson 1991.

17. A few inland cities, such as Wuhan in June 1988, also announced to adopt some of the preferential policies enjoyed by the coastal open cities (Howell 1993: 87).

18. "External Opening," posted at http://news.xinhuanet.com/ziliao/2003-01/23/content_704704.htm, accessed on August 13, 2005.

19. For an analysis of China's WTO accession and its implications, refer to Lardy 2002. For a detailed study on the conclusion and the context of the agreement, refer to Lai 2001b.

20. "External Opening," posted at http://news.xinhuanet.com/ziliao/2003-01/23/content_704704.htm, accessed on August 13, 2005.

21. The author's own observation in Sichuan, Xinjiang, and Guangdong as well as conversations with national and local officials in charge of economic affairs and China economic experts, 2003–2005.

3   Managing Elite Conflict and Policy Cycles

1. For detailed discussion of the role of top leadership in initiating reforms, refer to Harding (1987), Baum (1996), and White (1993). For empirical documentation of the role of top leaders in reform, refer to Baum (1996) and Ruan (1994).

2. For a thorough discussion on factions, refer to the articles on "The Nature of Chinese Politics," in *The China Journal*, July 1995: 1–208.

3. For discussion of the role of policies and ideology in defining factions, refer to Fewsmith 1994: 3–16; Baum 1996: 9–18.

4. As Lieberthal and Oksenberg (1988: 58–62) and Baum (1996: 9–18) suggested, factional identity could be fluid and in the case of a few leaders, not fixed. Members of the same faction might also compete against each other for advancement. For example, reformist Zhao Ziyang supported the ouster of liberal Hu Yaobang in order to move up the ladder of power. However, as Baum (1996), J. Huang (2000), Fewsmith (1994), as well as many China observers agree, factionalism, despite its fluidity, is a useful tool for analyzing Chinese elite politics.

5. The term "moderate reformists" is used to distinguish this group from *liberal* or *radical* reformists in Eastern Europe in the 1990s and Chinese liberal intellectuals, who embraced both democratization and rapid economic reform.

6. For a discussion on Chen's economic view, see Bachman (1985) and Lardy and Lieberthal (1983).

7. Conservatives might be further divided into moderates and the orthodox. *Moderates* such as Chen Yun believed that a softer approach toward dissidents in the form of admonitions or Party disciplines would protect both the Party's image and legitimacy. On the other hand, *orthodox* conservatives such

as Deng Liqun, along with *orthodox* reformists, valued stern law and strict order and urged stiff punishment of dissidents.

8. For further discussion on Deng-Chen relationship, refer to Fewsmith 1994: 3–18, 241–50.

9. The inflation rates during 1978–1980 and 1989–1991 might be regarded as two minor exceptions. During 1978–1980, Chen Yun and Deng Xiaoping orchestrated the reform initiatives in order to tame inflation during the first two years. Nevertheless, the averaged 2.9 percent was still unusually high by the Chinese standard at that time, for inflation during 1963–1976 ranged between −5.9 percent and 0.6 percent (SSB 1990b: 32). Although inflation in the second and third years of the retreat of 1989–1990 remained low at 2.1 percent and 2.9 percent respectively, unusually high inflation at 17.8 percent in 1989, however, skewed averaged inflation of this period upward to 7.6 percent. The impact of the ill-fated price reform of 1988, coupled with the Tiananmen turbulence in 1989, enabled high inflation to persist in 1989.

10. This is not to deny that during the early period of reform or over certain issues Chen and Deng did cooperate. For example, as Teiwes (1995: 72–77) pointed out, they cooperated in the early 1980s over economic reforms. They did so probably in an effort to defeat and demolish once and for all Maoists and Maoist opposition to economic reform. Likewise, they agreed on the need to reduce corruption and power abuse in the course of reform. Chen also never questioned Deng's "first-among-equals" position. In addition, Chen's reservation over Deng's reformist platform might not be entirely groundless, especially his stress on avoiding rush action and overly optimistic targets (Teiwes 1995: 72–77). Nevertheless, as many China watchers pointed out, their differences over economic reform policies were real and substantial. This point will be taken up in the coming chapters.

4   Installing Technocratic Young Leaders

1. For detailed discussion of the role of the top leadership in initiating reforms, refer to Harding 1987 and White 1993. For highly empirical documentation of influence of top leaders on reform policies, refer to Baum 1996 and Ruan 1994.

2. For an in-depth study of the retirement of cadres, see Manion 1993. For a detailed analysis of cadre rehabilitation, retirement, and recruitment in the 1980s, refer to H. Y. Lee 1991.

3. "The Organizational Line Guarantees the Implementation of the Ideological and Political Lines" (July 29, 1979), *Selected Works of Deng Xiaoping, Volume II (1975–1982)*, posted at http://english.peopledaily. com.cn/dengxp, accessed on October 25, 2003.

4. For discussion of promotion of cadres in Mao's era, refer to Lee 1991: 47–163 and Shirk 1982. Shirk characterized the promotion regime under Mao as virtuocracy, namely, awarding career opportunities to individuals who possessed the moral virtues promoted by the regime.

5. For a detailed explanation of these institutions and their operation, refer to J. Wang, 2002: 69–80 and Lieberthal, 1995: 158–63.

6. Wolfgang Bartke, ed., *Who's Who in the People's Republic of China*. New York: K.G. Saur, 1987; Wolfgang Bartke, ed. *Who Was Who in the People's Republic of China*. New York: K.G. Saur, 1997; *Zhongguo Renming Da Cidian: Dangdai Renwu Zhuan (Who's Who in China: The Volume on Contemporary Figures)*. Shanghai: Shanghai Cishu Chubanshe; and *Xiandai Zhongguo Renmin Cidian (Who's Who in Modern China)*. 1982. Tokyo: Gannando Overseas, Inc.
7. For discussion on political generations in China, refer to Yahuda 1979 and C. Li 2001: 6–14.
8. For a detailed discussion of this interior developmental strategy, refer to D. Yang 1990.
9. See Barry Naughton 1988 for detailed analyses.
10. For detailed discussion of this coastal developmental strategy, refer to D. Yang 1990 and D. Yang 1997.

5   Selective and Showcase Liberalization

1. In September 1980 Jiang Zemin, a deputy director of a national management committee on imports and exports, led a ministerial and provincial delegation to study six export processing zones in the world. The above history on SEZs is compiled from the following sources: Ye 2001; Yang 1998; Jing Tang, "Should the Wire Entanglement of Shenzhen Be Demolished," posted at http://www.chinanews.com.cn in December 2000.
2. Two youths in Foshan of Guangdong I knew personally were caught by the Chinese authority when attempting to illegally cross the border to Hong Kong in the late 1970s. They were sent to labor reform for sometime and then sent back home with their heads shaven. They were viewed by friends and neighbors as ex-criminals for their acts of illegal border crossing (called *tou du* in Chinese, literally, illegal crossing of territorial water).
3. For discussion on the general role of Guangdong's leaders in reform, refer to Cheung 1998a; Cheung 1998b; and Howell 1993.
4. Ye supported Hua during 1978–1980 out of the conviction that Mao entrusted him at his dead bed to support the politically fragile successor Hua and that he should follow the Chinese tradition of fulfilling the will of a deceased "emperor" and supporting the young successor (Yang 1998: 101). Nevertheless, Ye was also traditional in another sense—he was keen to support economic development of his home province Guangdong and supported limited opening and limited use of foreign capital.
5. Deng Xiaoping, "Emancipate the Mind, Seek Truth from Facts and Unite as One in Looking to the Future" (December 13, 1978), posted at http://english.peopledaily.com.cn/dengxp/vol2/text/b1260.html, accessed on November 8, 2003.
6. Ibid. For the significance of these ideas in the Chinese reform, refer to Ye 2001: 1765–66.
7. Chen (1998: 284–86) discussed some of the rationale in choosing the selective opening approach over the widespread opening approach.

8. For discussion of economic history of Guangdong, refer to Lau Yee-cheung 1998; for discussion on Fujian, refer to Lau and Lee 2000.

9. See "Xiamen, Your Name Is Special Zone," posted at http://www.csnn.com.cn/csnn0111/ca32504.htm, accessed on November 1, 2003.

10. "Devotion to Reform and Opening Up," posted at http://big5.xinhuanet.com/gate/ on August 19, 2003, accessed on November 1, 2003.

11. On the basis of his inside observation of the Chinese factional policies, Ruan Ming (1994) suggested that conservatives often employed a legalistic tactics to attack reformists. They would accuse reformists of committing economic crimes or violating the Party's regulations in pursuing liberalization and used it as a pretext to strip them of power.

12. "Devotion to Reform and Opening Up."

13. Ibid.

14. This behavior trait resembled the bandwagoning strategy elaborated in Avery Goldstein's discussion of factional politics in China. See Avery Goldstein, 1991.

15. Frederick Teiwes (1995: 72–78) discussed in detail the relationship between Deng and Chen. He made good points that Chen supported Deng's paramount leadership and agreed with Deng on the Party's rule and discipline. He might have underestimated their differences over economic reform and the complexity and ruthlessness of political conflict in China that many scholars on factional politics in China accept. As stated, Chen and conservative at times tried to slow down or halt liberal reforms through subtle means such as Party discipline or ideological rectification.

16. For the case of Xiang Nan, see the following reports by insiders of Chinese politics: Xu Jiatun, "Wrongful Treatment of Xiang Nan," posted at http://members.lycos.co.uk/sixiang000/author/X/XuJiaTun/XuJiaTun009.txt; Liu Zaifu, "My Mourning over Xiang Nan's Death," posted at http://www.tangben.com/Duyutianya/gy2xiangnan.htm; Wu Dong, "Poor Province and Rich People: Fujian Has the Potential for Free-and-Easy Tours to Hong Kong," posted at http://www.chinesenewsnet.com on October 5, 2003, accessed on November 1, 2003. "Good Servant for the People: Stories about Xiang Nan," posted at http://www.66163.com/Fujian_w/news/mzwz/030114/1_45.html.

17. I compute the remittance rate as the ratio of remittance (or subsidies) to the sum of provincial revenue and remittance. Data comes from Wei 1997: 333; SSB 1990b; 1996b.

6   Extending the Open Policy

1. For discussion on fiscal arrangements, refer to Wong, Heady, and Woo 1995: 81–134; Wong 1997: 44–60. For information that helped distinguish these types of provinces, see Oksenberg and Tong 1991.

2. Howell (1993: 53) argued that central opposition to make Shanghai a SEZ was strong because it contributed a significant portion of central revenue.

3. For discussion of local strategies to increase fiscal revenue after reform, see Wang 1995: 94–97.

4. Vogel and Cheung discussed briefly the central government's special fiscal arrangement for Guangdong in exchange for its experiment in reform. See Vogel 1989: 89 and Cheung 1998b.

5. Remittance rates are an average of the rates in 1980, 1982, 1983, 1985, 1986, 1988, 1990, and 1991. They are computed using data from Wei 1997: 333. The formula is as follows: Remittance rate = remittance / (remittance + local revenue). Negative numbers indicate subsidies. Data on provincial revenue prior to 1990 are from SSB 1990b; data since 1990 are from SSB 1996b.

6. In this and the following chapters, I use correlation and charts as a tool to investigate statistical relations. For three reasons, I refrain from using multivariate regression of the index of national opening of provinces on all the possible causal variables. First, it is unclear whether the relations are linear or curvilinear. The regression can hardly detect a curvilinear relation. Second, some of the variables (such as the coding of provincial leadership) use discrete measures, while others (such as distance) use continuous measures. It is not appropriate to apply OLS multivariate regression to data in discrete *and* continuous measures. Third, while a number of the variables have nearly a complete set of data, others (such as provincial leadership) do not. Uneven data sets obstruct the use of multivariate regression.

7. For theoretical discussion on the role of provincial leaders in reform, refer to Cheung, Chung, and Lin 1998. For close examination of the role of leaders in groups of provinces, refer to Cheung, Chung, and Lin 1998; Goodman 1997; Hendrischke and Feng 1999; Fitzgerald 2002. For single-province studies of provincial leaders, refer to Vogel 1989; Cheung 1998b; and Shieh 2000.

8. Among the eighteen provinces, information on leaders in Shanghai, Zhejiang, Shandong, Guangdong, Fujian, Shaanxi, and Sichuan come from Cheung, Chung, and Lin 1998. Data on leaders in Guangxi and Liaoning come from Goodman 1997; those on leaders in Jiangsu, Tianjin, Shanxi, Anhui, Jiangxi, and Hunan come from Hendrischke and Feng 1999; and those on leaders in Henan from Fitzgerald 2002. Information on leaders in Beijing came from "The Personality and Events of Chen Xitong," posted at http://lc-www.sd.cninfo. net/shuwu/jswx/cxt.htm, accessed on November 27, 2003. Additional information on Fujian is from Shieh 2000 and that on Hunan is based on the author's own interviews with residents from Hunan in October 2003.

9. For some provinces in the north, such as Ningxia and Jilin, Japan is identified as the nearby potential major trading partner. The other nearby economy, such as Mongolia, has too small a trade volume to bring significant trade benefits for Ningxia. For Jilin, even though South Korea is closer, yet Japan is identified instead because Japan's trade volume is nearly five times as large as that of South Korea. In addition, though the distance from Jilin through Dalian (the nearby major ocean harbor) to a major South Korean port (Pusan) is shorter than that to a nearby major harbor in Japan, it amounts to far less than the five times difference. Therefore, Japan would entail larger trade potential for the province.

10. For details on the construction of the average index of opening of provinces, refer to earlier discussion.

7 Provincial Reform Initiatives

1. For more discussion on provincial reform policies, refer to Goodman 1997; Cheung et al. 1998; Yang 1997 and other studies reviewed in chapter 1.
2. Interviews with a vice president of a provincial Party school, December 2003.
3. Interview with a former official of a municipal government in Guangdong, December 2003.
4. For this reason, Lieberthal (1992) suggested that the Chinese state was characterized by fragmented authoritarianism. Yasheng Huang (1996), on the other hand, argued that the national government specialized in political responsibilities whereas the local government specialized in economic responsibilities.
5. This was true even as late as in 1994.
6. For a critique of the Chinese official intervention in the economy for economic growth in the reform period, also refer to Hongyi Lai, "Economic Overheat and the Urge for Intervention," *United Morning Post (Lianhe Zaobao)*, May 24, 2004. This commentary was reposted on news websites of *Guangming Daily* and Business School of Beijing University. The Chinese Premier Wen Jiabao echoed the critique in his speech on June 3, 2004 that the market had yet to play a greater role in allocating resources.
7. Chung (2000: 9–10), for example, suggested personal networks with central leaders might condition local implementation of central policies.

8 Divergent Reform Paths in Two Provinces

1. Interview with a Jilin official supervising private enterprises, September 1998.
2. For a theoretical discussion of the revenue and the state, refer to Levi 1988.
3. The seemingly low tax rates on collective, private and foreign enterprises have much to do with the large denomination in computing the rates. These rates would go up dramatically if the denomination is the profits instead of the output of these sectors. Yet data on this category are unavailable for a number of years. In 1990 formal taxes and remittances accounted for as much as 67.1 percent of the profits of rural enterprises nationwide, but only 4.6 percent of the revenue of enterprises.
4. Interviews with officials in Changchun, Jilin, and Yantai, and Shandong in September and October 1998.
5. Interviews with officials in Jilin in September 1998.
6. For detailed accounts of provincial leadership in Jilin, refer to the activities on the provincial party committee and provincial government in *Jilin Nianjian (Jilin Yearbook)*, 1987–1994.
7. For literature on governance and development, refer to the World Bank 1992; Thomas, Dailami, Dhareshwar, et al. 2000; Bueno de Mesquita and Root 2000; OECD 2002.
8. In Shandong, the private ownership expanded rapidly, as a result of provincial tolerance and encouragement. Its share in gross industrial output expanded from 5 percent in 1988 to 16 percent in 1993, compared to no change in the share in Jilin from 1982–1993. Foreign and mixed ownership in Shandong,

a bit surprisingly, accounted for only 6 percent in 1993, compared to 7 percent in Jilin. This relatively small share in Shandong may be a result of the province's rapidly expanding economy.

9   How China's Leaders Made Reforms Happen

1. Earlier surveys showed that a significant portion of the population in Eastern Europe remained in poverty and that the portion was even higher than that in China, even though China's GDP per capita was lower. During the 1993–1994 period, 23.8 percent of the Polish, 30.9 percent of the Russians, and 8.6 percent of the Hungarians lived in the poverty, compared with 4.6 percent of the Chinese in 1998. The data comes from the World Bank, 2002: 232–40. For more discussion on unemployment as well as failing urban infrastructures and public health in Eastern Europe, refer to "Eastern Europe & Russia Brief," posted at http://www.makingcitieswork.org/urbanWorld/eastern-europe, accessed on June 17, 2004.
2. S. Giovanna Giacomazzi, "Putin's Grand Entrance at Okinawa," *Overseas Perspectives*, August 2000, posted at http://www.giogia.com/PutinOkinawa.html.
3. Conversation with Professor Ignatius Wibowo, the head of a center for China's studies at University of Jakarta on April 17, 2004 in Singapore. For his arguments, refer to Wibowo 2004.
4. Conversation with Chairman of the Supervisory Panels of Key and Large-Sized SOEs of China, May 7, 2004, Singapore.
5. *China Daily*, May 30, 2003; *The Standard*, 30 October, 2002; *International Herald Tribune*, 20 October, 2002. For an in-depth discussion on the NPL in China, refer to Wong and Chen 2003.
6. Interview with a mid-rank research official at China's central bank, November 22, 2002.
7. For detailed discussion of the Hu-Wen efforts at tackling these political, economic, and social problems, refer to Lai 2005a and Wong and Lai 2006.
8. Interview with the owner-manager of the largest joint-venture enterprise in Foshan, Guangdong, June 2004.

Data Sources and Bibliography

Statistical and Governmental Publications (Mostly Chinese)

The following are statistical yearbooks, yearbooks, and other publications by China's central and local governments and international organizations, as well as scholarly analyses published in China. They are data sources for *Database on Political Economy of Chinese Provinces* and for quantitative analyses in chapter 3 and case analyses in chapters 5 and 8. The building of the database was partly aided by National Science Foundation (grant number SBR-9709813) and Social Science Research Council grants in the United States. Statistical analyses in chapters 6–7 use the database.

ECLAJP (Editorial Committee of Local Annals of Jilin Province). 1991. *Annals of Jilin Province (Annuals* thereafter), *Vol. 15: Records of Comprehensive Economic Management: Industrial and Commercial Administration (Jilin Shengzhi, 15 zhuan: Jingji Zonghe Guanli Zhi: Gongshang Xingzheng Guanli)*, Changchun: ECLAJP.

——. 1992. *Annals, Vol. 25: Records of Rural Enterprises (Xiangzhen Qiye Zhi)*.

——. 1993. *Annals, Vol. 30: Records of Finance (Caizheng Zhi)*.

——. 1994. *Annals, Vol. 11: Records of Political and Personnel Affairs (Zhengshi/Renshi Zhi)*.

——. 1995. *Annals, Vol. 23: Records of External Economic Trade (Duiwai Jingmao Zhi)*.

ECLASP (Editorial Committee of Local Annals of Shandong Province). 1993. *Annals of Shandong Province (Annuals* thereafter): *Records of Labor (Shandong Shengzhi: Laodong Zhi).*, Ji'nan: Shandong People's Press.

——. 1995. *Annals: Records of Political Authority (Zhengquan Zhi)*, Vols. 1–2.

——. 1996. *Annals: Records of Finance (Jinrong Zhi)*, Vols. 1–2.

—— 1997. *Annals: Records of Rural Enterprises (Xiangzhen Qiye Zhi)*.

EDCAY (Editorial Department of Chinese Agricultural Yearbook), ed. 1986. *Chinese Agricultural Laws and Regulations of 1984 (Zhongguo Nongcun Fagui)*, Beijing: Agriculture Press.

Guangdong People's Government and Guangdong Statistical Bureau. 1999. *Fifty Years in Guangdong (Guangdong Wushinian)*. Shenzhen: China Statistical Press.

IMF et al. 1991. *A Study of the Soviet Economy*, Vol. 1. Paris: OECD.

Jilin Yearbook (Jilin Nianjian), 1987–1995. Changchun: Jilin Yearbook Publishing House.

Organization for Economic Cooperation and Development (OECD) 2002. *Public Sector Transparency and Accountability. Making It Happen.* Paris: OECD.

Research Institute of the Party Committee of Chinese Communist Party in Jilin (RIPC). 1986. *Basic Situation in Jilin Province (Jilinsheng Jiben Shengqing)*. Changchun: Jilin People's Press.

Research Office of the Party Committee of Chinese Communist Party in Shandong (ROPCCCPS). 1985. *Conditions of Shandong Province (Shandong Shengqing)*. Ji'nan: Shandong People's Press.

———. 1988. *Ten Years of the New Era in Shandong Province (Shandong Xinshiqi de Shinian)*. Ji'nan: Shandong People's Press.

Section on Investment in Fixed Assets of State Statistical Bureau (SIFA-SSB). 1950–1985, 1986–1987, 1990–1991. *Statistics on Investment in Fixed Assets in China (Zhongguo Guding Zichan Touzi Tongji Ziliao)*. Beijing: China Statistical Press.

Shandong Yearbook (Shandong Nianjian) 1987–1995. Ji'nan: Shandong Yearbook Press.

State Bureau of Industrial and Commercial Administration (SBICA). 1992–1995. *China's Industrial and Commercial Administration Yearbook (Zhongguo Gongshang Xingzheng Guanli Nianjian)*. Beijing: Industrial and Commercial Press.

———. 1992b. *Statistics on China's Industrial and Commercial Administration of Four Decades (Zhongguo Gongshang Xingzheng Guanli Tongji Sishinian)*. Beijing: China Statistical Press.

State Statistical Bureau of the People's Republic of China (SSB). 1981–2004. *China Statistical Yearbook (Zhongguo Tongji Nianjian)*. Beijing: China Statistical Press (Zhonguo Tongji Chubanshe).

———. 1989b. *The 40 Years of Mighty Advance: The Shandong Volume (Fenjin de Sishinian)*. Beijing: China Statistical Press.

———. 1990b. *A Compilation of Historical Statistics of All the Provinces, Autonomous Regions, and Directly-Administered Municipalities: 1949–1989 (Quanguo Gesheng, Zizhiqu, Zhixiashi Lishi Tongji Ziliao Huibian: 1949–1989)*. Zhengzhou: China Statistical Press.

———. 1996b. *China's Regional Economy*. Beijing: China Statistical Press.

———. 2005b. *Zhongguon Tongji Zhaiyao (China Statistical Abstract)*. 2005. Beijing: China Statistical Press.

The World Bank. 1992. *Governance and Development*. Washington, DC: World Bank.

———. 1997a. *World Development Report: The State in a Changing World*. New York: Oxford University Press.

———. 1997b. *Sharing Rising Income: Disparities in China*. Washington, DC: The World Bank.

———. 2002. *World Development Report: Building Institutions for Markets*. New York: Oxford University Press.

——. 2003. *World Development Report: Sustainable Development in a Dynamic World*. New York: Oxford University Press.

Xianmen Statistical Bureau. 1991. *A Statistical Collection on Coastal Open Cities, Special Economic Zones, and Line-Item Cities (Yanhai Kaifang Chengshi, Jingji Tequ, Jihua Danlie Chengshi Tongji Ziliao Huibian)*. Xianmen: Xianmen Statistical Bureau.

By Series or Titles

China Agricultural Statistics (Zhongguo Nongcun Tongji Ziliao), 1985–1994.

China Economic Yearbook (Zhongguo Jingji Nianjian). 1981–1999.

China Finance and Banking Yearbook (Zhongguo Jinrong Nianjian). 1992–1996.

China Industrial and Commercial Administration Yearbook (Zhongguo Gongshang Xingzheng Guanli Nianjian). 1992–1995.

China Industrial Economic Statistical Yearbook (Zhongguo Gongye Jingji Tongji Nianjian). 1988–1995.

China Labor Statistical Yearbook (Zhongguo Laodong Tongji Nianjian). 1990–1994.

China Population Statistics (Zhongguo Renkou Nianjian). 1994.

China Tax Statistics (Zhongguo Shuiwu Tongji), 1950–1994.

China Taxation Yearbook (Zhongguo Shuiwu Nianjian). 1992–1996.

China Transportation Maps (Zhongguo Jiaotong Ditu). 1979.

China Transportation Statistical Yearbook (Zhongguo Jiaotong Tongji Nianjian). 1986. Beijing:

China Urban Economic and Social Yearbook (Zhongguo Chengshi Jingji Shehui Nianjian). 1985–1992.

China Urban Statistical Yearbook (Zhongguo Chengshi Tongji Nianjian). 1985–1990.

China Urban Yearbook (Zhongguo Chengshi Nianjian). 1993–1996.

Development of the Transportation and Postal Services in China: 1949–1987 (Zhongguo Jiaotong Youdian Shiye de Fazhan).

Fifty Years in Guangdong (Guangdong Wushinian). 1949–1999.

Statistics on Labor and Wages in China (Zhongguo Laodong Gongzi Tongji Nianjian). 1978–1987.

Tabulations of China 1% Population Sampling Survey in 1987: National Volume (Zhongguo 1987 Nian 1% Renkou Chouyang Diaocha Ziliao).

10 Percent Sampling Tabulation on the 1982 Population Census of the People's Republic of China (Zhongguo 1982 Nian Renkou Pucha 10% Chouyang Ziliao).

10 Percent Sampling Tabulation on the 1990 Population Census of the People's Republic of China (Zhongguo 1990 Nian Renkou Pucha 10% Chouyang Ziliao).

Yearbook of China's Rural Enterprises (Zhongguo Xiangzhen Qiye Nianjian). 1987–1995.

Yearbook of the Opening of China (Zhongguo Kaifang Nianjian). 1995.

Yearbooks and statistical yearbooks of the provinces between 1976 and 1996. Most provinces have published their yearbooks and statistical yearbooks since 1985.

Interviews With Chinese Officials

(Used mainly in chapter 8 and also in discussion in a number of chapters.)

Interviews with central officials in charge of special economic zones and economic reforms in Beijing, August 1998.

Interviews with provincial officials in charge of external trade and foreign investment, economic zones, taxation, banking, rural enterprises, and private business in Jilin, September 1998.

Interviews with officials in charge of economic developmental zones in Yantai, Shandong; interviews with provincial officials in charge of external trade, developmental zones, and private business in Ji'nan, Shandong, September–October 1998.

Interviews with officials in Guangzhou and Zhuhai of Guangdong and with private entrepreneurs in Foshan of Guangdong, December 2003.

Bibliography

Alesina, A., and A. Drazen. 1991. "Why Are Stabilizations Delayed?" *American Economic Review*, vol. 81, no. 5 (December): 1170–88.

Aslund, Anders. 1991. "Four Key Reforms: The Eastern European Experiment Phase II," *The American Enterprise* vol. 2, no. 4 (July/August): 48–55.

Aslund, Aders, and Mikhail Dmitriev. 1990. "Economic Reform versu Rent Seeking," in Anders and Aslund and Martha Brill Olcott, eds., *Russia after Communism*. Washington, DC: Carnegie Endowment for International Peace.

Backman, David. 1985. *Chen Yun and the Chinese Political System*. Berkeley: University of California, Center for Chinese Studies.

Bao Xuelong, and Li Bin, eds. 1996. *Thinking, Solutions, and Outlook: The Prospect of the Development of Jilin Province in the Coming Fifteen Years (Silu, Duice, Zhanwang: Jilinsheng Weilai Shiwunian Fazhan Qianzhan)*, Changchun: Jilin People's Press.

Bates, Robert. 1981. *Markets and States in Tropical Africa: The Political Basis of Agricultural Policies*. Berkeley: University of California Press.

Bates, Robert H., and Anne O. Krueger. 1993. *Political and Economic Interactions in Economic Policy Reform*. Oxford and Cambridge: Blackwell Publishers.

Baum, Richard. 1996. *Burying Mao, China Politics in the Age of Deng Xiaoping*. Princeton, NJ: Princeton University Press.

Bentley, Arthus F. 1908. *The Process of the Government: A Study of Social Pressures*. Chicago: The University of Chicago Press.

Berg, A., and O. Blanchard. 1994. "Stabilization and Transition in Poland, 1990–1991," in O. Blanchard, K. Froot, and J. Sachs, eds., *Transition in Eastern Europe*, Vol. 1: 51–92. Chicago: National Bureau for Economic Research and University of Chicago Press.

Bo, Zhiyue. 1996. "Economic Performance and Political Mobility: Chinese Provincial Leaders," *Journal of Contemporary China*, Vol. 5, no. 12 (July): 135–54.

———. 2002. *Chinese Provincial Leaders: Economic Performance and Political Mobility Since 1949*. Armonk, NY: M.E. Sharpe.

Bueno de Mesquita, Bruce, and Hilton Root, eds. 2000. *Governing for Prosperity*. New Haven, CT: Yale University Press.

Bunce, Valerie. 1980. "The Succession Connection: Policy Cycles and Political Change in the Soviet Union and Eastern Europe," *American Political Science Review* Vol. 74, no. 4: 966–77.

Byrd, William, and Lin Qingsong, eds. 1990. *China's Rural Industry: Structure, Development, and Reform*. Washington, DC: Oxford University Press.

Chen Chien-hsiun. 2003. "China's Banking Reform One Year after WTO Accession," *EAI Background Brief No. 158*, Singapore: East Asian Institute, National University of Singapore.

Chen, Kang, Gary H. Jefferson, and Inderjit Singh, 1992. "Lessons from China's Economic Reforms," *Journal of Comparative Economies* Vol. 16, no. 2 (June): 210–25.

Chen Li. 2002. *The Third-Generation Leadership and China's External Opening. (Disandai Lidaojiti yu Zhongguo de Duiwai Kaifang)*. Chengdu: Sichuan Renmin Chubanshe.

Chen Xuewei. 1998. *An Investigation of Major Events and Decisions since the Third Plenum of the Eleventh Party Central Committee (Shiyijie Sanzhong Quanhui yilai Zhongda Shijian he Juece Diaocha)*. Beijing: Zhonggong Zhongyang Dangxiao Chubanshe.

Cheng Dunshi, Qu Dongtao, Qu Wengang, and Wang Yong. 1989. *Second Light Industry in Shandong in the Past Ten Years: 1979–1988 (Shandong Erqing Gongye Shinian)*. Ji'nan: Shandong People's Press.

Cheung, Peter T.Y., 1998a. "The Guangdong Advantage," in Cheung et al., eds. 1998. *Provincial Strategies of Economic Reform in Post-Mao China*, 89–144.

Cheung, Peter T.Y., 1998b. "Changing Relations between the Central Government and Guangdong," in Y.M Yeung and David Chu, eds., *Guangdong*, Hongkong: The Chinese University Press. 23–62.

Chung, Jae Ho. 1995. "Studies of Central-Provincial Relations in the People's Republic of China: A Mid-Term Appraisal," *China Quarterly*, no. 142 (June): 487–508.

———. 1998. "Shandong's Strategies of Reform in Foreign Economic Relations," in Peter Cheung et al., eds., *Provincial Strategies of Economic Reform in Post-Mao China: Leadership, Politics, and Implementation*, Armonk, NY: M.E. Sharpe. 253–301.

———. 2000. *Central Control and Local Discretion in China: Leadership and Implementation during Post-Mao Decollectivization*. New York: Oxford University Press.

CJ. 1996. *A Study of Opening-up and Regional Economy*. Changchun: Jilin People's Publishing House (in Chinese).

Collier, David and James Mahoney. 1996. "Insights and Pitfalls: Selection Bias in Qualitative Research," *World Politics*, Vol. 49, no. 1: 56–91.

Crane, George T. 1990. *The Political Economy of China's Special Economic Zones*. Armonk, NY: M.E. Sharpe.

Cukierman, A., S. Edwards, and G. Tabellini. 1992. "Seignorage and Political Stability," *American Economic Review*, Vol. 82, no. 3: 537–55.

Deng, Xiaoping. 1993. *Selected Works of Deng Xiaoping (Deng Xiaoping Wenxuan): Volume 3*. Beijing: People's Press.

Dewatripont, M., and G. Roland, 1992. "The Virtues of Gradualism and Legitimacy in the Transition to a Market Economy," *The Economic Journal*, Vol. 102, no. 411 (March): 291–300.

Dickson, Bruce J. 2003. *Red Capitalists in China: The Party, Private Entrepreneurs, and Prospects for Political Change*. New York: Cambridge University Press.

Dittmer, Lowell. 1990. "Patterns of Elite Strife and Succession in Chinese Politics," *China Quarterly* 123 (September): 405–30.

——. 1995. "Chinese Informal Politics," *The China Journal* 34 (July): 1–34.

——. 2000. "Informal Politics among the Chinese Communist Party Elite," in Dittmer, Lowell, and Peter N. S. Lee, eds., *Informal Politics in East Asia*. New York and Cambridge: Cambridge University Press. 106–140.

Dittmer, Lowell, and Yu-shan Wu. 1995. "The Modernization of Factionalism in Chinese Politics," *World Politics* Vol. 47, no. 4 (July): 467–95.

Du Haiyan, 1990. "Causes of Rapid Rural Industrial Development," in William Byrd and Lin Qingsong, eds. *China's Rural Industry: Structure, Development, and Reform*. Washington, DC: Oxford University Press, pp. 47–62.

Du Zhi. 1993. *The Choice toward Tomorrow: A Study of the Strategy of the Development of Rural Enterprises in Jilin (Zhuixiang Mingtian de Jueze: Jilinsheng Xiangzhen Qiye Fazhan Zhanlue Yanjiu)*. Changchun: Jilin Daune Chubanshe.

Evans, Peter. 1992. "The State as Problem and Solution: Predation, Embedded Autonomy, and Structural Change," in Stephan Haggard and Robert R. Kaufman, eds., *The Politics of Economic Adjustment*. Princeton: Princeton Dauxe Chubanshe.

Fan, Cindy. 1995. "Of Belts and Ladders: State Policy and Uneven Regional Development in Post-Mao China," *Annals of the Association of American Geographers*, Vol. 85, no. 3: 421–49.

Fewsmith, Joseph. 1994. *Dilemmas of Reform in China: Political Conflict and Economic Debate*. Armonk, NY: M.E.Sharpe.

Findley, Christopher, and Andrew Watson, 2001. "Surrounding the Cities from the Countryside," in Ross Garnaut and Yiping Huang, eds., *Growth without Miracles*. New York: Oxford University Press, pp. 189–204.

Fischer, Stanley, and Alan Gelb. 1991. "The Process of Socialist Economic Transformation," *Journal of Economic Perspective*, Vol. 5, no. 4 (Autumn): 91–105.

Fitzgerald, John, ed. 2002. *Rethinking China's Provinces*. London and New York: Routledge.

Frieden, Jeffry A. 1991. *Debt, Development, and Democracy: Modern Political Economy and Latin America, 1965–1985*. Princeton, NJ: Princeton University Press.

Frieden, Jeffry A, and Ronald Rogowski, 1996. "The Impact of the International Economy on National Policies," in Robert Keohane and Helen Milner, eds., *International and Domestic Politics*. New York: Cambridge University Press, pp. 25–48.

Fu Mali, Shen Guidi, Zhou Beiyan et al. eds. 1992. *The Latest Practical Atlas of China (Zuixin Shiyong Zhongguo Dituce)*. Beijing: China Map Press.

Fukui, Haruhiro. 2000. "Introduction: On the Significance of Informal Politics," in Dittmer, Fukui, and Lee, eds., *Informal Politics in East Asia*. New York and Cambridge. 1–20.

Gao Shangqun, Wang Mengkui, and He Chun. 1993. *An Encyclopedia of Events in China's Economic Reforms and Opening (Zhongguo Jingji Gaige Kaifang Dashidian)*, Vols. 1 and 2. Beijing: Beijing Gongye Daxue Chubanshe.

Gao Wenqian. 2003. *Zhou Enlai's Later Years (Wannian Zhou Enlai)*. Hong Kong: Mirror Books.

Gao Xin and He Ping. 1998. *The Premier with the Iron Face: A Biography of Zhu Rongji (Tiemian Zaixiang: Zhu Rongji Dazhuan)*. Hong Kong: Mirror Books.

Gaunaut, Ross, Ligang Song, Stoyan Tenev, and Yang Yao, 2003. *A Study of Firm Restructuring in China*. Washington, DC: The World Bank.

Geddes, Barbara. 1990. "How the Cases You Choose Affect the Answers You Get: Selection Bias in Comparative Politics," *Political Analysis*, Vol. 2: 131–50.

Gelb, Alan, Gary Jefferson, and Inderjit Singh. 1993. "Can Communist Economies Transform Incrementally? The Experience of China," *NBER Macroeconomics Annual*: 87–133.

Goodman, David S.G. ed. 1994. "The Politics of Regionalism: Economic Development, Conflict, and Negotiation," in Goodman and Segal, eds., *China Deconstructs: Politics, Trade and Regionalism*. London: Routledge, pp. 1–20.

——. ed. 1997. *China's Provinces in Reform*. New York: Routledge.

Goodman, David S.G. and Chongyi Feng. 1994. "Guangdong: Greater Hong Kong and the New Regionalist Future," in David Goodman and Gerald Segal, eds., *China Deconstructs: Politics, Trade and Regionalism*. London: Routledge, pp. 177– 201.

Goodman, David S.G., and Gerald Segal, eds. 1994. *China Deconstructs: Politics, Trade and Regionalism*. London: Routledge.

Gore, Lance. 1998. *Market Communism: The Institutional Foundation of China's Post-Mao Hyper-Growth*. Hong Kong: Oxford University Press.

Granick, David. 1990. *Chinese State Enterprises: A Regional Property Rights Analysis*. Chicago: Chicago University Press.

Griffin, Keith, and Azizur Rahman Khan, 1994. "The Chinese Transition to a Market-Guided Economy: The Contrast with Russia and Eastern Europe," *Contention* Vol. 3, no. 2 (Winter): 104.

Gustafson, Thane, 1999. *Capitalism Russian-Style*. New York: Cambridge University Press.

Haggard, Stephen. 2000. "Interests, Institutions, and Policy Reform," in Krueger, Anne, *Economic Policy Reform: The Second Stage*. Chicago and London: The University of Chicago Press: 21–59.

Haggard, Stephen, and Robert Kaufman, eds. 1992. *The Politics of Economic Adjustment: International Constraints, Distributive Politics, and the State*. Princeton, NJ: Princeton University Press.

——. 1995. *The Political Economy of Democratic Transitions*. Princeton, NJ: Princeton University Press.

Hamrin, Carol Lee. 1990. *China and the Challenge of the Future*. Boulder, CO: Westview Press.

Hannan, Kate. 1998. *Industrial Change in China: Economic Restructuring and Conflicting Interests*. London: Routledge.

Harding, Harry. 1987. *China's Second Revolution*. Washington, DC: Brookings Institution.

He Li et al. 1995. *A History of the People's Republic of China (Zhonghua Remin Gongheguo Shi)*. Beijing: Zhongguo Dang'an Chubanshe.

Hellman, Joel S. 1998. "Winners Take All: The Politics of Partial Reform in Postcommunist Transitions." *World Politics* Vol. 50, no.2 (January): 203–34.

Hellman, Joel S. and Mark Schankerman, 2000. "Intervention, Corruption and Capture: The Nexus between Enterprises and the State," *Economics of Transition* Vol. 8, no. 3 (November): 545–76.

Hendrischke, Hans, and Feng Chongyi, eds. 1999. *The Political Economy of China's Provinces: Comparative and Competitive Advantage*. London and New York: Routledge.

Howell, Jude. 1993. *China Opens Its Doors*. Boulder, Colorado: Lynne Rienner Publishers, Inc.

Hu Angang. 1994. *A Report on China's Economic Fluctuation (Zhongguo Jingji Bodong Baogao)*. Shenyang: Liaoning Renmin Chubanshe.

Huang, Jing. 2000. *Factionalism in Chinese Communist Politics*. New York and Cambridge: Cambridge University Press.

Huang, Yasheng. 1990. "Web of Interests and Patterns of Behavior of Chinese Local Economic Bureaucracies and Enterprises during Reforms," *China Quarterly*, no. 123 (September): 431–58.

——. 1994. "Information, Bureaucracy, and Economic Reforms in China and the Soviet Union," *World Politics*, Vol. 47 (October): 102–34.

——. 1996. *Inflation and Investment Controls in China: The Political Economy of Central-Local Relations during the Reform Era*. New York: Cambridge University Press.

Ickes, Barry. 1990. "Obstacles to Economic Reform of Socialism: An Institutional-Choice Approach," *Annals of the American Academy of Political and Social Science*, Vol. 507 (January): 53–64.

IMF, 2000. *World Economic Outlook: Focus on Transition Economies*. Washington, DC: International Monetary Fund.

Jao, J. C., and C. K. Leung. 1986. *China's Special Economic Zones: Policies, Problems, and Prospects*. Hong Kong: Oxford University Press.

Jefferson, Gary, Albert Hu, Xiaojing Guan, and Xiaoyun Yu. 2003. "Ownership, Performance, and Innovation in China's Large- and Medium-size Industrial Enterprise Sector," *China Economic Review*, Vol. 14, no.1: 89–113.

Jia, Hao, and Lin Zhimin, eds. 1994. *Changing Central-Local Relations in China: Reform and State Capacity*. Boulder, CO: Westview Press.

Jin Bei, and Chen Liying. 1996. *A Breakthrough across the Straits: An Analysis of China's Industrial Regions (Liang'an Tupo: Zhongguo Gongye Quyu Fenxi)*. Beijing: Jingji Guanli Chubanshe.

Jin, Hehui, and Yingyi Qian, 2001. "Public vs. Private Ownership of Firms: Evidence from Rural China," in Ross Garnaut and Yiping Huang, eds., *Growth without Miracles*. New York: Oxford University Press, pp. 219–43.

Jin Shihe. 1985. *A Study of Second Light Industrial Collective Enterprises in Jilin Province (Jilinsheng Erqing Jiti Qiye Yanjiu)*. Changchun: Jilin Renmin Chubanshe.

King, Gary, Robert O. Keohane, and Sidney Verba, 1993. *Scientific Inference in Qualitative Research*. Manuscript.

Kleinberg, Robert. 1990. *China's "Opening" to the Outside World: The Experiment with Foreign Capitalism*. Boulder, CO: Westview Press.

Kornai, Janos. 1980. *The Economics of Shortage*. Amsterdam: North-Holland.

——. 1990. *The Road to a Free Economy*. New York: W. W. Norton.

——. 2003. "Ten Years after The Road to a Free Economy: The Author's Self-evaluation of Privatisation," in Yelena Kalyuzhnova and Wladimir Andreff, eds., *Privatisation and Structural Change in Transition Economies*. Houndmills, Basingstoke, Hampshire; New York: Palgrave Macmillan: 13–28.

Kraus, Willy. 1991. *Private Business in China: Revival Between Ideology and Pragmatism*. Translated by Erich Holz. Honolulu: University of Hawaii Press.

Krueger, Anne. 1974. "The Political Economy of the Rent-Seeking Society," *The American Economic Review*, Vol. 64, no. 3 (June): 291–303.

Kuo, Cheng-Tian, 1992. "The PRC and Taiwan: Fujian's Faltering United Front," *Asian Survey* 32 (August): 683–95.

Lai, Hongyi Harry. 2001a. "Legislative Activism and Effectiveness of Provincial Delegates at the 1988 NPC," *Issues & Studies* Vol. 31, no. 1 (January/February): 73–101.

——. 2001b. "Behind China's World Trade Organization Agreement with the U.S," *Third World Quarterly*, Vol. 22, no. 2: 237–55.

——. 2002. "China's Western Development Program: Its Rationale, Implementation, and Prospects," *Modern China*. Vol. 28, no. 4, October: 432–66.

——. 2003. "Local Governments and China's WTO Entry," *American Asian Review*, Vol. XXI, no. 3, Fall: 153–86.

——. 2004a. "Surge of China's Private and Non-State Economy," *EAI Background Brief No. 187*, Singapore: National University of Singapore, April.

——. 2004b. "Emerging Features of China's Private Economy," *EAI Background Brief No. 188*, Singapore: National University of Singapore, April 19.

——. 2005a. *Hu-Wen under Full Scrutiny: A Comprehensive Inside Story of Governance under Hu and Wen and Prospects for Future China (Hu Wen Quan Toushi: Hu Wen Shizheng Neimu Quan Jiedu ji Zhongguo Weilai Zhanwang)*. Hong Kong: Wenhua Yishu Chubanshe.

——. 2005b. "Growth with Rising Income Inequality: China's Response to the Problem," *EAI Background Brief No. 227*, Singapore: National University of Singapore.

——. 2005c. "Contrasts in China and Soviet Reform: Sub-National and National Causes," *Asian Journal of Political Science*, Vol. 13, no. 1 (June): 1–21.

Lake, David A., and Robert Powell, eds. 1999. *Strategic Choice and International Relations*. Princeton, NJ: Princeton University Press.

Lan Shiyong, 2001. "China's Individual Economy during 1989–1999," in Zhang Houyi et al., eds., *A Report on the Development of China's Private Enterprises, 2001 (Zhongguo Siying Qiye Fazhan Baogao 2001)*. Beijing: Shehui Kexue Wenxian Chubanshe: 31–41.

Lardy, Nicholas R. 1992. *Foreign Trade and Economic Reform in China, 1978–1990*. Cambridge: Cambridge University Press.

——. 1998. *China's Unfinished Economic Revolution*. Washington, DC: Brookings Institution Press.

——. 2002. *Integrating China into the Global Economy*. Washington, DC: Brookings Institution Press.

Lardy, Nicholas R., and Kenneth Lieberthal. 1983. *Chen Yun's Strategy for China's Development*. Armonk, NY: M.E. Sharpe.

Lau, Yee-cheung, 1998. "History," in Yeung and Chu, eds., *Guangdong*, pp. 466–81.

Lau Yee-cheung, and Lee Kam-keung. 2000. "An Economic and Political History," in Yeung and Chu, eds., *Fujian*, 26–48.

Leamer, Edward. 1983. "Let's Take the Con out of the Econometrics." *American Economic Review*, Vol. 73: 31–43.

Lee, Hong Yung. 1991. *From Revolutionary Cadres to Party Technocrats in Socialist China*. Berkeley: University of California Press.

Lee, Jongchul. 1994. "Regional Differences in the Impact of the Open Door Policy on Income Growth in China," *Journal of Economic Development* Vol. 19, no. 1 (June): 215–34.

Lee, Kuan Yew. 2000. *From Third World to First—The Singapore Story: 1965–2000*. Singapore: Times Media Private Limited.

Legal Work Committee, National People's Congress (LWCNPC). 2002. *A Report on the Development of China's Private Enterprises*, 2001 (*Zhonghua Remin Gongheguo Zhongxiao Qiye Chujinfa*). Beijing: Fazhi Chubanshe.

Lever-Tracy, Constance, David Ip, and Noel Tracy. 1996. *The Chinese Diaspora and Mainland China: An Emerging Economic Synergy*. New York: Macmillan.

Levi, Margaret. 1989. *Of Rule and Revenue*. Berkeley: The University of California Press.

Li, Cheng 2001. *China's Leaders: The New Generation*. Boulder, CO: Rowman & Littlefield Publishers.

Li, Cheng, and David Bachman. 1989. "Localism, Elitism and Immobilism: Elite Formation and Social Change in Post-Mao China," *World Politics*, Vol. 42 (October): 64–94.

Lieberthal, Kenneth. 1992. "Introduction: The 'Fragmented Authoritarianism' Model and Its Limitations," in Lieberthal and Lampton, eds., *Bureaucracy, Politics, and Decision Making in Post-Mao China*. Berkeley: The University of california Press, pp. 1–30.

——. 1995. *Governing China: From Revolution through Reform*. New York: W. W. Norton.

Lieberthal, Kenneth, and David M. Lampton. 1992. *Bureaucracy, Politics, and Decision Making in Post-Mao China*. Berkeley: The University of California Press.

Lieberthal, Kenneth, and Michel Oksenberg. 1988. *Policy Making in China: Leaders, Structures, and Processes*. Princeton, NJ: Princeton University Press.

Lilley, James and Sophia Hart. 1997. "Greater China: Economic Dynamism of the Overseas Chinese," in Joint Economic Committee, ed., *China's Economic Future: Challenges to U.S. Policy*. Armonk, NY: M.E. Sharpe: 423–50.

Lin, Justin Yifu, and Cai Fang, 1996. "The Lessons of China's Transition to a Market Economy," *CATO Journal*, Vol. 16, no. 2 (Fall).

Lipton, David, and Jeffrey Sachs. 1990. "Creating a Market Economy in Eastern Europe: The Case of Poland," *Brookings Papers on Economic Activity*, no. 1: 75–147.

Liu Jianwen, and Yang Hanping, 2001. *Legal Protection for Non-Public Enterprises (Feigongyouzhi Qiye Falü Baohu)*. Beijing: Xiwan Chubanshe.

Liu Xianrui, Le Qinghe, and Zhao Chi, eds. 1993. *A Practical Guide on Policies, Laws, and Regulations regarding External Opening of the Coast and Interior (Yanhai Yanbian Duiwai Kaifang Zhengce Fagui Shiyong Zhinan)*. Beijing: Zhongguo Jingji Chubanshe.

Machiavelli, Niccolo. 1970. *The Discourses*. Edited by Bernard Crick, translation by J. Leslie, and S. J. Walker. New York: Penguin Books.

Manion, Melanie 1993. *Retirement of Revolutionaries in China*. Princeton, NJ: Princeton University Press.

Manzetti, Luigi. 2003. "Political Manipulations and Market Reform Failures," *World Politics*, Vol. 55, no. 3 (April): 315–60.

McMillan, John, and Barry Naughton. 1993. "How to Reform a Planned Economy: Lessons from China," *Oxford Review of Economic Policy*, Vol. 8, no. 1: 130–43.

Montinola, Gabriella, Qian, Yingyi, Barry R. Weingast. 1995. "Federalism, Chinese Style: The Political Basis for Economic Success in China,." *World Politics* Vol. 48, no.1 (October): 50–81.

Moore, Thomas. 2002. *China in the World Market*. New York: Cambridge University Press.

Mueller, Dennis C. 1989. *Public Choice II*. Cambridge: Cambridge University Press.

Murphy, Kevin M., Andrei Shleifer, and Robert W. Vishny. 1992. "The Transition to a Market Economy: Pitfalls of Partial Reform," *The Quarterly Journal of Economics* Vol. 107, no. 3 (August): 889–906.

Murrell, Peter. 1991. "Can Neoclassical Economics Underpin the Reform of Centrally Planned Economies," *Journal of Economic Perspectives*, Vol. 5, no. 4 (Fall): 59–76.

Naughton, Barry. 1988. "The Third Front: Defense Industrialization in the Chinese Interior," *China Quarterly*, Vol. 115: 351–86.

———. 1996. *Growing Out of the Plan: Chinese Economic Reform, 1978–93*, New York: Cambridge University Press.

Nelson, Joan, ed. 1989. *Fragile Coalitions: The Politics of Economic Adjustment*. New Brunswick, NJ. and Oxford: Transaction Books.

———, ed. 1990. *Economic Crisis and Policy Choice: The Politics of Adjustment in the Third World*. Princeton, NJ: Princeton University Press.

Odgaard, Ole. 1992. *Private Enterprises in Rural China: Impact on Agricultural and Social Stratification*. Aldershot, Brookfield, Vermont: Ashgate.

OECD (Organization for Economic Cooperation and Development). 2000. *Public Sector Transparency and Accountability*. Paris: OECD.

Oi, Jean. 1999. *Rural China Takes Off*. Berkeley: The University of California Press.

Oi, Jean, and Andrew Walder, eds. 1999. *Property Rights and Economic Reform in China*. Stanford, CA: Stanford University Press.

Oksenberg, Michel, and James Tong. 1991. "The Evolution of Central-Provincial Fiscal Relations in China, 1971–1984: The Formal System," *China Quarterly*, Vol. 125 (March): 1–32.

Olson, Mancur. 1971. *The Logic of Collective Action*. Cambridge: Harvard University Press.

———. 1982. *The Rise and Decline of Nations*. New Haven, CT. and London: Yale University Press.

Pang Xiuzhen, Lin Shuxiang, and Wang Yongchang, et al. 1996. *A Study of Shandong's Economy (Shandong Jingji Yanjiu)*. Ji'nan: Shandong Renmin Chubanshe.

Pearson, Margaret. 1991. *Joint Ventures in the People's Republic of China: The Control of Foreign Direct Investment under Socialism*. Princeton, NJ: Princeton University Press.

Pei, Minxin, 1994. *From Reform to Revolution: The Demise of Communism in China and the Soviet Union*. Cambridge, MA: Harvard University Press.

Peltzman, Sam. 1976. "Toward a More General Theory of Regulation," *Journal of Law and Economics*, Vol. 19 (August): 211–40.

Perkins, Dwight. 1988. "Reforming China's Economic System," *Journal of Economic Literature*, Vol. XXVI (June): 601–45.

Perry, Elizabeth, and Christine Wong, eds. 1985. *The Political Economy of Reform in Post-Mao China*. Cambridge, MA: Harvard University Press.

Pomfret, Richard. 1997. "Growth and Transition: Why Has China's Performance Been So Different?" *Journal of Comparative Economics*, Vol. 25, no.3 (December): 422–40.

Propaganda Department of the Chinese Communist Party of Jilin Province (PDCCPJP) and the Statistical Bureau of the Jilin Province, eds. 1989. *Forty Years of Courageous Advances: The Jilin Volume (Fenjin de Sishi Nian: Jilin Fence)*. Changchun: Zhongguo Tongji Chubanshe.

Przeworski, Adam. 1991. *Democracy and the Market*. New York: Cambridge University Press.

Putterman, Louis, 1992. "Dualism and Reform in China," *Economic Development and Cultural Change*, Vol. 40, no. 3 (April): 467–93.

———. 1996. "The Role of Ownership and Property Rights in China's Economic Transitoin," in Andrew Walder, ed., *China's Transitional Economy*. New York: Oxford University Press: 85–102.

Pye, Lucian W. 1981. *The Dynamics of Chinese Politics*. Cambridge, MA: Oelgeschlager, Gunn & Hain: 1–75.

———. 1995. "Factions and the Politics of Guanxi: Paradoxes in Chinese Administrative and Political Behavior," *China Journal*, Vol. 34 (July): 35–54.

Qian, Yingyi. 2003. "How Reform Worked in China," in Dani Rodrik, ed., *In Search of Prosperity: Analytical Narratives on Economic Growth*. Princeton, NJ: Princeton University Press: 297–333.

Qian, Yingyi, and Chenggang Xu, 1993. "Why China's Economic Reforms Differ: The M-form Hierarchy and Entry/Expansion of the Non-State Sector," *Economics of Transition*, Vol. 1: 135–70.

Ramo, Jashua Cooper. 2004. *The Beijing Consensus*. London: The Foreign Policy Center.

Reardon, Lawrence. 1998. "Learning How to Open the Door: A Reassessment of China's 'Opening' Strategy," *China Quarterly*, Vol. 155 (September): 479–511.

Ren Huiwen. 1997. *Inside China's Power Succession (Zhongnanhai Quanli Jiaoban Neimu)*. Hong Kong: The Pacific Century Institute.

Research Office of the Jilin Provincial Party Committee (ROJPPC). 1986. *Basic Conditions of Jilin Province (Jilinsheng Jiben Shengqing)*. Changchun: Jilin Renmin Chubanshe.

Riskin, Carl. 1987. *China's Political Economy*. Oxford: Oxford University Press.

Rodrik, Dani. 1995. "The Dynamics of Political Support for Reforms in Economies in Transition," *Journal of the Japanese and International Economies*, Vol. 9, no. 4: 403–25.

Rogowski, Ronald. 1989. *Commerce and Coalition: How Trade Affects Domestic Political Alignments*. Princeton, NJ: Princeton University Press.

——. 1995. "The Role of Theory and Anomaly in Social-Scientific Inference," (Review of *Designing Social Inquiry*). *American Political Science Review*, Vol. 89, no. 2 (June): 467–70.

Roland, Gerard. 2000. *Transition and Economics: Politics, Markets and Firms*. Cambridge, MA: The MIT Press.

Roubini, N. 1991. "Economic and Political Determinants of Budget Deficits in Developing Countries," *Journal of International Money and Finance*, Vol. 10: 549–72.

Ruan, Ming. 1994. *Deng Xiaoping: Chronicle of an Empire*. Boulder, CO: Westview Press.

Sachs, Jeffrey D. 1996. "The Transition at Mid Decade," *The American Economic Review*, Vol. 86, no. 2 (May): 128–33.

Sachs, Jeffrey and Wing Thye Woo. 1994. "Reform in China and Russia," *Economic Policy*, April: 102–45.

Samuelson, Paul A., and William D. Nordhaus. 1998. *Economics*. 16th edition, Boston, MA: McGraw-Hill.

Schamis, Hector. 1999. "Distributional Coalitions and the Politics of Economic Reform in Latin America," *World Politics*, Vol. 51, no. 2 (January): 236–68.

Schurmann, Franz. 1968. *Ideology and Organization in Communist China*. Berkeley, Los Angeles, and London: University of California Press.

Shi Qingwu, and Hao Lingyun, eds. 1990. *Economic Geography of Jilin Province (Jilinsheng Jingji Dili)*. Beijing: Xinhua Chubanshe.

Shieh, Shawn. 2000. "Centre, Province and Locality in Fujian's Reforms," in Yeung, and Chu, eds., *Fujian*, 83–118.

Shirk, Susan. 1982. *Competitive Comrades: Career Incentives and Student Strategies in China*. Berkeley: University of California Press.

Shirk, Susan. 1985. "The Politics of Industrial Reform," in Elizabeth Perry and Christine Wong, eds., *The Political Economy of Reform in Post-Mao China*, Cambridge, MA: Harvard University Press: 195–222.

——. 1993. *The Political Logic of Economic Reform in China*. Berkeley: University of California Press.

Shirk, Susan. 1994. *How China Opened Its Door*. Washington, DC: The Brookings Institution.

——. 1996. "Internationalization and China's Economic Reform," in Keohane and Milner, eds. *International and Domestic Politics*, pp. 186–208.

Shleifer, Andrei, and Robert W. Vishny. 1998. *The Grabbing Hand: Government Pathologies and Their Cures*. Cambridge, MA: Harvard University Press.

Shue, Vivienne. 1994. "Grasping Reform: Economic Logic, Political Logic, and the State-Society Spiral," *China Quarterly*, Vol. 144 (December): 1174–85.

Snyder, Richard. 1999. "After Neoliberalism: The Politics of Reregulation in Mexico," *World Politics*, Vol. 51, no. 2 (January): 173–204.

Solinger, Dorothy. 1984. *Chinese Business under Socialism: The Politics of Domestic Commerce, 1949–1980*. Berkeley, CA: University of California Press.

——. 1991. *From Lathes to Looms: China's Industrial Policy in Comparative Perspective, 1979–1982*. Stanford, CA: Stanford University Press.

Solnick, Steven L. 1996. "The Breakdown of Hierarchies in the Soviet Union and China," *World Politics,* Vol. 48, no. 2 (January): 209–38.

——. 1998. *Stealing the State: Control and Collapse in Soviet Institutions*. Cambridge, MA: Harvard University Press.

Steinfeld, Edward. 1998. *Forging Reform in China: The Fate of State-Owned Industry*. Cambridge and New York: Cambridge University Press.

Stiglitz, Joseph. 1999. "Whither Reform? Ten Years of the Transition," Keynote Address at the World Bank Annual Conference on Development Economics.

Svejnar, Jan, and Josephine Woo. 1990. "Development Patterns in Four Counties," in William Byrd and Lin Qingsong, eds., *China's Rural Industry: Structure, Development, and Reform*. Washington, DC: Oxford University Press: 63–84.

Tan, Qingshan Forrest. 2002. "Growth Disparities in China: Provincial Causes," *Journal of Contemporary China*, Vol. 11, no.33: 735–59.

Tang Yingwu. 1998. *The Choice: A History of China's Reform since 1978 (Jueze: 1978 Nian yilai Zhongguo Gegai de Licheng)*, Beijing: Jingji Ribao Chubanshe.

Teiwes, Frederick. 1995. "Paradoxical Post-Mao Transition," *China Journal*, Vol. 34: 55–94.

Thomas, Vinod, Mansoor Dailami, Ashok Dhareshwar, et al. 2000. *The Quality of Growth*. New York: Oxford University Press.

Tong, James. 1989. "Fiscal Reform, Elite Turnover and Central-Provincial Relations in Post-Mao China," *The Australian Journal of Chinese Affair*, Vol. 22 (July): 1–28.

Tornell, A. 1995. "Are Economic Crises Necessary for Trade Liberalization and Fiscal Reform? The Mexican Experience," in R. Dornbusch an S. Edwards, eds., *Reform, Recovery, and Growth: Latin America and the Middle East*. Chicago: University of Chicago Press: 53–73.

Townsend, James. 1991. "Reflections on the Opening of China," in Kenneth Lieberthal et al. eds., *Perspectives on Modern China*. Armonk, NY: M.E. Sharpe: 387–417.

Treisman, Daniel. 1999. "Political Decentralization and Economic Reform: A Game-Theoretical Analysis," *American Journal of Political Science*, Vol. 43, no. 2 (April): 488–517.

Truman, David B. 1971. *The Governmental Process: Political Interests and Public Opinion*. New York: Alfred A. Knopf.

Tsou, Tang. 1986. "Political Change and Reform: The Middle Course," in Tang Tsou, ed., *The Cultural Revolution and Post-Mao Reforms: A Historical Perspective*. Chicago: The University of Chicago Press: 219–58.

——. 1995. "Chinese Politics at the Top: Factionalism or Informal Politics?" *China Journal*, Vol. 34 (July): 95–156.

Unger, Jonathan. 1987. "The Struggle to Dictate China's Administration: The Conflict of Branches vs. Areas vs. Reform," *Australian Journal of Chinese Affairs*, no. 33 (July): 15–45.

United Nations Organization. 1997. *Human Development Report*. New York: Oxford University Press.

Vogel, Ezra. 1989. *One Step Ahead: Guangdong under Reform*. Cambridge, MA: Harvard University Press.

Wade, Robert. 2004. *Governing the Market: Economic Theory and the Role of Government in East Asian Industrialization*. Princeton, NJ: Princeton University Press.

Wake, David. 1998. *Commodifying Communism: Markets, Culture, and Politics in a South China City*. New York: Cambridge University Press.

Walder, Andrew. 1992. "Property Rights and Stratification in Socialist Redistributive Economies," *American Sociological Review*, Vol. 57.

——. 1995. "Local Governments as Industrial Firms," *American Journal of Sociology*, Vol. 101, no. 2 (September): 263–301.

Wang Guohua. 1989. *An Analysis of Economy in Shandong for the Past Forty Years (Shandong Jingji Sishinian Toushi)*. Jinan: Shandong Renmin Chubanshe.

Wang, Hongying. 2001. *Weak State, Strong Networks*. Hong Kong: Oxford University Press.

Wang, James. 2002. *Contemporary Chinese Politics: An Introduction*. Upper Saddle River, NJ: Prentice Hall.

Wang, Shaoguang. 1995. "The Rise of the Regions: Fiscal Reform and the Decline of Central State Capacity in China," in Andrew Walder, ed., *The Waning of the Communist State*. Berkeley: The University of California Press: 87–113.

Wang, Shaoguang, and Hu Angang. 1993. *A Study of China State Capacity (Zhongguo Guojia Nengli Baogao)*. Shengyang: Liaoning Renmin Chubanshe.

Waterbury, John. 1989. "The Political Management of Economic Adjustment and Reform," in Nelson, Joan. ed., *Fragile Coalitions: The Politics of Economic Adjustment*. New Brunswick, NJ, and Oxford: Transaction Books: 39–56.

Wedeman, Andrew. 2003. *From Mao to Market: Rent Seeking, Local Protectionism and Marketization in China*. New York: Cambridge University Press.

Wei, Yehua, 1997, "Regional Development in China, 1978–91," *Geoforum*, Vol. 27, no. 3: 329–44.

——. 2000. *Regional Development in China*. London and New York: Routledge.

White, Gordon. 1993. *Riding the Tiger: The Politics of Economic Reform in Post-Mao China*. Stanford, CA: Stanford University Press.

White, Lynn T. 1998a and 1998b. *Unstately Power. Vol. 1: Local Causes of China's Economic Reforms; Vol. 2: Local Causes of China's Intellectual, Legal and Governmental Reforms.* Armonk, NY., and London: M.E. Sharpe.

Whiting, Susan. 1999. "The Regional Evolution of Ownership Forms," in Jean Oi and Andrew Walder, eds., *Property Rights and Economic Reform in China.* Stanford, CA: Stanford University Press.

——. 2001. *Power and Wealth in Rural China: The Political Economy of Institutional Change.* New York: Cambridge University Press.

Wibowo, Ignatius. 2001. "Party Recruitment and the Future of the Chinese Communist Party," *EAI Background Brief No. 101.* Singapore: EAI, NUS, September 7.

——. 2004. *Learn from China: How China Grabs the Opportunity in the Era of Globalization (Belajar dari Cina. Bagaimana Cina Merebut Peluang dalam Era Globalisasi).* Jakarta: Penerbit KOMPAS.

Williamson, John. 1994. "In Search of a Manual for Technopols," in John Williamson, ed., *The Political Economy of Policy Reform.* Washington, DC: Institute for International Studies.

Winiecki, Jan. 1990. "Obstacles to Economic Reform of Socialism: A Property-Rights Analysis," *Annals of the American Academy of Political and Social Science,* Vol. 507 (January): 65–71.

Wolf, Thomas A. 1991. "The Lessons of Limited Market-Oriented Reform," *The Journal of Economic Perspectives,* Vol. 5, no. 4 (Autumn): 45–58.

Womack, Brantly, and Guangzhi Zhao. 1994. "The Many Worlds of China's Provinces: Foreign Trade and Diversification," in Goodman and Segal, eds., *China Deconstructs: Politics, Trade and Regionalism.* London: Routledge, pp. 59–98.

Wong, Christine. 1986. "The Economics of Shortage and Problems of Reform in Chinese Industry," *Journal of Comparative Economics,* Vol. 10: 363–87.

——. 1997. *Financing Local Government in the People's Republic of China,* Hong Kong: Oxford University Press.

Wong, Christine, Christopher Heady, and Wing T. Woo. 1995. *Fiscal Management and Economic Reform in the People's Republic of China.* Hong Kong: Oxford University Press.

Wong, John, and Chen Chien-Hsun, 2003. "How Serious Are China's Non-Performing Loans with Its State Banks," *EAI Background Brief No. 159.* Singapore: National University of Singapore, June.

Wong, John, and Lai Hongyi, eds. 2006. *China into the Hu-Wen Era: Policy Initiatives and Challenges.* Singapore: World Scientific, forthcoming.

Woo, Wing Thye. 1994. "The Art of Reforming Centrally Planned Economies: Comparing China, Poland and Russia," *Journal of Comparative Economics,* Vol. 18, no.3: 276–308.

Woon, Yuen-Fong. 1990. "International Links and the Socioeconomic Development of Rural China: An Emigrant Community in Guangdong," *Modern China,* Vol. 16 (April): 139–72.

Word Bank. 1987. *World Development Report 1987.* New York: Oxford University Press.

Wu Yufeng. 1993. "Development of Foreign Enterprises" (Waishang Touzi Qiye de Fanzha), in Gao, Wang, and He, eds., *Encyclopedia on the Major Events of*

Chinese Economic Reform and Opening Beijing: Beijing Gongye Daxue Chubanshe: 1704–18.

Xia Yulong, and Gu Xiaorong, eds. 1999. *Reforms of Political Structure and Democratic and Legal Construction in China in the Recent Two Decades (20 Nian lai Zhongguo Zhengzhi Tizhi Gaige he Minzhu Fazhi Jianshe).* Chongqing: Chongqing Chubanshe.

Yahuda, Michael. 1979. "Political Generations in China," *China Quarterly,* Vol. 80 (December): 792–805.

Yang, Dali. 1990. "Patterns of China Regional-Development Strategy," *China Quarterly,* Vol. 122: 230–257.

———. 1996. *Calamity and Reform in China.* Stanford, CA: Stanford University Press.

———. 1997. *Beyond Beijing: Liberalization and the Regions in China.* New York: Routledge.

Yang Jisheng. 1998. *Deng Xiaoping Era (Deng Xiaoping Shidai).* Beijing: Zhongyang Bianyi Chubanshe.

Ye Shuming. 2001. *Turbulence of One Hundred Years: Records of Guangdong in the 20th Century (Bainian Jidang: 20 Shiji Guangdong Shilu).* Guangzhou: Guangdong Jiaoyu Chubanshe.

Yeung, Y. M., and David K. Y. Chu. 1998. *Guangdong: Survey of a Province Undergoing Rapid Change.* Hong Kong: The Chinese University Press.

———. 2000. *Fujian: A Coastal Province in Transition and Transformation.* Hong Kong: The Chinese University Press.

Yin Dongqin, and Yang Zhenghui. 2004. *Tremendous Change: China's Journey of Economic Reform from 1978 to 2004 (Jübian: 1978 Nian–2004 Nian Zhongguo Jingji Gaige Licheng).* Beijing: Dangdai Shijie Chubanshe.

Young, Susan. 1995. *Private Business and Economic Reform in China.* Armonk, N.Y.: M.E. Sharpe.

Zhang, Le-Yin. 1999. "Chinese Central-provincial Fiscal Relationships, Budgetary Decline and the Impact of the 1994 Fiscal Reform: An Evaluation," *The China Quarterly,* Vol. 157 (March): 15–41.

Zhang Zhinei, Liu Kangtai, and Zhu Jiayuan. eds. 1985. *An Introduction to the Laws and Regulations regarding Individual Household and Professional Enterprises (Getihu, Zhuanyehu Jingying Fagui Changshi).* Shijiazhuang: Gongren Chubanshe.

Zhao Libo. 1998. *Reform of Governmental Administration (Zhengfu Xingzheng Gaige).* Ji'nan: Shandong Renmin Chubanshe.

Zweig, David. 2002. *Internationalizing China.* Ithaca, NY: Cornell University Press.

Index

abuse of power, 70, 244, 247,
    249, 280
agricultural cooperative movement, 32–4
Anti-Japanese War, 96–7, 105
Aslund, Anders, 4
autarky, 123, 127, 158
    see also self-reliance

bank
    non-performing loans, 246
    loans to non-state economy, 34–7, 42,
        46, 170–1, 192, 194,
        198
    loans to SOEs, 245
Bates, Robert, 9, 10
Baum, Richard, 15–6, 63, 69–73, 75, 78,
    80–1, 134, 180, 256–7
Beijing consensus, 1
big-bang (shock therapy) reform
    approach, 2–5, 5–8, 253
    see also incrementalists vs. shock-
        therapists
bourgeois liberalization, 65, 70, 71, 79, 84
Bo Yibo, 63, 65, 67
Bunce, Valerie, 13
bureaucracy
    agencies for and against reform,
        157–60, 181–2
    resistance to reform, 181–3, 196–7,
        210–15
    entrepreneurship in reform, 7
Byrd, William, 21, 34–5, 38

cadre promotion
    in Mao's era, 92, 100
    in the reform era, 91–4

cadre retirement, 91–4
Cai, F., 4, 7
CCCCP (Central Committee of
    the Chinese Communist
    Party), *see* Chinese Communist
    Party
center (central or national authority)
    definition, 253
    see also central-local relations; Chinese
        Communist Party
Central Commission for Discipline
    Inspection (of the Party), 132, 250
Central Committee, *see* Chinese
    Communist Party
central government, *see* central-local
    relations
central-local relations
    central appointment of local cadres,
        7, 17–8, 28–9, 32, 67, 92,
        120–1, 138–9, 168, 236, 238,
        241, 250
    central coordination of local reform,
        7, 17–8, 168
    central opening of provinces, *see* Open
        Policy
central-local fiscal relations
    central subsidies to provinces, 19,
        28–9, 140–1, 144–7, 166, 177–8,
        188, 197, 205–8, 225, 240–2,
        245, 248, 259–60
    local fiscal remittance (contribution),
        19, 28, 140, 144–7, 164, 166,
        176–8, 184, 188–9, 197, 205–7,
        240, 259–61
    local fiscal residuals (surplus), 11, 144,
        176, 208, 240–1

Central Military Commission (CMC), 49, 68, 98, 126
central planning, 15, 20, 22, 24, 48, 50, 254
Chen, Kang, 3,
Chen Li, 52–6
Chen Xuewei, 21, 34, 36–7, 39–41, 46–89, 51, 53–4,
Chen Yun
    as an arch conservative, 63, 65, 67,
    conflict with reformists, 63, 65–9, 70–3
    criticisms of Maoists, 64
    criticism of SEZs, 131–3
    economic view, 65–6
    persecution of reformists, 132, 137–8, 259 (notes 15, 16)
    political view, 67
    sources of power, 65–7
Cheung, Peter, T. Y., 7, 112–13, 130, 149, 153, 175, 179, 253, 258, 260–1
China
    gross national product (GDP), 1, 20, 22, 71, 81–2, 85, 86, 135, 247, 262
    incremental reform, 5–8, 13–7, 232–5
    reduction in poverty, 1
    structure of political power, 14–8, 62–3, 91, 94–5
    success in economic transition, 1
China's agriculture
    Collectivization of, 32–4
    decollectivization of, 6, 8, 21, 88
    reform in, 21, 88
    surplus labor, 21, 33
China's economic growth, 1, 61, 64–6, 68, 70–1, 72, 74–5, 77–8, 80–8, 90, 102, 114, 116, 123, 158, 171, 232, 246–7, 249, 251, 254
    as a criterion for official performance, 7, 17–8, 169, 239
    foreign direct investment and, 56, 134, 135
    non-state economy and, 20–2, 59, 220–1, 225–8, 233–4, 239
    trade and, 130, 135, 153, 165–7, 175–6
China's economic reform

big bang and incremental views of, 5–8
choice in, 12–24
compared to Soviet reform, 2, 5–8, 18, 20, 22, 23, 24, 231, 243, 254 (note 11)
conditions prior to, 20, 22, 23, 24
economic constraints in, 15, 20, 22, 24
political constraints, 14–8, 235
China's economic strategy for reform
definition, 254
grope for stones to cross a river (experimentalism), 15, 24
dual-track prices, 8, 232–3
liberalizing market entry (grow out of the state sector), 15, 20–2, 33–59, 232–3
local experiments of national solutions, 15, 24–5, 237–9
China's political strategies for reform, 14–9, 235–3
appointing able local leaders, 7, 15, 17–8, 28–9, 32, 62, 67, 120–21, 125, 138–9, 236, 238–9
competitive liberalization, 7, 12, 15, 25, 111, 114–15, 139, 141, 238
definition, 254
fiscal incentives to localities, 15, 19, 134–5, 140, 143–5, 177–8, 205–9, 241
management of elite conflict, 15–17, 67–73, 76–7, 88–90, 235–7
promotion of young technocrats, 15–16, 17–18, 28, 91–108
rewarding local leaders for reform and growth, 7, 17–18, 169, 239
selective liberalization, 18–19, 116–38, 138–40
"two steps forward, one step back", 15–17, 27, 61, 235
See also flaws in China's reform strategies
Chinese Communist Party (CCP)(or Party), 15, 16, 17, 21, 27–8, 35–42, 47, 49, 51, 53, 55, 62–107, 112, 118–19, 121–6, 131, 136–9, 162, 168–71, 182, 200, 204, 208, 213,

217, 235–8, 243–5, 249–50, 253–6, 259, 261
Central Committee of, 34–5, 46, 48, 53, 55, 67, 69, 92, 94, 112, 119, 125, 131–3, 136, 237, 249, 253
control of official appointment, 7, 17–8, 32, 139, 241, 245, 250
as coordinator of reform, 17–8
Eleventh Party Congress, 94
Fourteenth Party Congress, 35–6, 53, 73, 89–90, 92, 94
Fifteenth Party Congress, 37, 45, 74
Party Congress, 94, 96, 250
political dominance of, 17–8
Third Plenum of the Eleventh (Party) Central Committee in 1978, 34, 65, 119, 131
Third Plenum of the Twelfth Central Committee, 40, 136
Thirteenth Party Congress, 72, 92, 94
Third Plenum of the Sixteenth Party Central Committee in 2003, 38, 42, 255
Twelfth Party Congress, 92, 94, 98
Chu, David K. Y., 112, 130, 153
Chung, Jae Ho, 7, 149, 179, 200, 213, 215, 222–4, 253, 255, 260–1
coastal provinces/cities, 3, 7, 11, 15, 29, 47–9, 68, 73, 79, 88, 115, 130, 136, 142, 148, 153–4, 166, 168–70, 174, 176, 192, 222, 236, 239–40
coastal region (eastern region), 49, 59, 103, 106, 108, 136, 142, 168, 222, 239–41, 247–8
collective-owned enterprises, 33–9,
  see also township and village enterprises
  urban collective enterprises
competitive liberalization, 7, 12, 15, 25, 111, 114, 115, 139, 141, 238
conflict among top leaders
  over economic reform, 64–90, 131–7, 235–6
  over political reform, 65–72, 74–5, 79, 82–3, 85
  see also factions
conservative leaders, 2, 4–7, 13–7, 27–8, 47–8, 51, 61, 64–90, 97–9, 105,

108, 100, 120, 125, 131–9, 162, 164, 168, 173, 177, 179, 182, 215, 221–2, 226, 234–9, 243, 254, 256, 259
  removal of reformists, 137–8, 259
constitutional amendment to protect private economy, 21, 41, 42
corruption, 4, 9, 18, 67, 71, 73, 74, 79, 232, 244, 247–50
Crane, George, 47, 69, 112, 134
Cultural Revolution, 6, 24, 34, 88, 96, 100, 118, 122, 206, 254

decentralization, 5, 7, 11, 14, 18, 24, 31, 38, 105, 110, 133, 169, 253
  economic versus political, 11, 14, 18, 31, 253–4
democracy, 250, 251
democracy movement, 70–3, 79, 85, 87
democratization, 4–6, 9, 69, 85, 90, 243, 244, 254, 256
Deng Xiaoping
  appointing suitable leaders for Guangdong, 120–1, 138–9
  comeback to power in 1978, 64–5
  conflict with conservative leaders, 17, 67–3, 76–7, 88–90, 235–7
  conflict with Hua Guofeng, 64–5, 70, 91
  evaluation of Mao, 16, 68–9
  military and, 67–9, 89–90, 235–6
  orthodox reformism, 15, 65, 69, 76–7, 85
  political skills, 15–9, 28–9, 61–2, 67–9, 88–90, 235–7
  pragmatism, 8, 61, 77, 140, 165, 232, 251, 271
  as a pragmatist, 64–5, 70, 116, 235,
  promotion of technocrats, 62, 67, 91–108, 236, 238
  protection of private business, 40
  Pudong, 49–53
  pursuit of high growth, 76–78, 87
  reform in Guangdong, 112–40
  SEZs, 47, 70, 128–38
  Shanghai, 49–53

Deng Xiaoping—*continued*
  sources of power, 62–3, 67
  Southern Tour, 35, 53, 79, 84–5, 89–90, 222
  suppression of liberalism, 70–2, 76, 79–80
  Tiananmen crackdown, 72
  visit in Japan, 77
  visit in Singapore, 77
  see also Open Policy
Deng Liqun, 133, 257
Deng Yingchao, 63, 67
Department of Propaganda (or propaganda machinery), 63, 67, 78, 134
Dewatripont, M., 4, 12
Dittmer, Lowell, 63–4, 66–7, 75–7, 81–2, 90, 180
dual track price, 8, 232–3

economic crime, 47, 68, 88, 132–3, 137, 259
economic planning, 6–7, 21, 22, 25, 65–6, 109, 160–1, 182–3, 213, 221, 233
employment, 20, 29, 40, 44, 158, 160–7, 181–5, 188–9, 197, 199, 210, 219, 233–4, 244–5
  see also jobs
entry of markets, 3, 5, 8, 15, 21, 31, 57, 73, 199, 210, 225, 232–4
evolutionary school, *see* incrementalists
exports, 1, 31, 36–7, 47, 50, 54, 57–8, 64, 119, 123, 134–5, 139–40, 158–9, 165, 199, 202, 224, 238, 258

factions, 9, 27, 61–90, 97–9, 118, 235, 256
  origin, 63–4
  definition, 63
  see conservatives; moderate reformists; orthodox reformists; radical reformists; pragmatists; whateverists
Fan, Cindy, 253
Fewsmith, Joseph, 66, 113, 256
fiscal conditions, *see* central-local fiscal relations
fiscal incentives, *see* central-local fiscal relations
Fischer, Stanley, 4, 11

flaws in China's reform strategies
  outstanding bad loans at state banks, 246
  a significant number of inefficient SOEs, 244–5
  sluggish political reform, 243–4
foreign capital prior to reform, 45–6, 117–18
foreign direct investment (FDI), 45–59, 134–5, 140, 200–01, 212–14, 222–4
foreign enterprises (or joint ventures)
  classification, 46, 47
  development and presence, 45–59, 227
fortuna, 12, 90
four cardinal principles, 65, 70, 79
Frieden, Jeff, 9, 117
Fujian, 21, 29, 35–6, 40, 46, 48, 58, 70, 104, 110, 112, 129–42, 146, 153–4, 166, 218, 237–40, 259

Gang of Four, 97, 118–19, 125
Geddes, B., 192, 255
Gelb, Alan, 3–4, 8, 11, 21, 234
Gini coefficient, 248
Goodman, David S. G., 149, 153, 169, 175, 179, 253, 260–1
Gore, Lance, 7, 38, 254
governance, 15, 29, 65, 77, 100, 215–19, 226, 242, 245, 247, 261
Great Leap Forward, 24, 33, 34, 118
Gu Mu, 135
  opening of coastal region, 136
  special economic zone, 111–2, 119, 132
Guangdong,
  cleansing of Maoist influence, 125, 138
  conservative criticism, 131–3
  consolidation of reform, 134–6, 139–40
  economic take-off, 134–5, 140
  factor prices and, 117–19, 127
  history of commerce, 130
  illegal immigration to Hong Kong, 121–2, 125, 127
  local patrons, 123–5
  national patrons, 125–7
  open-minded cadres and population, 130–1, 138
  proximity to NIEs, 127–30

request to use foreign capital in 1956, 118
request for special policies in 1979, 119, 130
suitable reformist leadership in, 132–3
SEZs, 129–6
start of reform, 131–2
see also Shantou, Shenzhen, and Zhuhai
guanxi, 63

Haggard, Stephen, 5, 9–10
Hellman, Joe, 4, 5
Hong Kong, 117–18, 126–7, 247
development inspiration for China, 77, 118, 121–2, 153
as a neighbor of Guangdong, 19, 28, 36, 110, 117, 121–2, 127, 129, 138, 152–6, 237, 258
SEZs and, 21, 47, 51, 111, 119, 129–30, 133–4, 137, 165
capital for and trade with China's provinces, 131, 152–6, 175, 223
Howell, Jude, 21, 47–9, 51, 69, 74, 112–14, 120, 130, 132–3, 136, 142, 152, 154, 174–5, 253, 256, 258–9
Huang Guofeng, 258
differences from Deng in opening, 118–20
fall from power, 64, 92, 98, 119
orthodox Maoism ("whateverists"), 64, 97, 105
use of foreign capital, 64, 70, 111–12, 118–19, 125
Huang, J., 62–3, 256
Huang, Yasheng, 7, 17–8, 22, 25, 32, 80, 169–70, 239, 261
Hu Jintao, 84, 107
new policies, 244, 247–8
Hu Yaobang, 125, 131, 136–7
compared to radical reformists, 256
as a generalist leader, 63
as a moderate reformist, 65, 76, 98,
as Party General Secretary, 64
as a reformist technocratic leader, 98, 108, 236
opposition of political conservatism, 70,
replaced by Zhao as the Party Secretary, 71, 72, 79, 256

ideology (ideological control), 32, 63, 120, 255–6
conservative, 25, 259
as a criterion for promotion, 92, 97–9, 100
Deng's, 64
Maoist, 16, 68, 119
non-state economy, 32, 41, 125, 137, 139, 221
political business cycle and, 78–84, 87–8
political role of, 78, 110
promotion of young leaders, 93, 95, 97–8, 100, 105, 169
income disparities, 247–8
incrementalists vs. shock therapists, 2–5, 5–8
complementarities of reform, 3
conditions prior to reform, 2, 6, 8
democratization, 4–5
focus of reforms, 3–4
irreversibility of reform, 4
partial reform, 4–5, 7
reform of state-owned enterprises, 4
the role of the state, 5, 6, 7
uncertainty of reform, 3
view of China's reform, 6–8
incremental approach, 2–5, 5–8
see also incrementalists
individual household business (IHB), *see* private sector
inflation, 15, 17, 27, 47, 49, 61, 66, 68, 70–4, 77–8, 81–90, 114, 131, 233–4, 257
informal politics, 63–4
see also factions
inland regions (inland provinces, interior regions, central and western regions, or interior cities), 7, 21, 36, 49, 53, 59, 73, 106, 115, 136, 142, 148, 153–4, 174, 221, 256
institutions, 2–4, 6, 8–10, 12–3, 20, 31, 37, 53, 64, 118, 120, 125, 135, 160, 162–3, 169, 185, 210–1, 217, 255, 257
see also state
interest groups, *see* bureaucracy, sectors, heavy and light industry, state and non-state sectors
investment, 31, 34, 37, 39, 43, 45–9, 52, 54–5, 68, 72–3, 78, 80–5, 87, 106,

113–14, 129–30, 134, 147, 152,
    158–9, 165, 174–5, 178, 189, 193,
    198, 200, 204, 212–13, 223–4, 232,
    239–40, 249

Japan, 46, 52, 77, 130, 152–5, 175, 260
Jefferson, Gary H., 3, 8, 118, 234, 255
Jiang Chunyun, 213, 217
Jiang Zemin, 53–4, 258
    anti-corruption, 73
    leaders from Shanghai, 107, 151
    opening of Shanghai, 51, 139
    as orthodox reformist, 83
    outlawing of Falun Gong, 74
    post-Tiananmen retrenchment, 89
    replaced Zhao as Party Secretary, 72
    suppression of protests, 74
    three represents, 41–2, 255
Jiangsu, 25, 35–6, 38, 58, 104, 149, 151,
    155, 172, 199, 218, 260
Jilin
    bureaucracy and reform,
        210–5
    economic conditions, 194–96
    fiscal arrangement and conditions,
        205–09
    foreign trade, FDI and opening,
        200–01, 222–4
    governance, 218–19
    leadership, 215–19
    national opening of, 222–4
    non-state economy, 198–204
    policy effects on the economy
    policy toward non-state economy,
        192–4, 198–204
    state sector and influence, 219–21
jobs, 17, 19, 39–40, 43–4, 56, 68, 77,
    141, 158, 181, 212, 219–20, 226,
    246, 250

Kaufman, Robert, 5, 9–10
Kleinberg, R., 46–7, 69, 112–3, 121–2, 256
Krueger, Ann, 9–10
Kuomingtang (Nationalists), 96

leaders,
    four types, 62–3
    generations, 96–7
    see also factions

Lai, Hongyi H., 21, 44–5, 55–7, 169–70,
    239, 248, 254–6, 261–2
Law on Encouraging Small- and
    Medium-Sized Enterprises, 42
laws and rules on foreign enterprises, 46,
    48, 52, 55–6
Lee, H. Y., 91–2, 99, 100, 257
Lee, Jongchul, 100
Lee, K. Y., 77
liberals (political liberalism), 70–2, 74,
    75, 79, 256
Li, Cheng, 96, 100–1
Liang Lingguang, 121, 124
Liang Xiang, 123
Li Peng, 51, 63, 65, 89
Li Ruihuan, 16, 108, 236
Li Xiannian
    as conservative leader, 63, 65, 67
    and SEZ, 111, 119, 133
Lieberthal, Kenneth, 62, 66, 75, 77, 80,
    94, 253, 256–7, 261
Lin, Justin Y. F., 4, 7
Lin, Q., 21, 34–5, 38
Lin Ruo, 124
Liu Tianfu, 123–4
Lipton, D., 3–5, 7, 253
local government, see central-local
    relations; central-local fiscal
    relations; provincial reform
    initiatives

Machiavelli, Niccolo, 12
Manion, Melanie, 93, 257
Manzetti, Luigi, 9
Mao Zedong, 16, 24, 33–4, 62, 64, 66,
    67–9
Maoists (whateverists), 28, 63–5, 68,
    97–9
    orthodox, 97
    moderate, 97
marketization, 2, 13–6, 18, 20, 61, 68–9,
    73, 77, 88, 90, 108, 232, 234, 236,
    251, 254
McMillan, John, 3, 4, 20, 233–4
military, 16, 28, 49, 62–3, 67–9, 73, 79,
    89–91, 98, 100–2, 104, 126–7,
    235–6, 243–4
    see also Central Military Commission
        (CMC)

Ministry of Communications, 111–12
ministries for and against reform, 158–60
mode of growth,
    extensive versus intensive, 249
moderate reformists
    clash with conservative, 65–7, 69, 76, 77–85
    clash with orthodox reformists, 65, 67, 69, 76, 77–5
    view on economic reform, 65, 76
    view on political reform, 65, 256, 76
Montinola, Gabriella, 7
Murphy, Kevin M, 4, 6
Murrell, Peter, 3, 5

national government
    see center; central-local relations
National People's Congress, 41, 46, 67, 74, 102
national policies
    effects on provincial reform, 187–8, 198–204, 221–4
Nationalists, see Kuomintang
Naughton, Barry, 3, 4, 8, 20, 24, 70, 119, 233–4, 245, 258
necessita, 12, 90
Nelson, Joan, 9–10
non-state economy (non-state sectors)
    facilitation of price reform, 234
    growth of, 170–1, 175, 177, 188, 202, 203, 209, 214, 215
    restrictions on, 14, 21, 39, 70, 72, 113, 122, 160, 198, 203, 204, 215, 221, 250–1
    see also collective-owned enterprises, foreign enterprises, joint ventures, private sector (private business)

Oi, Jean, 7, 21, 33, 36, 38, 144, 176,
Oksenberg, Michael, 62, 113, 253, 256, 259
Olsen, Mancur, 9, 157
Open Policy
    demonstration effects and, 128–31, 134–5, 140
    existing explanations, 112–16
    local agents and, 120–5
    national patronage and, 125–7

national policy environment and, 117–20
    versus Open Door Policy, 109
    opening of coastal cities, 47–8
    opening of coastal areas, 48–9
    opening of Fujian, 46–8
    opening of Guangdong, 46–8
    opening of interior cities, 53–5
    opening of Pudong in Shanghai, 51–2
    selective opening versus widespread opening, 129–31
    see also special economic zones
opening of China, see Open Policy
opening of provinces
    bureaucracy and, 160–3
    distance from Beijing and, 147–8
    distance from the coast and, 154–6
    fiscal arrangement and conditions and, 143–7
    heavy industry and, 156–60
    light industry and, 156–60
    measure of, 143
    national patrons and, 150–2
    non-state sectors and, 156–60
    provincial leadership and, 148–50
    state sector and, 156–60
    trade potential and, 152–4
orthodox reformists
    alliance with conservative, 67, 69
    clash with conservative, 65–7, 76, 77–85
    clash with moderate reformists, 65, 67, 69, 76, 77–85
    eventual political dominance, 84–5, 98–9
    view on economic reform, 65, 76
    view on political reform, 65, 76

Party Congress, see Chinese Communist Party
patrons for provinces, 51–2, 105–7, 123–7, 150–2, 180–1
Pearl River Delta, 36, 38, 48, 118, 136, 240
Peng Zhen, 63, 66–7, 93, 98, 132–3
people's communes, 34–5, 147
planned economy, 2, 5, 14–5, 22, 24, 32, 64, 120, 178, 233

Politburo
    formation and power, 94–5
Politburo members
    age, 95–6
    education, 101–2
    functional background, 99–102
    ideological orientation, 97–9
    regional background, 102–7
    role in reform, 93–4, 108
    political business cycles, 69–90
        calls for democratization, see
            democracy movements
        growth versus inflation, 69–74, 77–87
        reform versus retrenchment, 69–74,
            77–87
        sources, 74–87
        subsiding of, 84–6, 89–90
political entrepreneurs, 18, 254
political reform (democratization)
    under Deng Xiaoping, 4, 17, 27, 62,
        69, 70, 73–4, 79–81, 85, 87, 235,
        243–4
    under Hu Jintao, 244, 251
post-Tiananmen syndrome, 85, 243
poverty, 1, 10, 68, 77, 168, 240, 248, 262
pragmatists, 64–5, 70, 235
pragmatism, xviii, 77
price reform, 49, 72, 79, 81, 88, 89,
    233–4, 257
private sector (private business)
    classification and definition, 43
    expansion in the reform era, 20–3,
        43–5
    individual household business (IHB),
        41, 43–4, 203
    local restriction of, 41, 203–4
    liberalization of, 20–2
    nationalization and collectivization of,
        39
    political protection, 21, 40–2, 203–4
    policy toward, 32–3, 39–42
    private enterprises, 32, 38, 40, 41, 59,
        43–4, 203–4, 215, 221, 255, 261
    prohibition and restriction of, 39, 70,
        203–4
private entrepreneurs joining the Party,
    41–2, 72
problems in contemporary China and
    remedies

abuse of power, 249–50
corruption, 249–50
income inequality, 247–8
limited social safety net, 248–9
restrictions on non-state sectors,
    250–1
social instability, 248
extensive mode of growth, 249
provincial bureaus for and against
    reform, 158–60
provincial reform initiatives
    distance from Beijing and, 172–4
    distance from a sea port and, 174–5
    fiscal conditions and arrangement and,
        175–8
    light and heavy industry and, 182–6
    measures of, 171–2
    national patronage and, 1980–81
    national policy and, 187–8
    non-state and state sectors and,
        182–6
    path dependency of non-state sectors
        and, 186
    power of provinces and, 168–70
    provincial bureaucracy and, 181–3
    provincial leadership and,
        178–9
    trade potential and, 175
    variation in, 167–8, 171–2
Przeworski, Adam, 5, 10
Putterman, Louis, 4, 7
Pye, Lucian, 64, 78, 180
Pudong, see special economic zones

Qian, Yingyi, 3, 4, 7, 8, 23–5, 38, 233–4
Qiao Shi, 16, 108, 236

radical reformists (liberals), 256
Ramo, Jashua Cooper, 1
reform in provinces
    see provincial reform initiatives
reformists, see also orthodox reformists,
    moderate reformists, and radical
    reformists
Ren Zhongyi
    appointed as leader of Guangdong,
        121, 124
    protection of reform in Guangdong,
        132–3, 138–9

research methods, 25–6, 191–2
retrenchment in reform, *see* political
      business cycles
Rogowski, Ron, 9, 117, 192, 255
Roland, Gerald, 4, 5, 7, 12, 24, 231,
      253–4
Ruan, Ming, 72, 75, 78, 80,
      256–7, 259
rule of law, 64, 80, 169, 170, 236, 243,
      251,
rule of man (rule by man), 91, 107, 236
rural enterprises,
      in central and western regions, 36
      commune and brigade enterprises
            (CBE), 34–5
      history, 33–4
      rural collective enterprises, 33–35
      see also collective-owned enterprises
      see also township and village
            enterprises

Sachs, Jeffrey, 3–7, 253
sectoral support for reform, 19, 28, 186,
      190, 238
selective and showcase liberalization,
      109–40, 237, 258
self-employed individuals, 32, 43
self reliance, 33, 46, 109, 118, 120
      see also autarky
Shandong
      economic conditions, 192–6
      economic growth, 227–8
      fiscal conditions and arrangement,
            205–6
      fiscal factor and reform initiatives,
            208–9
      foreign trade and opening, 200–1,
            222–4
      non-state sector, 197, 198–204
      policy toward foreign direct
            investment, 200–1
      policy toward private sector, 203–4
      policy toward rural enterprises,
            198–200
      policy toward urban collective sector,
            201–3
      policy effects on the economy, 226–9
Shandong's reform
      coastal proximity and, 221–3

fiscal conditions and arrangement and,
      208–9
foreign trade and opening,
      222–4
national opening and, 221–4
national policies and, 198–200,
      202–4, 221–4
non-state sectors and, 219–21
policy effects on the economy, 226–9
provincial bureaucracy and, 203–15
provincial leadership and governance
      and, 215–19
state sector and, 219–21
Shanghai, 66, 71, 79, 151, 155, 176,
      186, 218
      base for technocratic leaders, 51, 104,
            106–7, 151–2
      as a coastal open city, 47–8
      as a heavy fiscal remitter, 19, 140,
            177, 240, 259
      national patrons, 51, 104, 106–7,
            151–2
      non-state economy in, 44, 58, 172
      Open Policy and, 51–2, 53–4, 139,
            149, 259
      Pudong, 51–2, 142
Shantou, 46, 112, 123–4, 130
Shenzhen
      illegal border crossing, 121–2, 127
      SEZ designation, 112, 121–2, 129–31
      SEZ development, 45–7, 112, 131–6
Shirk, Susan, 7, 25, 65, 75–6, 81, 100,
      112–15, 117–18, 135, 157, 161,
      169, 182, 237, 253–4, 257
Singapore, 77, 153, 247, 254
Singh, Inderjit, 3, 8, 11, 234
Shleifer, Andrei, 4, 6
shock therapists
      see also shock therapy (big-bang
            approach)
Snyder, Richard, 9
social instability, 248
socialist transformation, 32, 96–7
social welfare (social safety net), 248–9
Solnick, Steven, 4, 6
South Korea, 152–3, 155, 175,
      200, 222–3, 246, 260
Southern Tour in, 1992, 35, 53, 79,
      84–5, 89–90, 222

Soviet Union, 2, 5, 6, 18, 20, 22–4, 155, 231
  economic aid to China, 32, 45, 46
  economic model for China, 156, 214
  see also China's economic reform compared to Soviet reform
Spark Program (*xinhuo jihua*), 36
special economic zones (SEZs)
  conservative criticisms of, 47, 50, 71, 131–3
  development of, 45–6, 49, 51–2, 54, 131–6
  establishment of, 45–6, 49, 51–2, 111–12, 129–30
  special treatment of, 47
  see also Pudong (under Shanghai); Shantou; Shenzhen; Xiamen; Zhuhai
spiritual pollution, 70, 79, 133
state, 8, 9, 21, 32–7, 39–46, 48–9, 53–7, 62–3, 72–3, 79–87, 93, 111, 114, 117, 122, 139, 142–3, 156, 158, 160, 162, 169–70, 205, 211, 231, 240, 243–8, 250–51, 261
  the role of, 4, 5, 7, 9–11, 84, 113, 232–3, 253–4, 259
State Council, 21, 34–6, 39–40, 46–8, 51–7, 67, 112, 130–2, 136, 142, 154, 200, 216, 222, 223, 250, 253
state-owned enterprises (SOEs)(or state sector), 15, 20–1, 35, 38, 44, 156, 158, 162, 164, 169–70, 181–4, 200–04, 215, 220–1, 225–7, 231, 232–34, 250
  reform of SOEs, 3, 73–4
  size of, 20, 22–3, 45, 58–9
State Planning Commission, 49, 63, 160, 213
Stiglitz, Joseph, 3–5, 11
student protests, 71–2, 76–7, 79, 85
studies on reform
  big-bang reform approach, 2–5, 6–7
  incremental reform approach, 2–5, 6–7
  interests groups and, 4–5, 7, 9
  political institutions, 4–5, 8, 9–12
  political studies on, 9–12

tariffs, 9, 47–8, 56, 73, 114
Tang Yingwu, 65–6, 70, 72–3, 80, 122

technocratic leaders, 91–108
Teiwes, Frederick, 62, 67, 90, 257, 259
three represents, 41–2
Tiananmen Movement, 49, 71–2, 74, 79, 243
top leaders
  four types, 62–3
  functional leaders, 63
  generalists, 63
  paramount leader, 62
  Party elders, 63
  sources of power until, 1990s, 62
township and village enterprises (TVEs)
  development, 35–9
  in inland regions, 36
  local government and, 38–9
  Pearl River Delta model, 36
  policies toward, 33–9
  privatization, 38–9
  promotion of exports, 37
  Sunnan model, 36
  technological program, 36
  Wenzhou model, 36
Tsou, Tang, 62, 64, 74

unemployment, 15, 17, 33, 35, 40, 71, 74, 87–8, 169, 203, 231, 234–5, 243, 248–9, 262
United States (also the U.S.), 46, 55, 56, 57, 109, 231, 247
USSR, *see* Soviet Union

virtu, 12–3
Vishny, Robert W., 4
Vogel, Ezra, 111–13, 127–8, 130, 147, 153, 172, 175, 179, 260

Walder, Andrew, 7, 21, 33, 36, 169
Wan Li, 63, 70, 89, 108
Wang Zhen, 63, 93, 98, 136
Weingast, Barry, 7
Wen Jiabao, 107, 244, 247–8, 261
Wenzhou, 25, 36, 38, 47, 186
whateverists (Maoists), 64, 97
White, Lynn T., 178, 253
Whiting, Susan, 38–9, 169–71, 176, 186, 239, 253–4
Williamson, John, 5, 102
Winiecki, Jan, 4

Wolf, Thomas, 3, 253
Woo, Wing Thye, 6, 144–5, 176–7, 253
World Bank, 1, 5, 8, 113, 247, 261–2
World Trade Organization (WTO), 54–7, 73, 246
Wu Nansheng, 122–4

Xiamen, 46, 112, 113, 130, 155, 259
    Special Economic Zone, 46, 112, 136
Xiang Nan, 137, 259
Xi Zhongxun
    biography, 125
    leadership in Guangdong, 120–25, 138–39
    as national patron for Guangdong, 127

Yang, Dali, 7, 114, 134, 147, 154, 172–4, 240, 258, 261
Yang Jisheng, 36, 48, 77, 89, 111, 118–19, 122, 130, 133, 135, 136, 142, 258
Yang Shangkun, 63,
    as a leader of Guangzhou, 120, 124–5, 138
    as a patron of reform in Guangdong, 127, 136

as a reformist, 15, 67, 98
Yangtze River Delta, 48, 51, 136, 240
Yao Yilin, 51, 89
Ye Jianying, 125–7
    and Hua Guofeng, 258
    opening of Guangdong, 126–7, 258
Ye Shuming, 123, 132–3, 136, 258
Ye Xuanping, 124, 138
Yeung, Y. M., 112, 130, 153
Yuan Geng, 111, 123, 127
Young, Susan, 39–40, 44, 255

Zeng Sheng, 126–27
Zhao Ziyang
    coastal developmental strategy, 49
    fall from power, 72
    moderate reformist, 65, 76, 98
    opening of the coast, 136
    reform in Guangdong, 125–7, 131–2
    as Party General Secretary, 72
Zhu Rongji, 51, 73, 107, 108, 139, 236
Zhuhai SEZ, 46, 130, 134–6
Zweig, David, 7, 112, 114–15, 154, 174, 253